MW01087290

Masterless Men

Analyzing land policy, labor, and legal history, Keri Leigh Merritt reveals what happens to excess workers when a capitalist system is predicated on slave labor. With the rising global demand for cotton – and thus, slaves – in the 1840s and 1850s, the need for white laborers in the American South was drastically reduced, creating a large underclass that was unemployed or underemployed. These poor whites could not compete – for jobs or living wages – with profitable slave labor. Though impoverished whites were never subjected to the daily violence and degrading humiliations of racial slavery, they did suffer tangible socio-economic consequences as a result of living in a slave society. Merritt examines how these "masterless" men and women threatened the existing southern hierarchy and ultimately helped push southern slave-holders toward secession and civil war.

Keri Leigh Merritt is an independent scholar in Atlanta, Georgia. Merritt's work on poverty and inequality has garnered multiple awards, and she is a coeditor of a volume on southern labor history.

Cambridge Studies on the American South

Series Editors:

Mark M. Smith, *University of South Carolina, Columbia*
Peter Coclanis, *University of North Carolina at Chapel Hill*

Interdisciplinary in its scope and intent, this series builds upon and extends Cambridge University Press's longstanding commitment to studies on the American South. The series offers the best new work on the South's distinctive institutional, social, economic, and cultural history and also features works in a national, comparative, and transnational perspective.

Titles in the Series

Masterless Men

Poor Whites and Slavery in the Antebellum South

KERI LEIGH MERRITT

CAMBRIDGE
UNIVERSITY PRESS

CAMBRIDGE
UNIVERSITY PRESS

University Printing House, Cambridge CB2 8BS, United Kingdom

One Liberty Plaza, 20th Floor, New York, NY 10006, USA

477 Williamstown Road, Port Melbourne, VIC 3207, Australia

4843/24, 2nd Floor, Ansari Road, Daryaganj, Delhi - 110002, India

79 Anson Road, #06-04/06, Singapore 079906

Cambridge University Press is part of the University of Cambridge.

It furthers the University's mission by disseminating knowledge in the pursuit of education, learning and research at the highest international levels of excellence.

www.cambridge.org
Information on this title: www.cambridge.org/9781316635438
DOI: 10.1017/9781316875568

First published 2017
First paperback edition 2017

A catalogue record for this publication is available from the British Library

Library of Congress Cataloging in Publication data
NAMES: Merritt, Keri Leigh, 1980 – author.
TITLE: Masterless men : poor whites and slavery in the antebellum South / Keri Leigh Merritt.
DESCRIPTION: Cambridge, United Kingdom ; New York, NY : Cambridge University Press, 2017. |
Series: Cambridge studies on the American South | Includes bibliographical references and index.
IDENTIFIERS: LCCN 2017003313 | ISBN 9781107184244 (hardback : alkaline paper)
SUBJECTS: LCSH: Poor whites–Southern States–Social conditions–19th century. |
Poor whites–Southern States–Economic conditions–19th century. | Slavery–Social aspects–Southern States–History–19th century. | Slavery–Economic aspects–Southern States–History–19th century. | Labor–Southern States–History–19th century. | Land tenure–Southern States–History–19th century. | Social conflict–Southern States–History–19th century. | Southern States–Social conditions–19th century. | Southern States–Economic conditions–19th century. | Southern States–Race relations–History–19th century. | BISAC: HISTORY / United States / 19th Century.
CLASSIFICATION: LCC F220.A1 M37 2017 | DDC 975/.03–dc23 LC record available at https://lccn.loc.gov/2017003313

ISBN 978-1-107-18424-4 Hardback
ISBN 978-1-316-63543-8 Paperback

For Henry

Contents

Acknowledgments

I owe countless thanks, and much appreciation, to many people. This book would have never come to fruition without their help. I was lucky enough to be one of the final doctoral students of James C. Cobb, to whom I remain indebted both professionally and personally. He continues to advise me on the important things in life, and for that I am forever grateful. Stephen Mihm, who served on both my Master's and doctoral committees, was like a second mentor in many ways. My knowledge about economic history was strengthened greatly due to his suggestions. I would also like to thank Stephen Berry, whose vast knowledge of the antebellum South helped bolster many of my arguments. Other faculty at the University of Georgia, Michael Kwass, Bethany Moreton, and Pamela Voekel, expanded my intellectual horizons, engendering my interest in the study of capitalism. Claudio Saunt prepared me to analyze and discuss race with his ethnohistory classes. I also owe much to Peter Hoffer, who helped direct my first graduate research paper and instructed me on the use of local court records. It was in his class that I first uncovered the lives of the South's poor whites.

Yet my history education did not start in graduate school. Emory afforded me an incredible education, and James Roark was an instrumental part of that. James Flannery, in the Literature Department, helped stimulate my love for other humanistic inquiries. I still consider both men important mentors in my life. But it was a young graduate student, Elizabeth Pollard (Hancock), who made me understand that I could actually *be* a historian. Her amazing teaching – and her faith in me – makes me even more aggrieved that she is no longer of this world.

I would also like to thank the St. George Tucker Society for the Bradford Dissertation Award, and Greg and Amanda Gregory for multiple research grants. Throughout the years, I also received very valuable feedback from conference presentations. Furthermore, scholars who have studied poor whites, such as Charles Bolton, Jeff Forret, and Victoria Bynum, have all greatly encouraged and supported my work, and I hope that I have made them proud. I also want to thank my good friend Bea Burton for indexing, and Kathi Nehls for helping me endure the many rejections and celebrate the few victories that come with this profession. I ultimately decided to publish with Cambridge University Press because of David Moltke-Hansen, who provided fantastic advice on transforming the dissertation into a book.

Finally, I never could have written this book without the support of my amazing husband, Henry Perlowski, or without the love of my sons, Henry and Cash.

Introduction: The Second Degree of Slavery

*The liberation of five millions of 'poor white trash' from the second degree
of slavery, and of three millions of miserable kidnapped negroes from the
first degree, cannot be accomplished too soon ... It now behooves us to take
a bold and determined stand in defence of the inalienable rights of ourselves
and of our fellow men, and to avenge the multiplicity of wrongs, social and
political, which we have suffered at the hands of a villainous oligarchy ... If
to-day we could emancipate the slaves in the Union, we would do it, and the
country and everybody in it would be vastly better off to-morrow. Now is
the time for action; let us work.*
   – Hinton Helper, 1857[1]

*The slave-holder knows wherein lies his power to enslave one class and
trample upon another. He scatters abroad prejudice ... And in order to do
this, he scatters abroad ignorance, shrouding the whole region in a veil of
mental darkness, debarring the poor freeman from the opportunity of
educating his children; for ignorance, prejudice and crime are a triumvirate
of tyranny, acting and reacting upon, producing and re-producing each other.*
   – J.G. Palfrey[2]

In the few years prior to the Civil War, Hinton Helper was one of the
most reviled names uttered among the slaveholders of the South. His
thoughts banned from the region, his likeness burned in effigy, and his
life threatened with death, Helper had published a book that struck fear
into the hardened hearts of slave masters everywhere, ultimately helping

---

[1] Hinton Rowan Helper, *The Impending Crisis of the South: How to Meet It* (1857; reprint,
New York: A.B. Burdick, 1860), 32–3.
[2] J.G. Palfrey, "American Slavery – Its Effects upon the Non-slave-holding Population of the
South," *The North Star* (NY), March 10, 1848.

push them to the brink of secession. While *The Impending Crisis of the South* certainly advocated the end of chattel slavery, its main argument was not focused on the plight of the nation's four million blacks. Instead, Helper crafted a statistically stacked, well-researched tome intended for the masses of white Southerners, calling upon them to join the antislavery movement out of concern for their own self-interest. As a non-slaveholder from North Carolina, Helper was one of the region's only outspoken abolitionists at this point, instantly becoming infamous throughout the country. By claiming that five million poor southern whites suffered "a second degree of slavery" precisely because of the enslavement of blacks, Helper made a variety of convincing arguments detailing slavery's detrimental impact on the lives of non-slaveholders.[3]

According to Helper, a small but very wealthy group of slaveholders lorded over the South, controlling politics and dominating the economy. Deeming the master class "a disgrace and a curse to humanity," he refuted the pro-slavery argument point by point, asserting that no free white could compete with slave labor. Contrary to planter claims that black slavery boosted the status of all whites, Helper realized that slave ownership mattered much more than white skin when determining southern social status. He thus classified non-slaveholders as a distinct economic class. In a frenzied quest to suppress anything that even mentioned abolition, slaveholders immediately banned *The Impending Crisis* from the South, clamoring for Helper's death and arresting or lynching anyone who brought a copy of his book into the region. Their overzealous reaction to Helper's ideas strongly suggests that his theories may have been more accurate than previously assumed.

While recent scholarly trends have involved minimizing Helper's impact on American history, without a thorough examination of his claims, a full understanding of the path to secession remains incomplete. Indeed, at an Organization of American Historians meeting more than forty years ago, Eric Foner urged a panel of Civil War students "to take a new look at the social and economic structure of the Old South." The best way to accomplish this massive undertaking, Foner asserted, was through innovative research on non-slaveholding whites, "the least studied of all our social classes." While much of the South's history has been interpreted through studies on slaves, planters, and even yeomen, poor whites

---

[3] Helper, *The Impending Crisis*, 32–3; 191; David Brown, *Southern Outcast: Hinton Rowan Helper and the Impending Crisis of the South* (Baton Rouge: Louisiana University Press, 2006).

still remain understudied – four decades after Foner's initial request. Generally defined as owning neither land nor slaves, poor whites comprised, at the very least, about one-third of the South's white population in the few decades preceding the Civil War. Since the mid-1990s, several good social histories about antebellum poor whites have been published, but they have yet to be synthesized, or incorporated into nineteenth-century history writ large. This book, therefore, attempts to answer Foner's call for research by situating poor white Southerners into America's broader political economy.[4]

Organized thematically, it explores how slavery impacted the lives of poor whites in the few decades before the Civil War by focusing on land ownership, labor, material realities, the southern legal system, and vigilante violence. It then argues that the plight of poor whites helped push slaveholders into disunion, and further shows how the active resistance or passive noncompliance of large numbers of poor whites added to the Confederate military's multitude of problems. Finally, it proposes that black emancipation actually freed poor white Southerners in a variety of ways. By integrating the story of poor whites into the broader narrative of the nineteenth century, the answers to some of the biggest questions in American history become clarified and nuanced.

With no direct ties to slavery, poor whites had long posed a threat to the maintenance of the peculiar institution. The tumultuous decade of the 1830s brought sweeping social changes to America, especially with the rise of abolitionism. As many slaveholders in the Mid-Atlantic and Upper South states began to disentangle themselves from the institution, over the next two decades close to a million slaves were sold farther South, flooding the labor market and pushing poor whites closer to the margins of society. Moreover, by the end of the 1830s, the land brutally stolen from Native Americans and sold cheaply to white settlers was no longer readily available in the older slave states, and land prices became too expensive for many poorer and lower-middling-class whites to purchase.[5]

---

[4] Eric Foner quoted in Fred Arthur Bailey, *Class and Tennessee's Confederate Generation* (Chapel Hill: University of North Carolina Press, 1987), 17; Charles C. Bolton, *Poor Whites in the Antebellum South: Tenants and Laborers in Central North Carolina and Northeast Mississippi* (Durham, NC: Duke University Press, 1994), 5. For a full discussion of how I arrived at (and why I use) this conservative estimate, see the Appendix.

[5] For the purposes of this book, the Deep South refers to South Carolina, Georgia, Alabama, and Mississippi. Louisiana's complex racial hierarchy was obviously too different from its sister states to be fully included, but examples from it, as well as from the bordering states of Tennessee and North Carolina, are occasionally used.

The Specie Circular Act of 1836 further helped solidify class distinctions, as the law required that all governmental land purchases be transacted with silver or gold, making it nearly impossible for the landless to enter the ranks of the landed. Supposedly ushering in an era of universal white male suffrage, the Jacksonian era ended with a significant financial crash that helped further concentrate wealth. Although, until recently, historians have tended to overlook the significance of the Panic of 1837, the breadth of its devastation cannot be overstated. As many smallholders lost their land due to foreclosure, bankruptcy, and tax liens, plantation owners began buying up the acreage around them, consolidating much of the region's landholdings.

Problems for non-slaveholding whites continued accruing throughout the 1840s, right on the heels of the economic recession. By this time, the profitability and profusion of plantation slavery had rendered most unskilled white workers superfluous, particularly in the Deep South, where higher percentages of slaves exacerbated the problem. Like their forefathers, most poor whites had spent their lives working in agriculture, only to find their services no longer required, except during the bottleneck seasons of planting and harvest. Shut out from much of the Deep South's agricultural work, many poor white laborers spent the late-antebellum period experiencing long bouts of unemployment or underemployment.[6]

The situation only grew worse with the cotton boom of the 1850s, as the richest slaveholders grew their wealth while non-slaveholders continued to flounder, increasingly shut out of the market economy. Agreeing with historian Gavin Wright that "antebellum southern agriculture was characterized by a highly unequal wealth distribution," economist Albert Niemi described the region as marred by deep levels of inequality, regardless of the cash crop produced. Slavery had already driven the wages of southern white laborers well below those of their northern counterparts, but even more detrimentally, it decreased the demand for white tenants,

---

[6] Most studies that focus on antebellum laborers in the South have tended to concentrate on a slightly higher class of workers, like those with artisanal skills. Other scholars have lumped poor whites into a broad non-slaveholder category. See Michele Gillespie, *Free Labor in an Unfree World: White Artisans in Slaveholding Georgia, 1789–1860* (Athens: University of Georgia Press, 2000); J. William Harris, *Plain Folk and Gentry in a Slave Society: White Liberty and Black Slavery in Augusta's Hinterland* (Baton Rouge: Louisiana University Press, 1985), Timothy J. Lockley, "Partners in Crime: African Americans and Non-Slaveholding Whites in Antebellum Georgia," in Matt Wray and Annalee Newitz, eds., *White Trash: Race and Class in America* (New York: Routledge, 1997), and Timothy James Lockley, *Lines in the Sand: Race and Class in Lowcountry Georgia, 1750–1860* (Athens: University of Georgia Press, 2001).

croppers, day laborers, and even mechanics, creating a large underclass of white people who were unable to find consistent work or earn a living wage. As poor white Isaac Grimes remembered, employment opportunities were "awful scarce. Couldn't hardly get work [and] wages [were] so low – I have worked that time for $5.00 a month and board. Worked with oxens, all [I] could get for work." Another laborer from Georgia complained that "the slaveholders could get the slave for almost nothing and the poor young men like myself could not get a job." Completely removed from many of the privileges of whiteness, poor whites were essentially masterless men and women in an increasingly hierarchical world held together by mastery. This fact deeply troubled the region's slaveholders.[7]

Indeed, poor white Southerners not only possessed class consciousness, but as the antebellum period wore on, they became overtly resentful of slaveholders. With their labor rendered almost unnecessary, some poor whites chose to drop out of society altogether, living off the land and often running afoul of the law. Others struggled to make ends meet with occasional odd jobs and seasonal agricultural work. Yet the nature of this type of labor kept many poor white men on the move in search of jobs, fracturing households and leaving many families headed by women, at least for portions of the year. Although they never experienced the brutality and abuse that African Americans did, poor whites still suffered obvious hardships – all because of slavery.

Unfortunately, poor whites made particularly inviting targets for a southern legal system dominated by slaveholders, who generally incarcerated them for behavioral, nonviolent "crimes" such as trading, drinking, and other social interactions with slaves and free blacks. On the eve of secession, slaveholders were still jailing poor whites for small amounts of debt, publicly whipping thieves, and auctioning off debtors and criminals (for their labor) to the highest bidder. In addition to the region's sophisticated legal system, the Old South also had an extremely effective extralegal system to keep the lower-class whites in their places. From vigilance committees to minutemen groups, these organizations helped maintain

---

[7] See Gavin Wright, *Old South, New South: Revolutions in the Southern Economy Since the Civil War* (Baton Rouge: Louisiana University Press, 1986); Albert W. Niemi, Jr., "Inequality in the Distribution of Slave Wealth: The Cotton South and Other Southern Agricultural Regions," *Journal of Economic History* 37, No. 3 (Sept. 1977): 747; 750; Colleen M. Elliot and Louise A. Moxley, eds. *The Tennessee Civil War Veterans Questionnaires*, Vols. 1–5. (Easley, SC: Southern Historical Press, Inc., 1985), Vol. 3, 966; Vol. 3, 1057.

both slavery and the southern social hierarchy, and ultimately forced a divided region to wage an unwanted war.

Class tensions between white Southerners in the Deep South, therefore, ultimately added to the causes of the Civil War. Angered by their lack of job prospects, poor white laborers – whose ranks were rapidly increasing in southern cities due to immigration – were becoming more and more militant in the decades leading up to secession. They began forming "associations," or labor unions, and demanded freedom from competition with slaves and even free blacks, whose wages always undercut their own. Vocal leaders of these groups threatened to stop supporting slavery if something was not done to help raise their wages. The master class was already strenuously defending the peculiar institution from attacks by northern abolitionists and by slaves themselves. When poor whites created a three-front battleground, slaveholders had few viable alternatives other than secession to protect their main source of wealth and revenue.

Attempting to frighten poor whites into supporting disunion, slaveholders predicted an impending race war following emancipation. Warning that freeing the slaves would drive down the wages of poor whites to "starvation levels," slave owners then prophesied that black men would marry the daughters of the white poor. Without slavery, masters cautioned, poor whites would become impoverished peons, the social equals of blacks. Still, despite slaveholders' racist rhetoric, many poor whites objected to the Confederate cause, but slave owners used threats of imprisonment, vigilante violence, and even death to impress the poor into service. During the Civil War, the extremely high rate of layouts and desertions among lower-class whites eventually helped lead to the Confederacy's demise.

Slavery certainly had been detrimental for poor whites, yet in a similar way, black emancipation ushered in several new freedoms for the white poor. Most importantly, poor white workers were finally able to compete in a free labor economy. But their increasing inclusion in the spoils of whiteness often came at the expense of blacks. While freedmen waited in vain for forty acres and a mule, some poor whites were granted land from the Homestead Acts. Emancipation also brought an end to the high rates of incarceration for poor whites who had threatened the stability of slavery. Instead, African Americans became the primary targets of the southern legal system, but their punishments were much more extreme and vicious than they ever had been for poor whites. The end of slavery, therefore, heralded many new freedoms for lower-class white

Southerners, while African Americans realized they now occupied poor whites' former place at the bottom of "free" society.

By simply stating these facts, one of the biggest and most persistent falsities of southern history is revealed: the myth of white unity over slavery. Poor whites consistently supported slaveholder policies, and even fought for the Confederacy, the argument goes, because they greatly admired the slaveholders and aspired to own slaves themselves. To be sure, there was certainly near-universal consensus among southern whites regarding racism, but support for slavery varied significantly, especially among members of lower-economic classes. Heeding the recent work of economists, however, shows that the vast majority of poor whites recognized the near-impossibility of eventually owning slaves.

With the research of the cliometricians appearing in the 1960s and 1970s, the long-accepted premise that the white South was united across class lines became more tenuous. Understanding wealth distribution and the price of slaves helped dispel the misconception that every non-slaveholder, no matter how impoverished, believed that one day they would enter the ranks of the master class. In 2011, the pioneering work of economists Samuel Williamson and Louis Cain established that by the later antebellum period, purchasing a slave was far outside of the realm of possibilities for poorer whites. By using different measures of economic value, these scholars arrived at a much more accurate analysis of the capital it required to become a slaveholder. Arguing that both economic status and economic power influenced the cost of slaves, Williamson and Cain wrote that "Even if they have not been elected to power, the wealthy often have disproportionate influence on those who do ... [and] Slaveholders as a group had considerable economic power." Therefore, while the average "real price" of a slave in 1860 was $20,000 in today's terms, that number is not an accurate indicator of how much capital a non-slaveholder needed to enter into the ranks of the slaveholding oligarchy.[8]

Instead, by using a "comparable value" based on three measures of worth, Williamson and Cain took into consideration (1) labor or income value, (2) economic status, and (3) real price. They found a threefold increase in slave prices following the long depression that started with the Panic of 1837 and ended around 1843. Using this new valuation process, they calculated that the average price of a slave in 1850 ($400) would be

---

[8] Samuel H. Williamson and Louis P. Cain. "Measuring Slavery in 2011 Dollars." Paper on MeasuringWorth.com.

$82,000 in 2011. As the price of slaves rose throughout the decade, and slave ownership became even more concentrated, on the eve of secession the "purchase of a single slave represented as much as $130,000 and more in today's prices." This astonishing fact – that in 1860 it took about $130,000 to purchase a single slave – combined with the reality that less affluent white Southerners had no access to loans, finally puts the slaveholder-aspiration illusion to rest. "Potentially all slaveholders ranked in the top one percent," Williamson and Cain concluded, "if economic power is used as the standard of comparison."[9]

By understanding that the lives of poor whites and blacks followed similar trajectories during the mid-nineteenth century, the far-reaching impact of slavery is finally revealed. Traveling through the South just a couple of years prior to the Civil War, one Northerner plainly stated that the rather pitiful status of the South's poor whites was a blight upon the entire country. A direct result of slavery, non-slaveholders' "poverty, ignorance, and debasement, are not merely sectional" problems, he wrote, but "constitute a national calamity, an element of impoverishment, a running sore in the body-politic. The whole Union is weakened by it." A century and a half later a team of economists revealed similar sentiments. Finding that the "historical use of slavery is significantly correlated with current levels of inequality," their research convincingly demonstrated that even today slavery's legacy is undeniably visible in the economic circumstances – and thus the material well-being – of all nonelite Southerners, both black and white. While the consequences were certainly far more severe and sustained for black Americans, it is important to recognize that the economic repercussions of slavery also greatly affected lower-class whites.[10]

---

[9] *Ibid.* Williamson and Cain also showed that "the holder of 10 slaves likely ranks in the top one percent of the distribution [of total estate], if economic status is used as the standard of comparison." Wealth grew by about 30 percent during the decade of the 1850s, but in the South, non-slave wealth grew at 25 percent, while slave wealth grew at 40 percent. By 1860, the top 1 percent of white Southerners held 27 percent of total estate, while the bottom 50 percent held 1 percent. Only 0.11 percent held more than 100 slaves, and "Those who owned over 500 slaves had a measure of economic power that compares to billionaires today."

[10] John S. Abbott, *South and North; or Impressions Received during a Trip to Cuba and the South* (New York, 1860), 145, Web; Rodrigo R. Soares et al., "A Note on Slavery and the Roots of Inequality," *Journal of Comparative Economics* 40, (2012): 578. "The correlation between slavery and inequality," they reported, "survives the inclusion of variables controlling for development, geographic characteristics, institutional quality, and provision of public goods ... [and holds true] still today."

In the Old South, the daily realities of this sizable poor white class clearly show how the institution of slavery was detrimental to their livelihoods. They consciously recognized its negative impact on their lives. Kept uneducated and mostly illiterate, poor whites had few chances to rise out of poverty. Industrialist-turned-historian James Ford Rhodes compared the South's poor whites to northern laborers, concluding that "they were in material things abjectly poor; intellectually they were utterly ignorant; morally their condition was one of groveling baseness." As the antebellum period wore on, some particularly disillusioned poor whites chose to drop out of the workforce altogether, preferring to live on the fringes of society. As Governor James Henry Hammond reported to the South Carolina Institute in 1850, many poor whites were able to "obtain a precarious subsistence by occasional jobs, by hunting, by fishing, by plundering fields or folds, and too often by what is in its effects far worse – trading with slaves, and seducing them to plunder for their benefit."

This illicit trading with slaves, coupled with the high numbers of young, property-less white men drifting from county to county in search of work, caused slaveholders to begin selectively enforcing behavioral laws, especially in places with both high slave populations and recent influxes of transient whites. By insisting that poor whites be arrested for vagrancy, buying liquor on Sunday, or engaging in lewd behavior, slaveholders were able to incarcerate non-slaveholders whenever they needed to reinforce subordination to their authority. Poor whites' increasingly frequent bouts with local law enforcement officials helped brand them as hardened, troublesome criminals, characterized, as A.N.J. Den Hollander put it, by "laziness, carelessness, unreliability, lack of foresight and ambition, habitual failure and general incompetency."[11]

Certainly by the late antebellum period, poor southern whites had few opportunities to rise above the economic station into which they were born. Under slavery, E.B. Seabrook wrote, "The poor white, instead of being an active, vital member of the organism of society, was merely an excrescence upon its body. Useless to others, he became helpless to himself." Because slavery's association with agricultural and manual

[11] James Ford Rhodes, *History of the United States from the Compromise of 1850 to the McKinley-Bryan Campaign of 1896*, Vol. 1, 1850–1854 (New York: Macmillan Company, 1920), 344, Web; quoted in George M. Weston, *The Poor Whites of the South* (Washington, DC: Buell & Blanchard, 1856), 3, Web.; A.N.J. Den Hollander, "The Tradition of 'Poor Whites,'" in W.T. Couch, ed., *Culture in the South* (Chapel Hill: University of North Carolina Press, 1935), 414.

labor "rendered toil ignoble in the estimation of the whites," poor white laborers adopted "a willful, determined indolence, which actually became the badge and ensign of their independence."[12]

The lives (and deaths) of poor white Southerners were often chaotic and unpredictable. For a meaningful proportion of them, some combination of material want, hunger, illiteracy, involvement in criminal activity, and problems resulting from alcohol abuse reinforced these self-perpetuating cycles of poverty. Writing almost one hundred years after Hinton Helper, Richard Morris critiqued the assumption that white skin entitled an individual to freedom in the slave South. Instead, he claimed, "two-thirds of that white population which was 'free' in name never fully enjoyed the fruits of that freedom." Slavery, Morris concluded, had "seriously undermined the economic security of white labor in the slave states and left ugly scars upon the character and temperament of the ruling class."[13]

The master class, of course, would never admit to the numbers of poverty-stricken poor whites in the region. How could they, William Jay incredulously asked, when they would be acknowledging that slavery was detrimental to a large percentage of free white citizens? William, the second son of John Jay, was an abolitionist lawyer who appealed to non-slaveholding southern whites in 1849. "It is amusing to observe how adroitly the slaveholders avoid all recognition of any other classes among them than masters and slaves. Who would suspect from their language, that they were themselves a small minority of the white inhabitants, and that their own 'white negroes' could, if united and so disposed, outvote them at the polls?" he prodded. "It is worthy of remark that in their denunciations of the *populace*, the *rabble, those who work with their hands*, they refer not to complexion, but to condition; not to slaves, but to the poor and laborious of their own color."[14]

Poor whites, therefore, are well hidden in the annals of southern history for a variety of reasons. Slave owners were very reluctant to publically acknowledge the poor's existence, as doing so would have nullified the pro-slavery charges of "wage slavery" in the North. By

---

[12] E.B. Seabrook, "Poor Whites of the South," *The Galaxy Volume*, Issue 6 (Oct. 1867): 685.

[13] Richard M. Morris, "The Measure of Bondage in the Slave States," *The Mississippi Valley Historical Review* 41, No. 2 (Sept. 1954): 240.

[14] William Jay, *Address to the Non-slaveholders of the South, on the Social and Political Evils of Slavery* (New York: William Harned, 1849), 18 (This tract is wrongly attributed to Lewis Tappan on the Web).

admitting the South had a very sizable percentage of its own poor – consistently plagued by unemployment, underemployment, and non-livable wages – the rosy ideal of the humanitarian, caretaking paternalist would have immediately dissolved. Both abolitionists and free-labor supporters frequently referred to the "poor, deluded, ignorant masses" of southern whites, but southern politicians and intellectuals were loath to respond. Poor whites were undoubtedly a basic part of southern society, but generally speaking, historians have also overlooked them in assessments of the nineteenth century. Who, exactly, qualified as a poor white has been debated for decades, and scholars still have not reached consensus. According to Mildred Mell, the earliest writer to have used the description was David Ramsay, who published *History of South Carolina* in 1809. The term gained widespread notoriety throughout the United States because of the works of Harriett Beecher Stowe, especially *Key to Uncle Tom's Cabin* and *Dred: A Tale of the Great Dismal Swamp*. Sociologist Matt Wray wrote that Stowe did more to "popularize, nationalize, and internationalize the phrase poor white trash than anyone in antebellum history." And while Stowe obviously harbored some sympathy for the slaves in her novels, she did not maintain similar feelings for the white poor. Instead, she regarded them as violent and prone to criminal activities, a "miserable class" who are "utterly ignorant, and inconceivably brutal."[15]

Beginning in the early 1900s, scholars like W.O. Brown, Paul Buck, Avery Craven, and U.B. Phillips wrote about poor whites, but their findings were often compromised by racism, as well as a desire to redeem the South through a subjective retelling of history. Casting the vast majority of white Southerners as either slaveholders or poor whites, these scholars rarely mentioned yeomen landholders or the burgeoning professional middle classes of the Deep South's towns and cities. Their analyses would remain unchallenged until an aggrieved southern apologist undertook to rewrite the historical record in an effort to redeem the tarnished memory of his beloved Dixie.[16]

---

[15] Mildred Rutherford Mell, "A Definitive Study of the Poor Whites of the South" (Ph.D. Dissertation, University of North Carolina, 1938), 92; Wray, *Not Quite White*, 57; quoted in *Ibid*.

[16] See W.O. Brown, "Role of Poor Whites in Race Contracts of the South," *Social Forces* 19, No. 2 (Dec. 1940): 258–68; Paul H. Buck, "The Poor Whites of the Ante-Bellum South," *The American Historical Review* 31, No. 1 (Oct. 1925): 41–54; Avery O. Craven, "Poor Whites and Negroes in the Antebellum South," *The Journal of Negro History* 15, No.1 (Jan. 1930): 14–25; U.B. Phillips, *American Negro Slavery: A Survey of*

In 1949, Frank L. Owsley effectively shifted the focus of generations of historians away from the numerically more significant poor whites and onto the South's rural middling classes. *Plain Folk of the Old South* challenged the traditionally accepted belief that the South was a land of three classes (black slaves, poor whites, and elite planters). Attempting to prove that slavery had had almost no effect on non-slaveholding whites, Owsley and the other Nashville Agrarians erroneously asserted that the vast majority of white Southerners owned land. Although never fully revealing his precise methodology, Owsley utilized "church records, wills, administration of estates, county-court minutes, marriage licenses, inventory of estates, trial records, mortgage books, deed books, county tax books, and the manuscript returns of the Federal censuses" to make his claims. Using a sampling technique, Owsley concluded that by 1860, 80 to 85 percent of the "agricultural population" owned land. "Plain folk" included herdsmen, small slave-holding farmers, non-slaveholding landowners, and even well-off tenant farmers. Owsley held that this amalgamation of white Southerners shared folkways and traditions, migratory patterns, and often, political beliefs. His most controversial ideas concerned patterns of southern migration and the plain folk's relative political and social equality with their planter neighbors.[17]

Owsley also deliberately excluded slavery from his analysis. Plain folk wanted to herd cattle and hogs, he argued, and had no desire to own land like planters. Once plantation owners began erecting fences and cordoning off land, it was only natural for the plain folk to withdraw farther into the woods and forests so their herds could roam free. "It was agriculture, then, and not slavery – as has been said repeatedly in the discussion of the pastoral economy of the frontier – that drove the herdsmen from frontier to frontier and finally into the pine barrens, hill, and mountains," he concluded. Realizing that other scholars might take him to task for such unsubstantiated claims, Owsley insisted that "because of the great forests [plain folk's] herds of cows and droves of hogs were seldom to be seen by anyone passing hurriedly through the country." Modern scholars have largely nullified Owsley's herding thesis. As Charles Bolton and others have found, the vast majority of

the Supply, Employment, and Control of Negro Labor as Determined by the Plantation Regime (1918; reprint, Baton Rouge: Louisiana University Press, 1966); and Phillips, "The Origin and Growth of the Southern Black Belts," American Historical Review Vol. 11, No. 4 (July 1906): 798–816.

[17] Frank L. Owsley, Plain Folk of the Old South (1949; reprint, Baton Rouge: Louisiana University Press, 1977), 6; 16.

Southerners from all classes historically had worked as farmers, farm laborers, and tenants.[18]

Furthermore, Owsley completely dismissed the possibility of class consciousness among poor or non-slaveholding whites. He wrote that "with rare exceptions they did not regard the planters and men of wealth as their oppressors. On the contrary, they admired them as a rule and looked with approval on their success." Thus, he claimed, plain folk "assumed, on the basis of much tangible evidence, that the door of economic opportunity swung open easily to the thrust of their own ambitions and energetic sons and daughters." For Owsley's subjects, economic and social mobility seemed possible and even likely. His sturdy landowners were supposedly independent, self-sufficient farmers, and the presence of racial slavery had little to no bearing on their lives. Instead, he attempted to prove how insignificant and benign slavery had been. "But the greater part [of southern whites] remained landowning farmers who belonged neither to the plantation economy nor to the destitute and frequently degraded poor white class," he concluded. "They, and not the poor whites, comprised the bulk of the Southern population from the Revolution to the Civil War."[19]

Owsley's motives for writing about plain folk instead of poor whites, however, were hardly above reproach. As one of the Nashville Agrarians, Owsley had committed himself to presenting the South as a land of Jeffersonian ideals. He romanticized the small landowning farmer and resisted almost every aspect of the New South, from industrialization to the changing racial hierarchy. More importantly, Owsley wanted to discredit neo-abolitionist historians who had emphasized the hegemony of the Old South's planter class and the resulting degradation of other whites.

The antebellum South, Owsley incorrectly asserted, was undoubtedly democratic in nature. Slavery, he claimed, was actually beneficial for all whites, regardless of economic class and social status. By maintaining that most non-slaveholders owned land, Owsley tried to refute writers, such as Hinton Helper and Frederick Law Olmsted, who recognized slavery's detrimental impact on non-slaveholders. Primarily owing to Owsley's influence, the majority of contemporary histories on nonelite white Southerners have focused solely on landholding (and often slaveholding) yeomen farmers, classifying them as plain folk or common whites.

---

[18] Owsley, *Plain Folk*, 51; 36; Bolton, *Poor Whites*, 8.   [19] Owsley, *Plain Folk*, 133; xx.

No matter the term, farmers who owned slaves and/or land had much more in common with planters than they did with poor whites.

Owsley's contentions were almost immediately repudiated in a *Journal of Negro History* article that appeared in 1946. Along with two other Confederate sympathizers, Harry L. Coles and Herbert Weaver, Owsley was taken to task by a young Harvard-trained economist named Fabian Linden. While Linden would go on to create the Consumer Confidence Index, earning accolades and notoriety within the field of economics, historians have usually relegated his work to a footnote. A few scholars, such as Eugene Genovese, used Linden's research as a way to sidestep Owsley's unsound claims, but more recent historians of the Old South have ignored Linden's comprehensive rebuttal altogether, assuring that studies of the antebellum period generally disregard class as a unit of analysis.

Focusing on arithmetical errors, incorrect sampling methodology, illogical assumptions, and misleading conclusions, Linden's article should have exposed Owsley and the other Old South defenders as academic frauds. First and foremost, Linden wrote, all of Owsley's findings were said to apply to "that segment of the population which was engaged in agriculture, as recorded by the census," yet "in no instance is data given showing what portion of the entire population was so designated." Without precise numbers or even an explanation of methodology, Linden could only estimate what percentage of the southern population Owsley and his colleagues failed to count. The estimate was high. By leaving cities out of their analysis, as well as unskilled and semiskilled laborers, they likely failed to include a fifth to a quarter of the region's enumerated white population in their analyses. In just one example, Linden used Roger Shugg's work on Louisiana to show that in 1860, 43 percent of the population was urban, with over four-fifths of urban whites classed as unskilled or semiskilled wage earners. Yet even among the rural whites, almost half the families were landless, "while roughly one out of every two owners tilled farms of 50 acres or less." Therefore, only about 14 percent of the state's whites could be classified as middle class. While other Deep South states varied in population stratification, Shugg's findings were nowhere close to the approximations of the southern apologists.[20]

After thoroughly dismantling both the methodology and results of the Nashville group, Linden went after the heart of their argument, showing

[20] Fabian Linden, "Economic Democracy in the Slave South: An Appraisal of Some Recent Views," *Journal of Negro History* 31, No. 2 (April 1946): 148; 142; 144; 155; 157–8.

that by the late antebellum period, many white Southerners had been pushed off the land and out of agriculture because of slavery. He contended that there was "a striking concentration of slave property" in the areas studied. More importantly, "[w]ithout exception the great majority of families were either slaveless or very small landholders owning in the aggregate only a meagre proportion of the colored population." Linden further argued that real estate holdings were similar in pattern to slave holdings, and issued an additional caveat regarding land quality. Southern land varied so much in value that it had been known to sell for as little as a quarter an acre on one extreme, and as much as $100 an acre on the other. Most non-slaveholders and small-holders owned the least desirable plots. Indeed, Linden concluded, "a very considerable proportion of the farm population, in the areas studied, owned an almost insignificant share of the land. In no instance ... did the lowest quartile of farming families own more than 1 per cent of the land." However, the top quartile in every sample region laid claim to between two-thirds and three-quarters of land wealth. Thus, the concentration of wealth – whether in land or slaves – was incredible, even in non-blackbelt areas with poorer soil, like the piney woods and northern hill regions. Regardless of which part of the Deep South Linden examined, "the coefficient of [wealth] stratification tended to be constant. Even in areas where there were few or none of the extensive slave estates this distribution pattern was distinct."[21]

Yet despite Linden's work, and other recent efforts by a handful of scholars, the larger narrative of southern history is not yet liberated from Owsley's myths. Historians have managed to free much of southern history from the distortions of Confederate apologists, but current scholars should take note that Owsley's musings on poor whites were also very much a part of the racial agenda revealed in his essay in *I'll Take My Stand*, which referred to freedmen "who could still remember the taste of human flesh." Later, in his 1940 presidential address to the Southern Historical Association, Owsley asserted that the primary cause of the Civil War was the "egocentric sectionalism" of Northerners. At the time, he was saying what many white Southerners – and white southern historians – wanted to hear. Owsley's idyllic version of history

---

[21] *Ibid.*, 151; 156; 165; 163–4. Linden found that in Alabama, "two-thirds of all acres in the black belt were held by 17 percent of the farming population and were part of plantations which claimed over 500 acres," (161) and in the Mississippi Delta, about 90 percent of all land was "parceled off in units of 500 or more acres." (159).

unquestionably helped restore the legacy of their forefathers, whether slaveholders or not, from historic reality.[22]

Only within the past couple of decades have scholars begun to focus specifically on poor whites. Led by the pioneering work of Charles Bolton, historians such as Victoria Bynum and Jeff Forret have already challenged the accepted "Old South" historical canon. The most commonly used definition of poor whites remains Bolton's, who estimated that they comprised 30 to 50 percent of the region's white population. He classified them simply as owning neither land nor slaves. However, using a strictly economic definition poses additional problems. As Den Hollander noted, while "[n]ot all [poor whites] were squatters or tenants ... the possession of some barren tract made small difference." Writing a dozen years after Bolton, Forret expanded the definition, accounting for the importance of "character and not wealth alone." Taking into consideration antebellum Southerners' uses of the term, Forret's definition combined both qualitative and quantitative factors. Following his classification, this book overwhelmingly refers to poor whites who were both landless and slaveless, although there were undoubtedly a few cases of very small property holders counted. Conversely, in an attempt to exclude middling-class Southerners who did not own real estate (mostly town and city dwellers), whenever it was possible to ascertain personal property, I include only those individuals who owned less than $100. All things considered, therefore, I have chosen to use a rather conservative estimate of the total numbers of poor whites. For reasons explained in the Appendix, I contend that scholars can safely assume that by 1860, at least one-third of the Deep South's white population consisted of the truly, cyclically poor.[23]

[22] Owsley quotes appear in James C. Cobb, "'On the Pinnacle in Yankeeland': C. Vann as a [Southern] Renaissance Man," *Journal of Southern History* 67, No. 4 (Nov. 2001): 732; see Frank Lawrence Owsley, "The Irrepressible Conflict," in Twelve Southerners, *I'll Take My Stand: The South and the Agrarian Tradition* (1930, reprint; Baton Rouge: Louisiana University Press, 1977).

[23] See Bolton, *Poor Whites*; Victoria Bynum, *Unruly Women: The Politics of Social and Sexual Control in the Old South* (Chapel Hill: University of North Carolina Press, 1992); and Jeff Forret, *Race Relations at the Margins: Slaves and Poor Whites in the Antebellum Southern Countryside* (Baton Rouge: Louisiana University Press, 2006). Bolton, *Poor Whites*, 5; also see David Brown, "A Vagabond's Tale: Poor Whites, Herrenvolk Democracy, and the Value of Whiteness in the Late Antebellum South," *Journal of Southern History* 79, No. 4 (Nov. 2013): 808; Den Hollander, "The Tradition of 'Poor Whites,'" 412; Forret, *Race Relations*, 10–11. Forret also estimated that one-fifth of all landless, slaveless whites qualified for the "trash" designation. These impoverished people lived a

Poor whites undoubtedly composed a completely distinct class from slaveholding yeomen and even from self-sufficient land-owning farmers. Still, most scholars have failed to distinguish poor whites from the middling classes, and have often made assumptions about all white Southerners based on the actions and privileges of propertied yeomen. This tendency likely originally stemmed from the infamous pro-slavery arguments, wherein slaveholding masters denied the existence of poor white Southerners altogether. Without acknowledgment of the dire circumstances of many poor whites, historians and writers have typically transposed the economic needs and political wants of propertied yeomen to less affluent whites, and in the process, they have obscured a very important aspect of American history.

W.J. Cash, the South Carolina-born journalist, serves as a perfect example of this common inaccuracy. He published *The Mind of the South* in 1941, but based important premises about the dictates of race and class in the antebellum period on his own contemporary experiences. Cash argued that even under slavery, a racist "proto-Dorian bond" united all southern whites, no matter how lowly or impoverished they were. Slavery may have been detrimental to poor whites in certain, limited ways, Cash admitted, but it still elevated their social status. Identifying a "very positive factor" of slavery, he presented the Old South as a region where "the old basic feeling of democracy was preserved virtually intact." Indeed, slavery elevated the common white to a position comparable to that of, say, the Doric knight of ancient Sparta. Not only were poor whites not exploited directly, Cash wrote, but most importantly, they shared membership in the master class. He failed to realize, however, that poor whites were far from masters. White skin, of course, granted them conditional freedoms, but as the burgeoning capitalist market further shut them out of southern society, they would better be described as masterless men and women.[24]

Writing exactly thirty years after Cash, George Fredrickson made similar claims, positing that a "herrenvolk democracy" united all classes of whites in racism. As long as poor whites had slaves to look down upon, Frederickson argued, they would always go along with slaveholders' wishes. He further held that the "savage ideal" of white supremacy kept poor whites from allying with blacks; instead, they were presented as rabid racists who chose to self-segregate. Even the poorest whites, both Cash and Frederickson believed, were content because they would never

dire hand-to-mouth existence, sporadically trading with slaves and free blacks in an interracial "underground economy" to supplement their meager incomes.
[24] W.J. Cash, *The Mind of the South* (1941, reprint; New York: Vintage, 1991), 38; 39; 39.

be at the bottom of the social pyramid, as long as blacks were enslaved or denied certain "white" rights and privileges. Frederickson and his intellectual successors, of course, were writing in response to the growing white backlash against the Civil Rights Movement. Their ideas concerning white solidarity over racism seemed natural given the realities of the times in which they were writing.[25]

Given this prior scholarship, subsequent historians – understandably – have tended to overlook poor whites, often basing theories about the white South solely upon the rights, privileges, and interactions of property-owning (and often very affluent) whites. Lacy Ford and Stephanie McCurry both argued that South Carolina had a democratic political culture that included the widespread participation of yeomen, who, they maintained, far outnumbered the more affluent planters. While Ford classified yeomen as owning up to five slaves, and McCurry expanded the definition to include up to nine slaves, *any* slaveholder, as well as the vast majority of landholders, had much more in common with planters than with poor whites. The master class naturally encouraged the political participation of men who shared their economic interests.[26]

Poor whites, conversely, were not engaged in an egalitarian, democratic society, and tensions with slaveholders ran deep for a variety of reasons. Instead, in the few years prior to disunion they coexisted with an increasingly hostile slaveholding class who sought to police and control their actions, speech, access to information, and even their beliefs. David Brown alluded to poor whites' dissatisfaction with their economic situation, but also suggested that the class be further divided into "two groups of rural propertyless white men ... one with yeomen aspirations; the other wedded to a culture of crime, backwoods fighting, and interracial fraternization that distanced them from the mainstream." While Brown's new classification offers important distinctions among the poor, it is necessary to note that many of the "aspirational poor whites" of whom he speaks were actually younger sons from families of wealth and property. Just beginning their professional lives, they had yet to accumulate wealth or inheritance. Certainly by the later antebellum period, there

---

[25] George M. Frederickson, *The Black Image in the White Mind: The Debate on Afro-American Character and Destiny, 1817–1914* (New York: Harper and Row, 1971).

[26] Lacy K. Ford, *Origins of Southern Radicalism: The South Carolina Upcountry, 1800–1860* (New York: Oxford University Press, 1988); and Stephanie McCurry, *Masters of Small Worlds: Yeoman Households, Gender Relations, and the Political Culture of the Antebellum South Carolina Low Country* (New York: Oxford University Press, 1995), 278.

were very few whites born to impoverished families who were able to gain an education and rise out of the lower classes. Slavery-driven capitalism made the slaveholders richer, while simultaneously ravaging the poor. The *National Era* ran an article in the fall of 1858 asserting that no other "country in the civilized world" had "such a wide, deep chasm" dividing "class and class as that which separates" the slaveholders and non-slaveholders "occupying this plantation district in the Southern States." To be sure, the writer continued, the two groups "are united by no common bond of sympathy or interest. On the contrary, a sour, sullen suspicion on the one side, and a proud and haughty bearing on the other, are likely to widen the gulf between them."[27]

To fully establish whether or not poor whites harbored class consciousness, two terms deserve more careful definitions. For both "class" and "class consciousness," this book follows the meanings set forth by E.P. Thompson in his seminal history of the English working class. "By class," he wrote, "I understand an historical phenomenon, unifying a number of disparate and seemingly unconnected events, both in the raw material of experience and in consciousness." Viewing class not as a thing, but instead as a relationship, Thompson claimed that in "the years between 1780–1832 most English working people came to feel an identity of interests as between themselves, and as against their rulers and employers." This feeling, of course, formed the basis of class consciousness, which Thompson defined as "the way in which these experiences are handled in cultural terms: embodied in traditions, value-systems, ideas, and institutional forms." According to these definitions, antebellum poor whites unquestionably possessed class consciousness, and class tensions had reached dangerous levels by the time of secession. Heavily influenced by the work of W.E.B. DuBois, David Roediger added racial nuance to Thompson's designation. "The problem is not just that the white working class is at critical junctures manipulated into racism," he concluded, "but that it comes to think of itself and its interests as white." As to Roediger's point, however, it seemed to be very difficult for impoverished white Southerners to consider their interests as "white." They were directly prevented from enjoying many of the privileges of whiteness.[28]

---

[27] David Brown, "A Vagabond's Tale," 806; "The Farming and Plantation System in the Southern States," *National Era*, Sept. 30, 1858.

[28] E.P. Thompson, *The Making of the English Working Class* (1963, reprint; New York: Vintage, 1966), 9; 11; 11; 10; David R. Roediger, *The Wages of Whiteness: Race and the Making of the American Working Class* (New York: Verso, 1999), 12.

As of yet no scholar has convincingly argued that poor whites exhibited a broad sense of class consciousness. Historians of middling and lower-class whites have long been divided over this issue. J. Wayne Flynt, for example, believed that poor whites were just as racist as other southern whites, and therefore inclined to rally to the defense of all southern institutions, regardless of how those institutions affected their wealth and livelihoods. Poor whites, Flynt held, "generally were neither exploited nor mistreated by the aristocracy; they were simply ignored ... not overtly oppressed." Conversely, both Michael Johnson and J. Mills Thornton concluded that class anxiety *did* exist in the Old South, but they also believed that by the time of the Civil War most of these tensions had been suppressed by race, republicanism, and fear of Yankee rule. Bolton and Bill Cecil-Fronsman basically agreed with these analyses, but they further posited that kinship ties and religion helped meld the various white classes together. Bolton, perhaps, went the farthest, suggesting that slaveholders also employed more overt and violent means to maintain the fidelity of the poor. Moreover, the emergence of a true southern middle class of merchants, lawyers, and doctors, along with a well-established class of sturdy land- and slaveholding yeomen, certainly complicated any kind of "common white" solidarity. Eugene Genovese and Elizabeth Fox-Genovese wrote that, because yeomen aspired to become planters, "they were led step by step into willing acceptance of a subordinate position in society." Poor whites, however, were not so easily led, as they had little incentive to follow.[29]

A small group of scholars, however, have long argued that poor whites possessed at least a degree of class consciousness. In 1964, Clement Eaton proposed that "[t]oward the close of the antebellum period, the mechanics and non-slaveholders were beginning to show some signs of class consciousness." Later, likely inspired by Genovese's theories on hegemony and class, historians like Fred Arthur Bailey more boldly claimed that "the poor, the plain folk, and the planters were [all] class conscious." The

---

[29] J. Wayne Flynt, *Dixie's Forgotten People: The South's Poor Whites* (Bloomington: Indiana University Press, 1979), 11; Michael P. Johnson, *Toward a Patriarchal Republic: The Secession of Georgia* (Baton Rouge: Louisiana University Press, 1977), 143; J. Mills Thornton, III, *Politics and Power in a Slave Society: Alabama, 1800–1860* (Baton Rouge: Louisiana University Press, 1978); Bolton, *Poor Whites*; Bill Cecil-Fronsman, *Common Whites: Class and Culture in Antebellum North Carolina* (Lexington: The University Press of Kentucky, 1992); Eugene Genovese and Elizabeth Fox-Genovese, *Fruits of Merchant Capital: Slavery and Bourgeois Property in the Rise and Expansion of Capitalism* (New York: Oxford University Press, 1983), 263.

situation of poor whites was similar to that of slaves in that there was no major, overt opposition to the existing order. However, just as slaves feigned illness, broke tools, or worked at a slow pace, poor whites also resisted affluent whites in similar ways. Walter Johnson's reconsideration of slave "agency" is completely applicable to antebellum poor whites. For decades, Johnson argued, most historians held three faulty premises about agency. First, scholars failed to recognize revolutionary aspirations among slaves. Second, many believed that a "'failure' to revolt must somehow be explained in reference to the slaves' own culture rather than the balance of force in the society – by reference, that is, to 'hegemony' rather than simple 'rule.'" Finally, historians of slavery needed to stop creating contradiction "between individual and collective acts of resistance."[30]

Thus, even without any generally recognized, well-coordinated acts of mass resistance, poor whites were still intellectually aware of the region's deepening inequality. Their daily realities made class differences painfully clear. Class consciousness, of course, does not always translate into action. It can simply be an awareness of inequity. "With all this, the mere blind instincts of human nature filled these people with a dim consciousness of the falsity of their position, and a vague sense of injury, which was displayed in a deep, sullen hatred of the upper class," Seabrook explained in 1867. Yet the influential "planters were always able to repress" this class tension, "at least so far as any active demonstration was concerned, by that power which intelligence of the highest order must always have over the grossest ignorance, and unbounded wealth over abject poverty." Indeed, as the Genoveses reminded the scholarly community in 2011: "Kindness, love, and benevolence did not define paternalism." It depended instead "on the constant threat and actuality of violence." The brute force of the all-powerful slaveholders was much more intense and calculated than most historians have previously believed. Recent histories concerning capitalism in the Deep South have revealed, to a certain extent, the vicious cruelty masters inflicted upon slaves. Yet these slave owners lorded over more than just blacks. In actuality, they maintained tight control over the vast majority of all Southerners – including poor whites. Dominating both the political and economic spheres, masters used both legal and extralegal means to keep other whites in line.

[30] Clement Eaton, *The Freedom of Thought Struggle in the Old South* (1940; reprint, Durham: Duke University Press, 1964), 40; Bailey, *Class*, 67; Walter Johnson, "On Agency," *Journal of Social History* 31, No. 1 (2003): 117.

As Richard Morris wrote, "it is impossible to ignore the extent to which arbitrary rule and even lawlessness flourished in the South, how it was fed by perverted paternalism, by the psychological unbalance of the master-servant relationship."[31]

By fully situating poor whites into the larger political economy, nuance is added to the old debate over whether the South was capitalist by the later antebellum period. Certainly by the 1840s, the upper-middling and upper classes had become strong proponents of modern capitalism and were full participants in the market-driven economy. Recent works by Edward Baptist, Sven Beckert, and Walter Johnson all attest to the fact that slaveholders were shrewd capitalists who treated their slaves accordingly. James Oakes, therefore, anticipated what would soon become accepted cannon within American history: the Old South was, in fact, fully capitalist.[32]

Yet, while all of these scholars were certainly correct in their assessment of the markets, their analyses tend to minimize the primary questions that Eugene Genovese raised decades ago. When actual laborers – whether slave or "free" – are brought back into consideration, the issue becomes more complicated. Indeed, while the markets were certainly capitalist, social relations within the region did not resemble *capitalist* social relations, making Genovese's "in-but-not-of" maxim much more accurate than some recent scholars have contended. Genovese, of course, wanted to show how labor and social control worked in a rural-but-market-driven, slavery-ridden economy. He argued that the "relations of production (slave labor) rather than relations of exchange (the world market in which slaveholders participated) shaped the nature of antebellum southern society." Therefore, "merchant capitalism gave rise to archaic systems of labor such as racial slavery ... but it also created the world market." Commerce, he insisted, "cannot be mistaken for capitalism." Unlike more recent scholars, Genovese relied on Marx's definition of capitalism, which is based upon the *relationship* between wage laborers

---

[31] Seabrook, "The Poor Whites," 866; Eugene D. Genovese and Elizabeth Fox-Genovese, *Fatal Self-Deception: Slaveholding Paternalism in the Old South* (New York: Cambridge University Press, 2011), 2; Morris, "The Measure of Bondage," 240.

[32] Edward E. Baptist, *The Half Has Never Been Told: Slavery and the Making of American Capitalism* (New York: Basic Books, 2014); Sven Beckert, *Empire of Cotton: A Global History* (New York: Alfred A. Knopf, 2014); Walter Johnson, *River of Dark Dreams: Slavery and Empire in the Cotton Kingdom* (Cambridge: Harvard University Press, 2013); James Oakes, *The Ruling Race: A History of American Slaveholders* (New York: Norton, 1998).

and their employers. According to that definition, the ability of workers to sell their own labor-power is critical.[33]

The enslaved – as laborers – must NOT be removed from this equation. But, if scholars wish to sidestep the issue of slavery, they still must deal with the South's other laborers. As soon as wage-earning poor whites are added into the analysis, the South cannot be considered to have had capitalist social relations. Marx defined labor power as the capacity to do work, and capitalist systems rely on the fact that the laborer has a choice of whether or not to enter into a contractual relationship. Labor power, therefore, should be understood as the ability of workers to choose how, when, where, and perhaps to whom to sell their labor. By definition it is not forced or unfree labor. While under capitalism, all laborers need to sell their labor power in order to live, Marx argued, they still maintained a modicum of control due to free will and choice.[34]

Under capitalism, labor power was the commodity of the laborer. Conversely, under feudalism, as well as under slavery, the ruling classes owned, either completely or partially, the labor power of the working classes. The system was predicated on elites coercing individuals to work, often by violent means. In the slave South, where white laborers were in competition with brutalized, enslaved labor, the laborers, whether legally free or not, had little to no control over their labor power. The profitability and profusion of plantation slave labor consistently reduced the demand for free workers, lowered their wages, and rendered their bargaining power ineffective, indeed generally (except in the case of specialized skills) worthless. In essence, they were not truly "free" laborers, especially when they could be arrested and forced to labor, for the state or for individuals.

The definitial issues do not stop there. While the term "capitalism" is bandied about freely, most scholars refrain from distinguishing precisely what type of capitalism they are referring to. The majority of readers conceptualize capitalism as being of the industrial variety, but the social relations in that type of society are completely different from the social relations under merchant capitalism. As early as the 1940s, Richard Morris argued that the type of capitalism in the Old South was merchant

---

[33] Manisha Sinha, "Eugene D. Genovese: The Mind of a Marxist Conservative," *Radical History Review* 88 (Winter 2004): quoted on 6. See Genovese and Fox-Genovese, *Fruits of Merchant Capital*.

[34] For critiques of the new history of capitalism, see Robin Blackburn, "White Gold, Black Labour," New Left Review 95 (Sept.–Oct. 2015): 151–60, and Peter James Hudson, "The Racist Dawn of Capitalism," *Boston Review*, March 14, 2016.

capitalism, *not* industrial capitalism. His theory, of course, would be championed several decades later by Genovese. This distinction is one of the keys to understanding labor relations in the nineteenth-century South. It also shifts our focus from economic and business transactions back to human beings – to relationships between masters or employers and slaves and free laborers. Indeed, the lack of this distinction between merchant and industrial capitalism has been a detriment to the field. Beckert has recently broken from this tradition, confirming that Dixie was ruled by merchant capitalism, although he rebranded merchant capitalism as "war capitalism." Indeed, war capitalism may become a very important notion in the future, but stopping there still obscures the concept of labor power and thus fails to provide an accurate version of social relationships between Southerners.[35]

As Genovese further pointed out, Marx believed that labor power was particularly potent in factory settings, where workers could band together in solidarity. Because of the rural nature of most the Deep South, laborers usually did not have the ability to share grievances over employment with fellow laborers. They were simply too isolated. On the other hand, some poor whites also had the ability to hunt, fish, forage, or steal instead of taking a wage paying job. These facts added to Genovese's contention that the plantation South was ruled by merchant capitalism (which then fed industrial capitalism).

Thus, as Oakes and others have argued, slaveholders operated an intensely capitalistic economic system, but, as Genovese theorized, most of the region's social relations were still predicated on premodern behaviors – and violence trumped everything. Simply put, owing to slaveholders' personal (and often very intimate) role in social discipline, labor relations in the rural South differed greatly from those in an industrial northern factory. In critical, meaningful aspects, therefore, precapitalist social mores differentiated the plantation South from the rest of America. The legacies of this fact remain undeniable today.

Precapitalist features, however, were not simply rooted in southern culture. Instead, they were codified and ingrained in a remarkably systemic way. The master class had a long-established, effective, and well-planned system of social control. They kept the white poor uneducated and illiterate on purpose. Refusing to invest in a system of public education, slaveholders used public money to fund law enforcement departments,

---

[35] In *Fruits of Merchant Capital*, the Genoveses argued that merchant capital was distinct from capitalism altogether.

creating an intricate and bureaucratic criminal justice system. This system allowed masters to incarcerate (at will) whites who failed to follow their social dictates. The owners of flesh understood that preserving slavery necessitated a society with near-constant surveillance, a harsh legal code, and vigilante groups ready to mete out "justice" whenever courts and jails failed. This brutal, terroristic system of extralegal violence reinforced the entire hierarchy. Indeed, as Genovese had long argued, the master class's "paternalist spirit readily extended beyond the black-white relationship and impinged upon the relationship of rich to poorer whites." And it involved "more than a pattern of deference. Rather, that pattern provided one element in a contradictory and potentially explosive whole." The Deep South housed two "potentially explosive" underclasses, one terribly and relentlessly oppressed and the other tangentially oppressed. As Helper penned, "The lords of the lash are not only absolute masters of the blacks, but they are also the oracle and arbiters of all non-slaveholding whites, whose freedom is merely nominal, and whose unparalleled illiteracy and degradation is purposely and fiendishly perpetuated."[36]

Despite the various heavy-handed forms of social control, hostilities between classes of southern whites had become so apparent by the later antebellum period that many abolitionists directly tried to channel poor whites' anger into a larger anti-slavery movement. One particularly well-reasoned harangue appeared in a Washington, D.C. paper in 1857, describing the ever-growing power of the slaveholders:

In the controversy now going on, the question lies ... between the few hundred thousand slaveholders and the many million non-slaveholders - between a Slave Oligarchy and a Free People. This Oligarchy is an absolute Despotism. *It owns black men and domineers over white men.* It claims to be the South, to represent Southern interests, to decide Southern policy, to determine Southern destiny. It controls the press, the pulpit, the rostrum; sends its own members to the State Legislatures, its own Senators and Representatives to Congress. Questions of public policy are regarded by it, first of all, as they affect its peculiar interests ... and yet so exclusive is it in its devotion to its own peculiar interests, it is forever seeking to absorb every foot of the common property of the Union for its slave labor.

Time after time abolitionists laid out the numerous ways in which slavery was detrimental to the lives of southern poor whites. Yet because the

---

[36] Eugene D. Genovese, *Roll, Jordan, Roll: The World the Slaves Made* (New York: Vintage, 1974), 92–3; Helper, *The Impending Crisis*, 43. Seabrook, "The Poor Whites," 684.

master class controlled access to education and literacy, and strictly regulated the flow of information through rigorous censorship laws, antislavery men were generally not able to communicate with their intended audience. In fact, during the 1850s, many of the diatribes against the slaveholders' abuses against poor southern whites became aimed at working class Northerners, as abolitionists implored them to care for their white co-laborers, even if they did not have sympathy for slaves.[37]

Still, some men continued trying to reach the non-slaveholding masses of the South. William Jay insisted that the slave owning aristocrats "fear the PEOPLE; they are alarmed at the very idea of power and influence being possessed by any portion of the community not directly interested in slave property. Visions of emancipation, of agrarianism, and of popular resistance to their authority, are ever floating in their distempered and excited imaginations. ... Hence it is their policy to keep down the 'mean whites.'" Poor whites unquestionably resented, and at times even hated, wealthy slaveholders. But perhaps more importantly to the larger narrative of American history is the realization of slaveholders' fears of poor whites. These often transient people received no benefits from slavery, and increasingly they came to realize that their own livelihoods were somehow intertwined with those of the slaves themselves. Although the overwhelming brunt of slaveholder brutality and cruelty fell upon the backs of African Americans, slavery was also a deeply injurious institution for a significant number of southern whites. These masterless men and women greatly threatened the existing southern hierarchy, and undoubtedly helped push the slaveholders towards secession. As Jay aptly concluded, "it is obvious to any person attentive to the movements of the South, that the slaveholders dread *domestic* far more than foreign interference with their darling system. They dread *you*, fellow-citizens, and they dread converts among themselves."[38]

Unfortunately, owing to their high rates of illiteracy, poor whites left virtually no written records. Instead of personal diaries and letters, therefore, this book utilizes a wide variety of primary records, from county-level sources like superior court minute books and court cases, to coroner's inquests, jail records, and "Poor House" reports. Newspapers, penitentiary records, state court documents, statutes and proposed laws, census

---

[37] "The Oligarchy and the People," *National Era*, Jan. 8, 1857 (italics mine).
[38] Jay, *Address to the Non-slaveholders*, 14–15; 39. N.B. on the title: "Masterless Men" is supposed to be universal – referring to both men and women, as I do discuss gender throughout the book.

records, petitions for pardons, petitions to southern Governors, slave narratives, Civil War veterans' questionnaires, travelers' accounts, and writings from abolitionists and slaveholders helped form a more complete picture of the lives of the Deep South's poor whites.

Three types of records require some explanation. First, the use of newspapers is always problematic, and antebellum papers were very pointedly political. As much as the Deep South's press nearly always represented the interests of slaveholders, the abolitionist press had its own agenda as well. It is always prudent to assume there was a degree of exaggeration in nineteenth century journalism. Next, both the Tennessee Civil War Veteran's Questionnaires and the Works Progress Administration (WPA) slave narratives were recorded more than half a century after the end of the Civil War. The Veteran's Questionnaires, gathered between 1915 and 1923, resulted in replies from 1,650 former soldiers. The vast majority of these former soldiers fought for the Confederacy, and the responses included men from every economic class. Furthermore, the questionnaires were sent to all veterans residing within Tennessee during World War I, so some of the surveys came from men who had grown up in the antebellum Deep South. Although the questionnaires rely heavily on memory, they are one of the only sources that allow the voices of poor whites to be heard. Each veteran was required to list how much property and how many slaves he or his family owned at the time of the Civil War. They were also pointedly questioned about issues regarding class tensions and labor relations.

Much like the Veterans' Questionnaires, the slave narratives were conducted long after emancipation. Between 1936 and 1938, writers and journalists employed by the Roosevelt Administration interviewed more than 2,300 former slaves. These accounts are even more problematic than the Veteran's Questionnaires because the WPA interviewers were almost exclusively white, causing many freed people to choose their answers carefully. This self-censorship was apparent in Liza McGhee's case. Having spent her childhood as a slave in Mississippi, McGhee told her interviewer that she "[w]as hesitant about talking freely as she feared the white people were planning to enslave her again." Still, these slave narratives are among the best sources historians have for people who left few written records in the antebellum period. Both of these sets of records provided invaluable information on the pre-War period, and also on Reconstruction, and the birth of the New South. Furthermore, because the veterans' writings are peppered with misspellings, missing punctuation, and incorrect grammar, and the slave narratives were written in a demeaning "dialect" style, following the lead of Steven Hahn, I have taken the liberty to change spellings and verb tenses, although I never altered a word's meaning.[39]

Finally, concerning the topic of racism among poor whites, I have chosen simply to allow the historical record to speak for itself. In the vast majority of cases, poor whites seemed far more likely to get along with slaves and free blacks than to self-segregate or demonstrate a vicious type of racism. Despite the few antebellum travelers who commented on the racist ways of poor whites, most of the conjecture about this supposed racism has come from historians who have based their analyses on Jim Crow era race relations. Rather than establishing a pattern of brutality and overt racism, poor whites continually interacted with slaves and free blacks on frequent bases, and likely considered those relationships a routine part of daily life.

The one antebellum topic that *did* produce a degree of racial tension between slaves and poor whites, however, was labor. While most of the time poor whites seemed to direct their anger at slave owners or hirers instead of at the slaves themselves, there were occasional instances of racial violence between the two groups of workers. Yet instead of recognizing labor relations as a complicating issue between black and white workers, past historians have generally presented both an incomplete and inaccurate version of the region's social relations. Stories of poor whites and slaves eschewing the dictates of racial etiquette by drinking, colluding, trading, and sleeping together are too prominent in the available primary sources to support overarching assumptions that poor white racism was as violent and pervasive as it appeared to be after emancipation. On the contrary, poor whites and blacks, both blocked from the formal market economy, formed their own economy, creating both business and personal relationships between the two groups – all while leaving slaveholders with the dreaded task of attempting to establish segregation. This mission would ultimately prove impossible, as Forret wrote, because "[i]ndividual poor whites may have at times identified with individual slaves, viewing them as darker-skinned reflections of themselves, brothers and sisters in a fraternity of shared economic deprivation."[40]

---

[39] Elliot and Moxley, *Tennessee*; George P. Rawick, ed., *The American Slave: A Composite Autobiography* (Westport, CT.: Greenwood, 1972–9); Liza McGhee, *American Slave*, Vol. 9 (MS), Supplement, Series 1, Part 4, 1402; see Steven Hahn, *A Nation under Our Feet: Black Political Struggles in the Rural South from Slavery to the Great Migration* (Cambridge: Harvard University Press, 2003), 10.

[40] Forret, *Race Relations*, 141.

Chapter 1 focuses on the single most important factor of self-sufficiency in rural antebellum America: land ownership. In the wake of the Specie Circular Act of 1836, the financial Panic of 1837, and the resulting land and wealth consolidation, many smallholders lost their land, and the ranks of poor whites grew. As it became more difficult for the lower classes to purchase land throughout the later antebellum period, they had two choices: move west and squat, hoping to one day purchase the land that they had improved, or stay at home and work for whatever wages were offered. But moving still required capital for the move itself, and some poor whites could not even afford that.

By focusing on the westward migration of poor white squatters, the southern origins of the Homestead Act become incredibly important, as do slaveholder objections to the bill. The master class may have made sure that homesteading never became law in the antebellum era, but because of their opposition, landlessness became cyclical for poor families. The resulting inequality, of course, lead to aggravated class tensions. An 1856 *New York Times* article reported that:

The owners of slaves command the markets ... they buy out the little plantations which in the earlier settlements surround them, and in the end the rich lands all become the domains of rich planters ... the poorer classes are either tenants at will, or, banished to the poor lands of the hills, take to the life of idlers, hunters or fishermen; or, at best, the more industrious among them become day-laborers, living from hand to mouth – in a word, they are stripped by the oligarchy of slave-owners, who command their wages, their tenements, and of course every thing. The class who hold a monopoly of the soil can command everything.

Less than a year after this article appeared, another financial panic would grip the nation, further exacerbating the crisis of the impoverished throughout the Deep South. As the proportion of poor whites grew, slaveholders faced an increasingly hostile populace; a populace with not one, but two, underclasses deeply resentful their respective oppressive states.[41]

Without the prospect of land ownership and self-sufficiency, this "dead peasantry," as the poor whites were referred to, had little choice but to tenant farm, sharecrop, or labor for wages. Chapter 2 thus examines the working lives of poor whites, who often cobbled together a meager existence with only occasional employment. Many poor white men were constantly on the move in search for work, leaving households to be

---

[41] "Philadelphia National Convention," *New York Times*, April 12, 1856.

headed by females for at least portions of the year. Examining the different types of jobs that poor whites held, this chapter reveals the beginnings
of white unrest over competition with slaves and free blacks – an issue
that would eventually reach near-crisis proportions by the time of secession. Pushed out of most agricultural work by the late antebellum period,
poor whites had begun to enter into jobs associated with construction,
infrastructure, and the extraction of natural resources, as well as the
burgeoning manufacturing industries.

A very large percentage of poor whites were left no choice but to pick
up piecemeal "mechanical work," a term understood by antebellum
Southerners to include most manual labor occurring outside of the realm
of agriculture. For the men who did secure this type of employment,
however, their wages were much lower than those of their northern
counterparts, because slavery's profitability, along with an oversupply
of laborers, kept wages depressed. All of these issues together led to a
crisis in work ethic among poor whites, who commonly refused to labor
for wages they deemed too low, or in jobs that were too dangerous, or if
they were supposed to work as equals alongside free blacks or slaves.

The prevalence of slave hiring in the 1840s and 1850s further exacerbated class tensions, Chapter 3 argues, just as an influx of impoverished
white immigrants into southern cities intensified racial tensions. When
poor whites finally had to accept the fact that slaves dominated the
southern labor market, some of them became so disillusioned that they
chose to drop out of the labor force entirely. Instead of futilely continuing
to try and participate in the formal economy, growing numbers of them
began living away from "civilized" white society, hunting, fishing, stealing, and trading with slaves in an informal underground economy. Thus,
lower-class whites became more than just a nuisance to masters. Slaveholders were tangibly losing assets, but more importantly, they were
losing control over their slaves. Alternatively, for those white laborers
who remained committed to trying to find wage-paying work, labor strife
continued to grow, and nascent unions began forming in every major
town and city across the Deep South. As one 1853 article reported, lower-
middling and poor white mechanics were advocating "to obtain a monopoly of the work for their respective trades, sometimes interfering by
force to prevent the employment of the negroes."[42]

---

[42] "The South: Letters on the Productions, Industry and Resources of the Slave States:
Number Four," *Ibid.*, March 4, 1853, 2.

Deemed "poor white trash" by planters and slaves alike, lower-class whites often lived a hardscrabble existence. Chapter 4 focuses on their daily material realities. From housing, food, and family structure to gender roles, sex, and religion, underprivileged whites had very different life experiences than other regional whites. Inadequate diets, accompanied by periods of hunger and want, added to the most impoverished whites' misery. Poor white children were still being "bound out" as forced laborers. And a masculine subculture of primal honor, predicated on substance abuse and frequent displays of aggression and violence, further helped distinguish poor whites from their more affluent counterparts. Perhaps most importantly, impoverished whites' daily realities demonstrate that they were, in fact, class conscious. Excluded from so many of the privileges of whiteness, how could they *not* realize how drastically their lives varied from the lives of those who owned land and slaves?

With no functioning system of public education in any Deep South state, poor whites were further barred from any chance of rising above the economic station into which they were born. Chapter 5 examines literacy, education, and disfranchisement, showing how the master class deliberately denied a system public education to the white masses. Preferring them to remain in ignorance, slaveholders knew that poor whites' access to information would eventually lead to greater discontent, especially when they learned about agrarian reform, workers' rights, and what life was like for working class whites in free states. As the Virginia-born abolitionist Moncure Conway lamented, "I have found among these wretched people a deep consciousness of their degradation, and have seen hardy men weep that there was no prospect for their children but to grow up as ignorant and besotted as themselves." Someday, Conway hoped, poor whites "will learn that, whilst they have had nothing but wretchedness and brutal ignorance at their homes, the lowest class of the North have comfortable homes and happiness and education; they will learn what Freedom does for the people who enthrone her, and recognize what Slavery has done for themselves."[43]

Finally, the chapter ends with a discussion of southern state and local governments, and voting rights. Far from a democratic region, the Deep South instead functioned more like an oligarchy or aristocracy. As DuBois wrote: "Even among the two million slaveholders, an oligarchy of 8,000 really ruled the South." Slaveholders wielded immense and pervasive

---

[43] M.D. Conway, *Testimonies Concerning Slavery* (London: Chapman and Hall, 1855), 122; 123–4.

power as lawmakers, law enforcers, judges, and even jury members. They dominated the region's politics and devised multiple ways to disenfranchise poor whites. From poll taxes to residency requirements, masters easily maintained control over the political privileges of lower-class whites. When the rich did allow the poor vote, slaveholders were still able to control the outcome of elections, as one man observed, by "means of the votes of the poor whites whom he owns, in owning all by which they can live for another day." Lamenting the miseries of the South's poor whites, E.B. Seabrook eloquently concluded that "It is impossible to elevate in the scale of mental improvements a people who are at the same time barred from material progress."[44]

Very much intertwined with the Deep South's problem of surplus laborers was its highly sophisticated criminal justice system. Chapters 6 and 7 focus on aspects of the region's judicial inequities. Chapter 6 demonstrates how slaveholders used their positions of power to keep tight control over the poor white population, policing and jailing those who could possibly cause trouble or disrupt the established hierarchy. Masters generally charged poor whites with nonviolent, behavioral "crimes" like vagrancy, trading with blacks, selling liquor to slaves, gambling, lewd behaviors, and public drunkenness. The point of many of these arrests was neither to punish nor to reform. Instead, slave owners used these laws to dominate and scare poor whites into docility, jailing

---

[44] W.E.B. DuBois, *Black Reconstruction in America: An Essay toward a History of the Part which Black Folk Played in the Attempt to Reconstruct Democracy in America, 1860–1880* (1935; reprint, New York: Free Press, 1992), 26; Conway, *Testimonies Concerning Slavery*, 121. Seabrook, "The Poor Whites," 687. Over the past few years the growing fields of neuroscience and biology have been scientifically confirming the work of historians and social scientists on poverty. One recent study seemingly proves that poverty does, in fact, directly interrupt and impair cognitive function. Defining poverty as the "gap" between an individual's material needs and having the resources to alleviate those needs, Anandi Mani and her team of scientists determined that "poverty-related concerns consume mental resources." In addition to life's everyday tasks and labors, poor people were constantly distracted by trying to balance expenses with income. They spent valuable time everyday making mental tradeoffs, juggling priorities, and worrying about the short-term future. Mani's team of researchers ultimately concluded that: "Being poor means coping not just with a shortfall of money, but also with a concurrent shortfall of cognitive resources. The poor, in this view, are less capable not because of inherent traits, but because the very context of poverty imposes load and impedes cognitive capacity." This cognitive deficit, the researchers found, was comparable to losing a full night of sleep, or the loss of thirteen IQ points. While these findings certainly do not absolve poor people from bad decisions, they do help explain *why* they may make those choices. Anandi Mani et al., "Poverty Impedes Cognitive Function," *Science* 341 (Aug. 2013): 976; 980.

them for months or years at a time – often without the chance to stand trial. By following more than 300 arrested poor whites through census records, studying hundreds of coroner's inquests, and examining scores of scattered local trial transcripts, the lives of the white underclasses become illuminated. The extent of their poverty is revealed, their raucous, intemperate worlds exposed, their pain and anguish laid bare.

Chapter 7 begins by explaining the southern system of punishment and incarceration. While most southern jails and penitentiaries were well-established by the late antebellum period, other more barbaric forms of punishment were still occasionally used. Perhaps most shockingly, there are multiple documented cases of poor white convicts being publically whipped as late as the 1840s and 1850s, generally for nonviolent crimes such as bastardy and simple larceny. Furthermore, several Deep South states continued jailing debtors up until the Civil War, including those individuals who could not pay court fines and fees from their own arrests. In some areas, poor white convicts were actually auctioned off to other white citizens in exchange for the use of their labor. Essentially indentured servants, these white men helped blur the lines of white privilege in a racially-based slave society. Indeed, the public whipping and auctioning off debt-ridden whites – practices usually reserved for blacks – likely frightened some poor and even middling whites into quietly accepting the deep inequalities inherent in the slave system.

Chapter 8 documents the various problems slaveholders faced as they attempted to establish segregation in a racially-ambiguous world. As Alexis de Tocqueville famously wrote, "There are parts of the United States where the European and Negro blood are so crossed that one cannot find a man who is either completely white or completely black; when that point has been reached, one can really say that the races are mixed, or rather that there is a third race derived from the two, but not precisely one or the other." Indeed, by the late antebellum period, generations of interracial sex had produced an entire class of people who were difficult to immediately categorize as either white or black. And in a world based on racial slavery, classification of individuals was imperative. With the prevalence of slave hiring, the presence of free blacks, and the darkened skin of poor whites who generally labored in the hot southern sun, the region's racial hierarchy was becoming unwieldy and unenforceable. Lines separating the supposedly dialectic categories of black and white, slave and free, were gradually becoming blurred, and in some cases, even indistinguishable. From advertisements for white slaves to court cases where poor whites were sold into slavery, the racial dynamic of the Deep South was growing ever more complicated and nuanced, undoubtedly adding to slaveholder concerns over the long-term maintenance of "black" slavery.[45]

As the master class scrambled to come up with solutions to an increasingly unwieldy hierarchy, some of them began to argue for slavery in the abstract. Essentially stating that slavery was philosophically just, slavery in the abstract completely divorced bondage from skin color. Fox-Genovese and Genovese wrote that "[p]roslavery logic cast enslavement, broadly defined, as necessary and proper for much of the white race, as well as for practically all of the black race." Slavery in the abstract rapidly won adherents throughout the Deep South in the 1850s, particularly in South Carolina. The issue gained such widespread support among slaveholders that in 1856 the Republican Party distributed handbills cautioning working class whites of the designing and devious plans of the master class – plans that eventually included enslaving poorer whites.[46]

The preservation of this multifaceted slave society, of course, required constant attention. By itself, the legal system could not assure the level of security slave owners needed to feel safe, so they employed extralegal means to buttress the criminal code. Sally Hadden convincingly demonstrated how masters used slave patrols for constant surveillance of both blacks and poor whites. Similarly, slaveholders also relied on extralegal groups like vigilance committees and minute men organizations. Precursors to the Ku Klux Klan, these terroristic groups used violence and threats of violence to maintain the southern hierarchy, and their ranks proliferated with the rise of the Republican Party. Violating a spate of civil liberties laws, the Deep South was a heavily censored society, where speaking of abolition, or reading about class issues, or listening to a sermon on the humanity of slaves could end in a swift death of the accused. Slaveholders' increasing intolerance for dissenting ideas revealed just how threatening they found Republicanism. Placed in the context of class tension between whites, it becomes easier to understand why the master class viscerally feared the emerging party. Founded on principles of free labor, agrarian reform, and a type of relatively egalitarian, small-scale capitalism, Republicans not only seemed like radicals to

[45] Alexis de Tocqueville, *Democracy in America* (New York, 1966), 356.
[46] Elizabeth Fox-Genovese and Eugene D. Genovese, *Slavery in White and Black: Class and Race in the Southern Slaveholders' New World Order* (New York: Cambridge University Press, 2008), 1; 24–5; 69.

slaveholders – they were truly revolutionary, and not solely because of their stance on slavery. The new party clearly elucidated the staggering differences between the two sections of the country, and the comparison did not bode well for the South, where large-scale, slave-labor capitalism reigned supreme. Offering land to the landless and workers' rights to wage laborers, the entire Republican platform would have been incredibly appealing to southern poor whites – a possibility that terrified slaveholders.[47]

Chapter 9 focuses on the lead up to secession, the presidential election of 1860, and the Civil War. Given all of the injustices that poor whites were facing by the late antebellum period, members of the class became increasingly upset – and more confrontational – about their exclusion from the southern economy. Poor white labor unions occasionally warned that they would withdraw their support for slavery altogether, making overt threats about the stability of the institution, and the necessity of poor white support for that stability. Indeed, as lower-class whites became more militant about their exclusion from the southern economic system, slaveholders realized the urgent need to finally address class tensions. By the eve of war, affluent Southerners used an insidious form of racism to try to scare lower-class whites into supporting secession, predicting that the poor would be slaughtered by the thousands in an inevitable race war following emancipation.

Once the Civil War began, some poor whites still actively refused to support the slaveholders' cause. Masters did not hesitate to use violent and aggressive methods to force dissenters to join the armed forces. Cases of lynchings and threatened jail time for desertion, treason, and vagrancy were widespread. Far from being actively pro-Confederate, most poor whites had little or no choice but to support the war effort – they were at the mercy of the master class. As poor white soldier John Dinsmore remembered: "When the Civil War began to come up the non-slaveholders wasn't allowed to say anything ... [t]hey was kept down as much as possible." In 1863, Benjamin Black from Washington County, Georgia, claimed that only 5 votes were cast for disunion in his district, and more than 100 against it. "In his regiment are many men like himself," the *New York Times* reported, "unwilling soldiers in the cause of the rebellion." Black explained to the paper that in the plantation South,

---

[47] Sally Hadden, *Slave Patrols: Law and Violence in Virginia and the Carolinas* (Cambridge: Harvard University Press, 2001).

a poor man who has to work at day's work for a living has a very hard chance in the world. Fifty cents a day was considered a big price for a laborer. ... He thinks that those who owned negroes and who started the secession business ou[gh]t to have been the men to right it out. Such men as him, having no ownership or interest in negroes, felt that they had no rights that were being injured, and only desired to be left at home with their families. ... He thinks there will be a terrible reaction in the South against the leaders once the rebel armies are overthrown.

By forcing poor whites to fight, the Confederacy suffered incredibly high rates of desertion. This fact, coupled with increasing numbers of small scale revolts by lay-about groups of non-slaveholders throughout the region, ultimately helped ensure the Union's victory.[48]

The Conclusion broadly considers the crucial postwar period, showing that former slaves were not the only Southerners who benefited from emancipation. In effect confirming Hinton Helper's claim that poor whites suffered a "second degree of slavery" in the antebellum period, the postbellum era freed poor whites in several critical ways. Finally able to compete in a free labor economy, poor whites at last possessed the opportunity to improve their economic situation. Furthermore, during Reconstruction poor whites also became beneficiaries of the federal government, and for the first time in the Deep South's history, free public education became widely available. Finally, while newly emancipated slaves waited in vain for their fabled forty acres and a mule, some poor whites took full advantage of the Homestead Act and the Southern Homestead Act, at last entering the ranks of landholders.[49]

As poor whites became gradually included in the spoils of white privilege, however, black Americans realized that they had emerged from one kind of slavery only to suffer the "second degree of slavery" that poor whites had long endured. Freed people became the former slaveholders' new targets for victimless crimes like vagrancy. Just as slaveholders had used several different methods to monitor and mitigate the behaviors of poor whites in the antebellum period, during the earliest years of Reconstruction, the master class and their heirs adapted these methods to gain control over postbellum freedmen and women – politically, socially, and economically. There was a critical distinction, however, concerning sentencing and punishments for white and black criminals. The consequences for blacks were much more extreme, vicious, and violent than they had

---

[48] Bolton, *Poor Whites*, 158; Elliot and Moxley, *Tennessee*, Vol. 1, 45–6; "Affairs in the South," *New York Times*, Aug. 16, 1863.
[49] Helper, *The Impending Crisis*, 32–3.

been for poor whites. The postbellum South was an extremely chaotic, violent, racist society for African Americans because they now stood as the principal threats to the prevailing order. Waters McIntosh, who spent his childhood enslaved in South Carolina, clarified who, precisely, benefited from emancipation. As a boy McIntosh sang a song called "Rather be a nigger than a poor white man." After gaining legal "freedom," however, he changed his tune. "It was the poor white man who was freed by the war," concluded McIntosh, "not the Negroes."[50]

---

[50] Mell, "A Definitive Study," 2–3; Waters McIntosh, *American Slave*, Vol. 2 (AR), Part 5, 20.

I

The Southern Origins of the Homestead Act

Thieves steal trifles from rich men; slaveholders oppress poor men, and enact laws for the perpetuation of their poverty. Thieves practice deceit on the wise; slaveholders take advantage of the ignorant.
– Hinton Helper[1]

There has been a considerable exportation of slaves to the newer Southern States; but the increase has been so great, notwithstanding, as to cut off all hope of employment for the poor whites, and to compel them to seek homes elsewhere ... in South Carolina the constant increase of a class of laborers who are compelled to work without wages deters immigrants from abroad, and compels the poor whites who were born on the soil, and who have hitherto managed to eke out existence by occasional jobs, to abandon their native land, and seek employment in States whose institutions foster free labor.
– National Era[2]

To this day, the Homestead Act remains the most comprehensive form of wealth redistribution that has ever taken place in America. Passed during the Civil War, after slaveholders who had long blocked the legislation had seceded, the Act awarded approximately 246 million acres of western land to settlers for nothing more than a small filing fee. As the most sweeping form of entitlement legislation ever to pass Congress, the law granted a gigantic land mass – close to the size of both California and Texas – to more than 1.6 million households. These settlers, of course, were almost exclusively white. Both native poor whites and white

[1] Helper, *The Impending Crisis*, 140.
[2] "Political Economy," *National Era*, Oct. 6, 1859.

immigrants greatly benefited. Homesteading offered them a chance to start fresh in a new area, often in places unstained by the legacy of slavery. Indeed, the importance of the Homestead Act cannot be overstated. Yet its humble southern origins are nearly always overlooked.[3]

Although the true father of the Homestead Act is Tennessee's Andrew Johnson, the bill was first introduced by another Southerner of modest means, Felix Grundy McConnell. Born into the lower-middling class in central Tennessee, McConnell received little formal schooling and worked for several years as a saddler. Likely unsatisfied with his economic situation, in his young twenties he moved to Talladega, Alabama, where he eventually became a lawyer and Democratic politician. Elected to the U.S. House of Representatives, McConnell proved himself a friend to the common man. Simultaneously, though, he also earned the reputation of a drunken rowdy. Just three years after he was elected to federal office, McConnell – a terrible alcoholic – tragically committed suicide by stabbing himself multiple times and slicing his own throat, likely during a hallucination from delirium tremens. Less than a year before his death, however, Felix Grundy McConnell had asked permission to introduce a Homestead Bill in the House of Representatives.[4]

Two months after McConnell attempted to first introduce the legislation, on March 27, 1846, future-President Andrew Johnson asked again to present the agrarian reform bill to Congress. Johnson would continue to reintroduce the Homestead Bill every year he served in the House. Having suffered through an even more impoverished childhood than McConnell, Johnson was a likely candidate to support such a measure. Although he had grown up in parts of the South with low percentages of slaves, Johnson still felt overwhelmed by the peculiar institution, and by the incredibly wealthy men who profited off it.[5]

---

[3] Trina Williams, "The Homestead Act: A Major Asset-Building Policy in American History," Paper commissioned for "Inclusion in Asset Building: Research and Policy Symposium," Center for Social Development Washington University, St. Louis, Sept. 21–23, 2000, 1; 6, Web; also see T.R.W. Shanks, "The Homestead Act: A Major Asset-Building Policy in American History," in M. Sherraden, ed., *Inclusion in the American Dream: Assets, Poverty, and Public Policy* (New York: Oxford University Press, 2005).

[4] Kim Long, *The Almanac of Political Corruption, Scandals & Dirty Politics* (New York: Random House, 2008); "Felix Grundy McConnell," Web; St. George L. Sioussat, "Andrew Johnson and the Early Phases of the Homestead Bill," *Mississippi Valley Historical Review* V, No. 3 (Dec. 1918): 277.

[5] *Ibid.*, 277; 280; George M. Stephenson, *The Political History of the Public Lands, from 1840 to 1862* (Boston: Richard G. Badger, 1917).

The master class, of course, continued deeming agrarian reform as an abolitionist measure. Fire-eaters branded Johnson "a traitor to the South," and condemned him as a radical socialist. His beliefs certainly did not warrant either claim, but his politics provided fodder for their invective. In a speech made before the House of Representatives in 1846, Johnson passionately advocated westward expansion, even if American imperialism caused a war with Mexico. To an impoverished white from Tennessee, there was no reason – logical or moral – as to why poorer whites were doomed to languish in cycles of poverty in the older slave states. Johnson fully realized that affluent, slave-owning politicians had the power to allow or prevent migration into the southwest, and boisterously argued against their immense powers. "He said he was a mechanic, and when a blow was struck upon that class, either direct or by innuendo, from Whig or Democrat, he would resent it," the Congressional record reported. The United States of America, Johnson bewailed, was undoubtedly ruled by "an illegitimate, swaggering, bastard, scrub aristocracy, who assumed to know a great deal, but who, when the flimsy veil of pretension was torn off from it, was shown to possess neither talents, information, nor a foundation on which you can rear a superstructure that would be useful." To understand Johnson's impassioned loathing of the master class, as well as his fervor regarding agrarian reform, his own economic background becomes relevant.[6]

Andrew Johnson undoubtedly remains the poorest man ever to rise to the American presidency, even to this day. He continues to be the only president ever to have been forced to labor, the only one who experienced a degree of bondage. The fact that he became anything more than an illiterate wage laborer is a testament to his dogged determination, incredibly disciplined work ethic, and a whole lot of luck. His grandfather, William Johnson, Jr., was poor enough to have been "Sold out at a sheriff's sale" for his labor in Raleigh, North Carolina. Due to this fact, William subsequently was unable to provide for his family financially, leaving the future-president's father, Jacob, landless and illiterate. Jacob found occasional employment working odd jobs, serving as a miller, a porter at a bank, and the city's bell ringer. Jacob married Mary (Polly) McDonough, a seamstress, laundress, and weaver, and together they may have eventually made their way into the lower-middling classes after a

---

[6] *Ibid.*, 161 (see speeches by McMullin of Virginia and Brown of Mississippi, July 24 and 25, 1850); *The Congressional Globe*, 29th Congress, 1st Session, House (Washington, D.C.: Blair & Rives, 1834–73), 885, Web.

lifetime of hard work and long hours. But Jacob tragically died after saving three other men whose boat had capsized, leaving Mary destitute and widowed with two young sons. Andrew was only three.[7]

Often referred to as "swarthy complexioned" to raise questions over his racial purity, Andrew never received a day of schooling throughout his life. Like the states of the Deep South, North Carolina had no system of public education, and his mother was far too poor to pay for his education. By the time Andrew turned fourteen, his impoverished mother no longer had the means to house, feed, and clothe her two sons. Bound out as apprentices to a local tailor named James Selby, Andrew and his brother William were repeatedly abused and treated cruelly – in addition to working twelve hour days, six days a week. As Johnson's biographer Hans Trefousse wrote, "North Carolina law placed apprentices in a position little better that that of slaves ... while serving their term they were entirely at their masters' beck and call." After a particularly humiliating punishment, the boys ran away, staying on the move throughout the Carolinas to evade capture. Their master, Selby, had taken out an advertisement in southern newspapers for their apprehension and return. The ad for the Johnsons' capture was uncannily similar to runaway slave ads. Given these types of experiences, it was unsurprising that during his lowest moments, Johnson himself became a vicious, acerbic, intemperate drunk. No matter how hard Johnson worked, and clearly, no matter what he accomplished, there would always be painful memories of a poor white boy who had been ripped from his home, forced to labor for a master, and beaten as if he were enslaved. Try as he might, he would never fully escape the indignities of his past – his own short-term version of white bondage.[8]

Johnson's master, however, was not the only white Southerner to whip Johnson. As a young boy, Johnson lived near a wealthy slaveholder named John Devereaux, described by Trefousse as an aristocrat whose "contempt" for the poor white family "was scarcely hidden." Apparently, Devereaux "habitually" whipped impoverished whites, and members of the Johnson family were not spared the rod. Once, as young Andrew and his cousins ran along the path separating Devereaux's land from that of his son, the slaveholder sent his coachman "to whip the boys back to their

[7] Hans L. Trefousse, *Andrew Johnson: A Biography* (New York: Norton, 1989), 18–9; 19.
[8] Trefousse, *Andrew Johnson*, 21: Ironically, Johnson surreptitiously learned to read while he was bound out as an apprentice, although not from his master. As he worked, an old man would read to the laborers, and Johnson was bright enough to teach himself to read and write; 22; 23; Sioussat, "Andrew Johnson," 271.

shanty." During another instance, John Devereaux himself gave Johnson a whipping, allegedly because Andrew attempted to steal some fruit from one of his daughters' trees. Regardless of the reasons for the lashings, the truth remained. As an impressionable young child, Andrew Johnson had been punished multiple times like a slave – by a slaveholder *and* a master. There were seemingly few privileges associated with Andrew Johnson's whiteness.[9]

Given his upbringing, it was no surprise that Johnson would champion the Homestead Bill. As nearly a million slaves were sold from the Upper South into the Deep South during the 1830s and 1840s, slaveholders unquestionably needed bigger tracts of land. Federal policy, along with slaveholders' tight control over state and local law, greatly aided this agrarian consolidation. As the wealthy master class multiplied their assets, however, the ranks of the landless grew as smallholders lost their real estate. It also became much more difficult for aspiring landholders to acquire loans. Class lines undoubtedly hardened. Upward economic mobility became increasingly rare as the wealth gap between southern whites continued to widen. Yet as men like McConnell and Johnson sought to alleviate some of the rising poverty in the slave South, slave-holders balked at the idea, realizing that the precarious balance of federal power would be at stake as western lands filled with non-slaveholding farmers, especially those who had been economically burdened by the peculiar institution. Powerful slave owning politicians were able to pre-vent the passage of the Homestead Bill the entire time they remained in the Union. Shortly after secession, of course, the federal government was able to authorize the legislation that the slaveholding oligarchy had long blocked.

To understand why the push for land reform originated in the slave South, it is necessary to recognize how economically stratified the region had become by the time of secession. In rural America, of course, land ownership was the primary key to self-sufficiency and even great wealth, but as the antebellum period wore on, smaller landholders lost their farms, while poor whites became increasingly barred from entering the ranks of real estate owners. As the large land- and slaveholders became richer, some impoverished whites sank down to a level unimaginable by most Northerners. During the third year of the Civil War, a young Yankee captain named George Pepper described the poor whites that he

[9] Trefousse, *Andrew Johnson*, 21.

encountered throughout the Deep South: "They resembled the images of a frightful dream, rather than living men, women and children," he began. "In fact, the poor of this section are as ignorant, filthy and wretched as can be found anywhere in the world." Pepper's observations represented a familiar refrain echoed by travelers and journalists in the few decades before the Civil War. Northerners and upper-class Southerners repeated the same several points about poor whites: they were lazy, dirty, ignorant, immoral, and often drunk. Some of these descriptions certainly had credibility, but the reasons and causes behind these labels need to be explored in historical context.[10]

Income is generally considered the determinative factor of class, but in reality, a study of *wealth* is absolutely essential to understanding economic inequality, especially in antebellum America. As the only slave society in the New World in which slaves naturally reproduced, the South's wealth was multiplied with the birth of every enslaved child. The more slaves a master owned, the more money he stood to make, simply by allowing nature to take its course. Thanks in no small measure to the cotton boom of the 1850s, affluent slaveholders grew wealthier as the value of slaves continued to rise. However, this rise in prices also made it increasingly hard for non-slaveholders to purchase slaves, thus barring them from entrance into the slave-owner class. Without slaves, and without the training or education to become members of the professional class, land ownership became extremely important, as it was almost exclusively the only avenue to avoiding dependency on others. By the 1830s, the U.S. government stopped selling public lands brutally stolen from southeastern Native Americans, and – for all intents and purposes – the Deep South's frontier was closed. Furthermore, landholdings in older eastern states such as South Carolina and Georgia continued to consolidate, blocking aspiring and enterprising men from entering the propertied classes. As white male suffrage expanded during the Jacksonian period, blurring the lines of class and privilege, factors such as financial independence became central to southern masculinity.[11]

Thomas Jefferson famously envisioned America as an idealistic vision of an agrarian republic. Yet the forefathers of many poor whites – indentured servants, debtors, and low-wage laborers – arrived in America

---

[10] George W. Pepper, *Personal Recollections of Sherman's Campaigns in Georgia and the Carolinas* (Zanesville, OH: Hugh Dunne, 1866), 271.

[11] Genovese, *Roll, Jordan, Roll*, 57; James P. Schmidt, *Free to Work: Labor Law, Emancipation, and Reconstruction, 1815–1880* (Athens: University of Georgia Press, 1998), 60.

without any wealth, and many of their heirs struggled for generations to rise out of poverty. Their attempts at upward mobility were thwarted at almost every turn by the inequities in wealth and power fostered by slavery. Historically, almost all non-landholding agricultural laborers, as well as the poorer landed farmers, suffered times of great hardship and hunger. By 1860, the average wealth owned by free adult males in the United States was $2,500. But extreme wealth inequality throughout the country meant that in reality, a small percentage of affluent people were very rich, and a large percentage of the lower class was very poor. In fact, the top 1 percent of the population held 30 percent of the nation's real estate. The top 2 percent owned 40 percent of all land. Conversely, the poorest Americans generally owned less than $100 in total personal wealth. Lee Soltow determined that about one-third of the country's population owned "little more than clothing and perhaps some petty cash," and were consistently unable to save any money in a given year. Many Americans, in fact, had "dissavings," as few poor people managed to obtain a semblance of economic or social mobility throughout their lives.[12]

Although the industrial North had a very economically stratified society, it could not rival the extreme disparity pervading the slave South. Wherever the peculiar institution existed, inheritable slave property created a nonporous class barrier. In the year before the Civil War, 56 percent of the country's aggregate personal estate was concentrated in the South. Cotton was king, slave labor was profitable, and slave prices were rising. Dixie had become the wealthiest region in America. Yet once again, the bulk of this wealth was concentrated in the hands of a very small group of slaveholders, while the pool of less affluent whites was growing larger by the day. "Despite the fact that the South boasted of its freedom from pauperism, because slavery was supposed to provide all white men with cheap labor and all colored men with subsistence," wrote Roger Shugg, "there were nevertheless many paupers, as well as the poor whites who constituted as a class the slum element of the South." The extent of their often-lifelong poverty was both pitiful and shocking, especially as they lived in one of the richest areas of the nineteenth-

---

[12] Lee Soltow, *Men and Wealth in the United States, 1850–1870* (New Haven: Yale University Press, 1975), 3; 93; 142–3; 44; 59; 25; 24. In terms of purchasing power, a dollar in 1860 would be worth about $28.50 in 2012 terms, meaning the average wealth for men in America was about $71,250. See measuringworth.com; Peter Wallenstein, *From Slave South to New South: Public Policy in Nineteenth-Century Georgia* (Chapel Hill: University of North Carolina Press, 1987), 19.

century world. Surrounded by extravagant wealth and pretention, Helper complained, many poor whites "grow up to the age of maturity, and pass through life without ever owning as much as five dollars at any time."[13]

For the wealthiest whites, however, life was completely different. In 1860, slightly more than a thousand families accounted for nearly half of the Deep South's wealth. By contrast, the region's poorest half of the population held only 5 percent of its wealth. Income levels were just as highly stratified as wealth. In stark numeric terms, William Dodd estimated that among the cotton states in 1850, "A thousand families received [a total of] over $50,000,000 a year, while all the remaining 66,000 families received only about $60,000,000." Several factors added to this extreme economic disparity, but each one ultimately stemmed from slavery. On the eve of the Civil War, slaves accounted for 60 percent of all agricultural wealth in the five cotton-producing states of South Carolina, Georgia, Alabama, Mississippi, and Louisiana. With such a large percentage of southern wealth tied up in slaves, whether or not someone belonged to the slaveholding class revealed a great deal about their economic status.[14]

Because slaves comprised the majority of slaveholders' fortunes, it is important to note that slaves were unequally distributed among masters, and were becoming more so in the decade before secession. Soltow found evidence of a "slight increase" in the concentration of slave ownership in the decade before secession, and John Boles' data indicated an even more pronounced concentration. The percentage of families belonging to the master class "decreased from 36 percent in 1830 to ... 25 percent in 1860, and the size of slaveholdings was increasing." The richest planters were buying up more slaves and increasing their numbers of laborers, while some of the smaller yeomen farmers slipped back to non-slaveholder status following economic hardship. The same dynamic was true in regards to landholding. And in the agrarian South, land ownership was essential for maximizing returns of slave ownership.[15]

---

[13] Roger W. Shugg, *Origins of Class Struggle in Louisiana: A Social History of White Farmers and Laborers during Slavery and After, 1840–1875* (Baton Rouge: Louisiana University Press, 1939), 59; Helper, *The Impending Crisis*, 381.

[14] David Williams, *Bitterly Divided: The South's Inner Civil War* (New York: The New Press, 2008), quoted on 11; Robert R. Russel, "The Effects of Slavery upon Non-Slaveholders in the Ante Bellum South," *Agricultural History* 15, No. 2 (April 1941): 113. Also see the Introduction about slave prices, particularly Samuel H. Williamson and Louis P. Cain, "Measuring Slavery."

[15] Quoted in Wright, *Old South, New South*, 19; Soltow, *Men and Wealth*, 142; John B. Boles, *The South through Time: A History of an American Region, Volume I* (New Jersey: Prentice Hall, 1999), 221; Wallenstein, *From Slave South*, 14.

But how did wealth become so highly stratified in the first place? As an overwhelmingly agrarian nation, real estate had quite a bit to do with it. In rural areas, how much land someone held – and the quality of that land – generally determined the quality of their lives, as well as the quality of their children's lives. Yet wealth had not always been as concentrated as it was in the later antebellum period, due to several factors. In the early years of the Republic, public lands were purchased in bank notes, specie, or on credit. During this time, of course, land was always available for white settlers to purchase, due to the brutal elimination of Native Americans. In the Deep South, the removal of the Creek natives in Georgia began in the spring of 1816, and lasted until 1827. Between 1829 and 1832, the Cherokees were forced from their ancestral homelands in Appalachia and the foothills; by the early 1830s, the Choctaws and Chickasaws had been driven out of Mississippi; and the Florida Seminoles were completely removed from the state in 1842. Soon after this violent and vicious elimination, tens of thousands of white families began squatting, hoping to secure rights to the most productive areas. The practice of squatting had become so common in America that politicians contemplated legal actions of fines and imprisonment for the settlers. Even when laws actually passed, however, they were incredibly hard to enforce, especially over such an expansive geographical area. Given the situation, politicians discussed preemption as a partial remedy. In short, preemption allowed squatters the right to first refusal when it came to buying government land, generally at a federally set minimum price, and always without the burden of competitive bidding. Instead of being a progressive agrarian measure, preemption was the only realistic way for the government to deal with so many illegal squatters.[16]

According to one scholar, from the time of the Early Republic, the North and the West had supported preemption, while southern slaveholders opposed the policy, as it "was in the way of the plantation system." Yet, during a brief alliance of the West and the South, the Preemption Act passed in 1830. Two years later, politicians passed a bill allowing the federal government to sell forty acre tracts to people willing to cultivate and improve it. Although these measures meant to deal with the twin problems of landlessness and westward migration, after a few short months the system had become overwhelmed with fraudulent

---

[16] Malcolm J. Rohrbaugh, *The Land Office Business: The Settlement and Administration of American Public Lands* (New York: Oxford University Press, 1968), 32; 118; Williams, *Bitterly Divided*, 18–9; Rohrbaugh, *The Land Office Business*, 201; 200.

claims, as speculators devised plans to buy up as much of the land as possible. Of course, once speculators owned the real estate, they would exponentially raise prices on all land, especially the most productive. Due to this rampant fraud, preemption helped line the pockets of the already-rich, and further preserved the grave disparities in American wealth.[17]

Shortly after preemption but before the Homestead Act took shape, other ideas about how to best address the problems of landlessness and white poverty were bandied about Congress. Quite interestingly, the first proposal for real change also came from a Southerner – a Representative from Mississippi. Franklin Plummer had been born in Massachusetts, but moved to Mississippi as a young man to teach school. After becoming a lawyer and a politician, Plummer turned his attention to the cause of the landless poor whites surrounding him. Crafting a petition signed by the people of the Magnolia state, Plummer pleaded with the U.S. government to offer the landless (who also owned less than $500) free tracts of 160 acres, on the condition that the homesteaders cultivate and improve the land for a period of five years. In an impassioned speech, Plummer compared the situation of poorer whites to that of Native Americans, concluding that Native Americans were actually better off: at least they collectively owned the lands of their tribes.[18]

Furthermore, at the request of Andrew Jackson, Congress had passed the Specie Circular Act in 1836, making it much harder for poorer farmers to purchase land. The act stipulated that the government would accept only gold or silver for land sales. Even banknotes were turned down, meaning that middling and poorer Americans could no longer buy on credit. Saving enough to buy land outright – especially good quality farmland – became extremely difficult for Americans who started life out with little or no wealth inheritance. And as land values rose, it was harder to parcel land out to multiple beneficiaries. This land shortage meant that many sons of yeomen farmers began their adult lives without owning any kind of real estate, causing them to fall into the category of poor white laborers and tenants. By the eve of secession, Steven Hahn discovered, much of the upcountry had a surplus of propertyless men wandering around in search of work. In fact, the white population in the area

---

[17] S. Lyle Johnson, "Fight for the Pre-Emption Law of 1841," *Arkansas Academy of Science Journal* 4 (1951): 166; 168; Rohrbaugh, *The Land Office Business*, 209; 213; 231; 234; Johnson, "Fight for the Pre-Emption Law," 168: "The nullification controversy developing out of the tariff in 1832 broke up the South and West alliance which had made possible the pre-emption act of 1830."

[18] Sioussat, "Andrew Johnson," 278–9, footnote 72.

increased by close to one-fourth in the ten years leading up to the Civil War.[19]

Amidst all of this land speculation, and the complications of the Specie Circular Act, America's economic situation became ominous. When financial disaster finally struck with the Panic of 1837, class lines between whites only hardened. The depression further concentrated wealth in the hands of the most affluent Americans. It also condemned many small landholding yeomen farmers to the ranks of landless poor whites.[20]

All of these factors – the economic panic, the end of inexpensive public land sales, and an influx of hundreds of thousands of slaves into the Deep South – eventually drove up the cost of land, especially in the newer states. In 1850, the minimum price for one acre of unimproved southern land was $1.25. Seemingly not exorbitant at that price, most land purchases were much larger and more expensive. Many land sales, including those from the federal government, specified a minimum number of acres for a single sale. This number was often set as high as 80 or 160 acres. In Alabama, for example, the smallest purchasable lot was forty acres. While some poor whites may have had enough money to purchase a small farm of ten or twenty acres, few had the cash available to purchase anything much bigger. But even at $1.25 an acre, lower- and middling-class Southerners simply could not compete with the spate of land speculators and slave owning planters, who often bought up the best tracts before they were even available to the public at auction.[21]

Improved farmland, of course, was completely out of reach for poorer Southerners, averaging $11.42 an acre. One scholar found that in Hancock County, Georgia in 1850, the value of large planters' land was "significantly higher" than the value of surrounding smaller farms. While the biggest plantations (valued at $10,000 and up) averaged $7.53 an acre, the smallest farms (valued $1,000 or less) only averaged $4.36. These discrepancies in value only worsened as soil exhaustion became more of a problem during the later antebellum period. Especially in older states like

[19] Williams, *Bitterly Divided*, 11; Steven Hahn, *The Roots of Southern Populism: Yeomen Farmers and the Transformation of the Georgia Upcountry, 1850–1890* (New York: Oxford University Press, 1983), 49.

[20] Peter L. Rousseau, "Jacksonian Monetary Policy, Specie Flows, and the Panic of 1837," *NBER Working Paper Series* (Cambridge, MA: National Bureau of Economic Research, 2000), 39–40.

[21] Soltow, *Men and Wealth*, 174; Bolton, *Poor Whites*, 23; Soltow, *Men and Wealth*, 24; Wayne Flynt, *Poor But Proud: Alabama's Poor Whites* (Tuscaloosa: University of Alabama Press, 1989), 4–5; Soltow, *Men and Wealth*, 22.

South Carolina and Georgia, over-farming practices had depleted the soil of essential nutrients, diminishing the quality of crop produced and ultimately driving down land prices. Many large slaveholders bought lands in the western states, establishing plantations upon fresh grounds that had not yet been covered by the sweat and blood of slaves.[22]

As William Barney found, much like areas in the older Deep South, soil exhaustion was also a significant issue in Alabama and Mississippi. In the Magnolia state, the most eroded lands sold for $5 an acre, while "fresher lands" cost between $10 and $20. In Alabama, Clement C. Clay lamented that "a country in its infancy ... is already exhibiting signs of civility and decay." To make matters even worse for lower-class whites struggling to become landowners, the value of improved farm acreage more than doubled during the cotton boom of the 1850s. The purchase of a few unimproved, paltry acres would have required an industrious poor white to save almost all family earnings over a period of months or even years.[23]

An 1847 article published in the *National Era* described the early settlement of the Carolinas. Originally, all immigrants lived near the waterways and all Southerners supposedly "got along well." Yet as the numbers of slaves began to rise, "the poor began to feel their degradation. A bitter hatred grew up between these classes. It led often to violence." Due to this constant tension, the article posited, larger planters "began to buy up the poor men's land, and the poor men, in turn, became anxious to sell." However, after selling their farms, these landless whites realized they had few ways to make a living. "They had no alternative left, as they thought, but to herd together on the sand-hills, and there they and theirs still live," the *Era* reported. Indeed,

Their choice of place is significant enough of their feeling, and of the cause of their removal. . . . They got where they could live without being disturbed or worried by the continued sight of slaves . . . often they 'squat,' as the phrase is, on the State's or other's property – it is difficult to say. But the best of it, on the average, would not return ten bushels of corn to the acre, the most of it not five. . . . But things are where they are, and as they are, because slavery, with its biting social ills, beats them away from the richer soil, and keeps them hopelessly down and debased on the barren hills.[24]

[22] Soltow, *Men and Wealth*, 22; James Bonner quoted in Linden, "Economic Democracy," 170–1.
[23] William L. Barney, *The Secessionist Impulse: Alabama and Mississippi in 1860* (Princeton: Princeton University Press, 1974), 12; Abbott, *South and North*, 181, Web; Barney, *The Secessionist Impulse*, 13.
[24] "The South," *National Era*, Nov. 25, 1847.

Originally, poor whites were scattered throughout the Deep South, primarily as squatters. But as the antebellum period wore on, they became increasingly concentrated in the foothills and mountains of Appalachia, and the pineywood, wiregrass regions. They also flocked to cities and burgeoning towns in search of work. However, the geographic mobility of the poor was not a matter of their own volition. Slaveholders were strategically buying up as much land as possible, pushing the least affluent yeomen off the land, turning them into tenants and day laborers, thus increasing the percentage of white Southerners who qualified as poor. Clement Comer Clay, who served as Governor of Alabama in the mid-1830s, wrote, "Our wealthier planters, with greater means and no more skill, are buying out their poorer neighbors, extending their plantations, and adding to their slave force. The wealthy few ... are thus pushing off the many who are merely independent."[25]

"Driven off the fertile lands by the encroachment of the planter," wrote James Ford Rhodes, poor whites therefore "farmed the worn-out lands and gained a miserable and precarious subsistence." At the same time, wealthy Southerners became highly mobile and sentimentally detached from their ancestral homelands. They moved frequently and invested as little as possible in their communities, as much of their tax money would have gone to infrastructural projects like building roads and bridges, or funding public school systems for poorer white children. As Wright aptly wrote: "the passionate southern attachment to the soil was a post-Civil War phenomenon. Slaveholding farmers and planters moved from place to place so often they seldom had time to sink roots." In the decades leading to secession, the rich became richer, but with slavery's profitability, it was a zero-sum game for less affluent whites. Without land or the opportunity to acquire it, lower-middling and poor whites sank more deeply into poverty, their employment prospects largely in the hands of the slaveholders.[26]

The master class also realized that buying up the small farms around their own homes would help keep their slaves more isolated from lower-class whites. George Henderson, who spent his childhood enslaved in Kentucky, remarked, "My folks was sure quality. Master bought all the little places around us so he wouldn't have any po' white trash neighbors." Likewise, Acie Thomas's interviewer noted that "it was the habit of the Folsoms to buy out these people whenever they could do so by fair

[25] Weston, *The Poor Whites of the South*, quoted on 5.
[26] Quoted in Bailey, *Class*, 12; Wright, *Old South, New South*, quoted on vi-vii.

means or foul, according to his statements. And by and by there were no poor whites living near them." According to other slaves and travelers, Thomas's "by fair means or foul" statement seemed to hold true. As he journeyed through Alabama, James Redpath met a poor farmer who had to move because his wealthy slaveholding neighbors bought up all the land surrounding his small homestead and then began charging exorbitant passage rent. The man claimed he could not even get to the main road without paying several tolls. The poor farmer alleged that the slaveholder was only charging passage rent in an effort to run him off the land. Furthermore, the neighboring slaves consistently stole from the poorer man's farm, and when he complained to the overseer, the overseer told him to shoot the slaves who were stealing. But if he shot the offending slaves, the poor farmer reasoned, he then would have to pay the market value of the slave, a fee he certainly could not afford. Poor farmers and small landholders, it seemed, had little recourse in their dealings with the powerful master class.[27]

Several former slaves confirmed that slave owners did, in fact, fleece small landowners of their holdings when they got the chance. Knowing they could almost always count on the backing of local judges and law enforcement officials, slaveholders were easily able to manipulate the system to their economic advantage. As one freedman recalled:

Sometimes the niggers would turn the white man up – when the white man say, "Take this sack of flour or sugar and hide it behind the bush, and I'll get it after dark," and the nigger would go and tell the master that he told him to get him a sack of something and hide it for him. ... And that night [the master] would come cross the old white man carrying a sack and say, "What is it [you] got in that sack. A pig, or a sack of corn?"

Apparently, after the slaveholder confronted the poorer man about receiving stolen goods from a slave, he would simply tell the offender that he would not press charges – if, of course, the thief would skip town immediately. Sam Stewart, who spent his childhood enslaved in North Carolina, also remembered slaveholders using this tactic. "Some of the slave owners, when a poor white man's land joined theirs and they wanted his place would have their Negroes steal things and carry them to the poor white man, and sell them to him," reported Stewart. "Then

---

[27] George Henderson, *The American Slave*, Vol. 7 (KY), 7; Acie Thomas, *Ibid.*, Vol. 3 (FL), 327–8; James Redpath, *The Roving Editor, or Talks with Slaves in the Southern States*, John R. McKivigan, ed. (1859; reprint, University Park: University of Pennsylvania Press, 1996), 255.

the slave owner, knowing where the stuff was ... would go and find his things at the poor white man's house. Then he would claim it, and take out a writ for him, but he would give him a chance. He would tell him to sell out to him, and leave, or take the consequences," he recalled. This tactic undoubtedly worked quite well. As Stewart concluded, "That's the way some of the slave owners got such large tracts of land."[28]

U.B. Phillips famously argued that territorial expansion occurred at the expense of the small farmer, who was forced westward by "economic pressure." Some of these formerly prosperous yeomen had been unable to keep up with state and local taxes. Some lost their lands after economic crises, others after an illness, accident, or death in the family. There were myriad ways to slip down into a lower-economic class in the Deep South. And just as the small landholders were losing their real estate, farm tenants, sharecroppers, and laborers increasingly were being pushed into nonagricultural work. James Bonner posited that "the landless farmer of 1850 ... was sometimes found, ten years later, among the low-paid industrial workers of the vicinity, or occasionally trying his hand at a semiskilled trade." Fabien Linden took these findings one step further, arguing that "those who were forced to become urban wage earners had in many cases fallen thought the very bottom of the agricultural hierarchy: psychologically they were twice removed from the soil." For the region's most impoverished whites, there were two choices: remain in the slave-ridden South and scrape together a meager living, or move west in search of new opportunities, hopefully away from competition with unfree labor. Of course, there was a class poor enough that they simply could not afford the trip out of the Deep South. These poor whites generally faced a bleak future. Charles Bolton discovered that "even the limited shifts toward commercial agriculture during the antebellum years ... had an immediate, strong, and negative impact on landless white households." One slaveholder bemoaned to the *Farmer and Planter* that soon "the only poor folks we will have amongst us will be those we can't run off or buy out – who expect to live by traffic with our slaves. – This is the most dangerous element in our society." Thus, as cotton assumed its place upon the southern throne, a great land consolidation occurred, completely changing the Deep South's labor system.[29]

---

[28] "When It's Right to Steal From Your Master," *American Slave*, Vol. 19 (Fisk), 34; Sam T. Stewart, *Ibid.*, Vol. 11 (NC), Part 2, 319.

[29] Phillips, "The Origin and Growth," 799–800; Linden, "Economic Democracy," Bonner cited on 145; 146; Bolton, *Poor Whites*, 18; quoted in Walter Kyle Planitzer, "A

It was within this atmosphere that abolitionists predicted that a strong sense of class consciousness among poor white laborers would spread, leading them to seek out better opportunities, mostly in the western free states. As early as 1849 *The Philadelphia Republic* called attention to the plight of poor white workers, viewed as the victims of the South's widening economic inequality:

Two-thirds of the free white people of these States have no interest in slave property, but on the contrary are directly interested against the continuance of the system. They are starving or emigrating because labor is degraded in character generally and underpaid in price. ... That all this is clearly understood, appears from the fact that the tide of emigration drifts steadily to the free western states. The poor white man who under this compulsion leaves the home of his birth, avoids the competition and taint of chattel slavery. ... There is nothing wanting but an effective array of the latent abolitionism of the southern States to accomplish a general emancipation.

Similarly, in an article published in 1856, another writer insisted that when poor whites saw "the nobility of the free working man of Kansas, [they] will desert the degrading service of their white masters of the Slave States."[30]

Indeed, the immigration of non-slaveholders to the free states had taken place for generations, and this steady tide of settlers remained strong in the few years leading up to the Civil War. The dream of western autonomy – far away from both their debts and the stain of slavery – must have been incredibly seductive. Elijah Millington Walker, the son of a Tennessee yeoman farmer, ascended into the professional middling classes as a doctor in Mississippi. Despite his class status, however, Walker still had several outstanding debts, making the possibly of westward migration much more enticing. He ultimately desired to move to South America, or at least Texas, "where I can neither see my creditors nor hear of my debts until I am able to liquidate all just claims against myself; this I think the best way to make a rise. Here I can never do it."[31]

Dangerous Class of Men, Without Direct Interest in Slavery: A Proslavery Concern about Southern Non-Slaveholders in the Late Antebellum Era," (Ph.D. Diss., Johns Hopkins University, 2007), 358.

[30] Editorial, *The Philadelphia Republic*, reprinted as "Anti-Slavery in the South," *Albany Patriot* (GA), Jan. 27, 1849, 2; "Letter from Washington," *New York Evangelist*, March 27, 1856.

[31] Elijah Millington Walker, *A Bachelor's Life in Antebellum Mississippi*, ed. Lynette Boney Wrenn (Knoxville: University of Tennessee Press, 2004), 252, footnote 4; 66.

Lower-middling- and middling-class whites may have had the economic means to pick up and move westward, but some impoverished whites attempted to migrate as well. Most slave owners were perfectly happy to allow the poor to leave the region. "The census returns show the tendency of the poor white population to abandon the slave States, in search of employment," reported the *National Era*, and "Notwithstanding the large preponderance of population in the free States, and its greater density, the census of 1850 exhibits the singular fact, that those States were largely the gainers in the interchange of population with the South." Still another article directly linked the westward migration of non-slaveholders to slavery's "demoralizing and degrading influence upon the whites, making of the master a tyrant, and of the poor white man a creature, infinitely below the slave in intellect, and all else, except the liberty to leave the slave states if he knew how to go and had the means to go with."[32]

Perhaps one of the biggest historical debates has concerned this westward migration into the heartland of America. A renewal of interest in Frederick Jackson Turner's frontier thesis beginning in the 1930s challenged the idea of migration as a safety valve. This theory argued that older portions of the United States used the West to unload their impoverished laborers, unwanted immigrants, and debtors and criminals. In one 1936 study, Carter Goodrich and Sol Davison determined that the supposed "avenue of escape," open "particularly during periods of economic distress," was not an accurate description of westward migration. However, they only studied *northern* wage laborers. John Barnhart disagreed with their theories, noting that Turner correctly identified most settlers to Indiana and Illinois as dispossessed Southerners. Many of these migrants had been "eliminated with the expansion of the plantation system." These poorer whites despised the system, whether they had been forced to supervise and discipline slaves or to compete with them for jobs. "Many mechanics," Barnhart wrote, "felt slavery to be a great curse ... and wanted to see it brought to an end in some way. The competition in which they were constantly made to feel themselves engaged with slave-labor was degrading to them." Indeed, land reform and migration were intertwined with the southern labor problem. As the *Niles' Weekly Register* put it: "The westward movement was considered as both a cause and a

---

[32] "Political Economy," *National Era*, Oct. 6, 1859; "Anti-Slavery Meetings in Chatham," *Provincial Freeman* (Canada), April 18, 1857.

result of the failure to establish a permanent and paying system of improved agriculture."[33]

Besides, regardless of who settled western lands first, by the time large slaveholders entered an area, they were still able to buy out smaller farmers when they coveted their lands. Calls for land reform continued to mount as more and more settlers poured into the West. As the Virginia-born abolitionist Moncure Conway wrote, poor whites "are really serfs of the soil, without the advantages of serfs; *orphaned serfs*, they may be called. Having no square foot of the earth that they can lease, much less own, they generally 'squat' down upon some landowner's estate, which the landowner is willing enough to permit; for no sooner does the poor *peinard* fix himself there, than he is virtually owned." Affluent land-owners could always evict poor tenants and renters, he lamented, "or even imprison him for trespass, unless distinct permission to settle can be proved. These *peinards* may in some cases be sold. ... They are worse off than the Negroes, being not so well dressed or fed."[34]

In a report on the Domestic Manufactures of the South and West, one politician found that the land which non-slaveholders "possess is almost universally poor, and so sterile that a scanty subsistence is all that can be derived from its cultivation." Due to this fact, he stated, "The acquisition of a respectable place in the scale of wealth appears so difficult, that they decline the hopeless pursuit; and many of them settle down into the habits of idleness, and become the almost passive subjects of all its conse-quences." Pointing to "an evident deterioration" among "this part of the population," the statesman bemoaned that the younger generations were growing up "less educated, less industrious, and in every point of view, less respectable than their ancestors." Traveler John Abbott agreed with this characterization, but he knew that the land monopoly was inextricably linked to slaveholding. "It is thus that slavery drags the whites with the blacks down into the gulf of ignorance and penury," he penned, "And it is impossible to rescue the poor white man without, at the same time, liberating the negro."[35]

It was within this contentious atmosphere that the poor white Andrew Johnson emerged, beholden to causes benefiting the white southern

[33] Carter Goodrich and Sol Davison, "The Wage-Earner in the Westward Movement," *Political Science Quarterly* (June 1935): 161–85, and Goodrich and Davison, "The Wage-Earner in the Westward Movement II," Political Science Quarterly (Mar., 1936): 61–116; John D. Barnhart, "Sources of Southern Migration into the Old Northwest," *Mississippi Valley Historical Review* 22 (June 1935): 49; 56; 58; quoted on 58.
[34] Conway, *Testimonies*, 120–1.   [35] Abbott, *South and North*, 146–7; 150.

laborer, the plain folk, and the common man. Having personally witnessed the evils of slavery, and the attendant ways in which slavery pervaded the lives of people who did not financially benefit from it, Johnson acutely understood that the slaveholders' power must be weakened, at least, for non-slaveholders to ever have a chance at economic mobility. Adopting the homestead cause in early 1845, he argued that agrarian reform was necessary to prevent growing antislavery sentiment among the landless. By tying the specter of abolition to land monopoly, Johnson artfully tried to win the support of slaveholders. Year after year, he worked stubbornly to achieve the Homestead Act's passage, at a high personal cost. Johnson's affiliation with the issue was frequently used by his political adversaries as evidence of his revolutionary radicalism.[36]

As a fierce Jacksonian Democrat, Johnson was, according to George Stephenson, "intolerant, dogmatic," and "jealous of his own rights and those of his class." Enemies deemed him the "mechanic statesman" the "prince of humbugs," as he fought vociferously for the middling and lower classes against the privileges of wealth and inheritance. During his long political career Johnson took on a diverse array of national causes, including the direct election of senators, limited terms for Supreme Court justices, and the complete abolition of both the Electoral College and the convention system of presidential nomination. On a state level, he desperately tried to limit the influence of the master class by calling for political representation to be based upon the population of whites alone. But the singular cause Johnson was most zealous about was land reform. When the Homestead Bill failed to pass the House of Representatives year after year, Senator Augustus Dodge of Iowa addressed the slaveholding opponents of the bill in Georgia, appealing "particularly to the southern origin of both the principles of the bill and of the emigrants who profited by it." Dodge further pressed for reform, calling the bill's "indomitable author," Andrew Johnson, "the type of the men for whom this bill is intended – now a most able and faithful member of Congress, once a mechanic struggling with poverty and working with the hands which God gave him, and expending the sweat by which it was the decree of the Almighty that man should obtain his bread."[37]

Still, while slaveholders bitterly contested the passage of the bill, there were Southerners who sincerely desired agrarian reform. While many

---

[36] Sioussat, "Andrew Johnson," 270; 273; 283, footnote 88.
[37] Stephenson, *Political History*, 158–9; Sioussat, "Andrew Johnson," quoted on 286–7.

poorer and lower-middling-class whites "had a direct interest in the enactment of such a law," Stephenson wrote, they unfortunately "were of the class of people who in the past have been unable to exercise a potent influence on legislation and who have left few records of themselves. The domination of the slaveholders in politics and journalism was so complete that the non-slaveholding interests had little voice." A few southern politicians fought on behalf of the destitute and downtrodden, including Representative Fayette McMullin of Virginia, who reveled over the thought of the wealthy landed class having to "go to work themselves" once poor white tenants and laborers migrated west. He pointed out that even for the laborers left in the South, wages would go up, because there would be less labor competition. Representative Albert Gallatin Brown of Mississippi reminded the affluent to consider the fates of thousands of "homeless," who "look out upon your vast domains, and see them tenanted only by wild beasts." Eventually, he held, these men will ask, "is my poverty so great a crime that my Government prefers these beasts to me? Am I to be kept in penury and in want, and leave to my children no inheritance but poverty, whilst my Government guards … this mighty wilderness, which God in his providence has created for man, and not for beasts?" Having lived as a squatter during his childhood, Brown clearly sympathized with landless Southerners who needed financial relief.[38]

Two Alabamans supported the measure as well. As Williamson R.W. Cobb campaigned throughout the state, he professed to be a friend to the common man. He ended each stump speech with a little song entitled "The Homestead Bill," which claimed that the U.S. government was rich enough to give every man a farm. Cobb's short tune was swiftly dubbed a "masterpiece of demagoguery" by wealthy slaveholding candidates. Finally, Alabama's Representative William R. Smith challenged Congress to "help the cities to disgorge their cellars and their garrets of a starving, haggard, and useless population." By moving the poor out of the Deep South and onto their own homesteads, he pandered, the affluent would rid themselves of many undesirable neighbors.[39]

For the vast majority of the Deep South's slaveholding legislators, however, the Homestead Bill was terrifying, as it could shift the balance of power in government in favor of free states. With slavery's fate at stake,

---

[38] Stephenson, *Political History*, 157–8; Fred A. Shannon, "The Homestead Act and the Labor Surplus," *American Historical Review* XLI, No. 4 (July 1936): quoted on 641–2.
[39] Eaton, *The Freedom of Thought Struggle*, 82; Shannon, "The Homestead Act," quoted on 641–2.

they vociferously condemned the prospect as a radical, socialistic meas-
ure. As Conway revealed, Virginia's politicians recoiled at the idea of land
reform. At a dinner in 1850 with U.S. Senators James M. Mason and
Robert Hunter, Conway inquired about their opinions on the Homestead
Bill. The slave masters "sneer[ed] at it as an agrarian project, apiece with
Abolitionism, and one which would never be passed by Congress."
Although there had always been slaveholder opposition to land reform,
as the country became increasingly divided in the decade prior to the Civil
War, the master class' opprobrium for the Homestead Bill grew. Masters
made multiple attempts to mute the conversation over land reform, but
the masses continued to press the issue. "The homestead sentiment continued to mount, like a tide," George Stephenson concluded, until "it
threatened to break through in spite of every possible makeshift the
opposition could devise to withstand."[40]

As the *National Era* reported, slaveholders had long despised the
Homestead Act, "but the poor white men of the South, who are held
down by the incubus of Slave Labor, for whose children the State provides
no common school instruction, who scarcely can hope ever to rise to
social equality with their aristocratic neighbors, will hail it as a measure of
relief." Whenever the bill's passage should "finally prevail," impoverished
whites would be able to "emerge from the degradation to which they are
now subjected. They could leave the cities, escape from the oppressive
competition and prejudices of their enemies, and distribute themselves as
settlers on the public domain." Once poor whites became homeowners
and "industrious producers," they would rise above the prejudices of the
slaveholders and finally receive respect. Without the prospect of homesteads, though, "so many" impoverished whites pursued "menial pursuits, or live in squalor and poverty, without any steady employment at
all." The Homestead Act clearly divided the country: on one side, the
Eastern Whig capitalists and southern slaveholders stringently opposed
the measure; on the other side, poor white Southerners, immigrants, and
western Democrats fought for the right to own land. The contentiousness
between the groups precipitously increased as agrarian reform became
tied to antislavery. As Fred Shannon found, "It was only when the
Republican party became militant over the free-soil question that the
South consolidated its ranks against the homestead policy."[41]

---

[40] Conway, *Testimonies*, 33; Stephenson, *Political History*, 147–8.
[41] "The Public Lands – Free Farms," *National Era*, Sept. 20, 1852; Shannon, "The Homestead Act," 643.

As troubling as sectional and class tensions were in the mid-1850s, the latter part of the decade witnessed an escalation in conflict. The Congressional record unmistakably highlighted this growing division. By 1858, Georgia-born Senator Robert Toombs, slave owner and future-secessionist, took to name-calling. Branding homestead advocates "demagogues," he aroused the ire of politicians from the northwestern free states. Ohio Senator Benjamin Wade perhaps delivered the best reply to Toombs. Lamenting how long it was taking to "get a straightforward vote upon this great measure of" agrarian reform, Wade chastised the slaveholders who continued to block the passage of the bill. "The question will be," he thundered, mocking their fanciful notions of re-opening the slave trade, "shall we give niggers to the niggerless, or land to the landless?"[42]

Two years later Representative William Windom of Minnesota continued confronting the master class, who were once again effectively preventing a vote on the legislation. He cast the divide as a "struggle between the Republican party, as the friend of the toiling millions of the country, and the Democratic party, as the champion of the aristocratic, pampered, purse-proud few, who regard the laboring man as a slave, and estimate his importance only by the amount of money they can wring from his hard-earned pittance." Admitting that this was "no new struggle," Windom grieved that "too often capital has prevailed in the contest, and labor has been crushed beneath the iron heel of oppression." Making sure that white workers and immigrants understood what was at stake politically, he tied land ownership to freedom, highlighting the growing call for other forms of unfree labor in the South. "The white laborer, in the opinion of these Democratic leaders, comes also within the principle upon which they justify slavery," he concluded, "and they claim that the right of one man to own another 'does not depend upon difference in complexion.'" With just a few sentences, Windom warned the underclasses that their future liberty – regardless of their race – was dependent upon economic self-sufficiency.[43]

Slaveholders' invective against agrarian reform reached a crescendo during the presidential election of 1860. Political banners intended to discredit the Republicans ridiculed Abraham Lincoln's lower-class upbringing, scorning him for ever having labored with his hands. Dubbing him "Old Abe – one of Hammond's mud sills," the slaveholders

---

[42] Stephenson, *Political History*, quoted on 195.
[43] *The Congressional Globe*, 36th Congress, 1st Session, House, 171; 172.

always found a way to link the politician's impoverished childhood to the fact that he supported the Homestead Bill. Constitutional Union candidate John Bell did not escape the wrath of the slave owners, either. Georgia's *Southern Watchman* published an article just weeks prior to the election accusing Bell of being "the poor man's friend" because he apparently advocated an amendment to the Homestead Bill making it more accessible and appealing to severely impoverished whites. "Connected with this idea of the homestead, of providing a home for the homeless, and the principle of elevating the condition of the poor families of the Union, who have no lands," Bell opined, "there are many families in the country who cannot leave where they now are to go off to the new lands. .... I want citizens in different portions of the Union to be put upon an equal footing with those who live in the land States." Subsequently, the southern papers lambasted Bell, angrily implying that he was antislavery, simply because he supported agrarian reform. After the *Southern Banner* described the Homestead Bill as an "abolition measure of the vilest kind," it then turned upon the moderate politician. Subtly acknowledging the power of *The Impending Crisis*, the writer asked: "Was not Mr. Bell helping the Helpers, when he thus furnished them with an 'assignable and transferable' claim to one hundred and seventy nine millions of public lands, to raise money upon to prosecute their iniquitous war upon the South?"[44]

Bell, of course, was not the only pro-land reformer labelled a "Helperite." Andrew Johnson proudly wore the title as a badge of honor, and often used facts from Helper's work when arguing for class-based legislation – especially concerning agrarianism. "Go to any one of those countries where the soil has passed into the hands of the few, and the mass of the people have become mere tenants and cultivators of the soil for an inflated and heartless landed aristocracy," Johnson avowed in 1850, before the House of Representatives. Indeed, he vigorously asserted, when this "violation reaches that point at which it can be no longer borne, revolution begins, and those principles are partially or entirely restored." After his thinly veiled threat of a popular uprising of the white masses, Johnson closed his speech by allowing the master class to redeem themselves – and retain their own sense of benevolent paternalism – by voting for the Homestead Act. "Pass this bill," the former

[44] Stephenson, *Political History*, 229; "The Homestead Bill," *Southern Watchman*, Aug. 30, 1860, 3; "Mr. John Bell and the Homestead Bill," *Southern Banner*, Aug. 16, 1860, 2.

impoverished white sincerely pleaded, "and you will make many a poor man's heart rejoice."[45]

Due to sentiments like these, Johnson and the other Homestead supporters became the target of the master class' polemic. Senator Louis Wigfall of Texas lambasted the future-President as the North's sycophant, labelling Johnson "The vilest of Republicans, the reddest of the Reds, [and] a sans-culotte." The issue of land reform, of course, was only one part of Johnson's broader, progressive plan. He obviously realized the significance of land ownership in regards to labor. If poor whites had access to becoming financially independent, they would no longer have to rely on slaveholders for jobs or wages. And as the antebellum period wore on, white southern laborers increasingly became discontented with their station in life. Surrounded by ostentatious displays of garish wealth, they found they had fewer and fewer options for solvency. Simply feeding and clothing a family became increasingly hard as formerly "white" jobs were transferred to slaves or free blacks. With their wages constantly undercut by unfree laborers, poor whites' anger grew, and tensions within the Deep South – between different classes of whites – continued to escalate. As W.E.B. DuBois so thoughtfully opined about the causes of the Civil War, the causes of secession were much more complex than a northern/southern, abolition/pro-slavery divide. Indeed, he wrote, "The result was war because ... the South was determined to make free white labor compete with black slaves, monopolize land and raw material in the hands of the political aristocracy, and extend the scope of that power." Perhaps just as importantly, though, the result was a bloody Civil War "because white American labor, while it refused to recognize black labor as equal and human, had to fight to maintain its own humanity and ideal of equality." Without land, and with having constantly to compete with slaves, whether for jobs or wages, poor whites were burdened – not elevated – by the peculiar institution. Given all of these reasons, there is little wonder why in 1864, two years after the passage of the Homestead Act and one year after the Emancipation Proclamation, Andrew Johnson deemed the deadliest conflict in our nation's history "a war that has freed more whites than blacks."[46]

[45] DuBois, *Black Reconstruction*, 243; *The Congressional Globe*, 31st Congress, 1st Session, House, 951–2.
[46] DuBois, *Black Reconstruction*, quoted on 242; 237: see chapter 8: The Transubstantiation of a Poor White; quoted on 243–4.

2

The Demoralization of Labor

In the South, unfortunately, no kind of labor is either free or respectable. Every white man who is under the necessity of earning his bread, by the sweat of his brow, or by manual labor, in any capacity, no matter how unassuming in deportment, or exemplary in morals, is treated as if he was a loathsome beast, and shunned with the utmost disdain.
– Hinton Helper[1]

Fearfully as slavery bears upon the blacks of the South, its effects upon the vast majority of the whites is no way less dreadful. Slavery degrades all labor, and with it all laborers.
– The North Star[2]

Ten years before Lincoln's election, former slave and abolitionist leader Frederick Douglass lamented that "by encouraging the enmity of the poor, laboring white man against the black," the slaveholder "succeeds in making the said white man almost as much a slave as the black slave himself." Douglass's interpretation, of course, was nowhere near novel. Throughout much of the antebellum period, poor white Southerners had been compared to (and at times even referred to as) slaves. The primary point of comparison for most commentators was simple: if slavery was primarily a system of labor, then in a slave society, all laborers suffered degradation and humiliation. When labor becomes synonymous with "slave work," the theory goes, all laborers are in some sense enslaved, whether to masters or capitalists. As Douglass clarified, "The difference

[1] Helper, *The Impending Crisis*, 41.
[2] "The Poor Whites of the South," *The North Star*, March 1, 1850.

between the white slave, and the black slave, is this: the latter belongs to one slaveholder, and the former belongs to all the slaveholders, collectively. ... Both are plundered, and by the same plunderers." This dual enslavement, he concluded, resulted from each white laborer being "robbed by the slave system, of the just results of his labor, because he is flung into open competition with a class of laborers who work without wages." Indeed, just a few years later, Hinton Helper made that specific argument his main call-to-arms for the masses of non-slave-owning whites. Asserting that no free white worker could compete with slave labor, Helper destroyed the pro-slavery argument, purposefully challenging the domination of the region's slaveholders. His main argument rested in large part on labor theory: poor whites simply could not compete – for jobs or for living wages – with profitable slave labor.[3]

Although life had never come easy for the region's poor, the financial upheaval of the Panic of 1837 devastated the vulnerable lower classes. Then, further concentrating wealth, more than 800,000 slaves poured into the Deep South during the 1830s and 1840s, displacing unskilled and semiskilled white laborers. Finally, the cotton boom of the 1850s helped the richest slaveholders become richer, while the poorest continued to flounder. Upward mobility was increasingly elusive. Charles Bolton found that in the North Carolina Piedmont, 90 percent of landless laborers in 1850 were still landless in 1860. With "very little chance of improving their economic situations," poor whites were required to become short-term or day laborers. Forced from performing the agricultural work their ancestors had engaged in for centuries, poor whites born into the post-Jacksonian South increasingly became involved in non-agricultural work. Yet even in new industries, there were simply not enough jobs to keep poor whites at a level of full employment. Rarely did they have long-term contracts; most were hired daily, weekly, or seasonally, leaving many of them underemployed for parts of the year. Moreover, growing numbers of white laborers had to travel widely to find job opportunities, abandoning their homes and families for periods of time to take short-term work. They often took the South's dirtiest, most dangerous jobs, deemed "too hazardous for Negro property." Yet as poor whites attempted to enter construction, mechanical, factory, and other jobs, they constantly were made aware of the thousands of readily available black strikebreakers

[3] Frederick Douglass, *Life and Times of Frederick Douglass* (Boston: De Wolfe & Fiske Co., 1892), 180; Helper, *The Impending Crisis*, 32–3.

waiting to take their places should they ask for better wages or request safer working conditions.[4]

For some lower-class white workers, the prospect of competing with slave labor for the rest of their lives was too unsettling to handle. Instead of continuing to work for poverty-level wages, some chose to migrate west, away from slavery and toward a better standard of living. However, moving an entire family was often unrealistic for the poorest whites. Left in the Deep South to compete with slave labor, their futures appeared quite grim. Effectively excluded from the labor market, some of them withdrew from society, preferring to hunt, fish, and forage for a minimal subsistence. Significant numbers of disaffected poor whites supplemented their meagre incomes with illegal activities, mostly by trading with slaves in the underground economy. A few gave in to their basest impulses, preferring to dull the harsh realities of their lives with vices like alcohol. Still others were so plagued by poverty that they spent periods of time desperately hungry.

In 1845, Georgia's *Columbus Enquirer* reminded its readers: "It is a solemn truth, to be remembered, that the poor are miserable, and often hungry sufferers, when they are compelled to go in search of capitalists, to ask for employment." These white laborers knew enough about the world to comprehend the influence of slavery on their lives. It drove down their wages and rendered their former agricultural jobs obsolete. It stunted business ventures outside the realm of agricultural growth, therefore impeding both technological and industrial development. Gavin Wright has argued persuasively that the antebellum South failed to industrialize significantly not simply because of a lack of manufactory expertise but because slave owning labor lords were reaping consistently strong returns by using their labor force to grow cotton. Affluent men had no need to focus their attentions on other forms of moneymaking; they were becoming rich off their slaves in terms of both annual earnings and rising slave prices, and without the added risk of opening and operating a new business.[5]

Interestingly, however, southern industrialists actually earned a higher rate of return than large slaveholders did throughout the late antebellum

---

[4] Robert Evans, Jr., "The Economics of Negro Slavery, 1830–1860," in National Bureau of Economic Research, *Aspects of Labor Economics* (Princeton: Princeton University Press, 1962), 186; Bolton, *Poor Whites*, 14; Morris, "The Measure of Bondage," 223; 228.

[5] "Let Us Reason Together," *Columbus Enquirer*, July 16, 1845, 1; Wright, *Old South, New South*, 19; 25.

period. One study estimated that in 1860, an "acceptable" rate of return for planters hovered around 10 percent, while southern manufacturers averaged profits of 26 percent. Slave owners' reluctance to take advantage of this larger profit margin, James Cobb wrote, was probably largely due to "a simple preference for a relatively secure investment (slaves and land) over a potentially more lucrative but also more risky one (stock in a new factory)." Still, there was a possibility that their decision also was driven by certain social or political concerns about industrialization. Slaveholders likely had legitimate concerns about transforming the mostly rural, agricultural South into a society that more closely resembled the manufacturing-driven North. According to Cobb, the "key to understanding the restricted size for the South's industrial sector was not the absence of viable investment opportunities but the tendency of planters and slaveholders, the region's wealthiest investors, to shun manufacturing in favor of agriculture."[6]

Ultimately, the South's failure to industrialize at a more rapid rate meant that poor, unemployed or under-employed whites had few available options to earn a living wage within the region. George Weston wrote that "the complaint of low wages and want of employment comes from every part of the South." But Southerners did not have to be educated or even literate to understand why lower-class whites continued to struggle throughout the region. As former slave James Deane put it, "The poor white people ... were worse off than the slaves, because they could not get any work to do, on the plantation the slaves did all the work." Because of this obvious preference for slave labor, class tensions became a very serious problem for slaveholders in the few decades before secession. Writing in 1954, Richard Morris was one of the earliest historians definitively to establish a link between the Deep South's slave societies and the nominal, quasi-freedom of poor whites. In language reminiscent of Helper, Morris concluded that "a significant segment of the southern labor force of both races operated under varying degrees of compulsion, legal or economic, in a twilight zone of bondage." Poor white laborers in the slave states, he claimed, "dwelt in a shadowland enjoying a status neither fully slave nor entirely free."[7]

---

[6] James C. Cobb, *Industrialization and Southern Society: 1877–1984* (Lexington: University Press of Kentucky, 1984), 8; 8–9; 8.
[7] Weston, *"The Poor Whites,"* 4; James V. Deane, *The American Slave*, Vol. 8 (MD), 9; Morris, "The Measure of Bondage," 220.

While heavy slave areas, such as the plantation belt of the Deep South, were especially rife with class conflicts, problems over inequalities arose between groups of whites wherever slavery existed. Fred Arthur Bailey uncovered a great deal of information concerning this friction between slaveholders and poor whites, especially over labor issues. Because his results were based on the Tennessee Veterans Questionnaires, the responses were probably more benign than they would have been in the more economically stratified Deep South, where class tensions were undoubtedly more amplified. But even in the Upper South, problems over slave competition, wages, and perceived work ethic dominated the minds of lower-class whites. The vast majority of non-slaveholders interviewed, it seems, had little respect for slave owners as productive, working members of society. Instead, about 1 in 5 non-slaveholding whites concluded that the masters of other men rarely worked at all, and a surprising 14 percent of slaveholders confirmed these observations.[8]

Conversely, and contrary to the persistent stereotype of poor whites as lazy and shiftless, only 4 out of 1,223 Confederate veterans "condemned [the poor] for their idleness." Often commenting on the haughty, disdainful manner of wealthy slaveholders and the dire, sometimes pitiful, circumstances of poor whites, respondents clearly understood class division in the Old South. Poor white Confederate veteran Robert Lackey observed this distinction, writing "Them that was able had slaves to work for them but the poor class of people was almost slaves themselves – had to work hard and live hard." Rosaline Rogers, who grew up enslaved in South Carolina and Tennessee, attempted to make sense out of the great divide between whites. She recalled, "The wealthy slave owner never allowed his slaves to pay any attention to the poor white folks, as he knew they had been free all their lives and should be slave owners themselves. The poor whites were hired by those who did not believe in slavery, or could not afford slaves." William Eskew, the son of a poor white, described how economic inequality unmistakably set the tone for social relationships, and even dictated political participation. "There was no neighboring with the poor man and rich man," he bluntly reported, and "No poor man held office. There was no chance for a young poor man for his wages was so low he could not save anything."[9]

[8] Bailey, *Class*, 68.
[9] *Ibid.*; Elliot and Moxley, *Tennessee*, Vol. 4, 1316; Rosaline Rogers, *American Slave*, Vol. 6 (IN), Part 2, 165; Elliot and Moxley, *Tennessee*, Vol. 2, 778.

By the late antebellum period, these respondents claimed, class tensions continued to rise. They even seemed to threaten the primacy of race, eroding the supposedly sacred bonds of white privilege. Problems over white labor – the absence of full-time work, the lack of opportunities in general, and the inability of many workers to earn a living wage – created a potentially explosive society. Complete with large percentages of slaves *and* a sizable, disaffected poor white underclass, a constant state of anxiety engulfed much of the Deep South in the years preceding secession. If these two classes ever banded together against their common oppressors – as they had before repeatedly throughout America's short history – they threatened the fortunes, the power, and even the lives of the region's masters.

Understanding this anxiety helps to explain why so many slaveholders became preoccupied with segregating the two groups. When it came to labor practices, this separatism made rational economic sense. Masters undoubtedly preferred slave labor to the work of poor whites. Time and time again slaveholders commented on blacks' superior work ethic and their willingness to follow commands. Marcus Toney, the son of a wealthy slave owner from Lynchburg, Virginia, admitted that only if they needed additional help would planters "engag[e] the whites. As a general proposition, the slaveholders, were a class unto themselves." Even non-slaveholding yeomen farmers showed surprisingly little inclination to hire other white workers. As one Confederate veteran remembered, "There were a family of free negroes whom father hired and they lived on father's place ever since ... father hired free negro and Indian labor and sometimes a white hired man or two." While there were myriad reasons why both planters and employers preferred slave labor, the most common was that poor whites were often defiant, refusing to take orders from a "master." The sense of emasculation bred by being driven like a slave fueled poor whites' insubordination, whether consciously or subconsciously.[10]

Indeed, one Virginian landholder exclusively employed free labor, but still held that black workers were more productive than whites. Although he rarely paid free white men more than $100 a year, he "thought them less worth the money than any" laborers he ever hired. Poor white workers, he contended, were more trouble than owning slaves, as they were "less docile and more given to drink." Northern comparisons of

---

[10] Mildred Rutherford Mell, *A Definitive Study*, 95–6; Elliot and Moxley, *Tennessee*, Vol. 5, 2066; Vol. 4, 1355–6.

black and white labor often focused on the degradation of poor southern whites, and the lack of options they had as workers within a slave society. An 1847 article entitled "White Slavery" held that "The poor negro must work for others, or be flogged; the poor white man must work for others, or be starved. The poor negro is subjected to a single master; the poor white man is subjected to many masters – to a master class." Moreover, the impoverished white had no one to turn to in times of crisis and extreme poverty. "The poor negro has a master both in sickness and in health," the article concluded, but "the poor white man is a slave only so long as he is able to toil, and a pauper when he can toil no more." This sentiment certainly was shared by one Nashville slaveholder during the Civil War. A Unionist who did not want to see his slaves used for the war effort, he believed "that there are too many poor white men in Tennessee already, and it would be a positive benefit to us if you would clean them out by drafting them into the army." His logic was cold and calculated, reducing human beings to profit margins – a common analysis in a land dominated by slavery. "The poor white men raise little or no cotton," he reasoned, and thus "are of no use to the great commercial world."[11]

As Robert Starobin wrote in 1970, "slave labor was not less efficient than the free labor available. ... Physical coercion, or the threat of it, was an effective slave incentive." Economists Robert Fogel and Stanley Engerman confirmed this fact, noting that the typical slave field hand was, on average, "harder-working and more efficient than his white counterpart." Violence was an extremely effective incentive. One Mississippi planter bragged that by using slaves, "there is no haggling or striking for wages, no contention about hours. Uniformity, obedience, and wholesome discipline, make the labor of the South." Indeed, slavery had become so profitable in the few decades before the Civil War that black labor commonly was employed in factories and even in the skilled trades. The demand for slave labor continued to grow as secession loomed, especially in cotton producing areas. In the decade before the Civil War, slave hiring increased in the Deep South at three times the rate that it increased in the Upper South. As early as the 1820s and 1830s, white southern artisans began having trouble finding employment. Although this fact was due in part to the ready availability of cheap, northern-made goods,

---

[11] "The South: Letters on the Productions, Industry and Resources of the Slave States: Number Four," *New York Times*, March 4, 1853, 2; "White Slavery," *Portage Sentinel* (OH), July 7, 1847; "Letter from Theophilius Iron-Clad, Esq., to President Lincoln on Negro Enlistments," *Nashville Daily Union*, Nov. 3, 1863.

much of the skilled tradesmen's problems arose from competition with slaves. Combining black and white workers in the same jobs, Michele Gillespie purported, was becoming "a far more common sight by the late antebellum period."[12]

Adding more problems to the growing tension between poor white and black labor, masters pursued the practice of hiring out slaves. Some of these slave hires were artisans possessing certain profitable skills, but many were simply excess laborers who could be worked during agricultural lay-by times. While this practice likely originated with slaves being hired out to neighboring yeomen and small farmers, in the two decades before the Civil War, Deep South state and local governments – as well as private corporations – all rented slaves. While a few states passed laws providing for the taxation of slave hires, most of these tax rates were never enforced. Georgia, for example, had strikingly high rates of slave-hire taxation, totaling over $100 per year per slave. The laws were intended to discourage slave hiring, as the practice was commonly considered a pathway to emancipation. However, there is no evidence of any slaveholder actually paying this expensive tax. Instead, the powerful master class simply chose to ignore laws that were economically detrimental.[13]

Unfettered by these laws, therefore, during the 1840s and 1850s slave hiring rose by 50 percent, a rate proportional to the increasing value of slaves. Hinton Helper numbered slave renters at 160,000 people, deeming these temporary masters "third-rate aristocrats – persons who formerly owned slaves, but whom slavery, as is its custom, had dragged down to poverty, leaving them, in their false and shiftless pride, to eke out a miserable existence over the hapless chattels personal of other men." Employers throughout the South, whether involved in construction, manufacturing, or agriculture, had concluded that using slave labor – even in the form of hiring – was more economically efficient than using poor white laborers. Brutalized slave labor would always be more efficient than non-brutalized free labor. Still, poor white and even skilled laboring Southerners took immediate notice of how the institution of slavery, which had already pushed them out of agriculture, was now

---

[12] Robert S. Starobin, *Industrial Slavery in the Old South* (New York: Oxford University Press, 1970), 154; Robert W. Fogel and Stanley L. Engerman, *Time on the Cross: The Economics of American Negro Slavery* (Boston: Little, Brown, & Co., 1974), 5; quoted in Starobin, *Industrial Slavery*, 210; Evans, "The Economics of Negro Slavery," 223; Gillespie, *Free Labor in an Unfree World*, 136; 131.

[13] Morris, "The Measure of Bondage," 234–5.

obstructing their employment in various other jobs. No matter how uneducated poor whites were, they still understood that competition with slaves drove the price of their labor down. As A.J. Ferrell, a poor white Tennessean replied, if masters "had not owned slaves a man working as I was could have secured better wages."[14]

Yet slaveholders did have another reason for keeping poor whites separate from their slaves. Many of them believed that poor whites "demoralized" slaves by laboring so infrequently. As one owner explained, "the intercourse of *these people* with the negroes was not favorable to good discipline." Poor whites, he thought, could not command slaves' respect, and thus would weaken the prevailing racial hierarchy. This idea of "demoralization" is important: if slaves realized how little poor whites had to work to lead lives that differed only slightly from their own material realities, surely they would become more discontented. Furthermore, if enslaved blacks recognized the absolute differences – both economically and socially – between poor whites and all other whites, they would naturally question the ideological privileges associated with the idea of white supremacy. Poor whites not only undermined slavery through crime, miscegenation, and personal relationships with African Americans, but they also served as a constant reminder that race in itself did not constitute any type of "scientific" superiority.[15]

Traveling through Fayetteville, North Carolina, Frederick Law Olmsted commented that "there is a large number, I should think a majority, of entirely uneducated, poverty-stricken vagabonds ... people without habitual, definite occupation or reliable means of livelihood. They are poor, having almost no property but their bodies." Yet, he critiqued, these impoverished whites were not employed at any steady, regular work, but instead labored "occasionally by the day or job, when driven to it by necessity." One wealthy gentleman stated that "the whole household property of families of this class" was "less than $20. If they have need of money to purchase clothing, etc., they obtain it by selling their game or meal ... [or they] will work for a neighboring farmer for a few days, and they usually get for their labour fifty cents a day." These sentiments seemed to have been shared by affluent men across the entire South. In northern Mississippi Olmsted reported that one aspiring

---

[14] Helper, *The Impending Crisis*, 147; 149; Starobin, *Industrial Slavery*, 155; Elliot and Moxley, *Tennessee*, Vol. 2, 806–7.

[15] Quoted in Frederick Law Olmsted, *A Journey in the Seaboard Slave States: With Remarks on Their Economy* (New York: Dix and Edwards, 1856), 674.

politician proposed a law to send idle, jobless poor white men to the penitentiary, "to make 'em work and earn something to support their families. I pity the women ... they work hard enough, I know; but the men. ... They just hang around groceries and spend all the money they can get – just go round and live on other people, and play keerds, and only go home at nights; and the poor women, they have to live like they ken."[16]

Given all of these testimonies, Olmsted maintained that the vast majority of northern workingmen lived much better material lives than their southern counterparts. The "citizens of the cotton States, as a whole, are poor," he wrote. "They work little, and that little, badly; they earn little, they sell little; they buy little, and they have little – very little – of the common comforts and consolations of civilized life. Their destitution is not material only; it is intellectual and it is moral." Moncure Conway agreed with Olmsted's assessment, but more directly connected poverty to poor whites' withdrawal from the formal labor force. They "are generally employed in doing nothing, and thereat are eminently successful," he wrote. "I have never been able to find out how they earned even the pittance with which they get drunk." Deemed a "dead peasantry" by several contemporary writers, poor whites came to be seen as obstinate "non-producers, except for the necessaries of their own existence." The *New York Times* reported in 1854 that "As soon as" poor whites earn "any money, they quit, and will not go to work again until they have spent it." One immigrant mechanic living in South explained why poorer whites turned down the prospect of work: "no man will work along side of a nigger, if he can help it. It's too much like as if he was a slave himself."[17]

As much as slaveholders would have liked to avoid it, however, bi-racial work did happen, and with relative frequency, especially during the bottleneck seasons of planting and harvesting. The nature of this type of work, of course, forced the poor white laborer to have *some* sort of a personal relationship with their African American co-laborers. One citizen of New Orleans wrote that white laborers were "generally regarded as of the lowest; and in a slave State, this standard is 'in the lowest depths,

---

[16] Frederick Law Olmsted, *The Cotton Kingdom: A Traveller's Observations on Cotton and Slavery in the American Slave States* (2 vols.; New York: Mason Brothers, 1861) Web. Vol. I, 188; Vol. II, 65.

[17] *Ibid.*, Vol. I, 13; Conway, *Testimonies*, 121; "The South," *New York Times*, Jan. 26, 1854.

a lower deep,' from the fact, that, by association, it is a reduction of the white servant to the level of their colored fellow-menials." Eugene Genovese uncovered a case in Mississippi where the sons of a poor white man were working as laborers on a big plantation. Apparently, they "became too solicitous of the slaves alongside whom they were picking cotton," and for that sin, the boys "were nearly lynched as 'Negro sympathizers.'" Their story was likely replicated in every county in the Deep South throughout the late antebellum period, as it became clear to masters that having two sizable underclasses within one society was potentially dangerous.[18]

Indeed, these instances of working side by side with slaves probably did more than anything else to solidify notions of white inequality and class consciousness among poor whites. Doing the same work as a slave – for very little remuneration – forced poor whites to confront how much privilege whiteness entailed. More importantly, this practice made it possible for poor whites to identify with slaves as fellow laborers, possibly becoming empathetic to their plight, and perhaps becoming abolitionists. Whether in the fields or in the factory, poor white workers had long noticed the fading distinctions between them and their enslaved co-laborers. Certainly by the 1840s and 1850s, masters were granting favored slaves more freedoms, like hiring out their own labor, learning artisanal trades, and selling produce they raised during their free time. Simultaneously, freedoms and opportunities that most white Americans generally took for granted were slipping out of reach for many of the Deep South's poor whites: wealth became even more concentrated at the top, prospects for upward class mobility dwindled, job competition increased, and extreme poverty seemed to worsen.

By the late-antebellum period, the jobs held by southern poor whites – and the terms of their employment – varied considerably. Whether being paid by the day to chop wood, or given room, board, and $10 a month to help out seasonally, or sharecropping a wealthy planter's extra land, poor whites earned their livelihoods in a variety of ways. They lived in a constant state of uncertainty, unsure of how long their current status would last and how they might procure the next job – and sometimes even the next meal. Seth Rockman found that in the more urban Upper

---

[18] Quoted in Helper, *The Impending Crisis*, 380; Eugene D. Genovese, "'Rather Be a Nigger Than a Poor White Man': Slave Perceptions of Southern Yeomen and Poor Whites," in Hans L. Trefousse, ed. *Toward a New View of America: Essays in Honor of Arthur C. Cole* (New York: B. Franklin, 1977), 85–6.

South, the "vagaries of the preindustrial urban economy almost assured that a wage-earning man would teeter" between "self-support and constant and absolute dependence." In the Deep South's slave states, poor whites were simply unable to count on any sureties in their lives, leaving them highly stressed.[19]

While few historians and economists have extensively studied wage rates in the antebellum South, these preliminary figures do show that wage rates were lower in areas where slavery thrived. Just as Helper had so forcefully argued, southern wages remained lower than northern wages throughout the entire antebellum period. As Stanley Lebergott tabulated, in 1850 a farm laborer residing in New England could expect to earn $12.98 per month, while the same worker in Georgia would only be earning $9.03, or $7.72 in South Carolina, or $7.21 in North Carolina. These wage differentials cannot be explained solely by regional differences in the cost of living, as there was also a sectional divide between real wages, an estimate of money's purchasing power. Margo explained that by the 1830s,

The South also lagged behind the North in real wage growth. . . . The timing of the emergence of the gap suggests an important causal role for early industrialization, which was concentrated initially in the Northeast. Although the North-South wage gap narrowed somewhat in the 1850s, the low-wage South was already a feature of the American economy before the Civil War.[20]

One the eve of secession, therefore, wages had risen slightly for southern laborers, but not enough to be competitive with the northern wage rates. Guion Griffis Johnson used census record statistics to compare average wages in 1860 for various types of laborers. She claimed that Alabama's averages were representative of most the South, and determined that Mississippi housed the highest paid laborers in the region because the population was far less dense. The higher wages offered by "frontier-like" states surely hastened western migration for laboring whites. Unfortunately, as slaveholders followed with their slaves, poor whites were pushed out of many agricultural jobs again, bringing wages down because of the labor surplus. Starobin estimated that the daily

---

[19] Seth Rockman, *Scraping By: Wage Labor, Slavery, and Survival in Early Baltimore* (Baltimore: Johns Hopkins University Press, 2009), 75.

[20] Stanley Lebergott, "Wage Trends, 1800–1900," in The Conference on Research in Income and Wealth, eds., *Trends in the American Economy in the Nineteenth Century*. Princeton: Princeton University Press, 1960), 457; 453; Margo, *Wages and Labor Markets*, 155.

wages of common laborers in the South in 1860 ranged from seventy-five cents to $2, averaging about $1 a day. By contrast, skilled workers earned between $2 and $5 a day, averaging around $3. The "bulk of unskilled white workers" that Starobin studied netted about $310 per year. While these figures provide a general understanding of wage rates, even historians' numbers fluctuate widely. According to Johnson's figures, a North Carolina farm laborer could earn less than $125 a year, working full time – a far cry from Starobin's average.[21]

During his many excursions into the Deep South, Olmsted met with a man who owned quite a bit of land – about 1,000 acres – but no slaves. Claiming to despise both slavery *and* the master class, this landed yeoman reported that white laborers only earned about $8 a month, and usually made less than $75 a year. It was "general for people to hire here only for harvest time," he explained, and the "fact is, a man couldn't earn his board, let alone his wages, for six months in the year." Throughout the other parts of the year, "they gets jobs sometimes, and they goes from one place to another." Not having any consistency in work, and thus income, must have been incredibly stressful for people who already had so little. As one *New York Times* article plainly explained, slavery "depreciates the value of labor. A laboring white man, throughout Southern States, receives but fifty cents a day and his board, and, what is worse, labor is there considered the badge of servitude." Impoverished white Southerners, it seemed, had few chances of even securing year-round employment.[22]

To be sure, many personal accounts by poor whites indicate that daily wages were actually much lower than scholars have estimated. Laborers in both South Carolina and Georgia complained of making less than forty cents a day without room and board. At times they were paid as little as twenty-five cents a day. One Tennessee politician claimed that in Lowell, Massachusetts, men were paid eighty cents a day, and women made $2 a week. Comparatively, in his home state, male laborers never earned more than fifty cents a day, while females capped out at $1.25 a week. U.S. Representative Thomas L. Clingman of North Carolina made similar statements, pointing out that a main difference between New England and the South was that in the slave states, labor was "one hundred per cent cheaper. In the upper parts of [North Carolina], the labor of *either* a free man or a slave, including board, clothing, &c., can be obtained for from $110 to $120

[21] Guion Griffis Johnson, *Ante-Bellum North Carolina: A Social History* (Chapel Hill: University of North Carolina Press, 1937), 70; Starobin, *Industrial Slavery*, 158.
[22] Olmsted, *The Cotton Kingdom*, Vol. II, 132; "Political," *New York Times*, July 11, 1856.

per annum." These numbers were closer to Helper's, who declared to have "found sober, energetic white men" in North Carolina earning only $84 a year for agricultural work, "including board only." Olmsted noted that most white domestics in the region earned a paltry $3 to $6 per month.[23]

Many Confederate veterans wrote about this income inequality, directly connecting the slave South's problems to its increasing class divisions. Non-slaveholders worked especially hard, they claimed, for wages that would not cover basic living expenses. These soldiers often explicitly linked unlivable wages to a more generalized class-driven discontent. Ezekiel Inman, the son of a non-slaveholder, remembered that "Negro and poor white men did the work. Slaveholders [were] above working class people ... [and] did not mingle with those that did not own slaves. They considered themselves in a better class." In stark opposition to the leisurely pursuits of slave owners, Inman remembered, poor whites scrambled to find work, even though the opportunities for wage laborers were "very poor. Fifty cents a day was the best wage." Another former soldier, J.W. Bradley of Sumner, Tennessee, stated that "The poor young man had a poor chance to save any money." With wages averaging twenty-five to forty cents per day, combined with the fact that it was "very difficult to get a job," he concluded that "The slaveholder never gave the poor young man but little encouragement." One North Carolinian, whose father owned one slave, made a similar point. "A poor man did not get enough for his work to clothe himself decent," he surmised. They only earned "$7 to $8 a month. Had to be a good hand to get that." Still another poor white claimed to have worked for $5 a month with board, confirming that job opportunities for non-slaveholders were "awful scarce." And when Charles Ross was asked about "a poor boy's chances" for rising out of the lower class, he stoically answered, "It was not good, [the poor boy] had to work his way at 50 cents per day and sometimes not that much. [It was] a life and death struggle for a poor boy."[24]

Furthermore, historians still have not determined how, precisely, white laborers actually were paid in much of the South. In all likelihood, most payments to laborers in rural areas involved a combination of credit and payment in kind, as the amount of actual currency in circulation

[23] Quoted in Weston, "The Poor Whites," 4; *Ibid.*, 5, italics mine; Helper, *The Impending Crisis*, 380; Olmsted, *Journey*, 99.

[24] Elliot and Moxley, *Tennessee*, Vol. 1, 368–9; Vol. 2, 522–3; Vol. 3, 966; Vol. 5, 1881–2. Starobin, *Industrial Slavery*, 158: Starobin estimated that with food, board, clothes, and "supervision," white industrial laborers cost industrialists about $335 a year, while slaves working the same jobs cost about one-third that price.

fluctuated greatly depending on time and place. Bolton found that a number of poor white laborers in North Carolina were compensated with country produce and flour. This method was strikingly similar to the way black freedmen would be paid after emancipation. Payment in kind was logical when bank notes and currency were scarce, but it also served a second purpose by controlling poor whites' economic choices. By limiting the amount of cash poor laborers could access, slaveholders received the added benefit of regulating their behavior.[25]

Daniel Hundley reported that among the South's poor whites, money "is almost a perfectly unknown commodity." While small amounts of cash did occasionally exchange hands, many laborers were given promissory notes, or "book debt," for amounts still owed to them. Local employers would allow the laborers to redeem their book debt in meat, corn, rent, or clothing. These promissory notes undoubtedly allowed the employer an incredible amount of power over the employee. White laborers already had a hard time quitting a job for fear of forfeiting wages they had accrued. But when a former employer essentially held a laborer's wages long after the work had been completed, the worker was bound to both the honesty and the financial solvency of his old boss. And as long as these employers had the power to decide whether or not to honor old promissory notes, poor white laborers were completely at their mercy.[26]

Slaveholding employers certainly had good reason to control the amount of cash that poor whites kept in circulation. They certainly did not want their slaves selling items or services to poor whites and amassing large amounts of money. They also wanted to keep poor whites from becoming societal nuisances by enabling cash-fueled alcoholic benders. Indeed, many of the harshly enforced alcohol laws in the South, including the rule of no alcohol sales on Sundays, may have been influenced by the fact that poor whites generally received their wages Saturday evenings. Given the scant information historians have gleaned about the daily transactional lives of poor white laborers, questions concerning what they earned, how they found jobs, and what type of contracts bound them to their employers, still remain unanswered.[27]

[25] Bolton, *Poor Whites*, 23.

[26] Daniel R. Hundley, *Social Relations in Our Southern States* (New York: Henry B. Price, 1860), 471; Rockman, *Scraping By*, 8.

[27] Timothy James Lockley, "Spheres of Influence: Working White and Black Women in Antebellum Savannah," in Susanna Delfino and Michele Gillespie, eds., *Neither Lady Nor Slave: Working Women of the Old South* (Chapel Hill: University of North Carolina Press, 2002), 109.

Before the lives and labors of poor white men are examined, however, it is important to note that, just like their northern wage labor counterparts, poor southern families were greatly dependent on the labor of women and children. While records on these mostly illiterate individuals are extremely rare, historians now know enough to establish several general theories about their lives, especially concerning labor. At the most basic level, poor white women had the same major problem as poor white men: besides planting and harvest seasons, they had trouble finding jobs outside of cities and large towns, and even those places had experienced a shift toward slave hires by the later antebellum period. Furthermore, women's wages were much lower than men's wages, as employers assumed that females' incomes were supplementary to each family's primary (male) breadwinner. Well-compensated poor white women could expect to be paid at least one-third less than men in similar jobs, but many women made less than one-half of what their male kinfolk earned. Although very few records give any insight into the working lives of the South's poor white women and children, certain things can be inferred from what is known about the lives of African American and lower-middling class white women. In general, most poor white women had the dual duties of working some type of manual labor during the day (while tending to and nursing the children), and then taking care of their homes at night. Because a sizable percentage of poor white men were absent from their families for periods of time, and given the apparent impermanence of some poor white "marriages," poor white women occasionally had the weight of their entire families on their shoulders.

Household duties for impoverished white women were similar to the chores faced by slave women after a day of field work – making sure there was drinking water, tending the fire, cooking for and feeding the entire family, spinning, weaving and sewing clothes and bedding, and generally keeping the household running. If the family had access to land for a small garden of potatoes, corn, and vegetables, in all likelihood poor white women took care of that, as well. Many accomplished these tasks on their "off" hours. During the days, some of them worked as farm or wage laborers. Just like poor white men, many women had to take multiple short-term jobs during any given year, especially during lag times in the agricultural season. As Bolton wrote: "Census records often list unmarried, landless white women who headed households as having no occupation, but most of these poor white women did work in a variety of occupations – as farm laborers, as seamstresses, and, perhaps most often, as domestics." These women generally worked in hard, physically intense

jobs, from heavy domestic labor to hoeing, picking cotton, cutting wood
and brush, and digging ore. One son of a grand planter remembered that
in addition to slaves, "a white woman lived at our home who did all the
weaving at so much per yard and I think it was 10 cents per yard."
Former slave Aleck Woodward talked about Sally Carlisle, a poor white
widow who "weaved and taught the slaves how it was done. Master gave
her a little house to live in, and a garden spot on the place, good woman.
She showed me how to spin and make ball thread, little as I was."[28]

Other poor women tried to make ends meet by working as hucksters,
selling homegrown vegetables and poultry in town or urban markets.
A sizable percentage of the peddlers were Irish, and they often resold
stolen goods they had purchased from slaves. Cyrus Jenkins encountered
these "poverty stricken women" in Savannah. While strolling through the
city, he wrote, he occasionally met a poor woman "with a basket on her
arm with a few tomatoes a cabbage and a few [I]rish potatoes, just from
the market house, perhaps with her forenoons earnings to feed a half
dozen hungry children and perhaps a drunken vagabond husband."
Children were useful as laborers, of course, but only after a certain age.
For at least the first five or six years of a child's life he or she was a
financial burden, consuming a woman's time, energy, and resources but
not yet contributing anything to the family. Furthermore, breastfeeding
an infant for the first year or two of life severely restricted a woman's
physical abilities and required her to consume many more calories.
Despite all of these complications, however, hundreds of thousands of
poor white women helped keep their families from dire poverty by
working wage labor jobs.[29]

In the two decades before secession, the Deep South's scattered industrial tycoons began hiring poor whites – especially women and children –
to work in the cotton mills. As Gillespie found, despite the South's slow
industrial start, by the 1850s development was "very much on the ascen-
dency." Poor white operatives from South Carolina's Graniteville mills
were interviewed in 1850. The local paper revealed that children as young
as eight years old were working hours as long as adults, "from 4:45 A.M.
to 7:00 P.M. in summer (with two forty minute meal breaks) and from
6:15 A.M. to 7:30 P.M. in winter (with a thirty-five minute dinner break)."

---

[28] Bolton, *Poor Whites*, 38; Craven, "Poor Whites and Negroes," 17–8; Elliot and Moxley,
Tennessee, Vol. 4, 1367; Aleck Woodward, *American Slave*, Vol. 14 (SC), Pt. 4, 254–5.
[29] Cyrus Franklin Jenkins, *Diary, June 11, 1861-March 30, 1862.* Troup County Archives,
LaGrange, Georgia, 13; Lockley, *Lines in the Sand*, 74.

Deeming this work schedule "a condition of slavery," the reporter's disgust over the exploitation of white child labor clearly was evident.[30]

Young, childless teenage girls were the industrialists' preferred workers, but employers could underpay all poor whites because they desperately needed jobs. In Randolph County, North Carolina, for example, women workers outnumbered men four to one in 1850, largely because the average monthly wage for a male operative was $11 to $15, while a female only earned between $5 and $8. This wage gap remained intact a decade later, when women earned about $10 a month to men's $20. Because they had so few other options for employment, poor white women were forced to accept whatever terms an industrialist offered. No matter how insignificant a sum, steady, reliable wages were nearly always preferable to none. Furthermore, the possibility of earning additional money for a child's labor must have been extremely attractive to single mothers.[31]

As the South was a society predicated on violence and domination, rape and other forms of sexual assault were common. The frequent rapes of slave women would surely suggest that poor white women workers were victimized also. With little recourse in the courts, poor women frequently had to accept that sexual violence would be a part of their lives. This likelihood, combined with few employment opportunities and no education, made prostitution a viable way for poor white women to make decent money in a short amount of time. For a small percentage of poor women, prostitution was a career. Some worked out of their own homes, and others lived at bawdy houses with other prostitutes. County court criminal records are peppered with arrests for women operating or living in "lewd" or "disorderly" houses, sometimes referred to as "houses of ill-repute." But the majority of white sex workers only sold their bodies occasionally, during incredibly dire times. Never intending actually to become prostitutes, they were simply unskilled laborers who needed to make quick money in an economy with very few jobs. For most impoverished women, prostitution was a short-term, rare job of last resort, not a long-term career.[32]

[30] Michele Gillespie, "To Harden a Lady's Hand: Gender Politics, Racial Realities, and Women Millworkers in Antebellum Georgia," in Delfino, *Neither Lady Nor Slave*, 266; quoted in Orville Vernon Burton, *In My Father's House Are Many Mansions: Family and Community in Edgefield, South Carolina* (Chapel Hill: University of North Carolina Press, 1985), 53.

[31] Bolton, *Poor Whites*, 40; Gillespie, "To Harden," 276; 271.

[32] Forret, *Race Relations*, 202–3. Census takers often listed prostitutes as "seamstresses."

As inexpensive as poor white women's labor was, child labor always undercut it. While the growing number of textile factories began employing some of these children in the 1840s and 1850s, others worked with their families as farm laborers. Additionally, throughout the late antebellum period, a small percentage of poor white children in the Deep South were bound out as indentures – just like Andrew Johnson. Binding out was an arrangement not unlike slavery in many respects. These poor white children were not even lucky enough to remain in the custody of their families. Under southern law, local authorities had the power to remove children from indigent homes and indenture, or "bind them out," to someone who paid the local government a fee.

According to an 1841 South Carolina statute, the children of paupers, illegitimate children or those who may become chargeable to the locality, and those who "are liable to be demoralized by the vicious conduct and evil example of their mothers," were all in jeopardy of being bound out as apprentice laborers. During their indenture, these children provided years of free labor in exchange for learning a trade. Beginning as early as five years old, poor white indentures worked until the boys reached twenty-one years old, and the girls until eighteen years old or marriage. Much like its neighbors, the Palmetto State offered no provisions about educating the indentured children, leaving the great majority of them illiterate and thus unable to escape the uneducated lower classes.[33]

In Mississippi, an 1840 law, which remained in place until Reconstruction, required overseers to enumerate "poor orphans" and children "whose parents they shall judge incapable of supporting them, and bringing them up in honest ways" twice a year. All that was required from the "person to whom such apprentice shall be bound" was the bare minimum for the child's survival – that is, adequate food and shelter, and instruction in a useful "business or occupation." While the practice of binding out poor white children was not widespread, it was not necessarily uncommon, either. Guion Johnson claimed that "numerous children of poor parents" in North Carolina "were apprenticed in almost every county of the State to serve their masters until they were of age," while Lockley found that the rural county courts of Georgia averaged indenturing about five children per year. Although few scholars have yet to explain truly the intricacies of this indenture system in a slave society, Richard

---

[33] *The Statutes At Large Of South Carolina* (Columbia, 1841) 10 vols. *The Making of Modern Law: Primary Sources*, Web. August 15, 2013; also see Morris, "The Measure of Bondage," 223–4.

Morris described these involuntary apprenticeships as "merely a device for cheap labor exploitation."[34]

In practice, binding out varied greatly from community to community and from case to case. Since "[s]outhern states vested a broad jurisdiction in the county courts to apprentice poor orphans," local judges determined how the system functioned at the local level, causing great inconsistency in every part of the process. Most of the Deep South had laws like Alabama's, in which courts bound out poor white children whose parents were judged to be profane or unfit, or simply because they were considered bad influences. The wording of these laws left county judges with a great deal of power – essentially they could decide to remove a child from his or her home upon suspicion (or even speculation) of a parent's "immorality." Also used as a punishment for poor white adults who could not pay their court ordered fines and fees, this archaic practice could have served the interests of the master class by allowing them to threaten or scare poor whites whenever they felt the need.[35]

The power of the upper class to take away someone's children without legitimate, convincing proof of abuse or neglect raised a terrifying prospect – one that slaves lived with every day. Slaveholding lawmakers had long justified the practice by claiming that they were providing the best life possible for poor white children by giving them honest work, keeping them out of trouble, and teaching them the value of hard work. This defense mimicked the paternalism involved in American slavery: depriving a human being of his or her freedom was somehow a positive good. Despite the rhetoric, slave owners were able to give even lower-level tradesmen access to a type of unfree, extremely cheap labor, thus granting them the ability to become masters to these poor white children. Needless to say, Lockley wrote, there was never "a shortage of people willing to accept the charge of these children." At the same time, slaveholders were

---

[34] Volney Erskine Howard, *The Statutes of the State of Mississippi of a Public and General Nature, with the Constitutions of the United States and of this State: And an Appendix Containing Acts of Congress Affecting Land Titles, Naturalization, &c, and a Manual for Clerks, Sheriffs and Justices of the Peace* (New Orleans: E. Johns and Co., 1840), 145–6. *The Making of Modern Law: Primary Sources*, web. August 15, 2013; Johnson, *Ante-Bellum North Carolina*, 70; Timothy James Lockley, *Welfare and Charity in the Antebellum South* (Gainesville: University Press of Florida, 2007), 25; Morris, "The Measure of Bondage," 223–4.

[35] James W. Ely, Jr., "'There are Few Subjects in Political Economy of Greater Difficulty': The Poor Laws of the Antebellum South." *American Bar Foundation Research Journal* 10, No. 4 (Autumn, 1985): 863.

able to use the prospect of indenturing a family's children as a tool of social and political control.[36]

Studying Charleston, economist John Murray wrote the only full-length study about the South's antebellum "orphans." These children were typically not orphans in the true sense of the word, as the majority of them had at least one living parent. Most of the time, the children's caretakers were simply too poor to care for them, and attempted to enroll them in the city's Orphan House, where they would subsequently become bound apprentices. Mothers sponsored the majority of these children, and the fathers who did so were typically unskilled or semiskilled laborers. Murray found that many parents "emphasized in their application letters not only poverty but their desire to instill some education in their children." For most children at the Orphan House, though, this desire remained elusive, as nearly three-fifths of all these children were bound out as indentures to local masters.[37]

Furthermore, in the decade before secession, the Charleston Orphan House began experiencing frequent problems with forcing children to labor. Increasing numbers of apprentices were either running away or being returned. Apparently masters "were willing to pay the Orphan House the standard penalty (sixty dollars for boys) to be rid of them." Hardly an insignificant sum, the sixty dollar penalty reveals that these indentured children were quite unruly, likely resentful of their station in life. More importantly, at some point they may have become unwilling to endure the brutality of a master who was too quick to punish and too heavy-handed when he did. Allegations of violent masters were just as common as claims of unruly apprentices. The viciousness and primal brutality so embedded in slave societies permeated every southern relationship.[38]

One chilling example from Laurens District, South Carolina revealed startling abuse. On October 30, 1853, a young boy named John Nickle was found beaten to death by his employer. He was only five or six years old. According to witnesses interviewed in the coroner's report, during the previous summer "the child's mother consented for the child to live with William Hazel for his victuals and clothes." Hazel appeared in census records a few years before the murder as a thirty year old landless farmer

[36] Lockley, *Welfare and Charity*, 25.
[37] John E. Murray, *The Charleston Orphan House: Children's Lives in the First Public Orphanage in America* (Chicago: Chicago University Press, 2013), 62; 85; 89; 146; 94.
[38] *Ibid.*, 23; 168.

with a wife and no children. Perhaps approaching the upper economic tier of poor whites, Hazel was likely trying to make his way into the landed yeomen class, as he also boarded or indentured an eighteen year old boy as a farm laborer. He also owned some livestock.[39]

Rebecca Hazel, William's wife, testified that John Nickle lived with the couple for about six weeks. At some point during that time the child had fallen from a horse, becoming badly hurt, and Rebecca tried to nurse him back to health. When her husband found the boy injured, he immediately began whipping the child for "lying out sick." Sometime later young John asked his master for permission to go and visit his mother. After consenting to the visitation, Hazel apparently realized the child was hiding out "near the spring," likely trying to avoid more violence. Upon finding the boy, William Hazel beat the poor child mercilessly with a "large" switch that "had prongs." Each witness claimed John Nickle had been "badly" or "severely" whipped on several occasions, and seemed unsurprised that these punishments finally culminated in the child's death. Perhaps if William Hazel had been a richer, more powerful slaveholder, or at least a respectable yeoman, the case would have been dropped. But the Coroner did decide to press charges, although the outcome remains unclear from the records. John Nickle's abuse and murder suggests that some poor whites endured childhoods that differed little from those of slaves, living in a state of bondage where corporal punishment was relatively frequent, and occasionally brutal enough to cause death.[40]

Although poor white men were paid more than women and children, they generally worked jobs that were just as demeaning and dangerous. Many poor white men labored in a variety of professions throughout their lives, picking up short-term work whenever and wherever they could. As these mostly-rural men were forced to abandon agriculture, they made their way into the nascent southern industries and, along with slaves, helped build the region's infrastructure of roads, bridges, and railroads. Realizing that towns and cities offered many construction opportunities, some poor whites moved to more urban areas. This shift – from a rural, agricultural existence to one based on machinery, industry, and construction – must have been a jarring transition for people who had largely survived on the margins of a capitalist society. Indeed, this change not only revolutionized

[39] Laurens District, Court of General Sessions, Coroner's Inquisitions, 1800–1901, SCDAH; U.S. Bureau of the Census. Population Schedules. Seventh Census of the United States, 1850: Laurens District, South Carolina.

[40] Laurens District, Coroner's Inquisitions.

the working habits and labor patterns of poor whites, it also led them, step by step, into modernity. This change in the labor force would create a deep rift between upper- and lower-class whites in the Deep South – a division that would eventually help lead the region's militant young slaveholders towards secession.

To understand fully the working lives of poor white men in the Deep South, a persistent myth must first be dispelled. While many historians assume that the ranks of overseers were filled with poor white men, this supposition is simply incorrect. Overseers generally came from the yeoman or middling classes. Sometimes the younger sons of affluent slaveholders spent parts of their early adulthoods learning to manage slaves, buying time until they could purchase their own land and slaves or acquire them through inheritance. Overseers often were paid well, and salaries that high would have priced a poor white out of the lower classes and into the middling classes. Furthermore, few poor men would have had the opportunity for employment as an overseer in the first place, because the vast majority of overseers needed to know how to read and write, and many were required to have basic math skills. As one of the WPA interviewers wrote, a good overseer was "supposed to have an education so that he could handle the finances of the plantation accurately, and to be possessed of a good moral character." The average pay "was from three to five hundred dollars a year." Taking the lowest figure, even $300 a year comes out to $25 a month, about twice as much as a poor white laborer could expect to earn if he found full-time employment.[41]

And while some slaves did refer to their overseers as poor white trash, those identifications were simply meant to degrade the overseer, demeaning his character and reputation by comparing him to "mean" and "low" whites – by deeming him trash. Such comments rarely had anything to do with the overseer's actual economic situation. As freedman George Fleming remembered, "No, they weren't poor whites. All Master Sam's overseers were good men. They lived with their families, and Master's folks associated with them, too. They had good houses to live in." Martha Colquitt echoed these sentiments, remarking that "Master Billie's overseer lived in a four-room house up the road a piece from the Big House. Nobody thought about none of Master Billie's overseers as poor white folks. Every overseer he ever had was decent and respectable.

---

[41] "Slavery – Compilation by Ruby Lorrain Radford," *American Slave*, Vol. 13 (GA), Pt. 4, 329.

Course they weren't in the same class with Master Billie's family, but they were all right." Still another woman, who spent her childhood enslaved in Alabama, remembered that "Mr. Munger was our overseer, but he had money of his own. He was better than most overseers, and there weren't no poor white trash, them ornery buckers lived further back in the woods." In South Carolina, Thomas Carlisle's overseer Wash Evans "wasn't no poor white trash, but he was kind of middling-like." And Melvin Smith, who had been enslaved in Georgia, recalled that his overseer "was mean." Still, Smith concluded, he "wasn't no poor white trash; he was up-to-date but he liked to beat on niggers."[42]

Shut out of overseeing jobs, poor whites had very few options for long-term agricultural work, leaving a sizable percentage of landless whites with no other choice but to tenant, sharecrop, or work as wage laborers. The majority of poor white agricultural workers were known generically as farm laborers. Hired for short-term work, by the job, or by the day, they often lived a precarious existence with no stability of income or promise of long-term work. As the son of a small yeomen farmer, Thompson Glenn knew that things were different for whites who did not own any land. "For poor young men there was not anything to do but to hire to work," he recalled.[43]

Although there are no reliable estimates indicating how many landless white Southerners sharecropped or tenanted before the Civil War, both practices seemed to have been relatively common.

Sharecroppers were generally considered wage laborers (not tenants), further complicating a full understanding of southern labor practices. More frequently practiced in Upper South states such as North Carolina and Tennessee, tenant farming involved a landless family "renting" land from a planter by essentially mortgaging a percentage of their future cash crop. This percentage typically ranged between one-third and one-quarter of the harvest. Frederick Bode and Donald Ginter used 1860 census returns to estimate that in Georgia's eastern Piedmont, about 20 percent of farms were tenanted, while in the North Georgia mountains the number was upward of 40 percent. Based on census records from the 1850s and 1860s, Bolton concluded that about one-quarter of all of

[42] George Fleming, *Ibid.*, Vol. 11 (NC & SC), Supplement, Series 1, 132; Martha Colquitt, *Ibid.*, Vol. 12 (GA), Part 1, 241; Dellie Lewis, *Ibid.*, Vol. 1 (AL), 257; Thomas Anderson Carlisle, *Ibid.*, Vol. 2 (SC), Pt. 2, 57; Melvin Smith, *Ibid.*, Vol. 13 (GA), Pt. 3, 292; Genovese, "Rather be a Nigger," 80.

[43] Elliot and Moxley, *Tennessee*, Vol. 3, 909.

North Carolina's farmers worked as tenants, especially near the fall lines of rivers. Tenancy was not a postbellum phenomenon; instead, it was a well-established practice even before southern secession.[44]

Southern planters, of course, used slaves to cultivate their best lands, and leased unimproved and soil-depleted lands to poor white croppers and tenants. Perhaps a few tenants were able to save small sums of money over time to buy land for themselves, but many more were ruined economically after one bad crop. Cycles of indebtedness to the landlord thus left many poor whites beholden to their affluent creditors in myriad ways, not simply from an economic standpoint, but also socially and politically. Trying to make an honest living by working hard seemed to matter little when trying to escape the blight of landlessness.[45]

But times had not always been as hard for less affluent whites. In the early antebellum period, a sizable percentage of poor whites, especially those who had access to a city or a town, helped make ends meet by peddling. Whether squatting on land or renting it, some lower-class whites were able to raise a variety of fruits, grains, and vegetables. When their truck patches came to fruition, or hunting season had been particularly good, poor whites sought to sell their excess wares in the marketplace. Gillespie noted that many Georgia "'crackers' ... pushed their two-wheeled carts loaded with eggs, chickens, hides, fruit, and tallow for as many as ten days through the piney woods to [Savannah and] sold their goods in the town market several times a year." However, during the mid-1800s masters began worrying about itinerant vendors trading goods, liquor, and abolitionist ideas with slaves.[46]

By the 1840s, several Deep South states had enacted legal codes completely banning peddling without a direct permit or license from each locality. This requirement kept the majority of poor whites from legally selling their goods at all, as permit prices were exorbitant. In Georgia, for example, mandatory licenses for peddling ran as high as $25 or $50 a year, rendering it impossible for poor whites to sell their wares legally. These laws effectively blocked the poor from participating in the burgeoning capitalist economy, and ironically encouraged the illegalities of the underground market between slaves and poor whites. While

[44] Frederick A. Bode and Donald E. Ginter, *Farm Tenancy and the Census in Antebellum Georgia* (Athens: University of Georgia Press, 1987); Bolton, *Poor Whites*, 37.
[45] Johnson, *Ante-Bellum North Carolina*, 69.
[46] Robert R. Russel, "The Effects of Slavery upon Non-Slaveholders in the Ante Bellum South," *Agricultural History* 15, No. 2 (April 1941): 113; Gillespie, *Free Labor*, 11.

exceptions to the licensing rules were made for a few "decrepit and infirm" or "infirm and indigent" men, these individuals were only allowed to vend their goods if they took an oath promising not to do business with slaves.[47]

Slaveholder hysteria over the spread of abolitionist ideas seemed to be at the heart of all of the licensing laws. Deep fears of slave (or bi-racial) rebellion, coupled with other more immediate fears over the loss of valuable property, seemed to intensify in the late antebellum period. Traveling peddlers came under extreme scrutiny. While many hawkers suspected of abolitionism were northern or European, slave owners were also highly suspicious of poor white Southerners who had no fixed abode, and no ties to a local community. In 1859, for example, the citizens of Lafayette County, Mississippi pleaded with local officials to rid their community of these salesmen, deeming them "an intolerable nuisance to the community." Itinerate peddlers, they held, were "irresponsible – having no interest in any locality – [and] commit any fraud in their cupidity may suggest, or avail themselves of the facilities afforded by the present system of license to tamper with, and corrupt the slaves – the fruitful source and the trunk of the underground railroad traffic." By directly linking hawkers to abolitionism, the region's slaveholders ended poor whites' occasional relationships with the wider economy, effectively shutting them out of the modern world of commerce and capitalism. Instead, personal relationships between slaves and poor whites multiplied, and the underground economy flourished.[48]

Prevented from peddling and shut out of much of the region's agricultural work, many poor white southern men started to consider themselves simply as generic "laborers." Advertisements for laborers in the late antebellum period provide some insight into these types of jobs, as well as the frequency with which these men worked side by side with slaves. Although blacks and whites had worked together on short-term, non-agricultural projects since colonial times, as the antebellum period wore on, employer preference for slave labor grew stronger. This trend became obvious as early as the Jacksonian period. In 1827, the Savannah, Ogechee and Alatamaha Canal Company reported, "There are now employed on the line, about four hundred and forty-nine laborers; and, in addition,

---

[47] *Acts of the General Assembly of the State of Georgia*, e.g. 1857: 282; 1859: 152; 156; 182.
[48] "Memorial of Citizens of Lafayette in Relation to Itinerant Peddlers," Folder "Peddler and Hawkers," MDAH.

a proportion of mechanics. The principle part of the laborers are blacks."
The reason for this hiring discrepancy, the company revealed, was largely
due to the fact that slaves provided "a very effective and manageable
force."[49]

Unlike poor whites, slaves could not negotiate for higher wages, nor
could they protest working conditions or decide to quit. Slaves could be
violently "incentivized" to work, and were quickly returned to their
masters without a chance of retaliation against the company should they
be fired. For all of these reasons, southern employers had few reasons to
seek out white laborers, except in cases of dangerous jobs where the loss
of a slave life would be economically detrimental to the owner.

While white laborers' anger over job competition and substandard
wages was generally latent, at times it emerged against a current or former
employer. Poor whites, much like slaves, would demonstrate their angst
by breaking tools, working slowly, and occasionally stealing from their
employers. Bertram Wyatt-Brown deemed these acts "Snopesian crimes"
after the infamous poor white Snopes family in William Faulkner's tril-
ogy. Whether destroying property, harming or killing livestock, or burning down buildings, poor whites sometimes used destructive means to
demonstrate their anger. As James Henry Hammond's son Spann complained in his diary, he recently had a disagreement with a local wagoner
he had employed. "Worthlessness & obstina[nt]," the wagoner had
begun to destroy Hammond's fodder. "White laborers," he concluded,
"are the hardest to get on with." Another disagreement over employment
in Mississippi ended in the murder of a laborer. Local papers reported
that "A fatal affray occurred ... between two young men." Robert
Shotwell had apparently hired William Benoit to do some work, but "a
difficulty arose about his services. Angry words ensued, when Shotwell
inflicted a wound upon the body of Benoit with a knife, of which he died
the following day." Despite their limited opportunities, therefore, white
laborers did fight back against unfair labor practices, unpaid work, and
other perceived slights from their employers.[50]

In isolated cases, poor white men succumbed to their violent tempers
and sought revenge. Poor white laborer Edward Isham was hanged for
murdering a former boss who refused to pay him back wages. Perhaps

---

[49] "Savannah, Ogechee and Alatamaha Canal Company," *Macon Telegraph*, April 2,
1827, 3.
[50] Quoted in Harris, *Plain Folk and Gentry*, 68; Betty Couch Wiltshire, *Marriages and
Deaths from Mississippi Newspapers* (Bowie, MD: Heritage, 1987), Vol. 2, 50.

unsurprisingly, the murder of the former employer was not the first time that Isham had reacted in a violent or destructive manner after suffering through a perceived wrong; he had previously destroyed the property of other bosses with whom he had disagreements. Olmsted held that "It is not slavery [poor whites] detest; it is simply the negro competition, and the monopoly of the opportunities to make money by negro owners, which they feel but dimly comprehend." While that may have been true for some poor whites, others fully blamed the master class as the harbingers of their economic deprivation. After Isham committed murder, he felt no remorse, deeming his former slaveholding employer "a damned dog." In fact, facing his own impending execution, he lusted for more slave owner blood. "It is hard to be killed for one damned dog," he regretted. "If I could kill one more I would die willingly."[51]

But Isham was not alone in his disdain for his employers. "Spite-work always cured my distemper," another convict reported after admitting he had cut off the manes and tails of his boss's horses. According to Joseph Reidy, because the incident occurred following yet another dispute over wages, the poor laborer felt he had little choice but to retaliate in some manner. "Withholding a man's wages threatened his honor," Reidy concluded, "which in turn required compensation in property or blood." These types of sentiments would come to find a new militancy in the 1840s and 1850s as white mechanics began forming nascent labor unions, demanding certain terms and conditions from slave owners. At times these white Southerners even threatened to withdraw their support for slavery.[52]

---

[51] Forret, *Race Relations*, 162; 184–5; Joseph P. Reidy, "The Worlds of Nineteenth-Century Condemned Men," in Charles C. Bolton and Scott P. Culclasure, eds., *The Confessions of Edward Isham: A Poor White Life of the Old South* (Athens: University of Georgia Press, 1998), 108; Olmsted, *The Cotton Kingdom*, Vol. II, 137; Scott P. Culclasure, "I Have Killed a Damn Dog," in Bolton, *The Confessions of Edward Isham*, 62.

[52] Reidy, "The Worlds," 108.

3

Masterless (and Militant) White Workers

Slavery is a shame, a crime, and a curse – a great moral, social, civil, and political evil – an oppressive burden to the blacks, and an incalculable injury to the whites – a stumbling-block to the nation, an impediment to progress, a damper on all the nobler instincts, principles, aspirations and enterprises of man, and a dire enemy to every true interest.

– Hinton Helper[1]

Already there is disposition to exclude [the slave] from the trades, from public works, from drays, and the tables of hotels ... when ... more [white] laborers ... shall come in greater numbers to the South, they will still more increase the tendency to exclusion; they will question the right of masters to employ their slaves in any works that they may wish for; they will invoke the aid of legislation; they will use the elective franchise to that end...and this the town of Charleston, at the very heart of slavery, may become a fortress of democratic power against it.

– Leonidas W. Spratt, 1861[2]

Just as hundreds of thousands of slaves had been forced to migrate from the Upper South to the Lower South during the 1830s and 1840s, by the 1850s states such as the Carolinas and Georgia lost significant numbers of slaves to the newer plantation lands of the southwest. As labor was

---

[1] Helper, *The Impending Crisis*, 183.

[2] L.W. Spratt to John Perkins in 1861, on black labor and white immigrants, reprinted in Ulrich B. Phillips, *Plantation and Frontier Documents: 1649–1863, Illustrative of Industrial History in the Colonial and Antebellum South*, Vol. II (Cleveland: Arthur H. Clark Co., 1909), 176–7, web.

scarcer on the frontier, western migration drove up the prices of the enslaved. Indeed, the cost of slaves skyrocketed over the decade, making the rich richer and widening the inequality gap. This increase prevented many landed yeomen farmers from entering the master class. It was becoming very difficult to join the ranks of slaveholders. Meanwhile, white immigrants continued to pour into southern port cities, eventually making their way to every town and city. As slave owners saw their slaves being drained to the West, they realized that native white and immigrant laborers would eventually fill their places. By law, masters could not brutalize and control white laborers the same way they did with enslaved blacks, and this fact troubled them greatly. As Leonidas Spratt wrote to another slaveholder in 1861, "almost every negro offered in our markets is bid for by the West," and "the drain is likely to continue." Anxious that more white "pauper labor may pour in," Spratt legitimately worried that even in South Carolina, "the purest in its slave condition, democracy may gain a foothold, and that here also the contest for existence may be waged between" poor white laborers and black slaves.[3]

The situation was daunting for many slaveholders who rushed to come up with different ways to preserve and expand the peculiar institution. Not only did they need more slaves to work their plantations, they also desired to reduce the numbers of troublesome poor white workers who consistently served to undermine the South's racial hierarchy. With South Carolina leading the way, the most ardent pro-slavery men first attempted to reopen the slave trade. When that plan ultimately failed, some members of the master class began to advocate for slavery in the abstract – essentially, slavery regardless of race. With this doctrine, slaveholders no longer had to fear the masterless whites that they long struggled to control. The powerful slave owning politicians further advocated abolishing democracy and republicanism, lest the lower classes gain some control of politics and thus, legal codes and statutes. In these ways, ironically, it was the spread of slavery that ultimately led to its demise. Slaveholders in the older states became increasingly fearful about their social and economic statuses in a world in which they were losing power politically. As western free states disturbed the balance of power in the federal government, and western slave states drained off black slaves and their attendant wealth, older slave states were left with an increasingly militant white labor force. The master class realized their fortunes were in danger – unless they proactively dealt with the increasingly

[3] *Ibid.*, 177.

unwieldy situation. They needed nearly complete control over the region if they were to continue to rely on slavery as the basis of their economy.[4]

At the same time, lower-class whites were attempting to distance themselves as much as possible from the brutalized, unfree labor of blacks. Forming loosely organized labor unions, groups of mechanics began demanding non-competition from both slaves and free blacks. These laborers seemingly became more aggressive and vocal throughout the 1850s, as some unions even threatened to withdraw their support of slavery altogether. Having to contend with potentially revolutionary slaves, free blacks, *and* poor whites, the master class's system of social control had to be expanded immediately. Although many lower-class white laborers attempted to challenge the southern hierarchy, the domination of slaveholders was comprehensive and effective.

Complicating matters for slaveholders, however, the numbers of poor white laborers continued to increase during the 1840s and 1850s, partly due to Irish and German immigration into the region. While Germans had been steadily moving to the Deep South since the 1830s, many were part of the lower-middling class, and had family connections in the states. Immigrating for economic reasons, some eventually bought small tracts of land and worked as yeomen farmers. Outside of large southern cities where the poorest Germans worked wage labor jobs, recent immigrants from the region did not cause slaveholders much concern. Their intent was to come to America, work hard, and hopefully improve their material circumstances. Only the poorest German immigrants suffered fates similar to the famine Irish. As one railroad contractor confessed to Olmsted, "he was substituting Irish and German labourers" for blacks "as rapidly as possible, with great advantage." This substitution was predicated on the dire poverty of these immigrants, who were prepared to risk life and limb to secure their next meal. Regardless of economic class, though, most German transplants sided with slaveholders as the possibility of secession loomed.[5]

The incredibly disastrous Irish Famine struck in 1845. Between 1850 and 1860, more than a million men and women left Ireland for

---

[4] For more on slavery in the abstract, see chapter 8, as well as Fox-Genovese, *Slavery in White and Black*.

[5] Ira Berlin and Herbert G. Gutman, "Natives and Immigrants, Free Men and Slaves: Urban Workingmen in the antebellum American South," *The American Historical Review*, 88, No. 5 (Dec. 1983): 1187; Andreas Dorpalen, "The German Element and the Issues of the Civil War," *Mississippi Valley Historical Review* XXIX (June 1942): 56; Olmsted, *The Cotton Kingdom*, Vol. II, 264, Web; Dorpalen, "The German Element," 60.

job opportunities in America. In urban areas, the Irish comprised greater than 50 percent of the foreign-born poor and 20 percent of all impoverished whites. But the Irish, like antebellum immigrants in general, overwhelmingly settled in the states north of the Mason Dixon. Even Southerners understood why this was the case. Georgia's *Columbus Enquirer* plainly stated in 1855 that "few immigrants come to the South; they remain at the North and are abolitionized. As a laborer, the negro stands in their way, and they know it." While fewer people immigrated to the South due to the presence of slavery, the region did receive a substantial influx, especially in the port cities of Charleston, Savannah, and New Orleans. Indeed, thousands of Irishmen and women immigrated to the antebellum South. By 1860, half of the Savannah's white residents were foreign-born, with one-third of that population from Ireland. Half of the city's working white women had been born on the Emerald Isle: 70 percent of Savannah's white washers and ironers were Irish, as well as 80 percent of white domestics and servants, and more than 80 percent of white chambermaids.[6]

Out of the 84,000 Irish Famine immigrants who settled in states that would become the future Confederacy, some certainly qualified as semiskilled laborers, but very few were skilled, well educated, or otherwise upwardly mobile. While some of them were literate to varying degrees, they were likely only able to read Irish, not English. Scholars have tended to downplay the significance of immigrants in the Deep South due to their relatively insignificant numbers, but perhaps the rate of increase is a more accurate indicator of why these poor whites were considered a threat to the prevailing social order. In the decade prior to secession, the Irish population in the South increased by more than 55 percent, with a 100 percent increase in Mississippi and Georgia. In port towns and cities, their numbers were high enough to be very influential. On the eve of secession, the Irish comprised 16 percent of Mobile's white population, 14 percent of Charleston's, and almost 23 percent of Savannah's whites. Yet, even in rural areas, their presence was obvious. These settlers often moved to areas where railroad building was burgeoning, as they could find work digging ditches and building levees.[7]

[6] Soltow, *Men and Wealth*, 44; "From the Savannah Republican: Know Nothingism," *Columbus Enquirer*, May 29, 1855, 2; Gillespie, *Free Labor in an Unfree World*, 167; Lockley, *Lines in the Sand*, 37; Lockley, "Spheres of Influence," 111.

[7] David T. Gleeson, *The Irish in the South, 1815–1877* (Chapel Hill: University of North Carolina Press, 2001), 2; 40; 27; 36; 34; 99: Many Irish backed the Democrats, especially in Whig towns like Savannah, Natchez, Vicksburg, Memphis, and Nashville.

Irish immigrants tended to be young and single. The vast majority were between 20 and 27 years old; it was rare for someone over 30 years old to set out for America. Generally remaining in large port cities for several years before setting out into America's interior, they shared a lot common to the South's poorest whites, both economically and socially. Indeed, both the English and Americans alike referred to the Irish as "nigger[s] turned inside out," an epithet meant to place them on a level just barely above slaves. In reality, many Irish immigrants associated freely with the South's slaves and free blacks, trading, working, loving, and even living together. In his seminal book on the Irish in the antebellum South, David Gleeson found that Irish non-slaveholders maintained a variety of relationships with African Americans. In New Orleans, slave artisans occasionally even hired Irish workers. And just as with native poor whites, the South's Irish often engaged in sexual relationships with free blacks and slaves. John Brown, who had been enslaved in South Carolina, told his WPA interviewer about his wife's Irish father, who had immediately taken "a fancy" to his wife's mother, "a bright mulatto gal."[8]

Unlike some native poor whites, however, as a group, the Irish usually became strong supporters of slavery. Many of them formed personal relationships with African Americans (especially free blacks), but Ireland's sons and daughters soon abandoned the idealism of social reformers and abolitionists such as Daniel O'Connell in exchange for a chance of upward mobility. In fact, many Irish Southerners likened abolitionists to their former oppressors, the English Protestants. Noel Ignatiev even suggested that the Irish's hatred of blacks was the crucial element of their acceptance into American society, both in the North and the South. Plantation mistress Fanny Kemble theorized in her letters that because the Irish "have been oppressed enough themselves," they tended to "be oppressive whenever they" got a chance.[9]

Planters repeatedly stereotyped the Irish as dirty, ignorant, and lazy. In one particularly telling quote, Kemble compared the "stench" of a "negro house" to that of an Irish "hovel," concluding that the Irish were "almost a degraded class of beings as the negroes." According to Genovese,

---

[8] Soltow, *Men and Wealth*, 13; Berlin and Gutman, "Natives and Immigrants," 1187; Gleeson, *The Irish in the South*, 123; 26; John C. Brown, Vol. 14 (SC), Pt. 1, 127.

[9] Gleeson, *The Irish*, 94; Noel Ignatiev, *How the Irish became White* (New York: Routledge, 1995); Frances Anne Kemble, *Journal of a Residence on a Georgia Plantation in 1838–1839* (New York: Harper, 1863), Web.

Kemble was simply echoing the prejudices of her peers, as many wealthy slave owners, "especially elite women, had difficulty in seeing Irish servants as white." One former slave even recalled the extremity of the destitution among local immigrants. He said that under slavery, "the white people used to be awfully mean to the Jews and to the Irish. Sometimes the Irishmen used to slip around the cabins and fields and beg the slaves to keep them. They would say 'Mr. give me a little something to eat or help me along a little.' Sometimes the slaves would help them and sometimes they wouldn't." Regardless of the slaves' beneficence, however, the freedman reported that the poor immigrants found no charity from the upper classes: "But whenever the masters would catch them on the plantation or around the cabins they would say, 'What do you want here? Get off this place.' Then they would kick and cuff them and drive them off. All the Irish would say, 'Oh, my lord! Oh, my lord!' and run away."[10]

Needless to say, many slaveholders attributed the poverty of the Irish to their undesirable work ethic. Several slave owners that Olmsted met on his travels reported that German immigrants were good, steady laborers. The Irish, on the other hand, always thought they "knew more" than their "master," and would often "directly disregard his orders." Employers frequently complained about the "sauciness" of the immigrants; they despised the fact that these laborers – unlike blacks – could talk back, quit a job, or even organize strikes. Still, while the southern gentry agreed that a slave "could do twice as much work, in a day, as an Irishman," they never hesitated to use disposable immigrant labor, especially when the jobs were dangerous or deadly. As W.O. Brown concluded in his study on poor whites, extremely perilous work was reserved for white laborers, as "A dead Irishman merely added to the Kingdom of Heaven, while the loss of a slave subtracted from the capital investment." Ditch digging, especially, fell to the "expendable" Irish, as accidents occurred frequently in this line of work. In 1839, the *Macon Georgia Telegraph* reported, "One of the laborers employed on the Brunswick Canal, was accidentally drowned in Ellis's Creek ... by the upsetting of a boat. His name was Michael Finnon, a native of Ireland." These short blurbs notifying the public of the death of laborers were quite common.[11]

---

[10] *Ibid.*; Genovese, *Fatal Self-Deception*, 41; "Slave Who Joined the Yanks," *American Slave*, Vol. 19 (Fisk), 121.

[11] Olmsted, *Journey*, 269; Genovese, *Fatal Self-Deception*, 41; Olmsted, *Journey*, 85; Brown, "Role of Poor Whites," 263; "Accident," *Macon Georgia Telegraph*, March 5, 1839, 2.

Slaveholders' expectations that these immigrants continue working for low wages in hazardous jobs led to some class tensions between employers and laborers by the 1850s. Worker unrest, of course, was to be expected. But several slave owners seemed fully cognizant of the fact that eventually, large numbers of impoverished whites threatened the institution of slavery. Christopher Memminger, a wealthy Charlestonian slaveholder, argued that white workers – especially foreign ones – were "the only party from which danger to our institutions is to be apprehended among us." Poor white laborers, who had to compete with unpaid and underpaid black laborers, "would soon raise the hue and cry against the Negro, and be hot abolitionists – and every one of those men would have a vote." Formerly enslaved Elijah Hopkins alluded to this rising class pressure between whites, blaming immigrants for much of the problem: "The slaveholders were hard, but those people who come here from across the water, they bring our trouble. You can't squeeze as much out of the poor white as you can out of the darkey."[12]

Yet the slaveholders still tried to "squeeze" both races, by pitting slave and white workers against each other in competition over jobs, thereby reminding lower-class whites that higher wages were an elusive dream, as both planters and industrialists could switch to slave labor. Masters had little incentive to build up other sectors of the economy, from industrial pursuits to the extraction of natural resources. However, in the decade or two before secession, the Deep South did make slow but steady progress towards building up those business sectors. Railroads were one of the region's burgeoning industries by the 1830s, and even yeomen profited substantially from them, since they were better able to send their goods to market in an inexpensive manner.[13]

The institution of slavery, therefore, helped encourage affluent whites to implement industrial capitalism. Finding a different, nonagricultural "type" of labor for poor whites – whether mechanical or industrial – became a matter of central importance to the maintenance of a slave society. As Tom Terrill explained, "A major factor in the industry's growth and strength was an ample supply of usable, cheap labor, most of which by 1860 was native white." While much of this labor was performed by poor white women and children, the mills did offer poor white men new employment opportunities, as well. Alabama's industrial

[12] Quoted in Gleeson, _The Irish in the South_, 124–5; Elijah Hopkins, _American Slave_, Vol. 2 (AK), Pt. 3, 315.
[13] Wright, _Old South, New South_, 28.

expansion in the 1840s and 1850s resulted in 10.5 percent of the state's white males being employed in manufacturing by 1860. Whether in railroading, textile mills, gristmills, or sawmills, the worlds of poor white Southerners were changing rapidly.[14]

South Carolina industrialist William Gregg knew that this untapped pool of white labor could make his mills very profitable. It was "only necessary to build a manufacturing village of shanties," he wrote, "to have crowds of these poor people around you, seeking employment at half the compensation given to operatives at the North ... [I]f they are too lazy to work themselves, [they] might be induced to place their children in a situation in which they would be educated and reared in industrious habits." By the late 1840s, a series of articles in the *Scientific American* examined the plight of poor whites in the Deep South, noticing the change in the attitudes of white workers. Georgia's laborers, the paper reported, "have no objections to working in cotton factories ... but agricultural labor they consider nigger's work." A later essay echoed similar sentiments, holding "They are poor because they consider manual labor degrading and being poor they are also ignorant. ... Crackers, as they are called, reclaimed from their idle lives in the woods, are settled [now in the factories], and white labor only is employed, and the result so far we believe is encouraging."[15]

At least for a period of several years, upper-class Southerners thought they had figured out a way to employ – and more importantly, pacify – poor white laborers. For the most impoverished poor whites, textile mills became their only hope for survival without some sort of charity or assistance. One historian wrote, "Those to whom mill work most appealed were the large class of whites whose poverty was so abject that any opportunity for improvement was welcome." Southern capitalists professed that the cotton mills "would be a greater charity than an orphan asylum, would serve to civilize and Christianize those who lacked opportunities to attend church or school, and become a haven for families ruined by drunken fathers ... [it] meant decent food, clothing, and shelter for the first time in their lives." One Union veteran who grew up the son of an unemployed drunkard in north-central Tennessee remembered having to work industrial jobs to help the family make ends meet. Indeed,

---

[14] Tom E. Terrill et al., "Eager Hands: Labor for Southern Textiles, 1850–1860," *Journal of Economic History* 36, No. 1 (Mar. 1976): 84; Flynt, *Poor but Proud*, 19.

[15] Quoted in Terrill, "Eager Hands," 90; "A Curious Race in Georgia," *Scientific American*, July 31, 1847; "Southern Cotton Mills," *Scientific American*, May 26, 1849.

child labor in the mills meant that his family did not have to seek shelter in a poor house or indenture their young. In the summer the young boy worked at a tobacco factory, and in the winter he labored at a carding factory. While criticizing slaveholders for not working, the disaffected Southerner also complained that "most of the poor class idled about until they had to jump out and work [for] a bushel of corn or a few pounds of meat."[16]

To understand fully the racial dynamics of antebellum factory labor, however, the economics of agricultural history require explanation. During the 1840s, cotton prices were down, leaving a less intense need for slaves working in the fields. Slaveholders began hiring out their surplus laborers, either as mechanics, artisans, or mill workers. By the 1850s, the cotton market was booming, and most slaves were pulled back onto the plantations to help grow the cash crop. Southern textile factories simply stopped hiring additional workers throughout the decade. Instead, the vast majority of the region's additional capital was shifted immediately to cotton production. By the time of the Civil War, the southern factories were dominated by white labor, but the industry simply did not employ enough people – or pay high enough wages – to help alleviate white poverty.[17]

According to one historian's best estimates, only about 5 percent of slaves ever worked in the industrial sector. Jeff Forret reasoned that a similar percentage of southern whites worked in the factories as well. And while the captains of industry, such as William Gregg, initially deemed the mills a solution to poor white unemployment, most factories employed slaves in some capacity prior to the 1850s, when agricultural labor became more valuable. While the overwhelming majority of southern factory workers were white, many industrialists still openly favored the supposedly "docile" labor of slaves. Gregg finally admitted that the majority of industrial "overseers ... give the decided preference to blacks as operatives." Abolitionist George M. Weston confirmed this fact, writing "The employment of slaves is common everywhere at the South, in factories and mining." And Starobin found that "many entrepreneurs were actually converting [sections of their labor force] from free to slave labor" during the 1840s, while a few others never converted to white labor in the first place.[18]

---

[16] Richard W. Griffin, "Poor White Laborers in Southern Cotton Factories, 1789–1865," *The South Carolina Historical Magazine* 61, No. 1 (Jan. 1960), 30; Elliot and Moxley, *Tennessee*, Vol. 1, 136–7.

[17] Wright, *Old South, New South*, 127; 128.

[18] Starobin, *Industrial Slavery*, vii; Forret, *Race Relations*, 43; quoted in George M. Weston, "The Poor Whites," 5, Web; *Ibid.*; Starobin, *Industrial Slavery*, 119–20.

Southern captains of industry quickly learned from slaveholders how to pit poor white and black laborers against each other, and commonly used slaves as strikebreakers. One particular strike in 1856 by several hundred white dock workers in Savannah demonstrated the great efficacy of such a strategy, as the poor white strikers were immediately fired, and slaves took their places. Southern courts, of course, were never sympathetic to the plight of workers, and in many cases, were openly hostile. Legally, strikers were only entitled to individual – not collective – rights, making the exploitation of "free" laborers easy. "As long as Negro slave labor was available," Morris concluded, "the freedom of white workers to bargain collectively and take concerted action would be substantially curtailed. At the same time the marginal economic status of the white workers constantly kept them in jeopardy of coercive controls."[19]

Thus, pushed out of former jobs in agriculture, and without enough industrial jobs to alleviate high levels of unemployment, poor white workers experienced a crisis of identity as laborers. Their jobs were rendered obsolete by cheaper, more exploitable labor, and they simply could not work hard enough to rise far out of poverty. Many of these jacks-of-all-trades who cobbled together livings with multiple short-term jobs throughout the year began describing themselves as "mechanics." By the 1840s, the term mechanic had come to encompass a wide variety of nonagricultural work. Although many historians use the word exclusively to describe skilled and semiskilled laborers, people who lived during the late antebellum period generally considered anyone who worked with tools in non-farming jobs – no matter how unskilled – as mechanics. Whether building bridges and roads, laying railroad tracks, digging canals, or working in the building trades, mechanics were an incredibly important part of the southern labor struggle. Yet just as the ranks of white mechanics were growing, the number of slave mechanics started increasing. As Ronald Takaki confirmed, the cotton overproduction of the early 1840s caused a surplus of slave labor "which planters began to divert into the mechanic trades and thus intensified the competition" with white workers. Even when the cotton boom of the 1850s pulled many slave hires back to the plantations, there were still enough black mechanics in southern towns and cities to elicit complaints from aggrieved white laborers.[20]

[19] Lockley, *Lines*, 74; Morris, "The Measure of Bondage," 229.
[20] Ronald Takaki, "The Movement to Reopen the African Slave Trade in South Carolina," *The South Carolina Historical Magazine*, Vol. 66, No. 1 (Jan. 1965): 41.

Although tensions between black and white mechanics were evident as early as the 1820s, in the two decades before the Civil War, white mechanics' associations became more militant, ultimately helping to push slaveholders towards secession. The leaders of these labor unions were usually skilled, artisanal "master mechanics" who possessed some level of literacy, but their speeches and demands were still representative of the poor white unskilled laborers who rallied around them, clamoring for less competition from African Americans.[21]

Slaveholders, of course, long considered mechanics "a great annoyance." For more than fifty years before Lincoln's election, white mechanics had petitioned their state and local governments for the right to unionize and for protection from competition with black labor. Law makers generally ignored most pleas from non-slaveholding white laborers. In South Carolina, for example, white mechanics won little more than the right to "form associations" by the end of the antebellum period. In 1858, the state's Mechanics' Association requested a tax on their free black competitors. Gaining little traction for their plan, they humbly admitted that they would accept "some other remedy" as long as it would "at least place us in such a position ... to compete with [blacks], if they are to be on an equality with us." Of course, the slaveholding lawmakers balked at the Association's request, doing nothing to help the cause of white laborers. In neighboring Georgia, U.B. Phillips reported a similar scenario, as "The white laboring men wanted to keep the slaves out of the skilled trades as far as possible, and to that end opposed their being hired out under any circumstances for artisan's work."[22]

But the animosity between laborers was not based solely on race. The requests of white mechanics against black mechanics were no different from their protests against competition with unpaid white prison labor. One group based in Jackson wrote to the Mississippi legislature in the 1850s, imploring them to "amend the law regulating the affairs of the State Penitentiary as to prevent their manufacturing mechanical and agricultural implements, machines of which come in competition with the mechanics working at their trades." Regardless of the race of their competitors, white mechanics did not want to contend with unfree,

---

[21] Murray, *The Charleston Orphan House*, 148.

[22] Johnson, *Toward a Patriarchal Republic*, 96; Planitzer, "A Dangerous Class of Men, 71; 72; Ulrich B. Phillips, "The Slave Labor Problem in the Charleston District," *Political Science Quarterly* XXII, No. 3 (Sept. 1907): 423.

unpaid labor of any sort – that practice could only hurt their chances of gaining employment and earning a living wage.[23]

Still, the vast majority of white mechanics' concerns were a direct result of slavery. In 1851, the Georgia Mechanics' Convention was held near Atlanta. Around 400 delegates and 2,000 more supporters traveled to the city to hear speeches and enjoy some camaraderie with their fellow laborers. In one particularly fiery speech, a white mechanic attempted to protect the trade from competition with free blacks and slaves, proclaiming that "A few urban negro mechanics can do more practical injury to the institution of slavery … than all the ultra abolitionists of the country." As these types of veiled warnings became more frequent throughout the 1850s, slaveholders had no choice but to pay attention. In fact, in response to the Atlanta meeting, one Georgia paper called upon the southern aristocracy to "look to their rights, as this action was taken to mean an attack upon them, for if [slaves were] driven from one field, they will drive them from all." Clearly agitated by the audacity of these white workers, the paper denounced the meeting "as part of a general system of attack upon Southern institutions and rights."[24]

Thus, in the 1840s and 1850s white labor unions *were*, in fact, active – and vocal – across the region. They often fought to prevent slave self-hire, and "board-money," which was a payment that allowed a slave to live apart from their workplace. Occasionally these groups even resorted to violence. Their growing militancy, however, only encouraged slaveholders to protect further their cherished institution. As Starobin concluded, "The net effect of most protests by white artisans was thus not to weaken slavery but to entrench it more firmly in southern society." Henry Wright, who had been enslaved near Atlanta as a young adult, remembered that his master trained slaves in masonry and carpentry so that he could sell them for higher prices if he needed quick money. "The slaves who were allowed to work with these white mechanics, from whom they eventually learned the trade, were eager because they would be permitted to hire themselves out," Wright stated. He also commented on a lesser-known benefit for the better-skilled white mechanics, explaining that the average white mechanic "had no particular objection to the slaves being there to help him, even though they were learning the trade, because he was able to place all the hard work on the slave which made his job

---

[23] "Petition of Mechanics," Folder "Mechanic," Petitions, 1817–1908, Mississippi Legislature, MDAH.

[24] *Ibid.*, quoted on 148; quoted on 159.

easier." Although this fact was certainly true for the period of time in which a mechanic taught a slave, as soon as the instruction period was over, the white worker had to sell his labor in competition with his enslaved former student, a predicament that naturally produced spite and a sense of injustice.[25]

Poorer white laborers, mostly led by skilled and semiskilled mechanics, continued to press for protection from competition with slave labor. They even attempted to end the practice of slave hiring altogether. Eventually, their protests, frequently peppered with threats to withdraw their support for the peculiar institution if slaveholding politicians did not readily respond, caused masters to truly begin fighting a two front war, protecting slavery from forces both within and without the South. Some masters proposed moving poor whites exclusively into new industrial and mechanical jobs, confining all African Americans to agricultural labor. Other pro-slavery men even attempted to reopen the African slave trade, because importing more slaves would make more white men slaveholders. Although ill-conceived, reactionary measures, both ideas confirm that on the eve of the Civil War, slave owners were scrambling to come up with a way to dominate and placate the southern masses, both black and white.[26]

U.S. Representative Thomas H. Bayly of Virginia opined that slavery "exclude[s] whites from employment. ... The next step will be to employ slave-labor in the factories, where again they will exclude the indigent whites." Recognizing that competition between the races in these new industries would cause problems, Bayly advocated the use of slaves but continued to point out how this labor preference would harm the white working poor. Indeed, "One of the great drawbacks on the employment of slaves in agriculture, is the fact that they are scattered about in their employment and the expense of supervision is proportionably great. In factories they are huddled together, and are always under the eye of the superintendent." After lauding his home state's successful use of slaves in tobacco factories, the Representative also admitted that the plan rendered white laborers practically worthless. Impoverished whites "will be excluded from most of the handicraft and mechanical employments," Bayly concluded. "It will be the indigent white men who will be injured more than the large slaveholder."[27]

[25] Starobin, *Industrial Slavery*, 211–2; 213; Henry Wright, *American Slave*, Vol. 13 (GA), Pt. 4, 196.
[26] Rockman, *Scraping By*, 7.   [27] "Untitled," *Southern Recorder*, March 9, 1847, 2.

The master class began discussing their options. One school of thought advocated confining blacks to plantation work, freeing up other, non-farm work for whites. As Judge H.F. Hopkins of Mobile, Alabama, explained, "many white mechanics have had good cause for complaining of the antagonism of labor growing out of the competition of so unpleasant companionship with negro mechanics. He must work as cheap as the slave, and associate in unnatural competition, which is degrading, and entirely at variance with out vaunted notion of the superiority of the race." He continued by linking non-slaveholders' support for slavery to job opportunities for poorer whites. "If we wish to foster Southern manufactories, in which the white men of the South are to seek employment," Hopkins wrote, "we must encourage white mechanics by removing the rivalry which now confronts them in our servile population. Confine negro labor to the cultivation of the soil, where it properly belongs, and we will strengthen the 'institution' ten fold, by the encouragement it will give to the non-slaveholding young of the South, who are not able to become planters, to become possessory of the mechanic arts."[28]

In 1858, a group of printers advised masters "to reflect upon the policy of continuing a system which may prejudice any class of white laborers" against slavery, because "Such a policy ... elevate[s] the negro at the expense of the white man; and makes the poor mechanic at the South the enemy of the negro and of the institution of slavery." Attempting to empathize with poor white laborers, the printers proclaimed that "if the rich man's negro was placed in competition with us at the printer's case, and by lowering our wages, take the bread from the mouths of our wife and children, a well of bitterness would spring up in our breasts against the negro and his master, that would render us the everlasting and uncompromising enemy of both." Considering themselves fortunate because the "laws of the State protect printers against this humiliation and degradation," the men then vowed that "what the laws fail to do in this respect for other mechanics, a wholesome public opinion should effect for them."[29]

To further complicate the Deep South's labor problems, overzealous slaveholders began promoting the reopening of the African slave trade. John Hope Franklin discovered that "As early as 1834, there were various unaffiliated groups, commonly known as the Southern Rights Clubs, that

---

[28] "Negro Mechanics," *Southern Federal Union*, July 23, 1861, 1.
[29] "Negro Mechanics," *Federal Union*, July 6, 1858, 1–2.

advocated the reopening of the slave trade and the extension of slavery into new territories. They had signs of recognition, met regularly, evolved a program for the development of the South, and even equipped and manned some slavers." By the 1850s, a small group of enterprising South Carolinians had begun the fight to import more slaves from Africa in earnest. They were led by Leonidas W. Spratt of Charleston, the editor of the *Standard* and one of the most influential members of the South Carolina House of Representatives. In 1853, Spratt, along with Governor James Adams and the wealthy slaveholding politician Robert Barnwell Rhett, began pushing to reopen the trade. Part of their reasoning was articulated by Spratt in 1856: "So many whites have come in since slaves have been restricted that this class of our population is greatly in excess. Many have taken to the walks of manual labor. They struggle for subsistence in competition with the slave, and already, even in this state, where there is still an excess of slaves, the proposition had been made and pressed to relieve the whites from the severities of such a combat." The growing numbers of non-slaveholding whites undoubtedly concerned the shrinking class of slaveholders, who realized they needed to act preemptively.[30]

With class tensions continuing to rise throughout the cotton boom of the 1850s, masters knew that they needed to create jobs for poor whites while appeasing the non-slaveholding yeomen class. According to Manisha Sinha, this controversial crusade gained enough support to make it "the central topic of heated debates" in the southern commercial conventions of 1858 and 1859. Indeed, the leaders of this movement felt the need to protect slavery from three main threats: the federal government, the moral "revolution" and humanistic enlightenment that swept across much of the nineteenth century western world, and an internal challenge from other southern whites – the non-slaveholders.[31]

This last threat was serious enough for Spratt to warn slaveholders that unless the price of slaves could be lowered, the masses of white laborers would eventually become frustrated enough to vote for abolition. Even the plan's detractors used economic class issues to argue their own side, correctly pointing out that importing more slaves would further drive

---

[30] John Hope Franklin, *The Militant South, 1800–1861* (1956; reprint, Boston: Beacon, 1970), 124; Harvey Wish, "The Revival of the African Slave Trade in the United States, 1856–1860," *The Mississippi Valley Historical Review* 27, No. 4 (Mar. 1941): 570; 571–2.

[31] Manisha Sinha, *The Counterrevolution of Slavery: Politics and Ideology in Antebellum South Carolina* (Chapel Hill: University of North Carolina Press, 2000), 125.

down the wages of the region's white laborers. As evidenced by the few public responses of non-slaveholders on reopening the trade, they, too, realized the dire consequences that would befall them. One letter from a "poor, very poor" white laborer attempted to dissuade South Carolina's lawmakers from importing more slaves by appealing to their humanity: "If we are to have negro labor in abundance, where will my support come from ... how can I live?" Reopening the trade, of course, would have reduced the overall wealth of slave owners by lowering the cost of slaves. But that was an economic loss that some masters were willing to take. They needed to preserve slavery, and they wanted to continue with their efforts to expand the institution's geographic reach. While the region's politicians never succeeded in reestablishing the African slave trade, debates over the issue revealed new fissures between classes of southern whites.[32]

Still, as late as 1860, Robert S. Hudson was urging large planters to sell one tenth of their slaves to non-slaveholding yeomen, to "make interest supply the deficiency of patriotism." Until they became slaveholders, white men in the Deep South had very few reasons to feel a sense of nationalism (or even white unity) with the master class. As Ronald Takaki found, the desire to reopen the trade had ultimately been driven by "an internal crisis of the Old South – a crisis based chiefly on the distressing awareness that slaveholding social mobility was tightening, and on the disturbing recognition that white Southerners themselves doubted the rightness of slavery." By the end of the 1850s, the issue of reopening the African slave trade had clearly divided the southern upper classes on policy and exposed the tenuousness of non-slaveholders' fidelity to the social hierarchy. It also became an integral part of the pro-slavery argument, encouraging both southern nationalism and secession.[33]

Regardless of the arguments supporting reopening the slave trade, poor white Southerners were still not convinced. Indeed, they not only noticed the inequalities inherent in the slave-based economic system, but they were also bothered by the social stratification and degrading treatment they experienced at the hands of more affluent whites. The fact that impoverished white workers were considered inferior for having to toil

[32] Takaki, "The Movement," 38–9; 48–9.
[33] Quoted in Paul D. Escott, *After Secession: Jefferson Davis and the Failure of Confederate Nationalism* (1978; reprint; Baton Rouge: Louisiana University Press, 1992), 29; Ronald Takaki, *A Pro-Slavery Crusade: The Agitation to Reopen the African Slave Trade* (New York: The Free Press, 1971), x; Sinha, *The Counterrevolution of Slavery*, 126.

alongside slaves (or in jobs that slaves usually occupied) was too much for some poor white men to handle. Whatever sense of honor they had drove them in one of two directions: they either became more ambitious and worked extremely hard to improve their economic station in life, or – probably far more commonly – they dropped out of the permanent work force altogether, eking out a meager existence on the fringes of society. While there is no way to accurately assess just how many poor whites abandoned the labor pool in the late antebellum period, their refusal of certain job offers was a frequent complaint from observers both within and without the region. Manual, unskilled, and agricultural labor were deemed so shameful that some white men chose the uncertainty of unemployment over the offer of a job. Certainly, the arduous nature of the work, the dangers involved, and the fairness of wages influenced a poor white's decision to turn down an opportunity, but according to contemporaries, the degradation of labor itself contributed significantly to the widespread under- and unemployment of thousands of poor whites.[34]

William Carson of Carroll Parish, Louisiana, was the son of a grand planter who owned more than 200 slaves. Carson wrote frankly about the privileges associated with wealth in the antebellum era, stating that "money and education went far towards making an aristocracy." However, he continued, "the fact that a man could do no better than make his living by manual labor was assumed to prove that he lacked brains, education, or money." White laborers, Carson admitted, received "no social recognition." Another observer noted, "That class which Slavery has created by dishonouring labour and abolishing wages," were "generally employed in doing nothing, and thereat are eminently successful."[35]

Historians from the first half of the twentieth century also noticed this demoralization of the white labor force. As Paul Buck wrote in 1925, "labor was considered disreputable because it was performed by slaves." More than a dozen years later Mildred Mell raised the same themes, claiming that slavery's existence caused the "attitude that any labor which is customarily performed by the slave thereby becomes beneath the dignity of the white man." Unfortunately, after the work of Frank Owsley in the 1940s spurred the refocusing of antebellum studies on the landowning yeomen, this very important labor theory has been largely absent from recent histories on the region. Although poor whites had very few chances

---

[34] Russel, "The Effects of Slavery," 124.
[35] Elliot and Moxley, *Tennessee*, Vol. 2, 464–6; Conway, *Testimonies*, 122; 121.

in life to earn a living wage and had even fewer chances of maintaining such a job for more than a few months, they sometimes turned down offers of work if they considered the pay too low, the job too dangerous, or simply because they still had enough food and whiskey to get by for another couple of weeks. As the court records in subsequent chapters confirm, it was not uncommon for poor whites to balk at certain types of labor or certain rates of pay. In May 1857, the *Southern Norfolk Argus* attempted to explain why this lack of work ethic arose in the slave states:

Slave labor and free labor, black labor and white labor, do not work well together. The white laborer assumes a superiority over his sable co-laborer ... [and] acts as the overseer rather than the laborer ... white laborers ... very soon fall into the idle habits of the negroes. ... They find themselves ranked with a degraded class, and giving up all hopes of improving their condition, are content to suffice to procure the bare necessaries of life.[36]

Indeed, poor whites' seeming contentment with "the bare necessaries" led to repeated charges of laziness. Many comments related to poor whites' apparent lack of ambition; upper- and middling-class observers just could not seem to comprehend why the white poor were unable to lift themselves out of poverty. "The Georgia 'cracker' ... seems to me to lack not only all that the negro does, but also even the desire for a better condition, and the vague longing for an enlargement of his liberties and his rights," wrote Whitelaw Reid, a Northerner who toured the state right after the end of the Civil War. "Such filthy poverty, such foul ignorance, such idiotic imbecility, such bestial instincts, such groveling desires, such mean longings; you would question my veracity as a man if I were to paint the pictures I have seen," he concluded. Fanny Kemble echoed similar sentiments, writing that the "filthy, lazy, ignorant, brutal, proud, penniless savages," otherwise known as the "pine-landers" of Georgia, comprised the most "degraded race of human beings claiming an Anglo-Saxon heritage." These "wretched creatures," she reasoned, refused to "labour for their own subsistence," because "labour belongs to blacks and slaves alone here."[37]

Clearly, this crisis in work ethic needs to be examined more closely by historians, especially when attempting to understand the socioeconomic disconnect between the wealthiest and the poorest southern whites.

---

[36] Buck, "The Poor Whites," 48; Mell, *A Definitive Study*, 138; reprinted in "Principles of the Nebraska Bill," *Southern Recorder*, May 19, 1857, 2.

[37] Whitelaw Reid, *After the War: A Southern Tour, May 1, 1865 to May 1, 1866* (New York: Moor, Wilstach, and Baldwin, 1866), 348; Kemble, *Journal*.

Slavery unquestionably devalued labor for poor whites, both financially *and* psychologically. And while many of them understood that the institution of slavery stifled their wages and prevented them from being hired in the first place, they were virtually powerless to do anything to affect change. Traveler James Redpath reported that he "met and conversed with many of the poorer class of whites in my journey. All of them were conscious of the injurious influence that slavery was exerting on their social condition. If damning the negroes would have abolished slavery, it would have disappeared a long time ago, before the indignant breath of the poor white trash."[38]

Instead, it seems, a percentage of the region's poorest whites may have simply refused to work more than they absolutely needed to survive. As Olmsted wrote, the South's poor white laborers were often drunk and always undependable; they simply refused to "work steadily at any employment." In one instance, a laborer had received some of his wages in advance – to buy some church clothes, he said – and absconded the next day, "right in the middle of harvest." Olmsted also reported that if a slaveholder requested certain types of work from poor whites, like fetching water or wood or taking care of the cattle, the laborer "would get mad and tell you he wasn't a nigger." Their "distinct and ... rather despicable class," he concluded, "are worse off in almost all respects than slaves." Slavery, Olmsted knew, was essential "in encouraging vagabond and improvident habits of life among the poor."[39]

While there had always been a substantial class of poor whites in the Deep South, their ranks were growing, especially in the decade before secession. Generally removed from the modern world and not fully involved or invested in the marketplace, poor whites simply did not fit the image of the white Southerner who was supposedly elevated by slavery. America's capitalist work principles had been lost on them. And while many of them descended from Protestant stock, that infamous work ethic, it seems, had also evaded them. Account after account describes poor whites as people who prized leisure above all else; as long as they had corn bread and a bit of meat, and enough whiskey to forget about their troubles, they seemed contented with a life of leisure. Regardless of how accurate these perceptions may have been, because poor whites were unable to change their job opportunities or demand a living wage, there

[38] Redpath, *The Roving Editor*, 88.   [39] Olmsted, *Journey*, 73; 83; 84; 452.

was little incentive for them to try to live according to a society controlled by an increasingly wealthy master class.

By 1851, South Carolinian William Gregg estimated that "the white people who ought to work, and who do not, or who are so employed as to be wholly unproductive to the State" totaled 125,000. All of the South's "capital, enterprise, and intelligence, is employed in directing slave labor," he continued, "and the consequence is, that a large portion of our poor white people are wholly neglected, and are suffered to while away an existence in a state but one step in advance of the Indian of the forest." Of course, Gregg had an ulterior motive for his interest in the lives of poor whites, as he planned to make a fortune by using their inexpensive labor in his textile factories. Still, it is interesting that during a time of great uncertainty over the future of black slavery, more affluent whites attempted to categorize poor whites as a separate race. To the southern gentry, poor whites may have been white in appearance, but they did not *act* white. Therefore, they did not completely qualify as members of the master race. Sometimes the differences between "respectable" whites and poor whites were blamed on pseudo-scientific theories of racial hierarchy, blood quantum, and the like. To other observers, however, poor whites were completely to blame for their station in life, as they frequently appeared to choose leisure over hard, grueling work. In an address to the Alabama State Agricultural Society delivered in 1842, Reverend Basil Manly forcefully made that point:

In our large cities, hundreds are congregated, without employment, and often without bread. ... If a farmer advertises for extra labor, with difficulty he obtains a reluctant offer. ... Pass through the streets of some of these towns – you will see groups of idlers mounted upon empty boxes, drumming with the heels of their boots, lounging about the doors of drinking establishments, whistling, and manufacturing tobacco-juice or puffing the fumes of a cigar, retelling the latest scandal, conning some new joke, discussing affairs of State, and all other subjects but what concerns them, *what suits their genius or station*, and what they might do to promote their own true welfare and that of the country.[40]

Reverend Manly was not alone in blaming the poor for their own poverty. Two years after the Alabama speech, a grand jury from Meriweather, Georgia complained after a spate of vagrancy arrests that "We cannot, therefore, tolerate the practice of many who are lounging

---

[40] Mell, *A Definitive Study*, 95–6; "Extract from an Address on Agriculture: Delivered before the Alabama State Agricultural Society, by the Rev. Dr. B Manly, President of the Alabama University," *Columbus Enquirer*, June 16, 1842, 1 (emphasis added).

about villages and places of public resort, and who seem to have no means of support." The average poor, underemployed white man "is ever on the lookout for something whereby he can kill time, and consequently often engages in those pursuits which ruin him and exert a bad influence upon others who would perhaps do well." Connecting unemployment to both poverty and criminal activity, the jury concluded that "The individual who is always consuming, and never, by honest employment, contributing to the stock necessary for human sustenance, cannot be viewed in any other light than a general disturber of society, and as a common burthen upon the good citizens of our county." Nevertheless, the jury's statements seemed outright kind when compared to a letter published in the *Columbus Enquirer*. After comparing the jobless to "drone bees" and noting that worker bees kill the drones, the writer reasoned, "We cannot kill the human drones that cumber society, and tumble them headlong out of the hive of mankind; but we can treat them as to indicate our conviction of their utter worthlessness." First, he advocated the complete social ostracizing of those who did not work, telling the upper and middling classes to pretend that the unemployed simply did not exist. By refusing to hear them speak and by pretending they were invisible, more affluent whites could shame the poor into fleeing their communities. "But your real idlers, your true drones, are those who to poverty add laziness," the letter persisted, and "If such a one cannot be killed, he should at least be thrown out of the hive."[41]

While the leaders of the slave states continued trying to scare non-slaveholders into supporting the institution, the rest of the United States, and indeed, the rest of the world, also took notice of the great inequalities between classes of southern whites. In the two decades prior to secession, the South's main labor problem – the competition between "free" white and slave labor – had become enough of an issue to make national headlines. Northern politician Thaddeus Stevens wrote that "The poor white laborer is the scorn of the slave himself; for slavery always degrades labor." Thus, he continued, "The white people who work with their hands are ranked with the other laborers – the slaves. . . . Their associates, if anywhere, are with the colored population. They feel that they are degraded and despised, and their minds and conduct generally conform to their condition." With just a few words Stevens had subtly suggested that poor whites' lack of work ethic functioned as a kind of self-fulfilling

---

[41] "Georgia, Meriwether County," *Ibid.*, Sept. 11, 1844, 3; "Drones," *Ibid.*, Nov. 25, 1840, 1.

prophesy: repeatedly told that inherent laziness caused their lack of wealth, some poor whites eventually gave up trying to lift themselves out of poverty. They simply trudged along through life, demoralized and disillusioned. Even Canadian papers commented on this southern issue, often using stronger language than their American counterparts. In an article entitled "White and Black Slavery," one journalist urged every white working man of the slave states "to feel how closely their interests, and those of the black working men were united. To feel that the mill stone they are permitting to be bound around the neck of the negro bondmen, is also twisted around their own, and that they are both being dragged downward to a condition of brutish ignorance, degradation and slavish dependence."[42]

A pamphlet from the Democratic League, published during the Civil War, forthrightly laid out the reasons for the "partial feud that had long existed between the slaveholding and non-slaveholding population." According to the League, "Southern white labor was continually annoyed with the appellation of 'white trash,' and other contemptuous epithets; but still was compelled to toil under the continuous insult. ...Too many of the accidental droppings of foolish and stupid arrogance were let fall within the hearing of white labor to make it fully reconciled to the pretended monopoly of respectability by slaveholders." The laborers who were able immigrated to the free western states, but those who remained in the South learned to live "[u]nder this corroded feeling." The degradation of poor whites, the Democratic League proclaimed, was the key to understanding the aristocratic intentions of the slaveholders. "It would require a volume to delineate the arts and hypocrisy resorted to, and the false reasoning employed," lamented the writers, "to impose upon the masses of white labor[ers in the] South, and to make them contented with their disparaged condition." Slave owners had, indeed, degraded common labor enough to threaten a working man's pride. When a poor white man's only employment option was to work for low wages alongside slaves, taking orders from a de facto master, at times he simply chose not to work at all.[43]

The story of the antebellum South's poor whites – both laborers and the unemployed – is, at its core, similar to the stories of millions of the

---

[42] "The Slavery Question," *National Era*, March 7, 1850; "White and Black Slavery," *Provincial Freeman*, Dec. 29, 1855.
[43] The Democratic League, "The Slaveholders' Conspiracy against Democratic Principles," (N.P., 1864?), MDAH, 4–5; 8.

world's poor, spanning different times and different places. There *is* a point at which labor becomes so degrading and demoralizing that some people may stop working, preferring to take risks with their futures to avoid the daily drudgery of their current lives. Sometimes this apathy is due to an individual's inability to earn a living wage in a sixty- or seventy-hour work week; sometimes it is because of the actual labor itself, which is typically characterized by boring, physically demanding, dirty, danger-ous, or demeaning jobs; and sometimes it stems from the fact that there is simply no other option available to certain sections of the community. This last factor, especially, creates a sense of nihilism and disgust among society's most disadvantaged. Resulting from factors ranging from a completely broken or nonexistent educational system, to a lack of access to health care and adequate nutrition, to a legal system that favors the rich and harshly punishes the poor, common wage laborers have always had a multitude of factors prodding them to drop out of a society that does not value them – as laborers or as people. The Deep South's slave-holders had more than disgruntled slaves to consider as they weighed reasons to secede from the Union. They also had to figure out how to appease (or overcome) angry poor whites. Perhaps Paul Buck explained the South's labor problem most elegantly:

Towards the close of the antebellum period, however, obvious defects of an undiversified economy caused a re-examination of industrial society, and in the process the antagonisms latent in the relations of the various elements of the white population came to the surface. As a consequence there took shape a movement of discontent which promised to wrest political leadership from the hands of the gentry and overthrow the industrial monopoly of the plantation system.

Slavery was being threatened on multiple fronts, both internally and externally, by diverse interests. Slaveholders had little choice but to react.[44]

Mere weeks after Lincoln's election, the *Southern Banner* published an alleged "want" ad they claimed originated in Rochester, New York. Appearing in an article entitled "The Practical Workings of Abolition," the advertisement was supposedly placed by a "respectable colored family" who was looking for "a white boy, 14 or 16 years of age, to wait upon the table and make himself generally useful about the house." Thus, with one scandalous advertisement, slaveholders attempted to frighten poor white laborers into supporting the peculiar institution. If they failed

[44] Buck, "The Poor Whites," 41.

to do so, they could fully expect soon to be working for emancipated blacks, waiting on them in a servile fashion. Slavery, the masters of men claimed, was much more important for poor whites than it was for the affluent, as it kept them from being the mud-sill of southern society. Poor whites, their argument ran, had much to lose if African Americans ever gained freedom. Their honor and dignity were at stake. The southern publishers of this incendiary want ad concluded by warning non-slaveholders about their futures in a free land – futures in which they could expect to be working for black masters. "We trust the time will never come when the children of the poor white man in Georgia shall be thus humbled or abased," they wrote. With emancipation, "our slave-holding population would or might lose money ... but the poor white man would lose much more, and what is all in all to him and to every man, viz: the consciousness of political and social superiority."[45]

What the pro-slavery writers failed to understand, however, was that assurances of poor whites' ostensible superiority over slaves did not always mollify people who were already treated as socially, politically, and economically *inferior* to members of their own race. There were few scenarios in which things could get materially worse for whites who had great difficulty finding work, keeping work, and earning a living wage. They had little reason to think abstractly about their social position relative to emancipated slaves. Instead, they were much more worried about how to obtain next week's food and whiskey. For poor white Southerners in the late antebellum period, freedom *was* just another word for nothing left to lose. And for the region's master class, this type of freedom, especially within a slave society, was potentially dangerous. As one industrialist wrote, slaveholders had a vested interested in ensuring that poor whites had jobs. Otherwise, he warned, *"It is this great upheaving of our masses that we have to fear, so far as our institutions are concerned."*[46]

---

[45] "The Practical Workings of Abolition," *Southern Banner*, Dec. 13, 1860, 2.
[46] Quoted in Weston, "The Poor Whites," 2, italics in original.

4

Everyday Life: Material Realities

The lords of the lash are not only absolute masters of the blacks, but they are also the oracle and arbiters of all non-slaveholding whites, whose freedom is merely nominal, and whose unparalleled illiteracy and degradation is purposely and fiendishly perpetuated.

— Hinton Helper[1]

The poor white man will learn that his rights are wrapped up in the same bundle with the black man's, and that the rights of the one cannot be violated without affecting those of the other.

— The North Star[2]

In an 1847 article simply entitled "The South," one abolitionist newspaper described the living conditions of the region's poor whites in stark terms. "They live in ill-constructed log-cabins, neither air-tight nor water tight, with no partition between hall and chamber, the whole family often tumbling into one bed," the writer began. During "snowy and icy winters," these impoverished whites would "sit shivering over miserable embers, sooner than take the trouble of obtaining an adequate supply of firewood from the adjacent forest. Scant fare, scant clothing, and scant housing, with little or no work, seem to constitute the climax of their felicity." Surviving by hunting, fishing, and foraging, the article continued, poor whites "are very ignorant. Not one out of fifty can read or write, and, what is worse, they change not." Indeed, non-southerners

---

[1] Helper, *The Impending Crisis*, 43.
[2] "American Slavery – Its Effects among the Non-Slaveholding Population of the South," *The North Star*, March 10, 1848.

often described the daily material realities of poor whites with great disdain, and almost always with a sense of pity. Northern traveler John Abbott toured the interior of Georgia, bewailing the fact that he felt "disappointed and pained to meet only forlorn-looking villages, miserable negro huts, and a white population sunk almost below the negro, and seemingly content with a degree of indolence and discomfort which hardly entitles them to the name of civilized beings."[3]

As one *New York Times* article estimated, poor whites populated about one-third of South Carolina's low country. Deeming them "that strange, cadaverous, shuffling, miserable race of mortals," the paper went on to claim that out of the impoverished, about "a half are small traders and persons who live by selling liquor and other things surreptitiously to the negroes, and purchasing what they pilfer – a class thoroughly despised and hated by the planters." Concluding that the more affluent slave-holders "despise all sorts and conditions of men but their own sort," the writer determined that the master class regarded "every kind of worker as – what one of these insolent nabobs dubbed them – but the 'mudsills' of society, of which they are the crown and crest." Poor whites, therefore, were only slightly above slaves in terms of social distinction, and slaveholders wanted nothing to do with them. The master class considered the impoverished as little more than nuisances. Still another article contended that poor whites lived in "extreme penury, from want of regular employment." Just barely scraping by, they "subsist upon course and meagre fare, which they derive in part from a wretched cultivation of corn patches on poor lands, with fishing, hunting and stealing. They are almost entirely illiterate."[4]

Countless non-slaveholding Civil War veterans confirmed the stereo-types portrayed in these articles, particularly concerning the lack of opportunities for lower-class whites. Poor white boys, George Wray of Sumner, Tennessee remembered, "had very little encouragement or help from the slave owners. If they made good it was by hard labor and careful management." Federal soldiers from the state echoed his sentiments: non-slaveholders were "not encouraged very much" because slave owners refused "to elevate the poor boy very high." Anderson Roach recalled that "when a slaveholder hired a non-slaveholder he was principally looked at as being no better than a slave and was treated as one. . . . The

[3] "The South," *National Era*, Nov. 25, 1847; Abbott, *South and North*, 128, Web.
[4] "Southern South Carolina and Its Social and Political Character," *New York Times*, Nov. 23, 1861; "Who Rule the South?," *New York Times*, Jan. 15, 1861.

slaveholders kept the poor class of people down as much as possible." Poor whites sometimes *did* compare their plight to slavery, and they occasionally spoke about worries that they might one day become slaves themselves. George Payne claimed that slaveholders "tried to keep" poor men "down so they could make slaves of them." Payne's sentiment, however dramatic, nonetheless expressed what likely was a common concern among poor whites. Indeed, as impoverished whites continued to teeter – precariously and uneasily – on the bottom rungs of an unfree society, they must have occasionally wondered what would happen should they fall.[5]

Thus, disparities in wealth – manifested in daily material realities – only exacerbated class tensions during the late antebellum period. It became exceedingly clear to poorer whites that the privileges of whiteness were class-specific. By studying housing, diet, sexuality, marriage, family, religion, and honor, it becomes quite obvious that the lives of poor whites were vastly different from the lives of more affluent Southerners. This distinction between classes of whites was extremely pronounced in heavy slave areas and seemed most intense in the Deep South's cities and the plantation belt. Living in the foothills of Appalachia, one slave owner noticed a clear difference in social relations between whites in the plantation region and the overwhelmingly non-slaveholding community of Sequatchie, Tennessee. "There was no clannishness, nor snobbishness here between these two classes, such as I witnessed farther south," he stated. People from the Deep South confirmed his observations.[6]

This grave economic stratification between masters and non-masters meant that in material terms, the poorest southern whites lived somewhat similarly to slaves. Historians have shown that slaves' material lives were not far removed from those of European peasants. As valuable property, though, slaves were generally protected from severe hunger and starvation. It was in the masters' best economic interests to keep their workers fed and healthy, and many of the wealthier planters regularly employed a physician to help sick and injured slaves heal and recover. Poor whites owned very little property and rarely had access to actual cash, and often scraped together a meager living based on bare subsistence. As Fredrika Bremer remarked, poor whites "live in the woods, without churches,

---

[5] Elliot and Moxley, *The Tennessee Civil War Veterans Questionnaires*, Vols. 1–5. (Easley, SC: Southern Historical Press, Inc., 1985), Vol. 5, 2242; Vol. 1, 1; Vol. 1, 107; Vol. 4, 1710–2.

[6] Elliot and Moxley, *Tennessee*, Vol. 1, 310.

without schools, without hearths, and sometime also without homes." Despite their scanty belongings, many of the impoverished seemed to preserve some sense of honor, she concluded, as they remained "independent and proud in their own way."[7]

Lee Soltow determined that on the eve of secession, about one-third of white Americans owned no more than clothing and small sums of petty cash. Possessing next to nothing meant that poor whites were removed even more from the day-to-day realities of the yeomen farmers and emerging southern middle class. Bolton found that by 1860, even slaveless yeomen in North Carolina's central Piedmont generally owned about four or five times as much personal property as their landless white neighbors. Evidence gleaned from debtors' records show that poor whites' most commonly owned property included farming tools, hogs, furniture, and kitchen utensils. In 1839, John Crosland applied for insolvency in South Carolina. His worldly belongings included eighty-seven cents, three pairs of scissors, and the "wearing apparel of self and wife." The same year William Griffin was listed as owning "1 fore plane, 1 jack plane, 1 smoothing plane, 1 handsaw, 1 iron square, 3 chisels, [and] the wearing apparel of himself and his two little children." And in 1857, Fairfield District officials listed Berry Swan as an insolvent debtor. His only possessions were his clothing. Former slaves also confirmed just how severely impoverished many poor whites were. In Mississippi, former slave Julius Jones recalled having white neighbors who "were sure bad off. When they moved, they put their belongings in little wagons and had dogs pull them ... they didn't have no other way to get from place to place."[8]

Given how little they actually owned, poor white homes were generally of very poor quality, commonly described as crude, one room shacks made of logs and mud. Travelers often commented on the horrible conditions of poor white dwellings. Impoverished whites "usually lived in one-room cabins, the logs unhewn and inadequately chinked. Frequently there was no window of any kind, and almost certainly there would be no glass window," reported one source. "There was no floor but the bare earth; the furniture seldom included more than a bedstead or two, a rough pine table, a rough homemade chair or two, and perhaps an

---

[7] Genovese, *Roll, Jordan, Roll*, 59; Fox-Genovese, *Slavery in White and Black*, quoted on 246.

[8] Soltow, *Men and Wealth*, 24; Bolton, *Poor Whites*, 34; Fairfield District, Court of Common Pleas, Petitions and Property Schedules of Insolvent Debtors, 1805–1861 (SCDAH); Julius Jones, *American Slave*, Vol. 6 (MS), Supplement, Series 1, Part 3, 1221–2.

improvised cupboard and sometimes a spinning wheel. . . . All were dirty and unkempt." Freedman Ed McCree confirmed this description, noting that "Slave quarters were lots of log cabins with chimneys of crisscrossed sticks and mud. Poor white folks lived in houses like that too." Yankee soldier George Pepper added his voice to the chorus, pointing out the extreme differences in white living quarters:

The state of the habitations of the poor in many parts of Georgia, is a libel on the humanity of their more wealthy superiors. A fine dressed lawn, surrounded with miserable cabins and hovels of the poor, nothing can reflect more discredit on the character of the dominant class, than such a contrast . . . at each opening of the prospect, your eyes are pained by dwellings for laborers not half so convenient as the wigwam of the savage.

Guion Griffis Johnson similarly described the deplorable abodes of poor whites. "They often lived in abandoned outhouses, some with only a clay floor and no means of ventilation or light except the door," she wrote. But they were rarely able to escape this extreme poverty, due to having very little personal property and being "constantly in debt either to their landlord or the keeper of the cross-roads store."[9]

Avery Craven identified several similarities between the material lives of poor whites and slaves. Their cabins differed "little in size or comfort," he wrote, as both were constructed from chinked logs and generally had only one room. Furthermore, these two underclasses "dressed in home-spuns, [and] went barefoot in season. . . . The women of both classes toiled in the fields or carried the burden of other manual labor and the children of both early reached the age of industrial accountability." Even the food they prepared and ate, Craven concluded, "was strikingly similar." While the majority of non-landowners experienced periods of hunger throughout the antebellum period, the most impoverished poor whites dealt with food shortages on a fairly regular basis. Because poor whites generally had little or no access to fertile land, they often had to purchase or trade for food. Although they obviously supplemented their diets by hunting, fishing, poaching, and foraging, not having enough to eat was a constant worry for a sizable percentage of the white population. Travelers often commented on the limited selection and quantities of food among the poor. One thought that poor white Southerners "lived almost

[9] Edgar W. Martin, *The Standard of Living in 1860: American Consumption Levels on the Eve of the Civil War* (Chicago: University of Illinois Press, 1942), 132; Ed McCree, *American Slave*, Vol. 4 (GA), Part 3, 58; Pepper, *Personal Recollections*, 271, Web; Johnson, *Ante-Bellum North Carolina*, 569.

entirely on corn bread and bacon." In Georgia, reported Craven, another visitor "was served coffee without sugar, fried bacon, and corn bread mixed with water only; there were no vegetables, butter, or other foods." When poor whites did grow or acquire vegetables, they closely approximated slave fare: the most common included sweet potatoes, Irish potatoes, cabbages, peas, beans, okra, and occasionally leafy greens like collards. Aside from liquor, pork was the most commonly purchased item by poor whites. Yet given the exorbitant prices set by monopolistic planters and grocers, some poor whites preferred to purchase less expensive food from slaves and free blacks in the underground economy.[10]

Not all slaveholding southern families were unsympathetic on this count, however. In several court proceedings involving poor whites, wealthier neighbors were asked how many times they supplied a particular person with meat or corn. It was not uncommon for each small community to have multiple families who would go door to door asking for food on a regular basis. Both slave narratives and Confederate soldier questionnaires referred to the frequency of edible donations from the region's rich. Robert Floyd claimed that slaveholders "would kill beef or mutton and send some to the [poorer] neighbors without any cost." Former slave Coleman Smith echoed this observation: "when my master killed beefs he divided it with poor white people." And Melvin Smith from Beaufort, South Carolina, said that poor whites had so little to eat that "Master all the time send them meat and bread and help them with their crop. . . . Sometimes they even come to see the niggers and eat with us. We went to see them, too, but we had more to eat than them. They were sorry folk." Adeline Jackson even remembered one "poor buckra . . . [who] was a God-forsaken looking man that master or mistress always give something." Still another freedwoman from Georgia recalled "a white widow woman who lived near our place, and she had two boys. Missus let them boys pick them some peas when we would be picking, and we would run them off, because we didn't like po' white trash. But Missus made us let them pick all they wanted." Wealthy slaveholders clearly had to help support poor whites through periods of severe deprivation.[11]

[10] Craven, "Poor Whites and Negroes," 16–17; Martin, *The Standard*, 59–60; 63; Forret, *Race Relations*, 81.
[11] Elliot and Moxley, *Tennessee*, Vol. 2, 826–7; Vol. 5, 1973–4; Melvin Smith, *American Slave*, Vol. 13, Part 3, 290; Adeline Jackson, *Ibid.*, Vol. 3 (SC), Part 3, 2; Georgia Smith, *Ibid.*, Vol. 4 (GA), Part 3, 283.

State and local governments made weak attempts to address the South's poverty problems through a series of poor laws in the late antebellum period. While most of the region's laws aimed to control or punish the poor white population, a minority of them offered small charitable concessions, from poor/common school funds to the construction of almshouses and orphanages. Originally, southern "poor houses" were built for children, the elderly, and the infirm, but by the 1820s and 1830s, poor able-bodied adults were seeking admission. Thus, just as the Jacksonian Era supposedly lifted up the common man, some of the South's white workers were applying for governmental assistance just to survive. The overwhelming majority of the Deep South's paupers, of course, were white women of various ages. Although many impoverished whites may have applied for some form of relief, less than 1 percent of them ever received help. Southern governments typically only helped the blind, "insane," and severely physically disabled, as well as certain orphaned or abandoned children.[12]

By 1860, as many as one-third of Georgia's counties – especially those with cities or towns – had established poor houses and asylums. The Muscogee Asylum for the Poor advertised that it would educate impoverished children, "at least in reading and writing." Hancock, a county in the heart of Georgia's black belt, probably had the most comprehensive program: it levied an extra tax to establish quarters for the poor that included dormitories, a kitchen, a chapel, and a school, as well as enough land for a garden, orchard, vineyard, and pasture for two milk cows. But Hancock's program was an anomaly. In most parts of the South, almshouses were generally filthy, underfunded cesspools of illness. "A list of the sick in the poor house" in Adams County, Mississippi revealed that diseases such as hepatitis and typhus and disabilities such as blindness were commonplace. A few of the "sick" were gunshot victims, but the large majority of the indigent were incapacitated by diarrhea. Physicians ran the poor house, but just being there was a virtual death sentence. The almshouses rarely sheltered healthy young males or even able-bodied females; they generally only contained "but a few imbeciles and cripples."[13]

[12] Rockman, *Scraping By*, 211; Forret, *Race Relations*, 197; Lockley, *Welfare and Charity*, 16.

[13] *Acts of the General Assembly of the State of Georgia*. Passed at Milledgeville, at a session in November and December, 1858: e.g., 185, 186, 190; 1845: 131; 1847: 133; 1858: 190; Wallenstein, *From Slave South to New South*, 48; Adams County, Poor House Records, 1821–3, MDAH; Lockley, *Welfare and Charity*, 195.

While the southern states continued to offer underfunded, lackluster, and vague "solutions" to the problems caused by extreme poverty, private charitable donations became an important part of white-on-white paternalism. Lockley documented more than 600 antebellum benevolent societies in the slave states. In the most comprehensive work on southern charity to date, he proposed that slaveholders used charity to "demonstrate to poor whites that there were some privileges to which they were entitled merely because of their race." Interestingly, women led the effort to build some sort of charitable safety net beginning in the early nineteenth century, sustaining their work throughout much of the antebellum period. Just as in the North, affluent men in the South did not increase their "interest and involvement" in local charities until the 1840s, although Lockley gave no real explanation for this timing. Well after the supposed great equalizing of white men during the Jacksonian era, the support of charitable efforts by the master class came on the heels of a decade of hardcore abolitionist sentiment and sectional strife. Likely prompted by the depression of the late 1830s, slaveholders realized they needed to find ways to keep the poor loyal to them – and to slavery. Even as wealth inequality continued to grow over the next two decades, masters could ensure that poor whites depended on them for survival. This gratitude, however misplaced, was likely effective.[14]

Although Lockley was correct in most of his analysis of southern charities, aspects of southern masculinity – namely, honor – should have had a more prominent role in his thesis. Olmsted observed that the southern poor "are not generally anxious to be admitted [to an almshouse]. ... They usually consider it a deplorable misfortune which obliges them to go to it." Young, able-bodied poor whites were surely more than a little humiliated to have to seek financial help. In a world of extravagance and extreme wealth, not to mention a world where manhood was defined by the ability to provide for one's family, they doubtless felt like failures, both as men and as *white* men. Private sources of aid may have been less public than governmental assistance, but the fact that most of the region's charities were run by women deserves greater scrutiny than Lockley afforded it. The southern code of masculine honor surely would have discouraged at least some impoverished (but still fiercely independent) white men from taking economic assistance from *women*. Still, a

---

[14] *Ibid.*, 3; 114; 6; 216. For another good study on antebellum charity, see Christopher L. Stacey, "Political Culture and Public Poor Relief in Louisiana and Mississippi," (Ph.D. Diss., Mississippi, 2007).

deep-set sense of white honor undermined the main point of Lockley's study, that charity and welfare provided poor whites "fewer reasons to feel disaffected with the status quo," functioning as "important elements in the creation and maintenance of the 'solid South.'"[15]

While very few poor whites ultimately received personal charity from the master class, a sizable percentage were still both figuratively and economically indebted to slaveholders. Some of the most important practices that continued to reinforce the paternalist relationship between rich and poor whites concerned money lending and the extension of lines of credit. Banks were relatively scarce in the rural Deep South, and even if poor whites lived in cities or towns, they would rarely have the collateral to qualify for a loan. Planters had loaned money or granted credit to less affluent whites for generations, and the practice seemed to grow in accordance with the diversifying economy in the late antebellum period. Loans inextricably bound poor whites to the plantation gentry, economically, legally, and even politically. It is certainly conceivable that a lender would threaten to call in overdue debts if the debtor began to displease him in some manner. At the very least, the creditor would rack up court and legal fees owed by the poor white, who would be declared insolvent and put in jail. It is easy to imagine multiple scenarios in which the lending planter would advise – or even threaten – a debtor into voting a certain way, especially if the debtor was a tenant.

Furthermore, being dependent on a member of the master class for housing and food surely guided the way a debtor lived his life. Essentially foreshadowing the crop lien system, these types of credit relationships became cyclical and perpetual. Once the initial debt was established, the creditor could easily raise interest rates or sell or rent goods at exorbitant prices. Without other means of establishing credit, the debtor was forced to take the slaveholder's terms – terms that often financially bound the poor white to the master for his entire life. Richard Morris held that the "Principle forms of coercive labor service to which the poor whites of the South were subject stemmed from peonage, a relationship based upon debt." Bolton confirmed these findings decades later, writing that many employers used their "economic clout as a creditor to encourage poor debtors to sign on as laborers." The bonds of debt were incredibly tight, and the only way for poor whites to escape "such debilitating credit relationships was to move farther west. Many did." Indeed, there was a

---

[15] Olmsted, *A Journey*, 700; Lockley, *Welfare and Charity*, 217.

mass exodus westward of small farmers who had lost their land and grown tired of being in debt and working for others.[16]

At times, charitable contributions from wealthy Southerners included the "lending" of slaves. Masters would allow a slave or a small group of slaves to go over and work for a less fortunate white – either for a period of days to help him with planting or harvesting, or for a specific job, such as construction of a house or barn. William Pursley, the son of a slave-holder, remembered that his father would "take a bunch of slaves to help a neighbor less fortunate in log rolling and other work on the farm. Mother has sent negro girls for weeks to stay with a sick neighbor." Of course, it was probably more common for slaveholders to send these resources to a struggling but landowning yeoman farmer than to a truly impoverished white who did not own land. But the practice tied the beneficiary of the charity to slavery. Even if the poorer or lower-middling white did not own a slave, "borrowing" forced laborers from a master inexorably linked the non-slaveholder to the peculiar institution. At the very least, this exchange gave the poorer person a feeling of importance. Not only were they recognized by slaveholders as members of society worthy of charity, they also became – but for a brief moment – masters themselves. This singular event was likely transformative for a non-slave owner, especially in terms of his attitude toward slavery.[17]

Although there is an obvious history of private charitable acts in the antebellum Deep South, the vast majority of poor whites never received any form of relief or assistance, from either the upper classes or the government. On the contrary, it must have seemed to them that the slaveholders were only concerned with their own interests, and they quickly realized they would have to fend for themselves. In this cruel, hard world, some poor whites turned to illegal activities in order to survive. Understanding the extent of poor white poverty helps determine how commonly poor whites and blacks must have interacted in the underground economy. Poor whites often needed food, and slaves had access to plantation property, and at times had their own produce to sell. Thus, state governments frequently drafted laws preventing poor whites from having contact with slaves, and the most obvious regulations concerned peddling and trading. In his study on bi-racial crime in the Carolinas and Virginia, Forret unsurprisingly found an "inverse relationship

---

[16] Morris, "The Measure of Bondage," 225; Bolton, *Poor Whites*, 26; 105.
[17] *Ibid.*, Vol. 4, 1783.

between a white person's wealth and his or her likelihood of engaging in the unlawful trade with slaves."[18]

The presence of the underground economy only strengthened slaveholders' desire to keep slaves and poor whites separate. In fact, the southern gentry often encouraged their slaves to loathe poor whites; if blacks felt superior to poor whites, masters hoped, they would likely avoid having contact with them. In the few decades before secession, slaves regularly ridiculed poor whites, even face to face. Henry Bibb, a fugitive slave, wrote that poor whites "were generally ignorant, intemperate, licentious, and profane." Eugene Genovese theorized that it "was probably the slaves who dubbed the poor whites 'trash'" because blacks considered them "the laziest and most dissolute people on earth."[19]

Countless interviews with freedmen, along with fugitive slave narratives and third-party accounts, seem to affirm Genovese's conclusion. Many times blacks' disrespect and disdain for poor whites seemed to center on poor whites' illiteracy, work ethic, and moral habits, not their economic worth. Traveler Whitelaw Reid spoke to one newly freed man who weighed in on poor whites' lack of both education and ambition: "They haven't learned, because they don't care; we, because they wouldn't let us." Slaves also realized that poor whites' alleged immoralities added reasons for strict segregation. One African American woman recalled that her masters "didn't never allow us niggers to mix with what they called the po' white trash; they always said they would learn us how to steal and drink; it was the truth, too." Nan Stewart remembered that her "poor white neighbors weren't allowed to live very close to the plantation as Marse Hunt wanted the cultured slave children to be raised in proper manner." Telling slave children that they needed to act socially "better than" or "above" poor whites surely challenged slave owner teachings of inherent racial inequality. This type of hierarchy – predicated on ever more complicated formulas of race and class – likely caused many African Americans to reflect on their masters' pro-slavery theories based on the notion of white racial superiority. These concepts became less and less convincing with the unavoidable recognition of the South's white poor. Ella Kelly, enslaved in South Carolina, attempted to make sense

[18] Jeff Forret, "Slaves, Poor Whites, and the Underground Economy of the Rural Carolinas," *Journal of Southern History* LXX, No.4 (Nov. 2004): 785.
[19] Cecil-Fronsman, *Common* 89; John W. Blassingame, *The Slave Community: Plantation Life in the Antebellum South* (New York: Oxford University Press, 1979), quoted on 306–7; Genovese, *Roll, Jordan, Roll*, 22.

of the region's competing prejudices against both blacks and poor whites. Kelly proposed that "there are three kinds of people. Lowest down is a layer of white folks, then in the middle is a layer of colored folks and on top is the cream, a layer of good white folks. Suspect it'll be day way 'till Judgment day."[20]

Of course, slaveholders' main motivation for keeping the two groups separate was more serious than concerns over simple larceny and trading in the underground economy. Upper-class Southerners recognized the danger in poor whites' nonconformity and disconnectedness from slavery. Several of the African Americans interviewed after the Great Depression talked about the strained relationships between whites of different classes, demonstrating how easily disaffected poor whites could disrupt the lives of their masters. Samuel Andrews told his interviewer that he ran away twice, but his owner declined to whip him upon his return because "he was apprehensive that he might run away again and be stolen by poorer whites and thus cause trouble." The richer whites, Andrews related, "were afraid of the poorer whites"; if the latter "were made angry they would round up the owners' sheep and turn them loose into their cotton fields and the sheep would eat the cotton, row by row." He concluded that "the relationship between the rich and poor whites during slavery" was comparable to "that of the white and Negro people today." Undoubtedly, slaveholders' greatest fears involved blacks and poor whites forming *personal relationships*. Any hint of a growing empathy and compassion between the two underclasses surely terrified the master class. Reverend Squire Dowd remembered that "We looked upon the poor white folks as our equals. They mixed with us and helped us to envy our masters. They looked upon our masters as we did."[21]

Other freedmen and women commented on the deep social divide between rich and poor whites, pointing out some of the humiliations poor whites suffered. Jesse Williams, who had been enslaved in South Carolina, reported, "We had a good master and mistress. They were big buckra, never associated with poor white trash." And John Smith, a North Carolinian, remembered that "The poor white folks done tolerable well but the rich slave owners didn't allow them to come on their plantations." Instances of slaveholders denying poor whites access to their

---

[20] Nan Stewart, *American Slave*, Vol. 12 (OH), 88; "Now Supported by Children She Raised" *Ibid.*, Vol. 18 (Fisk), 215; Ella Kelly, *Ibid.*, Vol. 14 (SC), Part 3, 82.
[21] Samuel Simeon Andrews, *Ibid.*, Vol. 3 (FL), 13; Reverend Squire Dowd, *Ibid.*, Vol. 11 (NC), 267.

homes seemed particularly to delight slaves, as they often pointed such incidents out to their interviewers. Rosa Starke's master "Had a grand manner; no patience with poor white folks. They couldn't come in the front yard; they knew to pass on by to the lot, hitch up their horse, and come knock on the kitchen door and make their wants and wishes known to the butler." For all the pleasure slaves seemingly took in criticizing poor whites, however, very real friendships and relationships between the two groups continually threatened to traverse the boundaries of race. Market-driven interracial dealings were exceedingly common, particularly in grog shops, brothels, and gambling houses. Forret described the relationship between the two underclasses as a complex, "curious mix of love and hate, equality and inequality. At times, shared economic deprivation and impoverishment tempered racial hostilities and drew slaves and poor whites together into civil, cordial, and even intimate and loving relationships." Thus, he concluded, "slave and poor white interaction both reinforced and challenged southern racial boundaries."[22]

Despite masters' best efforts, therefore, slaves and poor whites in plantation areas, towns, and cities had quite a bit of interaction – and some of those relationships, of course, were sexual. Although there were cases of relationships between poor white men and black women, most historians have studied the more commonly reported sexual interactions between poor white women and black men. Ira Berlin found that beginning in colonial times, the largest incidence of interracial sex in America occurred between white servant women and black men. By the late antebellum period, Genovese asserted, "white women of all classes had black lovers and sometimes husbands in all parts of the South, especially in the towns and cities." Poor white women participated in the underground economy to a large extent, certainly more frequently than slave women. Forret estimated that impoverished women comprised about a quarter of all whites involved in the bi-racial trading network. Given how commonly they engaged in commerce with free blacks and slaves, miscegenation was all but inevitable. Whether abandoned, widowed, or simply alone while their men were gone for weeks or months at a time, these women had to make ends meet as best as possible. Sometimes they turned to black men as romantic lovers, and sometimes sexual favors were used

[22] Jesse Williams, *Ibid.*, Vol. 14 (SC), Part 4, 204. John Smith, *Ibid.*, Vol. 11 (NC), Part 2, 273–4; Rosa Starke, *Ibid.*, Vol. 14 (SC), Part 4, 147–8; Lockley, *Lines in the Sand*, 29; Forret, *Race Relations*, 15.

as payments for goods. But one thing is certain: interracial sex between the lower classes happened with relative frequency.[23]

Former slaves sometimes commented about these mixed-race relationships. One woman remembered an African American man who had been lynched in her community: "He was just like a heap of other young fool men, he was fooling around with the 'po' white trash,' and he had been putting up with this old white woman." Yet it seemed as if the poor white woman had real feelings for her black lover, because "the very morning he was to be hung, this old white woman hussy come to the jail and said he was innocent." Freedwoman Adeline Johnson recalled another incident that happened near her plantation. A particular poor white woman "had no living. Nigger men steal flour or a hog, take it and give it to her. She be hungry. Pretty soon a mulatto baby turned up. Then folks want to run her out of the country." During his travels through Georgia, Olmsted took notice of poor white "harlots," noting that "very slight value is placed on female virtue among this class." There must always be enough women so poor that "their favors can be purchased by the slaves." Even worse, he reasoned, the biracial offspring of these poor white women "must be constitutionally entitled to freedom." Because infants born in the antebellum period automatically took on the status (slave or free) of their mothers, any baby born to a poor white woman would be considered free, even if the baby was biracial. Poor white women's potential to augment the free black population doubtless disturbed slave owners a great deal. Poor white women' sexuality, therefore, caused antebellum masters great worry, and women suspected of selling their bodies were routinely prosecuted throughout the Deep South, especially if they were suspected of sleeping with black men.[24]

In one particularly cruel case argued before North Carolina's Court of Appeals, Nancy Midgett sued to gain back custody of her two young children, who had been bound out by the county level court as laborers. While Midgett, an unskilled single mother, technically qualified as a poor white, her children were not taken away simply due to her economic circumstances. Instead, the forced binding out of her mixed race children – a practice just one step removed from selling a slave's children to a

---

[23] Ira Berlin, *Many Thousands Gone: The First Two Centuries of Slavery in North America* (Cambridge, MA: Harvard University Press, 1998), 44–5; Genovese, *Roll, Jordan, Roll*, 422; Forret, *Race Relations*, 88.

[24] "Sold from the Block at Four Years Old," *American Slave*, Vol. 19 (Fisk), 70–1; Adeline Johnson, *Ibid.*, Vol. 2 (AK), Part 4, 56; Olmsted, *A Journey*, 507–9.

different master – was primarily intended as a punishment for Midgett's sexual improprieties across racial lines. She had already given birth to two free black children, and she still had the ability to birth more. Slaveholders must have felt the need to teach her a lesson. As Nancy Midgett pitifully pleaded for mercy, she successfully demonstrated to the Court "that for the last three years she has been living near her father, in a house built by him for her; that he has during that time taken charge of her children, and kept them diligently and industriously employed; that he is himself an honest, respectable and industrious man, well able to take care of her and her children." Despite abundant evidence demonstrating that the children were being well cared for, the presence of free black children (as well as the possibility of more) was too much for the state's slave owning judicial officers to bear. Their racist judgement was affirmed. Considerations about a parent or guardian's "honest and industrious occupation," the Court held, did not apply when the "child is a bastard."[25]

Often directly related to interracial sex is the little-explored prevalence of infanticide in the plantation South. A full-length study of the topic would undoubtedly add a new dimension to historians' understanding about race and the frequency of interracial sex. Just a cursory review of coroner's reports and inquisitions from the late antebellum period reveals that among white women, infanticide was far from an uncommon occurrence. Even though, as Genovese noted, "With childbirth deaths so common from natural causes, the deed could not easily be detected," many cases reveal the obvious, brutal murders of mixed-race babies by their white mothers. Perhaps these killings were meant to protect the woman's honor or save her from legal prosecution, or perhaps they were supposed to "save" the baby from having to grow up as a black individual in a white world. One fact, however, was obvious: the birth of an interracial child could completely ruin a white woman's entire life, essentially causing her to be banished from society. Some women, therefore, took drastic measures to control their own futures.[26]

Giving birth to a mixed race child in the antebellum Deep South, it seems, was a very risky and traumatic undertaking, as two cases out of South Carolina affirm. Matilda Reynolds was investigated for killing her newborn in Edgefield District. Reynolds was around 30 years old,

---

[25] *Midgett v. McBryde*, 3 Jones NC 21, Dec. 1855 [22], in Helen Tunncliff Catterall, *Judicial Cases Concerning American Slavery and the Negro*. Vols. I-V, (1926–37; reprint, Buffalo: William S. Hein & Co., 1998), Vol. II, 192.

[26] Genovese, *Roll, Jordan, Roll*, 497.

married to a landless farmer in his mid-50s, and the mother to numerous children. In April, when Matilda Reynolds went into labor, Amanda Riddle attended her. She was present for the birth of a "very large and healthy" baby boy, who was so animated that he "sucked on a piece of meat." The next time she saw the child, Riddle claimed he looked "darker," prompting her to declare, "I am of opinion it is mixed blood and thought so from the first moment I saw it." Another witness who lived with family admitted that the new mother had requested laudanum from the local doctor. Laudanum, a common prescription for sickness and pain in the antebellum period, was opium dissolved in alcohol. Upon receiving the laudanum, Reynolds mixed it with catnip tea, and spit it into her baby's mouth, killing the infant instantly with an overdose of opioids. Dr. Matthew M. Abney testified as the final witness. He said that Matilda's older son came to him for laudanum, and inquired if his mother could give some to the baby. "I told him not a drop, the child had no use for laudanum to give it <u>none</u>," Abney reported. The doctor concluded his testimony with another damning piece of evidence, confirming that Matilda's child had "all the marks and appearances [that] indicate mixed or African blood." Despite overwhelming evidence of infanticide, however, it does not seem as if any further legal action was taken against Matilda Reynolds. While her personal life was likely left in shambles, she escaped from the ordeal legally unscathed.[27]

In 1854, a similar scenario took place in the state's upcountry. There, Elizabeth Campbell, a poor white girl about 17 years old, had given birth to a baby girl. Quite morbidly, when she had been asked several weeks prior to delivery if she was pregnant, Campbell responded that "if she was nobody should ever see it." Although Campbell was alone when she delivered the baby, testimony from the midwife, who arrived sometime after the birth, indicated that the baby *was* born alive – and killed maliciously. The midwife reported that by the time she got to Campbell's home, the infant was dead. Yet her tiny body was still warm, and marked by finger-sized bruises. Another witness scandalously provided the motive for the infanticide by professing she "cannot say whether the child was or is a white child or a colored child." With Pandora's Box wide open,

[27] "April 19, 1857 – Infant Male of Matilda Reynolds," Edgefield County, Coroner's inquisition books, 1844–1902, SCDAH (underlining in original); W.J. Rorabaugh, *The Alcoholic Republic: An American Tradition* (New York: Oxford University Press, 1979), 177; "April 19, 1857 – Infant Male of Matilda Reynolds"; Seventh Census of the United States, 1850: Edgefield County, South Carolina.

subsequent witnesses all weighed in on whether or not they thought the baby girl was mixed race. Finally, against overwhelming evidence to the contrary, the inquest ultimately declared that the infant had died "by misfortune or accident." Perhaps the jury wanted to downplay the topic of interracial sex as much as possible. Maybe they were tacitly approving of what these women did to protect southern society from the menace of "free black" children.[28]

Unfortunately, there are literally scores of these interracial infanticide cases throughout every county of the Deep South. Victoria Bynum rightly demonstrated in *Unruly Women* that the prospect of poor white women giving birth to free black babies was too fearsome for some slaveholders to bear. Indeed, relationships involving black men and poor white women often led to arrests. But slaves and free black men were rarely charged with raping white women of any class before the Civil War. Forret found that between 1830 and 1865, not many more than three dozen slaves were hanged for rape (or attempted rape) in Virginia. Even fewer were executed in the Carolinas. Poor white women "proved far more likely" than upper-class women to allege sexual assault by a male slave, Forret claimed, adding that "[s]urely some of these allegations were false." Seemingly, a few poor white women attempted to use rape as a deflection of their guilt in interracial relationships.[29]

If the woman conceived a child, however, the rape defense generally was negated, as medical literature at the time held that the female orgasm was necessary for conception. Overall, masters seemed likely to give black men a chance at defending themselves against rape charges in the antebellum period, generally allowing them trials (unlike during the postbellum era, when due process would be denied systematically). Because the slave was first and foremost a valuable laborer, if the slaveholder wanted to punish the accused rapist, they likely did it without the interference of government. From the economic perspective of a slave owner, whipping the offender was much preferable to hanging him. Masters had no desire to needlessly execute a valuable laborer for the rape of a lowly white

[28] "Dead Female Infant of Elizabeth Campbell," Greenville County, Court of General Sessions, Coroner's Inquisitions, 1849–1941, SCDAH; Seventh Census of the United States, 1850: Greenville County, South Carolina; Eighth Census of the United States, 1860: Greenville County, South Carolina. Despite her young age, Campbell had a 3-year-old son already, and had previously said if she "ever had another child she would kill it." Turner Duncan, the poor white man who had first found the infant's lifeless body, claimed the baby was "a black child."

[29] Bynum, *Unruly Women*; Forret, *Race Relations*, 190.

woman until after emancipation, when poor white women finally enjoyed the many privileges of whiteness, and black men were no longer financial assets.[30]

Conversely, when poor white men raped or slept with slave women, their offspring would be considered slaves, legally, socially, and economically – factors that likely helped relax the attitudes of the master class towards poor white male/enslaved female sexual relationships. Forret claimed that these interactions took place far more commonly than the legal records would lead historians to believe. Poor white men, it seemed, did have the social prerogative – as white men – to rape black women, who in turn, had no legal recourse. When the relationship was born of mutual desire and choice, these pairs were rarely charged with sexual criminal acts at all, with one exception. When poor white men slept or lived with *free* black women, their offspring would be free blacks, too, occasionally prompting local officials to charge the lovers with criminal acts.[31]

Poor whites' sexual relationships with upper-class white Southerners were seemingly infrequent when compared to their interracial relationships, and they were usually limited to wealthy men and poor white women. Although occasional relationships and even rare marriages between the two groups occurred, whites in the Deep South generally courted and married people from the same socioeconomic class. Upper-class men, however, had the power and the money to engage in various sexual relationships with poor white women, from outright rape to prostitution to a concubine-type of relationship. These relationships could be economically beneficial to the female, but they could also be based solely on the overwhelming power of the wealthy white male. In a world where rape was a daily fear among slave women, it is not hard to imagine that poor white women had similar fears when coming into contact with powerful men. Christine Stansell found that in antebellum New York, working class women often had to go outside the household economy to help the family earn a living, putting them into frequent contact with upper-class men, many of whom paid their wages. Rape in this type of power dynamic was common and almost psychologically accepted as a part of life for the seemingly powerless. Women in these situations, Stansell argued, faced dual hurdles of dependency – being female *and*

[30] *Ibid.*, 206.
[31] *Ibid.*, 189. See Chapters 5 and 7 for more information on the criminality of interracial sex.

Everyday Life: Material Realities

being poor. They had no real recourse in the legal system, whether for justice in rape cases or for issues concerning child support. A similar situation seemed to have existed in the South. Poor white John Hank reported that his mother "was a lone woman with seven children to maintain – the man that was said to be my father had negroes and property and never did anything for me."[32]

Bynum theorized that poverty "defeminized" antebellum southern women in several ways; they were considered sexually "deviant" or depraved as a matter of course, and always assumed to be promiscuous. Formerly enslaved South Carolinian Sena Moore confirmed this assertion, recalling that a "good white lady told me one time, that a bad white woman is a sight worse and more 'low downer' than a bad nigger woman can ever get to be in this world." Poor whites' sexual relationships and marriages to other poor whites likely formed the foundation to these types of sentiments, for a variety of reasons. Perhaps most importantly, the majority of poor whites never formally married – in the church or legally. As the *New York Times* reported in 1854, "the number of illegitimate children among" southern non-slaveholders "was very great; and that many of them living together as man and wife, are never ceremoniously married." Scholars like Bynum deemed these "informal and fleeting marriages" consistent with "the precarious nature of domestic life in a region known for its economically distressed and highly transient laboring population."[33]

In an ever-changing, sometimes violent, often drunken environment, poor whites needed to be flexible in their living arrangements. In contrast to the low divorce rates of the upper class, poor whites' relationships were similar to slaves' in some respects. Many of the men lived "abroad" for at least part of the year working short-term jobs or looking for employment, leaving women and/or oldest children alone to head households. And poor whites were far more likely than the upper or even yeoman classes to have multiple partners, or short-term "spouses" throughout their lives. Slaves, of course, generally had no choice in these matters, and – in some ways – poor whites did not have much of a choice, either. Their circumstances dictated behavior that made simple survival the paramount

[32] Christine Stansell, *City of Women: Sex and Class in New York, 1789–1860* (New York: Knopf, 1986); Elliot and Moxley, *Tennessee*, Vol. 3, 996.

[33] Bynum, *Unruly Women*, 109–10; Sena Moore, *American Slave*, Vol. 3 (SC), Part 3, 211; "The South," *New York Times*, Jan. 26, 1854; Victoria Bynum, "Mothers, Lovers, and Wives: Images of Poor White Women in Edward Isham's Autobiography, in Bolton, *The Confessions of Edward Isham*, 68.

objective. Edward Isham's "wife," for example, was abandoned by her husband as he escaped the law. It was only natural for her to find another man to support and provide for her – regardless of the institution of marriage. When Isham and her new lover fought over her, she relished the attention, as they confirmed her worth in a world that rendered her valueless. As Bynum wrote, poor white women often found the "ability to manipulate or instigate male struggles over 'ownership' of them" as a "major sphere of power." Watching two men engage in violence over them likely gave poor white women a special sense of importance.[34]

Poor white men, however, did not just fight *over* women. At times, they fought *with* women. At other times, they were simply abusive. Cases of egregious domestic violence, while relatively infrequent in southern court papers, appear with regularity in coroners' records. Despite the various restrictions on poor white men's autonomy and power, it seems they were given free rein to control their wives and children in violent fashion. Local governments and the criminal justice system were slow to intervene in domestic disputes. Even when they finally did, abusive men often had a decent chance of walking away from murders without being charged. The prevalence of binge drinking by the middle antebellum period certainly contributed to incidents of domestic violence, especially in severe cases. James Pitts, a mechanic from Memphis and the son of overseer, admitted that out of the poor whites in his community, there "were a few who would lie and steal, get drunk and lie in the gutter and abuse their families."[35]

Pitts's claims are well supported by the hundreds of cases appearing in coroner's records across the region where horrific domestic violence seemed to go hand in hand with severe alcohol abuse. In Laurens District, South Carolina, Maria Stephens suffered a miserable existence in constant fear for her own safety. She and her husband Robert appeared to be from the upper-economic tier of poor whites. Robert was a very violent man, and his abuse escalated until he finally murdered his wife in 1833. At the coroner's inquest, one neighbor testified that she had recently found Maria hiding out in the briar patches, claiming "her husband was in a state of intoxication, and had been in a great rage, and seemed to vent it at her." Confessing that she "would have killed herself" long ago "if she had not believed in the existence of God," Maria Stephens was truly ready to flee her dangerous situation. Tragically, before she made it to safety, her

---

[34] *Ibid.*, 89.   [35] Elliot and Moxley, *Tennessee*, Vol. 4, 1739–40.

short life ended. As reported by a poor white boy who was bound out to the Stephenses, on the day of her death Maria's husband Robert had beaten "his wife with a wagon whip, for about half an hour, sometimes turning the butt and striking her on the head." Later that night, he "swore that he wished she was dead and in hell." A final witness corroborated that the abuse in the Stephens's household had been frequent, as Robert often "beat her until she could not stand ... running her off and keeping her out at nights."[36]

Just a few years later in the same county, Jenny Smith died from similar circumstances. The coroner described bruises on Jenny's corpse that were three to four weeks old, as well as new bruises on her neck "about the size of the end of a man's finger." Although one witness testified that Jenny's husband John had severely choked her two days before her death, and another witness told of how John had thrown Jenny onto a rock, wounding her abdomen and breast, John Smith was absolved of all wrongdoing. Once again, despite overwhelming evidence to the contrary, the coroner's report concluded that Jenny Smith died from "disease."[37]

In an uncertain world filled with death and violence, physical pain was an accepted part of poor Southerners' daily lives. And physical brutishness, it seems, was fully tolerated in a slave society. Stephanie McCurry proposed that yeoman farmers derived their sense of white masculinity from the "inviolability of the household, the command of dependents, and the public prerogatives of manhood." As the undisputed master of his home, she argued, the yeoman was able to experience a modicum of the power that the patriarchal planters held, and that was enough to keep their interests aligned. Poor whites, however, were constantly on the move searching for work, and thus could not always function as masters of their own homes. When they were home, local law enforcement clearly allowed them some leeway and autonomy – but only when it came to reprimanding their wives and children.[38]

Domestic violence, of course, was not limited to women; anger could turn physical and be directed at anyone less powerful, especially young children. Thomas Woolbright, a notably abusive man from Union District, South Carolina, brutally killed his son Henry in 1843. Henry's short life had been filled with constant terror and frequent assaults from his father. One of the first witnesses in the coroner's inquest testified that

---

[36] "April 20, 1833," Laurens County, Court of General Sessions, Coroner's Inquisitions, ca. 1800–1901, SCDAH.
[37] "Jan. 7, 1839," *Ibid.*   [38] McCurry, *Masters of Small Worlds*, 304.

Thomas "was generally cruel and hard on the deceased and often abused by language some of his children calling them bastards and [there] have been bruises on the deceased before." Henry's mother Milly admitted that Thomas had "disowned" Henry "as his child and had always a great spite at it and often whipped it for groaning and pulled its hair." The pitiful child was so terrified of his father that he "was never inclined to eat anything often Tom abused him so bad."[39]

In a chillingly similar story, young Warren Kirkland of Edgefield, South Carolina, was beaten to death by his father William Kirkland in 1858. The 1850 census listed William as a propertyless farmer from Georgia with five children to feed. At the time of the murder, William would have been in his early 30s; Warren was only 9 years old. As the coroner's inquest into Warren's death unfolded, witnesses recounted his father's violent history, which also included the murder of his wife. Mrs. Benjamin Barton recalled that on the day of Warren's passing, the boy's father "had beaten him severely that morning." She further claimed that Warren's recently deceased mother, Mrs. Kirkland, had fully realized that she eventually would die at the hands of her violent husband. Mrs. Barton then testified that William "was in the habit of severely beating" young Warren, and the abuse had become especially frequent since his mother's death. The inquest ended with the questioning of William Kirkland, Jr., the older brother of Warren. After confirming that his father used to beat his mother "very severely," William Jr. explained that one week before his brother's death, his father beat the boy "very severely of the head with an old heavy chain." Then, two days before Warren died his father beat him with the chain over the head yet again. The poor child likely died from excessive bleeding of the brain, yet somehow the inquest ruled that the young boy came to his death "by means unknown."[40]

While many poor whites doubtless never experienced such abuse, a poverty-ridden, often-weakened family structure still left the majority of poor children with few opportunities at ever improving their station in life. Disparities in inherited wealth left the playing field so unequal that poor whites had very little hope of ever rising above the class into which he was born. A southern child born into affluence in the antebellum

[39] "1843 Henry Woolbright," Union County, Court of General Sessions, Coroner's Inquisitions, 1806–1965, SCDAH.
[40] "Nov. 16, 1858," Edgefield County, Coroner's inquisition books, 1844–1902, SCDAH; Seventh Census of the United States, 1850: Edgefield County, South Carolina.

period generally could count on living in a two-parent household, having a warm place to sleep, adequate clothing, and enough to eat. Because their diets were better, they were much healthier than their poorer white counterparts, who commonly suffered from pellagra, rickets, hookworm, and other vitamin deficiencies. Wealthy children not only benefitted from the finest material goods, but they also had the ability to spend their formative years getting an education – not laboring in a field to make the families' rent, or attempting to help keep the family fed.

Education and literacy among impoverished whites is discussed at length in the next chapter. It should be noted, however, that poor whites' illiteracy was often mentioned in tandem with their apparent lack of religion. While it is incredibly hard to estimate how many poor whites attended church, and how many considered themselves Christians, evidence suggests that the number is low. There was certainly a percentage of the upper-economic tier of landless whites who identified with a church, but the truly impoverished masses seemed to rarely attend religious services. The inability to read the Bible, combined with insufficient finances to actually buy the book, certainly added to their indifference. On rare occasions when poor whites do appear in church records throughout the Deep South, it is often in reference to their being reprimanded. From the more benign offenses of drinking to excess, fighting, and living a sexually sinful life to more overt acts of defiance such as defecating in the middle of the sanctuary, poor whites were occasionally suspended or ejected from congregations and sometimes even charged with crimes.

Perhaps more importantly, because they often lived in the backwoods and on the outskirts of town, many poor whites would have had a long journey to church. As Union soldier George Pepper explained, much of their lack of religion stemmed from isolation: "The country is comparatively barren, and little inhabited." He recalled talking to one "family from North Carolina, who never saw a church, never heard a sermon, and had never heard of the Redeemer." Although it is likely that most poor whites believed in a monotheistic God and perhaps even considered Jesus as their Christ and Savior, organized religion did not seem to be an important factor in many of their lives, perhaps less important than folklore and ethnic traditions. "Of course they have among them nothing that can be called religion or education. The nearest approach to these is, that sometimes a Methodist or Baptist meeting may be held near them – say, once or twice in three months," Pepper wrote. "And to these meetings they add an hour of Sunday-school on each visit. In a collection of eighteen families, I found but one person who could read, and none that could write."[41]

Industrialist William Gregg raised this point in 1851. Claiming that nearly one-half of all of South Carolina's whites were idle and unproductive, Gregg recommended that "Christianizing" the poor would help turn them into useful factory laborers. As Orville Vernon Burton found, Gregg practiced what he preached, as "The majority of workers at Graniteville were church members, especially so for people who were promoted to weavers, spinners, and loom fixers." Becoming a Christian – and adopting the attendant chaste and industrious behaviors associated with evangelicalism – clearly helped some poor whites secure jobs with slightly better pay. For the majority of poor whites, however, labor was yet another factor that may have kept them from Sunday morning services.[42]

While illiteracy, physical distance, and social segregation explained part of poor whites' seeming apathy toward organized religion, it is also important to note that Sunday was a working man's only day off. Considering that employers usually paid wages on Saturdays, some workers were likely too exhausted to be bothered with anything other than resting or indulging in earthly pleasures, like drinking, gambling, and carousing. Others were simply too hung over to show up to a Sunday morning service. Well known for their weariness toward anything "organized" or "institutionalized," poor whites may have viewed the church in the same way they viewed government: with unease and trepidation. As Bertram Wyatt-Brown observed, "Many ... displayed indifference, if not overt hostility, toward 'institutional religion' generally. Evangelicals' unwavering strictures against the sinfulness of drinking, fiddling and dancing – all among many poor whites' favorite pastimes – deterred them from embracing evangelical religion en masse. And poor whites as a group never proved particularly dogmatic."[43]

Given all of the reasons poor whites had to eschew organized religion, they frequently participated in tent revivals and mass meetings, likely due to social reasons. Whether visiting with old friends and family members, courting new beaus, or selling alcohol and produce to other revivalists, mass religious meetings undoubtedly attracted many poor whites, if only

---

[41] Pepper, *Personal Recollections*, 242; Conway, *Testimonies*, 122, Web.
[42] Quoted in Weston, *The Poor Whites*, 3, web; Burton, *In My Father's House*, 54; 60: Burton further noted that the majority of interest in evangelizing poor whites occurred after the Civil War.
[43] Wyatt-Brown quoted in Forret, *Race Relations*, 65.

for the "frolic." While historians will probably never arrive at an accurate estimate of how many poor whites attended church on a regular basis, they do know that some poor whites clung to beliefs and superstitions attributable to the premodern era. A small number of this population was staunchly opposed to any type of organized religion. Poor white Edward Isham recalled a tiny town on the north Georgia/Alabama border, reporting that "No preacher could ever live in Pinetown, one lived there once and they tore down his fences and run him off." Some poor whites were more than just intolerant of organized religion; they even took drastic measures to keep it out of their communities. The majority of poor whites, however, were not as overt in their behaviors. They simply had no reason to be involved in church. They could not read, they likely did not have decent Sunday attire, and some may not have understood the Scriptures. As late as 1852, Georgia's Honorable J.H. Lumpkin described poor whites as that "degraded, half-fed, half-clothed, and ignorant population—without Sabbath Schools, or any other kind of instruction, mental or moral."[44]

Hinton Helper, of course, based part of his argument on the premodern ways of the uneducated and illiterate poor whites. "Poverty, ignorance, and superstition, are the three leading characteristics of the non-slaveholding whites of the South," he opined. Poor whites' superstitions appeared similar to the ones reported in slave narratives. "All are more of less impressed with a belief in witches, ghosts, and supernatural signs," Helper wrote. "Few are exempt from habits of sensuality and intemperance, nor have anything like adequate ideas of the duties which they owe either to their God, to themselves, or to their fellow-men." Thus, from the few accounts concerning religion and superstition, a decent percentage of poor whites probably still viewed the world in certain premodern ways on the eve of the Civil War. Perhaps this mindset helped further isolate the poor from the problems of the wider, capitalist, rapidly modernizing world. As an 1855 editorial out of Washington, D.C. pointed out: "Anti-Slavery men have long insisted that Slavery is almost as much the curse of the poor white man as of the slave – for it deprives him of education, of labor, of freedom of thought, and religious instruction." However, the writer lamented, "it has been impossible to reach this class ... we trust that the day is not distant when they will begin to act."[45]

---

[44] Bolton, *The Confessions of Edward Isham*, 10; quoted in Helper, *The Impending Crisis*, 378.

[45] *Ibid.*, 381; "Mobbing the Methodists," *The National Era* (D.C.) Aug. 2, 1855.

Unquestionably, poor whites were ostracized from white society in significant ways. Planters treated them very differently than they treated slave- and land-holding yeomen. And even though small land-holders were hardly seen as equals to the large slave owners, the Genoveses concluded that because they aspired to become plantation owners themselves, yeomen "were led step by step into willing acceptance of a subordinate position in society." Every slaveholder, it seemed, no matter if he owned but one slave, cast his lot with the region's affluent planters. Ownership of human property led a man to believe that his interests were inextricably bound to those of other slave owners. Moreover, a true southern middle class of merchants, lawyers, and doctors had become well established in the Deep South by the middle antebellum era. The strong presence of these middle classes signified the financial success of slavery. Almost all of the men in this class either directly or indirectly made their money from the region's cash crop economy, linking them to the wealthy master class. The Proto-Dorian Bond *did* bind the new middle and upper classes together in white solidarity. Any "pandering" by affluent planters – for votes, support, or anything else – was generally done at this level; wealthy slaveholders had almost no direct involvement of this sort with poor whites. According to David Brown, Hinton Helper, the "only southern intellectual to theorize and conceptualize non-slaveholders fully as a distinct class," also realized that the poorest whites were illiterate and "cut off from wider society." Because the truly poor made such unlikely class revolutionaries, Helper directed *The Impending Crisis* at the more affluent yeomen farmers, who could actually influence the future of the region.[46]

This deep division within white society – land- and slaveholders on one side, lower-middling and poor whites on the other – helps explain the difference between the classes and their conceptions of honor. The pre-eminent scholar on southern honor, Wyatt-Brown, argued that the South differed fundamentally from the North because of honor's prevalence. From the late colonial period through the end of the nineteenth century, he held, the South was distinctive because it contained elements of pre-modern culture. The North had evolved and industrialized by the Jacksonian period, shattering the bonds of order and deference that existed in a traditional, agricultural society. The South, by contrast, remained largely rural, leaving primitive, masculine honor as one of the very few ways to

[46] Brown, "Hinton Rowan Helper," 49; 42; Genovese, *Fruits of Merchant Capital*, 263; Brown, "Hinton Rowan Helper," 39; 44.

make society predictable. Living in smaller, agricultural communities, a man's honor was his worth; it was his credit, almost independent of his wealth. Its importance cannot be overvalued. In face-to-face societies, honor determined a man's rank and place. Physical manifestations of honor were vital, and many whites defended or proved their honor with violence. The "type" of violence chosen by the men was generally indicative of their class. From the time of the early republic, slaveholders attempted to distinguish themselves as upper class by a genteel code of manners. By the later antebellum era, dueling became the socially appropriate way for the upper class to solve disputes over honor. No bodily contact with one's adversary occurred. Much like the whip, the gun allowed the region's elite to punish and mete out revenge without ever having to touch another human being. Touch – the feel of another person's skin – may have made the humanity of the victim too hard to deny. Yet as the upper classes further removed themselves from hand-to-hand combat, poorer whites seemed ever more likely to engage in extremely vicious brawls. Rough and violent fighting, therefore, functioned as a way for the lower classes to prove their social significance. Thus, according to Wyatt-Brown, wealthy whites ruled themselves according to the tenants of gentility, while the poor remained wedded to the brutal concept of primal honor.[47]

Although Wyatt-Brown's theories about southern honor are certainly compelling, his analysis does not allow for a full consideration of the ways slavery influenced notions of honor. The horrific daily violence necessary simply to maintain the slave system surely added the vitriolic nature of the region. Violence was *the* essential component of both slavery and slave societies, and there were no limits as to who that violence affected. As Nell Irvin Painter wrote, "slavery rested on the threat and the abundant use of physical violence," which extended beyond the relationship of master and slave, straining every social bond in the South, whether between employer and laborer, husband and wife, or parent and child. Connecting the viciousness of southern honor to the bloodiness of the peculiar institution confirms the extremely high degree of social control necessary for the perpetuation of chattle slavery in America.[48]

---

[47] Bertram Wyatt-Brown, *Honor and Violence in the Old South* (New York: Oxford University Press, 1986).

[48] Nell Irvin Painter, *Southern History Across the Color Line* (Chapel Hill: University of North Carolina Press, 2002), 6: "Any sojourn in southern archives covers the researcher in blood, and slavery, particularly, throws buckets of blood in the historian's face."

Furthermore, simply living in the early to mid-nineteenth century was enough almost to numb an individual to violence and death. For the overwhelming majority of Southerners, life was predicated on hardship, sickness, and the loss of loved ones. Honor thrived in places like the rural South, penned Wyatt-Brown, because it developed from "a fatalistic world view" in which pain and suffering were an accepted and expected part of life. No white Southerners, of course, suffered more than the poor. Elliot Gorn noted the strong correlation between poor white men and the most brutal types of violence. "Rather than be overwhelmed by violence, acquiesce in an oppressive environment, or submit to death as an escape from tragedy," he asked, "why not make a virtue of necessity and flaunt one's unconcern? To revel in the lore of deformity, mutilation, and death was to beat the wilderness at its own game." Owning no slaves, no property, and little else, poor white men's culture of drunken fights and grog shop brawls provided a way socially to structure their worlds. It gave some sense of meaning and order to lives that were generally chaotic and unpredictable. Choosing "not to ape the dispassionate, antiseptic, gentry style but to invert it," lower-class white men rejected dueling for the "rough-and-tumble," or, simply, "gouging." These incredibly brutal fist fights, which ended when one opponent was knocked out or unable to continue, were "no holds barred" affairs that often involved biting, choking, head butting, and the "sine qua non of rough-and-tumble fighting," gouging out an opponent's eye. "Eye gouging," concluded Gorn, "was the poor and middling whites' own version of a historical southern tendency to consider personal violence socially useful – indeed, ethically essential."[49]

Among the white underclass, therefore, fighting and drinking and generally acting "tough" became the way by which poor white men gauged their honor. The liquor trade and alcoholism are discussed at length in a later chapter, but the importance of alcohol to many of these bloody fights cannot be overstated. As one scholar wrote, "a group's preference for a particular drug and appreciation of its properties were determined by the group's ideology, values, and psychological set. The caste that valued aggressive behavior drank alcohol." Gorn further explained this common connection between liquor and violence:

---

[49] Quoted in Elliot J. Gorn, "'Gouge and Bite, Pull Hair and Scratch': The Social Significance of Fighting in the Southern Backcountry," *American Historical Review* 90, Supplement to Vol. 90 (Feb. 1985): 40; 32; 41; 20; 42.

With families emotionally or physically distant and civil institutions weak, a man's role in the all-male society was defined less by his ability as a breadwinner than by his ferocity. The touchstone of masculinity was unflinching toughness, not chivalry, duty, or piety. Violent sports, heavy drinking, and impulsive pleasure seeking were appropriate for men whose lives were hard, whose futures were unpredictable, and whose opportunities were limited.

Fights within the poor white community provided relief from the boredom of daily life. They were a form of free and lively entertainment. More importantly, however, they helped create a way of measuring a man's worth without relying on occupation or wealth.[50]

[50] Rorabaugh, *Alcoholic Republic*, 179; Gorn, "'Gouge and Bite,'" 36.

5

Literacy, Education, and Disfranchisement

There is but one way for the oligarchy to perpetuate slavery in the Southern States, and that is by perpetuating absolute ignorance among the non-slaveholding whites.

— Hinton Helper[1]

The interests of slavery cannot be made at one with the interests of free society; there cannot be any legitimate institution of free society — as the free press, free speech, free school — which is not a bomb for Slavery.

— Moncure Conway[2]

"In the South," proclaimed the abolitionist Henry Ward Beecher, "ignorance is an institution. They legislate for ignorance the same way we legislate for school-houses." To protect and preserve slavery, the master class understood that preventing education among poor whites helped stifle the spread of abolitionist ideas. Illiterate or semiliterate, the white masses remained largely uninformed and politically apathetic. Slaveholders realized that allowing non-slaveholders access to information would disrupt their own fortunes, and thus imposed a strict system of censorship throughout the region. As Beecher concluded, "Knowledge is not only power in the South but powder, also, liable to blow false institutions to atoms."[3]

The overwhelming majority of poor southern whites, it seems, were grossly uneducated. Many of them did not receive enough of an education even to sign their names. Left wallowing in ignorance, the impoverished

---

[1] Helper, *The Impending Crisis*, 373.   [2] Conway, *Testimonies*, 118.
[3] "Anti-Slavery Lectures," *New York Times*, Jan. 17, 1855, 5.

had little chance to become anything else in the world besides unskilled, low-wage laborers. By continuing to allow the illiteracy of the white masses, slaveholders wittingly or unwittingly reinforced this cycle of poverty. They obviously knew that this lack of education among the poor would help them maintain their position at the top of society. This pervasive ignorance undoubtedly decreased poor whites' ability to understand the more complicated arguments against slavery, and certainly precluded them from clearly formulating their own reasons to oppose the institution. One abolitionist from western North Carolina expressed his frustration over being unable to communicate with poor whites about class issues and economic interests. "The more I think and see of slavery the more I detest it. . . . I am determined to oppose slavery somewhere," he lamented, "But for the unfathomable ignorance that pervades the mass of the poor, deluded, slavery-saddled whites around me, I would not suppress my sentiments another hour."[4]

Slaveholders' obsession with censorship further suggests that they preferred to keep the masses in ignorance. Upper South states had censorship laws as well, but the Deep South's penal code carried savage penalties. Most of this legislation was passed in the 1830s, likely in response to the proliferation of abolitionist literature. These laws were so resolute and comprehensive that the master class did not have to strengthen them throughout the late antebellum period. During John Abbott's travels through the South, he was struck by the high levels of illiteracy, and linked that issue to the region's pervasive censorship. "It is very rare that I see here any newspapers offered in the cars; there is no aspect of intelligence at the stopping places, and the poor whites seem as totally destitute of ambition as are the slaves," he wrote. Numbering illiterate white South Carolinians in the "scores of thousands," he recognized how "it is easy for unprincipled men to rouse the masses to any violence." Indeed, "These wretched dupes are taught that those at the North, who are in favor of equal rights for all men, are their bitterest foes, that they wish to make them 'no better than the niggers.' . . . These unprincipled men do every thing in their power to prevent the poor whites from being undeceived." As a very well-traveled man, Abbott had some legitimacy in concluding that "There is not another spot on the globe where the censorship of speech, and of the press, is so rigorous." It was not until after the conclusion of the war that Northerners really began to

[4] Helper, *The Impending Crisis*, quoted on 375.

understand how extensively the South had been deliberately veiled in ignorance. As *The Christian Recorder* reported, "So completely had the power of free speech been subdued as one of the necessary means for the security of slavery, that no man dared to utter a public warning against the danger of such an experiment; and the poor white classes, as ignorant as the slaves, were easily led as sheep to the slaughter."[5]

Northern abolitionists had derided the South's strict system of censorship for decades prior to the Civil War, rightly noting that poor whites would have made likely allies – had they been literate and educated. "Anti-Slavery men have long insisted that Slavery is almost as much the curse of the poor white man as of the slave," an article from the *National Era* claimed, "for it deprives him of education, of labor, of freedom of thought, and religious instruction." However, "it has been impossible" for abolitionists "to reach this class. They rarely read, even if they have the faculty, there being no institutions or usages in the South calculated to cultivate a taste for knowledge among the poor." Yet given the "insolence of the slaveholders," the writer warned, "we trust that the day is not distant when" poor whites "will begin to act." According to another northern paper, the master class had good reason to prevent impoverished whites from reading about slavery. "They fear that a discussion of it would enlighten and awaken the poor white man to his interest, and that the 'patriarchal institution' would be doomed," the journalist penned, "hence his censorship of the press, this fettering of speech and mind."[6]

Indeed, the most staggering hurdle for poor white children to overcome was that they received little to no education, and most of them remained illiterate or only-barely-literate throughout their entire lives. As Helper famously wrote, "Thousands of them die at an advanced age, as ignorant of the common alphabet as if it had never been invented." Travelers and writers never hesitated to comment on the entrenched ignorance of the region's poor whites. During the Civil War, Union soldier George Pepper wrote that the Deep South's poor "are the most illiterate and depraved creatures I ever saw – mentally and morally. I don't remember of ever having seen their equal. Their conception of God, of redemption, and of this war, are heathenish." Northerners had long heard about how

---

[5] Eaton, *The Freedom of Thought Struggle*, 129–130; Abbott, *South and North*, 156–8, Web; "The War and Its Effects," *The Christian Recorder* (PA), July 22, 1865. The topic of censorship will be thoroughly covered in Chapter 7.

[6] "Mobbing the Methodists," *National Era*, Aug. 2, 1855; "American Slavery – Its Effects among the Non-Slaveholding Population of the South," *The North Star* (NY), March 10, 1848.

slaveholders refused to implement comprehensive education systems, but confronting the reality of the slave South's class divide was surely jarring. Pepper continued writing, in apparent disgust, over a Georgia family "who were so ignorant that they could not tell their ages. Captain Hill ... tells me that he conversed with an old woman of seventy years, who could not tell the ages of her children. She had never seen a shirt-collar." Even a fellow Southerner admitted poor whites "have among them nothing that can be called religion or education."[7]

William Eskew, the son of a non-slaveholder, described his education as "very poor for it was pay school and poor children could not pay the price per head." Former slaves also commented on the exclusivity of a formal education among whites. George Ward of Mississippi reported, "At first the rich white folks sent children to the female college, and the poor white people didn't go to school." If impoverished white children were lucky enough to receive some sort of education, it was often just for a couple of weeks or months of the year. One poor white from Tennessee explained that "A poor man had a hard time to qualify himself for business. When I began going to school our free schools never went longer than two months in the year. My parents was poor [so] I hardly ever [had] more than one month and a half schooling in the year." Freedman Isaac Johnson confirmed this lack of literacy. Out of all whites, he reckoned, "only about half or less than half, could read and write then. There were very few poor white folks who could read and write." Many thousands of antebellum court records support Johnson's contention. The vast majority of people charged with crimes, as well as many witnesses to crimes, were only able to provide an "X" –their mark – as a signature. More than 50 percent of white mill workers at Graniteville signed their names with a mark, despite having access to schools there. And though Helper numbered illiterate native white Southerners at approximately half a million, his figures were likely low given their basis on census returns.[8]

Surely, this lack of formal education became such a dividing line between the white classes that some poor whites did begin using their lack of education as a point of pride, attempting to instead glorify manual

---

[7] Helper, *The Impending Crisis*, 381; Pepper, *Personal Recollections*, 242–3, Web; Conway, *Testimonies*, 122.

[8] Elliot and Moxley, *Tennessee*, Vol. 2, 778; George Ward *American Slave*, Vol. 10 (MS), Supplement, Series 1, Part 5, 2177–8; Elliot and Moxley, *Tennessee*, Vol. 3, 969–70; Isaac Johnson, *American Slave*, Vol. 11 (NC), Part 2, 17; Richard M. Morris, "White Bondage in Ante-Bellum South Carolina," *South Carolina Historical and Genealogical Magazine* 49, No. 4 (Oct. 1948): 195, footnote 17; Helper, *The Impending Crisis*, 291.

labor, and living off the land. Unfortunately, dismissing the need for an education often became a self-fulfilling prophesy: some impoverished whites came to regard education with distain rather than disinterest. It seemed as if a small percentage of the poor would rather their children run free – hunting, fishing, and foraging – than becoming educated and then stuck inside a factory, working for the dreaded slaveholders. In the few areas where some sort of public schooling was available, most poor white children still stayed home, even during times they were not necessarily needed as laborers. Scattered records from schoolteachers reveal that some of the impoverished dropped out of school completely after being mercilessly teased by other, richer children.

An 1847 *National Era* article explained other reasons why poor whites may have preferred no formal schooling. Possessing "some notions of personal freedom," the writer noted, they still remained "very crude." They hated labor because it "degraded them, because it put them on an equality with the slaves." Using an anecdote to illustrate his point, the journalist told the story of a very smart poor boy, whom members of the upper class thought worthy enough to educate properly. Slaveholders proposed apprenticing him to "Mr. C," the local carriage maker, but the boy's father immediately balked:

"Never," he quickly, almost fiercely, rejoined, with a harsh oath, "My son shall never work by the side of your negroes, and Mr. — 's negroes, (calling certain planters' names whose slaves were being taught the trade,) and be ordered about by Mr. C., as he orders them about." He was fixed. No argument, entreaty, appeal to interest, could move him. The idea uppermost in his mind was the idea of class - that labor was degrading; and he would rather his son should be free in the forest, if ignorant, than debased in the city, though educated, by a menial task.

Thus, as poor whites continued to associate working for a boss with working like a slave, formal education supposedly became less and less important to them.[9]

The accuracy of this claim is highly suspect. Surely, for a portion of the poor white population, education seemed unnecessary, and they likely viewed the changes that followed literacy as unwanted. But for most of the region's impoverished, there was simply no choice regarding whether or not education was important or valuable. Even Orville Vernon Burton, who believed there was general harmony among whites in Edgefield District, South Carolina, admitted that poor white children rarely

---

[9] "The South," *National Era* (D.C.), Nov. 25, 1847.

received an education. Indeed, he wrote, "a striking correlation existed between illiteracy and poverty on the eve of the Civil War," and even those people listed as literate in the census included a percentage of individuals who could not read or write "distinctly."[10]

Helper similarly remarked that poor white children were "effectually excluded from the institutions of learning by their poverty." For instance, the relative isolation of many poor whites certainly added to their difficulty in attaining an education. Living on the fringes of communities and in the backwoods and mountains was hardly conducive to traveling to and from the school house, if there was one. But geographic isolation was not the only problem. Several other factors helped preclude many poor whites from ever achieving functional literacy. First, because poor white families often depended on the labor of their children for survival, impoverished children rarely had the luxury of actual time for education. Whether at home, in the fields, or hired out for wages, most children were essential to poor white households as laborers. If these children were fortunate enough ever to have attended school, they generally attended short-term public and subscription schools, which met for mere weeks in between planting and harvesting seasons. Second, a public school system needed funding, meaning that wealthy Southerners would have to raise the tax money. Not surprisingly, very few members of the slaveholding gentry wanted to pay more in taxes to educate the children of poor people who paid little to no taxes at all.[11]

Elijah Millington Walker, a young, self-made doctor living on the Mississippi frontier, had been born into a lower-middling class family in Tennessee. Although much of his modest success in moving into the professional middling classes came from his dogged determination and late nights spent reading and studying, his early educational experience provides some insight into the opportunities for the children of the lower-yeomen class. When Walker turned 5 years old, his father paid a man to teach him to read. Up until he turned 10 years old, Walker primarily worked in the fields with his father, but he was lucky enough to attend school for a few months each fall and winter. After his family moved to the Chickasaw Nation, Walker remained without any formal schooling until he was 13 years old, when enough whites had settled in the small area to hire a teacher, "who was as little qualified as an African to teach the English." In five weeks, he learned how to write and do arithmetic.

---

[10] Burton, *In My Father's House*, 83; 89.   [11] *Ibid.*, 399; Bailey, *Class*, 46.

Completely self-taught after that point, Walker occasionally had enough money to purchase a few textbooks and often attempted to borrow history books from a wealthy planter in town.[12]

Despite his humble upbringing, once he attained an education and rose into the middling class, Walker tried time and again to psychologically distance himself from the uneducated poor whites surrounding him. Wanting to move far away from Mississippi, primarily to escape paying several debts, he often reminded himself that he – an insolvent debtor – differed greatly from the truly indigent. "The people here are of a class that will never satisfy me nor can I live satisfied among them," he wrote in his diary. "They are, to speak generally, an ignorant people, complying with the dictates of honor at the end of the law, disregarding all the whisperings of conscience." But at least Walker had some sympathy for the uneducated and impoverished. In 1850, as he watched the intricate and expensive set up for a camp revival meeting, he criticized how the church's resources were profligately wasted. Both the time and money, Walker contended, would have been better spent to "build a house and give a teacher a good salary to teach the children of the neighborhood in all the departments of literature. Something of this nature is needed, the children are growing up in ignorance even of the first rudiments of our mother tongue."[13]

Still, most impoverished children did not benefit even from the limited opportunities that Walker received. "Thousands of poor families in Georgia are entirely dependent upon the labor of their children, for food, clothing and habitation," one paper lamented. "These children, composing a large class, can never be educated under this free school," it continued, if it "does not furnish food, clothing and habitation for the families to which such children belong." With just two sentences, the dire poverty of many of the Deep South's poor whites was laid bare. In reality, some were no doubt too lazy to get an education, but for the vast majority of illiterate children, there was never a chance to go to school. The outspoken Republican publisher Horace Greeley deemed the "great bulk of the poor whites of the South" as "altogether too ignorant to have any precise idea of the extent of their own degradation, and still less of the causes of it, and the means of its removal." Comparing their depravations to those of slaves, Greeley bemoaned that the impoverished were "unable to educate their children, hopeless of rising, and degraded by the very

---

[12] Walker, *A Bachelor's Life*, 4.   [13] *Ibid.*, 13; 90.

labor by which they earn their bread." Because the master class led "the poor whites by the nose," they effectively terrified non-slaveholders "with raw-head and bloody-bone stories about the Abolitionists." Slaveholders easily preserved the status quo "among people who cannot read and who are not permitted to hear. It is well known that in every country and every age," Greeley concluded, "the most degraded and the most ignorant have been the most opposed to needed reforms, especially if those reforms were to begin with asking a sacrifice of them."[14]

To understand truly the ramifications of high levels of illiteracy in the antebellum South, scholars first must arrive at a more accurate definition of literacy itself. Native Southerners and travelers alike typically estimated white illiteracy at rates much higher than census records indicated. This discrepancy was likely attributable to two factors. First, the census returns were deeply flawed, and second, the meaning of "literate" added to the confusion. A *New York Times* article from 1861 alleged that census records were of little use when it came to quantifying literacy rates. "These people, by their own confession to the United States Marshals, can neither read nor write; but we have no means of knowing how often the question as to education was omitted – how often a false or evasive answer was given, or how often the literary attainments were of a character to warrant a certificate of proficiency," the journalist proclaimed. Indeed, measuring literacy by asking individuals whether or not they can read and write is a deeply unsound policy from the start. Few people freely admit their own ignorance to a stranger, especially one employed by the government, and particularly so when they live in a prideful, honor-based society.[15]

As Clement Eaton pointed out, "Within the classification of 'illiterates,'" scholars *should* include those "who could barely read and sign their names, yet who were, to all practical purposes, as ignorant as the completely unschooled." The education reformer Horace Mann believed that the statistics of illiteracy during the late-antebellum period should be increased by one-third in recognition of this fact. Henry Ruffner, the antislavery President of Washington College, found the literacy part of census returns "to be grossly inaccurate." Refusing to rely on the erroneous statistics, he estimated that in antebellum Virginia, more than one-third of white adults

---

[14] "Public Education," *Daily Federal Union*, Dec. 11, 1858, 2; No Title, *Daily Tribune*, Jan. 30, 1856, 4.
[15] "Who Rule the South?," *New York Times*, Jan. 15, 1861. See the Appendix for a full explanation on flawed antebellum census records, and on how many poor people were never enumerated in the first place.

were completely illiterate. But W.E.B. DuBois surely claimed the highest estimate of illiterate whites. Calling poorer whites "largely ignorant and degraded," he believed that only one-quarter of southern whites were able to fully read and write. Perhaps more troubling, however, were reports that illiteracy and ignorance among non-slaveholders continued to increase over the course of the late antebellum period. An "evident deterioration is taking place" among poorer whites, an 1856 article reported, with "the younger portion ... being less educated, less industrious, and in every point of view less respectable than their ancestors."[16]

Basing her analysis partially on census records and partially on sales of reading materials, Beth Barton Schweiger claimed that by 1850, the South "boasted one of the highest rates of literacy in the world. More than 80 percent of free adults in the slave states could read." While Schweiger was certainly correct in her assessment of the learnedness of affluent Southerners, a thriving print culture among the upper-middling and wealthy classes reveals virtually nothing about overall literacy rates within the region. One might judiciously add that even the claim of a "high" southern literacy rate completely discounts the lives of nearly 4 million African Americans who were barred almost universally from ever having a chance to learn to read or write. Although she admitted that "Voices from across the region called for free public schooling to correct the 'brutish ignorance' of poor white people," Schweiger never questioned the veracity of the census records, or the truthfulness of its prideful respondents. "It has been difficult to see the South as a place full of readers and books because our convictions about reading cannot easily accommodate the idea of a literate slave society," she purported, because "Literacy is a metaphor for modernism." Indeed, to academics and intellectuals, literacy is modern. But in many ways, the unfettered capitalists running the southern slave system were prototypical modern men. Yet for the workers abused and debased by slavery, and the displaced laborers rendered unnecessary by an exploitative system, illiteracy has proven that it, too, can be fully and completely modern. In fact, capitalism generally thrives when the masses are kept illiterate and uneducated.[17]

[16] Eaton, *The Freedom of Thought Struggle*, 64; quoted on 64; quoted on 64–5; DuBois, *Black Reconstruction in America*, 26; "Philadelphia National Convention," *New York Times*, April 12, 1856; also see Harvey J. Graff, *The Literacy Myth: Cultural Integration and Social Structure in the Nineteenth Century* (New Brunswick: Transaction, 1991).

[17] Beth Barton Schweiger, "The Literate South: Reading before Emancipation," *Journal of the Civil War Era* 3, No. 3 (Sept. 2013): 331; 333; 337.

Regarding African Americans, historians have estimated that only 5 to 10 percent were at least partially literate by 1860. This number is quite striking, as literacy restriction laws for both slaves and free blacks were incredibly harsh and violently punitive. Enacted in the 1830s on the heels of the abolition movement, black anti-literacy laws existed in every Deep South state. Literate slaves and free blacks historically had been the instigators and leaders of slave rebellions, and slave owners devised strict legal codes preventing African Americans from becoming literate. Closely correlated to the master class's fears over black rebellion was the possibility that literate poor whites could teach black Southerners to read and write. Slaveholders had a vested economic interest in keeping slaves illiterate, but poorer whites did not. And even some slaves would have had the ability to pay impoverished whites – either in cash or in kind – for the education. As an article in the *Savannah Daily Republican* claimed, in the middle of the night slaves would escape to "the cabin of some poor white man, who teaches them to read and write by the light of the pine splinters, and receives his pay in massa's corn or tobacco."[18]

Moreover, slaveholders needed to keep non-slaveholders from reading the tracts of abolitionists, agrarians, and labor organizers. Instead, they wanted the poor masses dependent on them for information, moral guidance, and political beliefs. The master class had rational economic reasons for never funding a system of universal education for whites. Clearly, the singular, most important incentive for keeping impoverished whites illiterate was the maintenance of the slave system. One traveler to the region echoed the sentiments of many of the abolitionists from the 1830s and 1840s: the "destruction of slavery would follow inevitably the education of the poor whites." This belief had become a refrain for northern and European radicals and was touted even by Helper, but slaveholders still managed to keep the vast majority of the poor illiterate throughout the antebellum period. Even with all of their censorship laws, masters still worried the poor would read about universal rights or land reform policies, discover how badly they were being treated, and band together with people of the same economic class. The information poor whites might have gleaned from reading could have been shared with

---

[18] Janet Duitsman Cornelius, *When I Can Read My Title Clear: Literacy, Slavery, and Religion in the Antebellum South* (Columbia: University of South Carolina Press, 1991), 8–9: DuBois said 5 percent of blacks were literate prior to emancipation, but other historians such as Carter Woodson accepted the higher rate of 10 percent. "Remarkable Case of Instinct in a Bird," *Savannah Daily Republican*, Sept. 30, 1842, 2.

black Southerners, bringing the chances of a black/poor white coalition to a very uncomfortable level.[19]

Moncure Conway further revealed how mass illiteracy benefitted slaveholders, scandalously alleging that slaveholders deliberately kept poor whites uneducated. After publishing a pamphlet on the necessity of free schools in his home state, Conway's work was "virulently attacked as an effort to introduce into the South the worst phase of New-England society – as an effort to make a 'mob-road to learning.'" The slaveholders "plainly declared" that poor whites "must be kept ignorant; for if they were educated, they would revolutionize Southern society," he lamented. "After this I felt that the wretchedness and ignorance of the poor whites around me ... w[as] deliberately fostered by the higher classes. The matter assumed the nature of the battle between two classes." While many other southern politicians were loath to discuss the ignorance of the poor white masses in the first place, pro-slavery ideology tacitly endorsed the illiteracy of all whites not directly involved in slavery. To maintain safely the peculiar institution, the spread of knowledge had to be controlled and curtailed.[20]

Certainly, in a slave society, both ideas and words *were* dangerous. Any utterance against the southern labor system – a system predicated on slavery – could have endangered the job prospects, lines of credit, and even the life and liberty of the speaker. Given the master class's overt defensiveness, *any* complaint was liable to be misinterpreted. Poor whites and other non-slaveholders had to monitor carefully what they said, and the complete absence of a universal education system denied them the option of privately, or even anonymously, committing their thoughts and opinions to pages. They must have found it incredibly difficult to amass knowledge or to express opinions without worries over slaveholder retaliation. Bishop Whipple traveled throughout the cotton South in the early 1840s, and quickly realized that because of poorer whites' lack of literacy, southern politics easily remained the domain of the rich. He candidly admitted that "the backwoods people are easily gulled and made the dupes of for the benefit of designing men."[21]

William Jay, the abolitionist-attorney son of Chief Justice John Jay, attempted to reach the South's lower-middling and poorer classes in

[19] Edmund Kirke, *Among the Pines, or, South in Secession Time.* (New York: J.R. Gilmore, 1862).

[20] Conway, *Testimonies,* 33; 34; quoted on 33.

[21] Eaton, *The Freedom of Thought Struggle,* quoted on 83.

hopes of making them aware of the extent to which they were being fleeced. To accomplish this, he pointed out the deep inequities inherent in the slave system, accounting for every tactic the master class used to keep non-slaveholders in line. "The maxim that 'Knowledge is power,' has ever more or less influenced the conduct of aristocracies. Education elevates the inferior classes of society, teaches them their rights, and points out the means of enforcing them. Of course, it tends to diminish the influence of wealth, birth, and rank," he appealed. Slave owners' power "depends on the acquiescence of the major part of the white inhabitants in their domination. It cannot be, therefore, the interest or the inclination of the sagacious and reflecting among them, to promote the intellectual improvement of the inferior class." Instead, Jay purported, slaveholders "are careful not to afford the means of literary improvement to their fellow-citizens who are too poor to possess slaves, and who are, by their very ignorance, rendered more fit instruments for doing the will, and guarding the property of the wealthier class."[22]

With all of the master class's concern over literacy and public education, it is important to understand to what extent the South lagged behind the rest of the United States regarding these issues. In 1850, the United States listed one in ten men as illiterate. The future Confederacy clearly had the worst rates of white illiteracy in the nation, due to the lack of a comprehensive educational system. As James C. Cobb found, only 35 percent of region's whites were enrolled in school in 1860, compared with 72 percent throughout the rest of America. The average school year was also 70 percent longer outside of the slave South. While some Upper South states attempted establishing free schools throughout the later antebellum period, the majority of the Deep South's poor whites received little or no education. Yet even the few states that made overtures toward universal education faced challenges from every direction, especially concerning funding. North Carolina's school system, one of the South's only publicly funded ventures, was unfortunately both ineffective and rife with fraud. Established in the 1840s, much of the program's money was embezzled. Other public funds were used by private schools for wealthy children. Similarly, Louisiana's Constitutional Convention of 1845 provided for the permanent endowment of free schools, but it funded the endeavor by placing a $1 poll tax on white males, effectively disenfranchising thousands of poor whites and ensuring the schools would be

---

[22] Jay, *Address to the Non-slaveholders*, 8–9; 10, Web.

underfunded. Tennessee's fledgling system was fraught with problems as well; the 1860 census revealed that the yearly per capita expenditure for children attending private schools was $25.93, compared to only $2.02 for children in public, or "subscription," schools.[23]

While South Carolina never implemented a system of universal education for white children, the city of Charleston passed a law in 1856 to establish common schools. Again, the attempt was highly ineffective, as census records reveal that very few students ever attended these schools. In Mississippi, late-antebellum Governor Albert Brown tried to establish schools for poor white children, but his efforts proved fruitless. And in antebellum Georgia, only about half the state's enumerated white children were receiving any type of formal education in the decade before the Civil War, and the 1850 census listed more than 40,000 illiterate adults. Instead of establishing common or public schools, Georgia created a "Poor School Fund" to help offset the cost for students without the money to attend the aptly named "pay schools." Basically, poor children could attend any school, and the teachers would then bill the Poor School Fund, "just as they charged the parents of paying pupils." Governor Crawford declared that "not half of the counties applied for their proportion of the state funds for free schooling." Because the state's laws tended to read more like guidelines that ceded the majority of details to the counties, local officials could choose how to spend the money, causing great discrepancies in how they used the funds.[24]

Interestingly, in the decade before secession, a few prominent slaveholders began advocating for the universal education of white children. This campaign coincided with growing concerns over the widening chasm between the master and non-slaveholding classes, which could ultimately threaten the long-term stability of slavery. William H. Stiles of Georgia promoted the cause of common schools "to elevate the indigent white." Indeed, he admitted, slaveholders' "failure to educate the poor whites among us, and thus fit them for employments better suited to their caste" left them "driven to similar occupations with slaves." This perilous labor issue led poor whites to believe that "the existence of the negro among us was injurious to them." Thus, as the possibility of disunion and war

[23] Soltow, *Men and Wealth*, 22; James C. Cobb, *Away Down South: A History of Southern Identity* (New York: Oxford University Press, 2005), 51; Bolton, *Poor Whites*, 55; Shugg, *Origins of Class Struggle*, 70; Bailey, *Class*, 46.
[24] Lockley, *Welfare and Charity*, 186; 192–3; 195; Wallenstein, *From Slave South*, 63; Eaton, *The Freedom of Thought Struggle*, quoted on 66; Wallenstein, *From Slave South*, 48; 67–8.

arose, slaveholders attempted to win the support of poor whites, who would be expected to provide the bulk of any significant southern military force. By offering the poor the possibility of an education, and better-paying, "non-slave" jobs, affluent Southerners actively, though quite belatedly, courted increasingly disaffected whites.[25]

Given the tumultuous state of affairs concerning southern education, it was hardly surprising that as the reality of secession loomed, the Deep South's slaveholders began proposing several new ideas in an effort to appease the white masses. Local leaders and politicians began holding educational "conventions" and meetings in every state. One such convention, held in Marietta, Georgia in 1851, directly linked the "right of the poor to be educated" to their potential (perhaps impending) military duty. If the impoverished "be under obligation at the call of his country to risk his life and to pour out his blood in defence of those institutions, which secure to the rich man his dearest rights and most valued possessions," the writer professed, then "the rich man is under obligations to contribute of his wealth, to give the children of his defender an education." Because the newspaper published the article less than two months after the Nashville Convention (in which southern states met to consider what to do if Congress banned the expansion of slavery), this sudden desire to do something beneficial for impoverished whites surely had strings attached. Slaveholders needed non-slaveholders to fill the ranks of their armed forces, and began making symbolic gestures in anticipation of these ends.[26]

As secession became a real possibility, some slaveholders began to rethink their strategy completely. Yet plans to reform each Deep South state's public education system all remained inchoate prior to Reconstruction. Most of the push for change occurred in relatively progressive states, such as Georgia. Although Georgia did not adopt a system of free public schools until 1877, on the eve of secession a group of politicians from the northern part of the state (including Governor Joseph Brown) outlined a proposal to educate most of the state's non-slaveholders. Committing $100,000 from the Western & Atlantic railroad earnings to the school fund, the bill was passed by the Georgia legislature in 1858 over adamant planter opposition. But it was never implemented. Still, the simple fact that southern politicians needed legislation like this to appease less affluent whites reveals the intensity of underlying class conflict. One wealthy

---

[25] Quoted in Johnson, *Ante-Bellum North Carolina*, 79.
[26] "Educational Convention," *Federal Union*, July 29, 1851, 1.

slaveholding legislator even claimed he voted for the Common School bill because "he thought this a Southern Rights measure." Members of the master class were scrambling to preserve slavery by making these types of emblematic propositions to poor whites.[27]

Occurring simultaneously – and actually embedded within the push for public education – was a nativist movement with widespread support among slaveholders. This xenophobic plan sought to rid all southern schoolhouses of northern-born or even northern-trained teachers. Once this was accomplished, each state would select male teachers trained in southern universities, but only after they had been thoroughly "instructed" (that is, "indoctrinated") in pro-slavery theory. As one editor out of North Carolina opined, "in nine cases out of ten, when you employ Northern teachers, you press a viper to your bosom, that will sting you by infusing into the minds of the pupils his thoughts, feelings, and tastes opposed to Southern interests and Southern institutions." That same year, a Georgia paper made very similar arguments. Governor Herschel Johnson claimed that the "educational wants of" the state were apparent in the "many thousand adults, in our midst, who can neither read nor write, and as many poor children who must be forever debarred the blessings of education, in consequence of the poverty of their parents." With seemingly insurmountable barriers to universal education, Georgia instead was weighed down by "the crime that burdens our criminal dockets … by the violence and corruption that desecrate the ballot box, at all our popular elections." Public schooling and widespread literacy, the Governor appealed, "will prize out the poor from the mire into which innocent poverty has sunk them … it will dignify labour." Thus, he proposed creating a new college to train native-born men as teachers. The inferior courts of each county would choose one promising boy to be educated in "southern" rights, after which he would return to his home and run the public school. This plan, the Governor hoped, would "render us independent of those itinerate adventurers from other States, who are too often hostile to our peculiar institutions."[28]

Yet just as some members of the master class finally accepted the fact that they must attempt to appease poor whites every now and then, other

---

[27] Eaton, *The Freedom of Thought Struggle*, 66; Wallenstein, *From Slave South*, 68; "House of Representatives," *Daily Federal Union*, Nov. 20, 1858, 2.

[28] Russell B. Nye, *Fettered Freedom: Civil Liberties and the Slavery Controversy, 1830–1860*, (1963; reprint, London: Forgotten Books, 2012), 97; quoted on 99; No Title, *Federal Union - Extra*, Nov. 5, 1857, 1; Nye, *Fettered Freedom*, quoted on 99.

slaveholders became bolder in their resistance to widespread literacy. In the few years prior to secession, some southern papers openly touted the benefits of keeping the general public uneducated. According to Virginia's *South Side Democrat*, the southern elite despised "everything with the prefix FREE. ... But the worst of all these abominations is the modern system of FREE SCHOOLS ... the cause and prolific source of the infidelities and treasons." New England's system of public schools, it continued, "have turned her cities into Sodoms and Gomorrahs." Farther south in Georgia, another editorial revealed why slaveholders did not concern themselves with educating non-slaveholders. "There is, however, a prejudice existing against common schools arising from the fact that they have their most perfect development in sections of the Union most hostile to the South," the writer bemoaned, "and characterized by the wildest vagaries from truth, reason and common sense." These "heresies," he concluded, "are a natural growth or incidental result of the common school system." Although the language was coded, the message was clear. Educating the masses could possibly lead to a large percentage of white Southerners questioning – or even opposing – slavery.[29]

Conversely, William Taber, a wealthy young aristocrat from Charleston, openly attacked the theory of universal education. Claiming literacy would only make white laborers "idle and vicious," he vocally advocated a system in which only the affluent children of slaveholders would get to attend school. Benjamin Perry of Greenville, located in the state's rural Appalachian upcountry, immediately took the rich firebrand to task over the contentious issue. Despite owning slaves himself, Perry was opposed to disunion and sought to protect the natural rights of his poorer, non-slaveholding neighbors. Taber and other pro-slavery men, Perry charged, remained "not only against human liberty," but also opposed republicanism at a theoretical level. A northern editorial plainly explained how the dismal education system in the South continued to worsen throughout the later antebellum period. In many Confederate states, the article alleged, pro-slavery men like Taber "took the strongest ground against all education for working people, white as well as black, arguing that it only rendered them more wretched, and less content with, their lot in life and

[29] The Young Men's Fremont and Dayton Central Union, *The New 'Democratic' Doctrine: Slavery Not to be Confined to the Negro Race, But to Be Made the Universal Condition of the Laboring Classes of Society: The Supporters of This Doctrine Vote for Buchanan!* (Ithaca, NY: 1865), quoted on 2, Web; "Common Schools," *Georgia Telegraph*, May 19, 1857, 2.

position in society." This particular issue, like so many issues that plagued poor southern whites, was "the result of slavery and the peculiar social order of the South," the journalist concluded. To be sure, the maintenance of the slave system was the main reason "that the great bulk of the Southern whites grew up without education, knowledge or intelligence."[30]

The master class's apprehension over poor whites' allegiance to the peculiar institution was further revealed in North Carolina, where Calvin Wiley delivered a report on public education in 1860. Essentially warning that there was as much danger from the prejudice existing between rich and poor whites as there was between master and slave, Wiley first established that "The peace of every social and political system depends on a just recognition of the mutual dependence of every rank on each other, and of the mutual obligations which this interest imposes." However, by denying basic services like education to a large percentage of southern whites, slaveholders were ultimately putting their property – and perhaps their lives – in jeopardy. A deepening divide between the region's haves and have-nots needed to be dealt with, even if it meant affording more governmental services to the poor. These actions were necessary, Wiley concluded, because any attempt "to widen the breach between classes of citizens [was] just as dangerous as efforts to excite slaves to insurrection."[31]

Between 1864 and 1865, the pro-Lincoln *New York Times* published a series of articles revealing the North's shock at the high levels of illiteracy among soldiers in the Confederate Army. One correspondent near Newbern, North Carolina held that even most of the small-landholding yeomen farmers were unable to read and write. "Before the war these were, of their class, well-to-do people, owning a little land, a few cattle, and some household stuff, but now having scarcely anything beyond the Government ration," the writer began, "They are generally, almost universally, illiterate to a degree inconceivable to a Northern mind; on an average, not more than one out of eight can read or write. They have suffered more than the negro from the blighting influence of Slavery, and they know it." Another article complained about the reliability of the

---

[30] Dan T. Carter, *When the War was Over: The Failure of Self-Reconstruction in the South, 1865–1867* (Baton Rouge: Louisiana University Press, 1985), quoted on 42; "What We Owe to the New South The Prevalence and Density of Popular Ignorance," *New York Times*, June 24, 1865.

[31] *Ibid.*, quoted on 79.

census on literacy in the South. It contended that a witness to the Confederate surrender "declared that less than a fifth of the privates could sign their own name. It was this want of popular education and intelligence that gave the Southern leaders and planters such great power in their respective States, and enabled them to practice such terrible deceptions upon the masses."[32]

Just two months after the fighting had ceased, still another article contended that "the great body of the poor whites" had "always been in the densest ignorance. The common-school system and the universal popular education of the free States, have never been appreciated or imitated in the Southern States." The rich privately educated their own children, it continued, "but the generality of the poorer white classes of Virginia and North Carolina, as well as of the cotton States, were absolutely destitute of even the primary elements of knowledge." Prior to secession, northern "schoolmasters – although there were hardly any other schoolmasters but Northern ones in the South – were looked on with suspicion, denounced as Abolitionists, and not unfrequently driven away or lynched. There was no law for their protection and little encouragement for their labors." Certainly, the *Times* concluded, "The planting aristocracy did not desire the education of the poorer classes, and the latter cared little for it themselves."[33]

By the winter of 1865, even southern papers were commenting on the former Confederacy's rampant white illiteracy and lack of a public school system. The *Savannah Republican* quoted Reverend Thompson from the American Union Commission, a charitable organization run by Northerners who aided the South during the years of greatest suffering following the war. The minister reported that "only one in fifteen of the poor whites could read. In Tennessee there were eighty-three thousand five hundred whites who could not read or write." Concluding that "ignorance was the main cause of the rebellion," the Commission vowed "to teach poor whites and blacks, and thus prepare them for the duties and responsibilities of men." In the aftermath of an incredibly bloody, destructive war, perhaps the South's truth finally was revealed to the world. Shrouded in ignorance and controlled by both legal and extralegal means, poor whites had little choice when it came to secession. Many of

---

[32] "Horrors of the Rebellion," *New York Times*, March 18, 1864; "What We Owe to the New South the Prevalence and Density of Popular Ignorance," *Ibid.*, June 24, 1865.

[33] "What We Owe to the New South The Prevalence and Density of Popular Ignorance," *Ibid.*, June 24, 1865.

them, it seems, did not fully comprehend the reasons for disunion, let alone the reasons for war.[34]

For many years, abolitionists claimed slaveholders had several ultimate goals, including reopening the slave trade, expanding slavery throughout the United States and beyond, and – as Russell Nye put it – removing from "the free white man those constitutional and traditional guarantees of liberty which stood in the way of the control over the middle and lower classes by a privileged aristocracy of slaveholder and capitalist." Whether the means involved disenfranchising poor whites, keeping them uneducated and illiterate, heavily policing them and monitoring their behaviors, or simply leaving them to wallow in cyclical poverty, the ends were always the same: the South's master class continued to lord over the region, attempting to control an increasingly unwieldy hierarchy. Slaveholders' worst fears were coming to pass as the ranks of disaffected poor whites grew. As one editorial out of South Carolina contended, the biggest danger to southern society was neither northern abolitionists nor black slaves. Instead, the owners of flesh needed to concern themselves with the masterless men and women in their own neighborhoods – this "servile class of mechanics and laborers, unfit for self-government, and yet clothed with the attributes and powers of citizens."[35]

The fact that slaveholders felt the need to oversee the actions of poor whites is hardly surprising. The rise of the underground economy, coupled with white laborers' growing unrest, gave masters good reason to be suspicious of poor whites' loyalty. Ronald Takaki found upper-class Southerners identified three main threats to slavery: "the external threat of the federal government, the internal threat of the Southern non-slaveholders, and the moral threat of the sentiment of the nineteenth century world." That second threat – the internal dissent of non-slaveholding whites – mattered much more than most historians have realized. The divide between the classes was deep, and the move toward disunion had much to do with extreme inequalities in wealth and income. To fully understand how this "gulf" continued to grow throughout the late antebellum period, the functioning of the Deep South's state and local governments, as well as its system of suffrage, need to be studied.[36]

Scholars still remain relatively uninformed about the voting process in the antebellum South. Questions over how many impoverished whites actually voted, and how many were *permitted* to vote in the first place,

[34] "American Union Commission," *Savannah Republican*, Nov. 21, 1865, 1.
[35] Nye, *Fettered Freedom*, 299; quoted on 248.   [36] Takaki, "The Movement," 39.

remain unanswered. Some poor whites, of course, were disinterested in political matters, likely due to their own desires to remain detached from wider society. And widespread illiteracy and semi-literacy among the lower classes – as well as the South's stringent censorship laws – further prevented their involvement. "How little the 'poor white trash,' the great majority of the Southern people, know of the real condition of the country is, indeed, sadly astonishing," Helper lamented. "The truth is, they know nothing of public measures, and little of private affairs, except what their impervious masters, the slave-drivers, condescend to tell, and that is but precious little." William Henry Brisbane of South Carolina, a former slaveholder turned abolitionist, published a pamphlet in 1849 under the pseudonym "Brutus." In it he condemned the slaveholders' complete control over southern politics and law, claiming that "The great mass of the people are virtually disenfranchised, their interests utterly disregarded, and their voice not heard in the Councils of the State." Southern constitutions were intentionally crafted to tie the interests of the government to the elite, Brutus continued, and the resulting inequality quashed the "interests of the free laborer." Poor whites simply could not attain decent jobs, wages, or even civil rights without some sort of access to the political system.[37]

Although each state had slightly different laws, in the Deep South, both state and local governments were dominated by a small but powerful group of wealthy slaveholders. Slave- and land-owning yeomen certainly participated in politics, and even some of the "respectable," more well-to-do poor whites became involved on a minor level. But for a majority of the truly poor, political power was never within reach, and it became more elusive throughout the late antebellum period. While members of the affluent master class occasionally paid lip service to democracy in the 1830s, by the 1850s many of the region's leaders were openly touting the benefits of oligarchy and aristocracy, while condemning the free states for rule by mobocracy. Within slave societies, these dens of "oligarchal despotism," as Helper referred to them, the entire system was set up to serve slaveholders. Indeed, he implored:

Non-slaveholders of the South! farmers, mechanics and workingmen, we take this occasion to assure you that the slaveholders, the arrogant demagogues whom you have elected to offices of honor and profit, have hoodwinked you, trifled with you, and used you as mere tools for the consummation of their wicked designs. They

[37] Planitzer, "A Dangerous Class of Men, quoted on 49; Helper, *The Impending Crisis*, 42.

have purposely kept you in ignorance, and have, by moulding your passions and prejudices to suit themselves, induced you to act in direct opposition to your dearest rights and interests. By a system of the grossest subterfuge and misrepresentation, and in order to avert, for a season, the vengeance that will most assuredly overtake them ere long, they have taught you to hate the abolitionists, who are your best and only true friends.

Not surprisingly, by primarily aiding the richest and most powerful, the government offered few benefits to the hundreds of thousands of white poor, many of whom remained cut off from politics altogether. As Bolton pointed out, the Jacksonian era's purported democratic reforms did very little to change the balance of power in southern politics. An affluent elite controlled both political parties. These men worked together across factional lines to prevent wider access to electoral politics, ultimately preserving their own political power. Slaveholders not only tightly limited the pool of potential candidates, they also restricted political debate and speech to issues they deemed proper and important.[38]

Thus, despite the popular fantasy of America as a flourishing democracy, a handful of scholars have long held that the South – particularly the Deep South – was an aberration. Bernard Mandel proclaimed that the South was nothing close to a democracy, and Manisha Sinha further asserted that "the proslavery, antidemocratic discourse pioneered by Carolinian planter politicians during nullification would form the theoretical foundation of southern nationalism." As the *National Era* reported, many southern politicians believed that popular suffrage was the "root of all the mischief" over the question of slavery. "This is a favorite theory with the Slaveholding Caste," the article continued, as "They dislike popular institutions." South Carolina Senator Andrew Butler had recently called the ballot-box "Pandora's box," a conviction rather common among the master class. "For we are all aware," the *Era* concluded, "that by various constitutional contrivances in that State, popular power is greatly restricted, and all but slaveholders are rendered virtually ineligible to a seat in the Legislature or to the office of Governor."[39]

During the few years prior to secession, the call for a southern political system other than democracy grew stronger. One Georgia editorialist passionately advocated for republicanism instead, claiming it "safer ...

---

[38] Helper, *The Impending Crisis*, 153; 120; Bolton, *Poor Whites*, 116.
[39] Bernard Mandel, *Labor, Free and Slave: Workingmen and the Anti-Slavery Movement in the United States* (1955; reprint, Chicago: University of Illinois Press, 2007), 41; Sinha, *The Counterrevolution of Slavery*, 33; "Land Reform in the Senate," *The National Era*, Feb. 7, 1850.

just because a government that is carried on by the agents of a consti-tutional constituency may be guarded and regulated by wise conservative statues. A pure and simple republic may have a constituency with limits to its elective franchise rights – just as the courts have had general limits within which they draw for their grand and petit juries." Continuing his argument, he plainly stated that suffrage had long been restricted in the slave South, and legal codification would simply be making the long-standing practice law. "Every body knows there has been a discriminative line all the time in operation here, and that in as far as the ends of justice are concerned, it is a necessary distinction," he continued, also pointing out the hypocrisy of politicians who "bawl and thunder from their stump-stands, on the equal rights of men, in order to procure a right to vote for a man he would not use on his farm or lot as a ditcher or groom." "Do all white men – no matter their class, education, beliefs, or upbringing – deserve to vote?," he asked. "Ought this trust to be deposited into the hands of every freeman?"[40]

The actual antebellum voting process itself largely remains a mystery. Many southern states apparently used the ancient practice of voting viva voce, or "by word of mouth." The problems inherent in this methodology are self-evident, as there was no right to privacy or secrecy concerning political allegiances. Simply put, under the practice each man's vote is read aloud at the election hall, while a local official recorded both the voter's name and the candidates for whom he voted. As to be expected, the process of voting viva voce could be incredibly time consuming – so much so, in fact, that many citizens waiting in line lost their chances to vote once the polls closed. As the *New York Evening Post* explained in 1849, poor white Southerners had little choice but "to labor by the side of the slave when they may, and starve or steal when they must. ... For political rights, even the right of suffrage – the only one they nominally possess – is legislated away from them, for the system of voting viva voce prevents its being an expression of their own will."[41]

The southern slave power, of course, had long dominated the federal government. Controlling the presidency, the legislature, and even the judiciary, slaveholders and their allies wielded wildly disproportionate power. As DuBois pointed out, slave owner aims to protect the peculiar

---

[40] "Political," *Southern Recorder*, May 31, 1859, 3.
[41] David Grimsted, *American Mobbing, 1828–1861: Toward Civil War* (New York: Oxford University Press, 1998), 181–2; "Non-Slaveholders in Slave States," *New York Evening Post*, reprinted in *The Examiner*, Nov. 3, 1849.

institution directly infringed upon the civil rights of non-slaveholding whites at both the federal and state levels. Indeed, the three-fifths compromise greatly skewed legislative apportionment in the favor of slave owners. In their hands, "the political power of the South was concentrated, by their social prestige, by property ownership and also by their extraordinary rule of the counting of all or at least three-fifths of the Negroes as part of the basis of representation in the legislature," he wrote. "It is singular how this 'three-fifths' compromise was used, not only to degrade Negroes in theory, but in practice to disenfranchise the white South." Unequal representation, however, was only a small part of a much larger issue, one encompassing (among other things) property ownership clauses, poll taxes, residency requirements, felon disfranchisement, intimidation, and outright fraud. One antislavery newspaper reported that poor southern whites were particularly "degraded" because they were "deprived of a vote, unless he possesses a certain amount of property, whilst his neighbor, the wealthy planter, often controls an entire county by voting on his slaves."[42]

While more than half of the region's legislators were farmers and planters, an additional fourth were lawyers. The majority of popularly elected local officials throughout the Deep South were slaveholders, and in most areas, well over 90 percent of them owned land (the remaining percentage often lived in cities and urban areas). The precise statistics ranged from state to state, but all the Deep South's statistics were more similar than different. In South Carolina, for example, four out of five state legislators owned slaves, and that percentage continued to climb in the decade before the Civil War. District and county governments, too, were controlled decidedly by the upper classes. Affluent politicians could pass laws to protect their wealth and slaves, as well as laws to monitor and control the poorer classes. Slaveholders also held the power to decide which whites were eligible to vote, and held great sway over every aspect of the election process. Men who had been convicted previously of certain crimes, or who did not have a long period of continuous residence in a certain state and locality, or could not afford to pay a poll tax of close to a day's wages, were liable to become disenfranchised. Poor white men's lack of education and literacy further hindered their chances of casting a ballot. For most lower-class white men, having a say in the South's political matters was an unrealistic dream. As one historian concluded,

---

[42] DuBois, *Black Reconstruction*, 33; "Anti-Slavery Address in Washington," *National Era*, April 3, 1856.

"Suffrage or representation, and sometimes both, were arranged to exclude a majority of the people, white or black, from effective control of their government. They were ruled by a minority made up of planters, merchants, and lawyers."[43]

Although Louisiana had a different type of racial hierarchy than did the rest of the Deep South, the state's voting restrictions were similar to those of the other cotton states. Louisiana's original Constitution barred about two-thirds of all white men from the polls. Roger Shugg plainly declared, "The right to vote and to stand for office depended on the possession of property." Adopting a new Constitution in 1845, the state abolished all property requirements for both voting and holding elective office. But the document also extended the residency requirement to vote from one to two years, which effectively disenfranchised transient laborers and many immigrants. Furthermore, the Constitution began allocating seats for the House of Representatives on the basis of *total* parish population, including slaves. Louisiana was not the only southern state to base representation on total population – Georgia and Florida did so as well. This practice obviously stacked legislative representation in favor of the slaveholders, essentially conferring political power to the richest third of the white population. With slaveholders wielding so much power within Louisiana's government, non-slaveholders had little chance of becoming politically relevant. And even though poor whites technically had the franchise, Shugg determined that most of them were not voting, whether because they were uninterested, unwilling, or were actively disenfranchised by the master class. A multitude of possible causes for their seeming political apathy abounded:

In the country, 'mechanics, artisans and overseers' frequently failed to qualify for the franchise, even by a year of residence, because they moved from place to place in search of employment. Hunters, fishermen, and a multitude of poor farmers in the backwoods either lived too far from the polls or were too indifferent to attend them. In New Orleans hardly 7 per cent of the white people were registered voters, and one-third of this fragmentary electorate was sometimes kept from voting by violence and intimidation – generally directed against those who were immigrants.

Indeed, Louisiana's poor whites were so removed from the voting process that Shugg considered the state an oligarchy. Despite touting universal

[43] Ralph A. Wooster, *The People in Power: Courthouse and Statehouse in the Lower South, 1850–60* (Knoxville: University of Tennessee Press, 1969), 33; 27; 117; 92; 102; 98; Shugg, *Origins of Class Struggle*, 121.

white male suffrage, Louisiana did not qualify as a democracy. Instead, a very wealthy slaveholding minority ruled the state.[44]

Like Louisiana, Tennessee's state and local governments were dominated by slaveholders, despite the state having a much lower percentage of them. As Fred Arthur Bailey established, by the late-antebellum period, *all* of Tennessee's state officials and judges, with one sole exception, were slaveholders. Neighboring North Carolina had even less egalitarian laws, with wealth requirements for most state offices. And even though there was a movement in the early nineteenth century against property qualifications for voting and for holding office, it was not until North Carolina's 1835 Constitutional Convention that the office of governor became elective. Up until 1857, white men were required to own a minimum of fifty acres to be eligible to vote for state senators. This single restriction disenfranchised about half of North Carolina's voters. Guion Griffis Johnson recognized "a constant effort on the part of the yeomanry to take from the upper classes the control of public offices. They constantly demanded the popular election of justices of the peace, constables, and of other petty office-holders, but these reforms did not come until after the ante-bellum period." Middling classes, too, noticed the severe inequalities embedded within the system, but their efforts to change things were always rebuffed. If the landed yeomanry could not engage the master class politically, poor whites were surely out of luck.[45]

Ostensibly, at least, Texas and Mississippi were the most democratic of the antebellum slave states. Neither had property qualifications for voting, and in both, all offices were elective, and legislative apportionment was reasonably equitable. In Mississippi, however, these factors still did not render the system fair. The state's requirements for voting were relatively standard for the Deep South. The white male voter had to have been a resident of Mississippi for one year and a resident of the county/city/town for four months. Indeed, these types of residency requirements, common in every southern state, probably served as the easiest way to disenfranchise poor whites whom officials did not want voting. Because so many impoverished men had to travel around in search of work, meeting strict residency requirements would have been difficult, if not impossible. According to a Mississippi statute, the prospective voter also could be disenfranchised if he had ever been "convicted of bribery,

---

[44] Shugg, *Origins of Class Struggle*, 122; 125; 128; 139; Wooster, *People in Power*, 15; Shugg, *Origins of Class Struggle*, 130–1.

[45] Bailey, *Class*, 75; Bolton, *Poor Whites*, 114; Johnson, *Ante-Bellum North Carolina*, 77.

perjury, forgery, or any other crime or misdemeanor for which the loss of the right of suffrage shall or may be imposed as a part of the penalty by any law of this State." This clause undoubtedly rendered a decent percentage of the poor white population ineligible to vote.[46]

Seemingly, Mississippi should have been a relatively egalitarian state, given its frontier-like status. But it was not. During the 1850s, the percentage of Southerners who owned slaves fell, yet they comprised an increasing majority of the state legislators. Over the course of one decade, the numbers of slaveholding lawmakers skyrocketed from around 60 percent to more than 80 percent. The Deep South was such a highly stratified society that it "accepted, even celebrated, inequality," Christopher Olsen argued. Local politics "was much less democratic or ideological than is often assumed." This divide clearly was evident in one complaint to Jefferson Davis from an appalled Mississippi legislator in 1849. With great distaste, James B. Smith wrote that a few candidates debased themselves by campaigning among poor whites, a "perfectly disgusting" display "with bowing & shaking hands as intimate as if they considered themselves among their equals, when in fact they think very differently."[47]

Like its neighboring state Mississippi, Alabama did not have property requirements for men to hold office. However, both Alabama and Georgia used poll taxes to disenfranchise poor voters, up through the time of the Civil War. Southerners well understood that these taxes prevented many of the poorest citizens from exercising the franchise. Because very few scholars have even acknowledged the role of poll taxes in antebellum elections, little is known about their historical importance. A full-scale study is still needed, but the evidence currently available suggests that the tax did help disenfranchise significant numbers of white men. In 1851 in Columbia County, Georgia, nearly one-fourth of all taxpayers owned no taxable property, and were thus only required to pay a poll tax. But as Peter Wallenstein wrote, "Small as the poll tax on whites might appear, it represented a heavy burden on people with little or no cash income or property." On the eve of secession, for example, one newspaper article claimed that the percentage of adult white men who paid their poll taxes

[46] Wooster, *People in Power*, 107; William Lewis Sharkey, *The Revised Code of the Statute Laws of the State of Mississippi* (Jackson, Mississippi: E. Barksdale, State Printer, 1857); *The Making of Modern Law: Primary Sources*, 23. Web. 15 August 2013.

[47] Williams, *Bitterly Divided*, 20; Christopher J. Olsen, *Political Culture and Secession in Mississippi: Masculinity, Honor, and the Antiparty Tradition, 1830–60* (New York: Oxford University Press, 2000), 14–5; quoted on 122.

ranged from about 77 percent of those enumerated in Greene County, Georgia (located in the heart of the state's blackbelt), to less than a quarter of white men enumerated in Chatham (the county containing Savannah). With poll taxes, it became quite obvious that the cotton South's slaveholding lawmakers desired to keep certain economic classes from voting. Simply put, when poor men could not come up with the tax money, and they had no property for the sheriff to seize, the counties listed them as insolvents, and they lost the right to vote in the elections for that year.[48]

Beginning as early as the mid-1820s, Georgia's legislators introduced bills to reduce or abolish the poll tax for all whites. In the 1830s, these bills started appearing annually, but they were never passed by the majority-slaveholding government. The few state politicians who were anti-poll tax continued to raise the topic throughout the next few decades. When their efforts to abolish the poll tax failed year after year, they even tried to put some restrictions on the tax – on who was required to pay, or how they would use the funds. By 1845, state legislators made it illegal for poll taxes to exceed 1 dollar for whites. The taxes usually fluctuated between 25 to 39 cents in the mid-1800s, close to a day's wages for many poor white laborers. Still, the anti-poll tax politicians pushed on, proposing several innovative strategies to make the tax more equitable. In 1851, for example, one bill proposed to add the poll tax revenue to the poor school fund. Among other calls for complete abolition of the tax, Representative Kimbrough of Stewart County sought to exempt whites who owned no personal property in 1858. That same year, a House member from Marion County tried to end the practice altogether by pointing out how difficult the tax was for poor men to pay. Not only did he assert that the poll tax failed to bring in revenue to the state, the Representative argued that it "is felt by the bone and sinew of the country. While the rich man does not feel a tax of 25 cents, yet the poor man does. Men cannot vote because they are not able to pay poll tax – it is oppressive and wrong." As the idea of secession became more likely,

---

[48] Wooster, *People in Power*, 21; Wallenstein, *From Slave South*, 14–5; 45; "To the Members of the House of Representatives of Georgia Legislature," *Daily Federal Union*, Dec. 9, 1859, 4: In Chatham, out of 5,515 enumerated white men (no children included), 1,339 paid poll tax (24.3 percent); in Greene, out of 1,008 enumerated white men, 780 paid poll tax (77.4 percent); and in Columbia, out of 1,031 enumerated white men, 711 paid poll tax (69 percent).

other legislators introduced bills exempting whites older than 45 years old from paying. None of these bills ever picked up any traction, however. Not a single one of them ever became law. "The poor white man is also degraded because, in some of the states, he is deprived of a vote unless he possesses a certain amount of property," the *National Era* opined. All the while, "his neighbor, the wealthy planter, often controls an entire county by voting on his slaves." Indeed, up through the Civil War, the poll tax remained a legitimate way to disfranchise poor white men.[49]

This strategy seemingly worked quite well. The master class dominated Georgia's state and local governments. At least four-fifths of state legislators were slaveholders, and a decided majority held a large number of slaves. And on the eve of secession, wrote Ralph Wooster, "among justices of inferior courts in the one-quarter of Georgia's counties most densely black, at least 40 percent held a minimum of twenty slaves." As bad as Georgia was for poor men, however, South Carolina was worse. The Palmetto State was undoubtedly the most aristocratic or oligarchic state in the United States. The democratization of other parts of America never occurred there. Even voting restrictions were more intensive than other neighboring states. South Carolina required voters to be 21 years old, a citizen of the state for two years, and a resident of the district for the previous six months. Paupers were singled out particularly as ineligible for the franchise.[50]

Apportionment for South Carolina's political representation was also completely different from that of any other state. The 1790 Constitution set the number of legislators in the lower house at 124. But the number of representatives from each district was based upon both the population *and* the value of the property in the

[49] For example, see: "Bills Rejected," *Southern Recorder*, Nov. 14, 1829, 3; "Bills Reported," *Georgia Journal*, Nov. 19, 1832, 2; "Mr. Hazzard's Speech," *Southern Recorder*, Dec. 19, 1837, 2; Wallenstein, *From Slave South*, 45; "Friday, December 26," *Southern Recorder*, Dec. 30, 1851, 3; Bills Introduced (House)," *Ibid.*, Dec. 7, 1858, 2; "House," *Daily Federal Union*, Nov. 18, 1858, 2; "In Senate, Monday, November 5," *Southern Recorder*, Nov. 15, 1859, 2–3; quoted in "Anti-slavery Address in Washington," *National Era*, April 3, 1856.

[50] Wallenstein, *From Slave South*, 21; Wooster, *People in Power*, 4–5; 9; *The Statutes At Large Of South Carolina*. Columbia, 1841. 10 vols. *The Making of Modern Law: Primary Sources*, 210, Web.

district, giving the very wealthy low-country planters a greatly disproportionate amount of political power. Furthermore, all of South Carolina's legislators were required to own a great deal of property. Michael Hindus asserted that the state had "exceedingly deferential" politics, and "elaborate measures were taken to stifle all popular input." In a moment of unabashed honesty, Governor James Henry Hammond even bragged that in the Palmetto State, the right to vote had been exercised "very negligently ... from time immemorial." Manisha Sinha, questioning whether South Carolina could even be considered democratic, described local politics as such:

> An all-powerful, planter-dominated state legislature lay at the heart of a highly centralized system of governance with weak local political organization. ... State representatives were required to have 500 acres and 10 slaves or real estate valued at 150 pounds sterling clear of debt, while state senators had to have a minimum of estate valued at 300 pounds sterling, also clear of debt.

Thus, the lawmakers and law enforcers of South Carolina truly represented the interests of one class. And this master class knew, in no uncertain terms, that democracy could eventually lead to abolition.[51]

Certainly many pro-slavery men openly endorsed the tenets of aristocracy and oligarchy, especially on the eve of secession. One planter proudly wrote that "The power in the South is where it ought to be always, in the hands of the men of property and education." Another slaveholder unashamedly advocated the restriction of suffrage while condemning the principle of "equality." And Leonidas Spratt, the vocal champion of reopening the African slave trade, claimed that throughout history, the most successful societies depended on "the greatest political inequalities." Instead of black slavery uniting whites across class lines, theories about racial inequality only served to strengthen notions of inequality in general. By the 1850s, a growing group of incredibly wealthy men, usually born into slaveholding families of great privilege, were brazenly identifying themselves as aristocrats or oligarchs – they simply did not believe in the benefits of "pure democracy." The famous writer George Fitzhugh actually argued for hereditary aristocracy, entail, and primogeniture,

---

[51] Michael S. Hindus, *Prison and Plantation: Crime, Justice, and Authority in Massachusetts and South Carolina, 1767–1878* (Chapel Hill: University of North Carolina Press, 1980), 244; 249; quoted on 244; Sinha, *The Counterrevolution of Slavery*, 34; 13; 221.

hoping these measures would help curb the scourge of democracy. South Carolina planter David Gavin "bitterly resented the fact that lower-class whites had the right to vote," calling universal white male suffrage "the most pernicious humbug of this humbug age." Even female planters like Keziah Brevard, who did not have the right to vote herself, prayed that "some thing be done to check this mobocracy. ... Democracy has brought the South *I fear* into a *sad, sad* state." The fire-eaters of the slave South envisioned something more than just a slave-ridden country modeled on the principles of the United States. They wanted a return to hereditary privilege, caste systems, and rule by the wealthy few. Indeed, James De Bow obstinately declared that property alone was "the basis of sound representation," since the poor's right to vote so often "degenerates into licentiousness."[52]

As seemingly tasteless as De Bow's description was, it may not have been terribly far from reality. Voting Day in the Deep South was a raucous, drunken, hedonistic affair, at least on its surface. Behind the scenes, of course, powerful slaveholders were in complete control of the day's events. The actual process of voting did vary slightly among the states, but most elections had several aspects in common. White male electors were usually required to be 21 years old, with certain residency requirements for each state and county. Generally, these periods ranged from three months to two years. After a voter's "qualifications as an elector" were approved by a panel of inspectors, the voter placed his paper ballot into the ballot box as the clerks took down his name. The entire process was public, which greatly influenced the votes of poor men. A lower-class man who owed money to one of the county's affluent men, or was in his employ, or lived as a tenant or renter on his land, surely felt compelled to support the rich man's political causes. Whether this influence was subtle or overt (or even coercive), poor white men's voting habits were carefully monitored. In some states like Alabama, a man's right to vote could be challenged not only by the election inspectors, but also by "any qualified elector." According to an 1852 statute, inspectors were charged explicitly with the duty to "challenge any person offering to vote, whom he knows, or suspects, not to be qualified as an elector." The number of men who possibly could be disqualified was high. A suspected criminal history, a failure to pay poll tax, or even

---

[52] *Ibid.*, quoted on 225–6; quoted on 224; quoted on 227; 141; 225; quoted on 225; quoted on 225 (italics in original).

"disorderly" action at the polling place could immediately disenfranchise a potential voter.[53]

While there have been few comprehensive studies on antebellum southern voting practices, Olsen's work on Mississippi provided insight into the process, as well as the voting behaviors of the state's population. He found that only the "wealthiest, most prominent men in each precinct" served as election inspectors, overseeing every aspect of suffrage in their counties. Even though the most affluent southern men tended not to run as politicians themselves, they were still able to control elections, and thereby, politics. Inspectors wielded remarkable authority. Not only did they have the power to decide who was and was not allowed to vote, they were also able to imprison disorderly voters or fine them as much as $500. It is difficult for modern Americans to understand how intimidating it must have been for non-slaveholders to cast ballots publicly right under the noses of three of the most powerful men in the county. These inspectors controlled the local economy. They oversaw many of the area's employment opportunities. And they had great influence over the criminal justice system. "Especially in small rural neighborhoods," Olsen wrote, "planter-inspectors potentially held vast power. Not everyone voted alike, but most did – some out of genuine class bonding or a shared masculine perspective but others because they felt pressured by elites." Lower-middling and poor whites, of course, faced many factors that left their voting experiences far from the Jacksonian ideal of a white male democracy. As Olsen concluded, "The distribution of election-day duties especially suggests Mississippians' faith in an organic, deferential society and reveals the gentry's influence in a supposedly democratic, free process."[54]

Whether poorer Mississippians really had faith in a deferential society or whether they were coerced into voting a certain way based on slaveholder influence may never be known. It seems, however, that on Election Day planter behavior could go one of two ways: they could actively court the votes of poor whites, offering liquor and barbeque in return, or they could intimidate non-slaveholders into casting ballots for their chosen candidates. Masters had the power to disenfranchise large numbers of

[53] For example, see Sharkey, *The Revised Code of the Statute Laws of the State of Mississippi*, 22, and John J. Ormond, *The Code of Alabama* (Montgomery, Brittan and De Wolf, State Printers, 1852), 270; 96–7. *The Making of Modern Law: Primary Sources*, Web. 15 August 2013.

[54] Olsen, *Political Culture*, 125; 127; 125; 129; 130; 125.

poor whites with a handful of effective strategies that were likely utilized with relative frequency. Slaveholders, it seemed, commonly used their positions as men of means and power to heavy-handedly influence non-slaveholders' votes.

Much of this political pressure centered on employment opportunities or the ability for a poor white to maintain an existing job. A white laborer from Charleston claimed that being a mechanic was "only better than the slave because he is entitled to vote and must give that sometimes for promise of a job." David S. Reed, a gubernatorial candidate for North Carolina, reminded the state's elite that "The landlord will always exercise a sufficient influence over his tenants without having an additional vote," because "those who do not own land can never ... remain here long, unless the land holder permits him to do so." Tenants and share-croppers undoubtedly felt pressure from land-owners. Slaveholders controlled so much of southern society that some poor white workers had no choice but to conform. Deference and intimidation, concluded Olsen, survived democratic reforms and persisted in the Deep South throughout the antebellum period.[55]

Challenges to universal white male suffrage, therefore, existed everywhere the late antebellum Deep South, entrenched in both local and state politics in a variety of ways. As Edmund Ruffin wrote, southern governments had historically disenfranchised "all of the lowest and most degraded classes, who, whether slaves or free, white or black ... are and must be incapable of understanding or caring to preserve the principle or the benefits of free government." Slaveholding politicians proposed a variety of different methods to aid in the retraction of voting rights for white citizens. South Carolinians, for example, began pushing for complete disfranchisement for poor whites convicted of trading with slaves. Other states followed suit, and additional convictions – for infractions ranging from vagrancy to larceny – were added quickly to the list of crimes that could possibly revoke the civil liberties of non-slaveholding whites. In 1858, one Georgia House member introduced a bill into the legislature seeking to disenfranchise anyone who appeared to be intoxicated at the time he cast his ballot. The "presiding Magistrates" should have the power to determine who was or was not intoxicated, he declared, and those men who were deemed drunk would immediately be fined 5 dollars. Adding insult to injury, the names of those voters would

[55] Morris, "White Bondage," quoted on 206; Bolton, *Poor Whites*, quoted on 126; Olsen, *Political Culture*, 130.

be read aloud at the next Grand Jury, "as dishonored at the ballot box."[56]

Men occasionally turned up in county minute books for "illegal voting," a term that could refer to a number of different infractions. Whether the men were immigrants, did not meet local residency requirements, or had not paid their poll tax, the term was a catch-all used to invalidate and imprison a variety of potential voters. As Olson found, illegal voting, tampering with ballot boxes, and the appointment of "unlawful supervisors" were not at all uncommon, as both public offices and money were at stake in antebellum elections. David Grimsted further established that multiple districts in South Carolina were complaining about the "many illegal voters" plaguing the polls in the 1850s. Grand jury presentments railed against the "species of bribery" and the "bribery and corruption" of local elections, as poor men frequently sold their votes, sometimes for cash, but far more commonly, "for the last drink of Grog."[57]

The Grand Jury of Jasper County, Georgia also recommended a crackdown on illegal voters. "In times of political excitement like the present," they wrote, the local officials needed to be on the lookout for "transient persons and frequently young men in our own county [who] vote illegal [ly], by traveling to distant parts of the county from where they reside, and impose their votes on the managers." Likewise, the *Georgia Journal* reported that complaints about illegal voting resounded from every part of the state. Prosecutions had taken place in several counties, and two men were currently serving sentences in the state penitentiary for the crime. As several local courts issued additional indictments, the paper used the offense as "a warning at the coming October elections, and that, for once, in Georgia, the legal will protect the rights against illegal voters." Blaming crop shortages in the Carolinas for an influx of landless whites in "dread of famine," the *Journal* drummed up fear of "immigrant" suffrage: "But we fear, for we have seen indications of it, that an effort will be made to induce many to vote, who are not qualified to do so, by reason of their short residence in the State. The law should be made known to the intended victims, and if then violated, let them suffer its

---

[56] Mandel, *Labor, Free and Slave*, quoted on 40; Forret, *Race Relations*, 105; "Sober Voting," *Southern Recorder*, Dec. 7, 1858, 1. For information on felon disfranchisement, see Pippa Holloway, *Living in Infamy: Felon Disfranchisement and the History of American Citizenship* (New York: Oxford University Press, 2014).

[57] Olsen, *Political Culture*, 126; Grimsted, *American Mobbing*, quoted on 196–7.

penalties!" Reiterating the qualifications for Georgia voters, the paper concluded by reminding potential illegal voters that the punishment for their crime would be hard labor in the penitentiary for one to two years.[58]

Probably more common than direct voter intimidation, wealthy slave-holders courted poor voters with material goods and favors, plying them with whiskey and cigars and providing transportation to and from the polls. Robert Russel believed that slave owners "took little interest in and felt little responsibility for their poor-white neighbors, except, perhaps, at election time." One poor white from Bedford, Tennessee, remembered, "First vote I ever cast a slaveholder came and carried me to the polls." Alcohol clearly played a prevalent role in all antebellum elections, and slaveholders easily manipulated the drunken masses. "At our public elections the disgusting spectacle is frequently presented," opined a Mississippi petition, "of a free citizen tottering to the polls, so drunk that he is utterly incapable of appreciating the important duty he is about to perform." Bolton further noted that this "social aspect of Election Day helped insure large turnouts, even if some voters became so intoxicated that they required assistance in exercising their suffrage rights." While the outright purchase of votes (with cash) did very occasionally occur in the antebellum period, most votes seemed to have been "bought" with liquor, barbeque, and a hedonistic atmosphere.[59]

Indeed, the Deep South's Election Day shenanigans were infamous: "penning" was a common enough practice to be called the "peculiar institution of Muscogee County," Georgia. Basically, on the day before elections, campaign workers would gather as many white men as they possibly could, pay for their boarding near the polls, and then proceed to get them completely drunk. The political party with the largest "pen" usually triumphed. In South Carolina, both sides particularly focused their efforts on illiterate poor whites, realizing that the impoverished would likely sell their votes. By beneficently distributing copious amounts of liquor, passing around cigars and meat, and transporting people to and from the polls, slave owners usually achieved the political results they wanted. Despite the fact that some poor whites voted (under differing

---

[58] "Presentments of the Grand Jury of Jasper County, October 1840," *Federal Union*, Nov. 24, 1840, 3; "Illegal Voting," *Georgia Journal*, Sept. 2, 1845, 3.

[59] Robert R. Russel, "The Effects of Slavery upon Non-Slaveholders in the Ante Bellum South," *Agricultural History* 15, No. 2 (April 1941): 123; Elliot and Moxley, *Tennessee*, Vol. 2, 723; "Petition for Prohibiting the Sale of Liquor," Folder "Temperance," Petitions, 1817–1908, Mississippi Legislature, MDAH; Bolton, *Poor Whites*, 123; 124.

levels of duress and coercion), the Deep South was unquestionably much more oligarchic than it was democratic.[60]

The few times poor whites were given a platform to discuss antebellum government, they had negative things to say about the master-dominated political process. Federal soldier James T. Wolverton grew up the son of non-slaveholders in Tippah County, Mississippi. His father, a carpenter and mechanic, was opposed to slavery but could do little about the situation, as slaveholders controlled the government. "It was considered slaveholders was allowed a vote for each slave owned," Wolverton remembered. Poor white S.P. Larkins from Dickson, Tennessee confirmed the sentiments of the Mississippian. "The slaveholders thought they was better than the poor people and would not have anything to do with the poor class," Larkins alleged. Instead, "the poorer class of people was look[ed] upon about like slaves was. ... My father would not vote for a man that owned slaves nor would he have anything to do with them."[61]

Thus, as poor whites entered the later antebellum period, the privileges of whiteness seemed to slip farther and farther out of their reach. "A cunningly devised mockery of freedom is guaranteed to them, and that is all," Helper bemoaned. "To all intents and purposes they are disfranchised, and outlawed, and the only privilege extended to them, is a shallow and circumscribed participation in the political movements that usher slaveholders into office." Taking all of these topics together – land, labor, wealth, income, material realties, religion, education, and politics – the extent to which the impoverished had been removed from southern white society becomes very clear. Wayne Flynt, one of the only scholars to confirm this self-awareness among poor whites, wrote that they "had a profound understanding of their own self-interest. They also had a fierce class consciousness that even casual observers noticed." Abolitionists had long attempted to use this class consciousness to their advantage. By playing upon the fears and interests of poor whites, they tried to forge feelings of common interest between slaves and poor white laborers. But their attempts generally failed, for two reasons. First, there were problems with distribution of anti-slavery materials due to strict censorship laws. Second, the masses generally remained illiterate or just-barely-literate. Still, the dichotomy between whites who owned slaves and whites who did not remained ominous in the antebellum period, growing worse during the

[60] Williams, *Bitterly Divided*, 20; Eaton, *The Freedom of Thought Struggle*, 81–2.
[61] Elliot and Moxley, *Tennessee*, Vol. 1, 143–4; Vol. 4, 1132.

cotton boom of the 1850s, and reaching truly troubling proportions following the economic recession of 1857. Combining impoverished whites' deprivations in education with their rejection or manipulation at the voting booth, it is nearly impossible to discount tensions over economic class as an important factor of the Civil War.[62]

[62] Helper, *The Impending Crisis*, 43; Flynt, *Poor but Proud*, 7.

6

Vagrancy, Alcohol, and Crime

They are now completely under the domination of the oligarchy, and it is madness to suppose that they will ever be able to rise to a position of true manhood, until after the slave power shall have been utterly overthrown.
– Hinton Helper[1]

A certain class of white men ... ha[s] been suffered to remain in our midst too long, and [their] intercourse with the slave population is altogether too intimate. So long as their presence is tolerated it will be found a difficult matter to preserve the decorum so essential among slaves. ... There must be ... new white laws as well as new black laws.
– Pointe Coupee Echo[2]

In 1858, Jacob Waddel was convicted of vagrancy in Marion, a county in the heart of the western Georgia blackbelt. Waddel appealed his case to the Georgia Supreme Court on the ground that the verdict was "contrary to evidence." Although he owned no real estate or personal property, Waddel was a 33–year-old farmer with a family to support. While he had been seen plowing a potato patch and "doing some other small jobs," the local superior court concluded that Waddel's "fancy" seemed to have been walking along the highways, "strolling about in idleness." In a unanimous opinion delivered by Chief Justice Joseph Henry Lumpkin, the Court acknowledged that the offense itself was "somewhat anomalous"; every other offense involved "doing something," but Waddel's "doing nothing" caused him to be sentenced to hard labor in the state penitentiary. Yet in the only vagrancy case to reach the appellate level in

---

[1] Helper, *The Impending Crisis*, 382.   [2] Quoted in Shugg, *Origins of Class Struggle*, 95.

the antebellum South, the justices wanted to make Waddel an example for other southern poor whites on the eve of the Civil War. "It is time, perhaps, to give them a scare," Lumpkin wrote, "to admonish them of the old adage, that the bird that can sing, and won't sing, must *be made* to sing."[3]

But was Jacob Waddel really arrested for being a "do-nothing"? Or was he merely a victim of circumstance, a poor white man in a slave-holder's world? Waddel's "crime" – vagrancy – accounted for many of the criminal cases involving the antebellum South's poor whites. By definition, vagrants owned no property and thus had nothing to lose, and their "wandering about" made it easy for them to have contact with both blacks and other white rabble rousers. Conceivably, when committed in a slave society, vagrancy was more than just mere idleness. Instead, it was a potentially subversive act that exposed the tenuousness of the upper class's position. Apprehension over the behaviors of poor whites was especially acute in areas with high percentages of blacks. Young, able-bodied whites with no ties to the southern hierarchy, who spent their days strolling about, could easily "wander" into trouble – by colluding with slaves to commit crimes, by forming intimate (and sometimes sexual) relationships with blacks, and by their propensity for drinking, fighting, gambling, and carousing.

Antebellum laws were geared to the preservation of slavery, and the peculiar institution permeated every legal decision made. The stain of racial slavery extended well beyond the master-slave relationship, making the maintenance of a stable, well-ordered society – in which poor whites and blacks were socially separated – imperative. Because masters were never able to achieve complete segregation between the two underclasses, the Deep South's slave owners were compelled to police the non-slaveholding population heavily, incarcerating lower-class white people for a variety of relationships with African Americans. While one of the most common charges was vagrancy, thousands of poor whites were imprisoned (and sometimes killed) for crimes ranging from slave stealing to "lewd behavior." Poor whites had long been involved in the lives of slaves and free blacks, and as hard as slaveholders tried, they simply could not stop this interracial interaction. Most historians purport that behavioral crimes like vagrancy were created during Reconstruction to control

[3] *Jacob Waddel vs. The State of Georgia*, 27 Ga. 262 (1859 Ga. Lexis 50); Seventh Census of the United States, 1850: Marion County, Georgia; *Waddel vs. Georgia*, italics in original; Eighth Census of the United States, 1860: Chattahoochee County, Georgia.

the labor and activities of African Americans. In reality, many of the same laws had been used for decades to control poor whites.[4]

Vagrancy offers an instructive example of affluent slaveholders using the criminal justice system to their advantage by jailing poor whites at will. Again, vagrancy is a peculiar crime: while every other offense involves the perpetrator doing *something*, the vagrant was arrested for doing *nothing*. Early modern Europeans initially used vagrancy as a way to control the labor of the lower classes. England's first vagrancy law was passed in 1349 in response to the end of feudalism and the onset of the Black Death, which killed 50 percent of the population and thus decimated the country's labor force. These early statutes were created for one reason: to guarantee landholders an adequate supply of low-wage labor. Some historians even dubbed the laws a "substitute for serfdom." Margaret Rosenheim wrote that these statutes ensured "labor *immobility* and concomitant wage fixing," while A.L. Beier proposed that vagrancy was originally a "crime of status" that caused people to be arrested "not because of their actions, but because of their position in society." Essentially, vagrants rebelled against social and cultural norms, becoming "masterless men" who could not be controlled by the local hierarchy.[5]

Thus, in early modern England most vagrants did not belong to the criminal underworld – they were simply economically dislocated. According to Forrest Lacey, after the Enlightenment, England passed a law that "placed almost exclusive emphasis on *conduct* and did not purport to attach criminality to *status* alone." But the new British law was not the one adopted by American colonies. Instead, almost all of them implemented versions of the common law offense, which simply stated that itinerants without a visible means of employment could be arrested. But antebellum American laws also varied widely from state to state. For example, Virginia law classified nine types of vagrants, while

---

[4] For information on postbellum southern vagrancy, see Eric Foner, *Reconstruction: America's Unfinished Revolution, 1863–1877* (New York: Harper Collins, 1988), 55, 62, 200–1, 206, 208–9, 363, 372, 519, 593; Lawrence M. Friedman, *Crime and Punishment in American History* (New York: Basic Books, 1993), 94, 100, 102–4, 201, 385–6; Alex Lichtenstein, *Twice the Work of Free Labor: The Political Economy of Convict Labor in the New South* (New York: Verso, 1996); and Douglas A. Blackmon, *Slavery by Another Name: The Re-Enslavement of Black Americans from the Civil War to World War II* (New York: Anchor, 2008).

[5] Margaret K. Rosenheim, "Vagrancy Concepts in Welfare Law," *California Law Review* 54, No. 2 (May 1966): 523; A.L. Beier, *Masterless Men: The Vagrancy Problem in England, 1560–1640* (London: Methuen, 1986), xxii.

Florida identified twenty groups. Many states, both North and South, considered a wide variety of people vagrants, including prostitutes, able-bodied beggars, gamblers and bootleggers, common drunkards, fornicators, associates of "known thieves," men who abandon or fail to support their families, and those who simply refuse to work: the "idlers." Two states even condemned jugglers and "common pipers and fiddlers."[6]

As America adopted versions of British statutes, a subtle but definite division between northern and southern vagrancy statutes became apparent. Northern vagrancy laws depended mainly on the need for labor – rapid industrialization caused an ever-increasing demand for workers. Northern states enacted longer, more detailed vagrancy statutes, but for all of their wordiness, they identified fewer categories of vagrants than did the much more terse southern laws, and they tended to focus on maintaining a productive population. The slave-based South, on the other hand, always had a surplus of labor; it was unnecessary to force any non-slave to work. And because the South's gentry had so much power over the region's laboring population, southern vagrancy statutes focused more on the prevention of undesirable activities – especially social interaction between poor whites and blacks. Because southern lawmakers crafted their vagrancy statutes in extremely vague ways, these non-descript definitions of the crime allowed slaveholders to justify the lengthy jailing of suspicious people – whether because of their habits, their occupations, their beliefs, or their resistance to the established hierarchy. Lacey found that, in modern vagrancy trials, it is commonly necessary to prove "evidence of prior acts, in most cases a series of such acts, to show that the accused has the personal condition he is charged with having," and this tenet seemed to hold true in the antebellum South. The typical poor white vagrant, therefore, was arrested not for a specific action, but rather for having "a certain personal condition" or being "a person of a specified character." Justice Hugo Black wrote that vagrancy had always been defined in "terms of *being* rather than in terms of *acting*." Considered a crime of status, arrests were based largely on the accused's economic class. In fact, class functioned as the only universal among southern vagrants. Most statutes stipulated that the offender be

---

[6] Forrest W. Lacey, "Vagrancy and Other Crimes of Personal Condition," *Harvard Law Review* 66, No. 7 (May 1953): 1206; Arthur H. Sherry, "Vagrants, Rogues and Vagabonds – Old Concepts in Need of Revision," *California Law Review* 48, No. 4 (Oct. 1960): 559; 564, italics in original; Lacey, "Vagrancy," 1207–9; Sherry, "Vagrants, Rogues," 559; 560.

without means of subsistence, and many declared that property ownership negated the crime.[7]

One of Georgia's first statutes to explicitly describe vagrancy came in
1816, condemning "[a]ny person wandering or strolling about, able to
work or otherwise to support himself or herself in a reputable way, or
leading an idle, immoral, or profligate course of life." The statute allowed
the courts to determine entirely the penalties for offenders. The law
remained untouched until 1847, when legislators added two important
clauses. First, the new statute specified that the accused "has not property
to support himself or herself." Second, punishment guidelines were set
between two and four years of hard labor in the state penitentiary. This
prison sentence was extreme in relation to the offense. Manslaughter
convictions generally warranted the same sentences, and prison terms
for assault were usually much shorter. Clearly, vagrancy frightened the
region's lawmakers. They made sure that convicts would be locked up for
several years.[8]

Paradoxically, if the offender could post bond "for his or her good
behavior and future industry for one year," he or she would be released.
Because most laws stipulated that vagrants could not own any property,
the bond clause was seemingly absurd. Statutorily the bond had to be less
than $400, but even if it averaged between 5 and 10 dollars, very few
impoverished whites could afford to pay it. Thus, such bonds as were
posted came largely from benefactors, resembling the ways in which well-
respected whites "vouched" for the behaviors of free blacks in local
courtrooms. This practice obviously served to strengthen the culture of
southern paternalism, and under this application, masters controlled
more than blacks and women – they dominated other white men as well.[9]

It is difficult to understand how vagrancy threatened the existing
southern order, though, without knowing more about the vagrants
themselves. Occasionally free blacks would be charged with vagrancy
(especially in South Carolina), but overwhelmingly the law was applied
to poor whites. In fact, one particular ruling seems to confirm that poor
whites were the intended targets of vagrancy laws throughout much of
the Deep South. In 1860, an Alabama appellate court ruled that "An

---

[7] Quoted in Lacey, "Vagrancy," 1214; 1224; 1203–1204; italics in original.
[8] Cobb, *Penal Code*, 38–9. *Acts of the General Assembly of the State of Georgia.* 1816,
pp. 181–6; 1835, pp. 332–4; 1847, pp. 199–200; 1855–6, pp. 344; 1857, pp. 314; 1859,
pp. 69–70; 1860, pp. 44–5; 1866, pp. 234; 1868, pp. 122. All Acts can be found online at
http://docsouth.unc.edu/imls/gagenas/georgia.html.
[9] Cobb, *Penal Code*, 38.

ordinance for the punishment of vagrants and disorderly persons" did not apply to slaves.[10]

Superior Court Minute books for fourteen Georgia counties indicate that more than 230 poor whites were charged formally with vagrancy in the forty years prior to the Civil War. Vagrancy cases appear frequently in local court documents in South Carolina and Mississippi as well. These numbers suggest that thousands of poor whites were charged with this offense throughout the antebellum South. Perhaps more importantly, extant jail records show that many poor whites were arrested and incarcerated without ever being formally charged with a crime. Yet, owing to the dearth of antebellum jail records, it is impossible to know just how many people were deprived of liberty without due process. Some of the most complete Deep South jail records come from Savannah, and they verify that many vagrants spent time in and out of the city jail before ever being arraigned. Indeed, it appears that the vast majority of vagrancy arrests led only to confinement; often there was no demonstrable intention of bringing these cases to court. Richard Morris found that in New Orleans, "the recorder's courts sentenced thousands of vagrants to the workhouse without proof, trial, or in most cases, opportunity of appeal." One grand jury even protested "against this failure to grant due process" to the accused. Several short statements in the Deep South's county minute books confirm Morris's research. People arrested for vagrancy frequently sat in jail for weeks and months awaiting indictment hearings.[11]

William Bishop, a poor white arrested for vagrancy in Bibb County in 1847, was finally released after being "confined to jail for more than a year and no person appearing to prosecute." The grand jury ordered him "discharged without payment of costs he having taken the oath of insolvency." And Benjamin Farrell, a farm laborer in his 30s, served an undisclosed amount of time in Camden County's guardhouse. When he finally was arraigned, the Solicitor General failed to appear in court, so the jury ordered Farrell discharged. In yet another example, Chatham County's officials twice charged George Horlbeck with vagrancy. After his first arrest, the judge described Horlbeck as "a prisoner in the county jail for some months," and ordered him "discharged for want of bond to prosecute."[12]

---

[10]   *Withers v. Coyles*, 36 Ala. 320, June 1860, in Catterall, *Judicial Cases*, 242–3.

[11]   Merritt, "Poor Whites," ch. 2; Lacey, "Vagrancy," 1214; 1224; Morris, "The Measure of Bondage," 224.

[12]   William Bishop: Bibb County, Superior Court Minutes, 1846–52, GDAH. Benjamin Farrell: Camden County, Superior Court Minutes, 1820–42, GDAH; Sixth Census of the United States, 1840: Decatur County, Georgia. George Horlbeck: Chatham County,

These stories, along with Savannah's jail records, suggest that slaveholders frequently used vagrancy as an excuse to imprison poor whites
without the intention of ever formally charging them. While some
vagrants were only held for a week to ten days, many offenders were
held without trial for several months, and some were even detained for a
full year. In cyclical fashion, other poor whites were jailed over and over
again. Some were imprisoned again just a day or two after being
released. Slave owners could use vagrancy laws to lock away anyone
who posed a threat to the southern system, even if no crime had been
committed.

Some southern officials even targeted entire families as vagrants,
arresting different relatives repeatedly over a period of ten or twenty
years. In more rural areas, slaveholders commonly cycled two or three
extended families through the criminal justice system over and over
again. In South Carolina's Anderson District, for example, the Chastain family served as some of the community's social pariahs. Federal
census records show that several households of Chastains lived near
each other, and all of the adults were listed as illiterate. Females
headed several of the homes, and the predominant male occupation
was farm laborer. Poor whites in every sense of the word, the Chastain
family became victims of Anderson's overzealous judicial system. In
1846 the district court found James Chastain guilty of vagrancy. Sent
to jail on the charge, Chastain apparently did "not get his support
honestly," although precisely *how* he managed to survive was unclear.
Many men in this rural community repeated this vague testimony, but
still, no one claimed that James Chastain was doing anything overtly
criminal. The most damning thing reported about Chastain was simply
that he owed a small amount of money to J.T. Broyles, who offered to
let him work off the debt. When Chastain refused to work for Broyles,
whether because the wages were too low, or the work was too dangerous, or simply because he did not want to, he was arrested and
imprisoned.[13]

James's case, however, was only one of the first in a string of late-
antebellum arrests among the Chastains. In 1849 and 1854, Cooper
Chastain was charged with the crime; in 1851, Sarah, Harriett, and

Superior Court Minutes, 1826–36, GDAH; Fifth Census of the United States, 1830:
Charleston County, South Carolina.
[13] Anderson District, Court of Magistrates and Freeholders, Vagrancy trials, 1829–1860,
SCDAH; Seventh Census of the United States, 1850: Anderson District, South Carolina.

Louisa Chastain were all arrested; in 1854 Martha was incarcerated; and in 1856 warrants were issued for the arrests of Emeline, Benjamin, and Mary Chastain. While some of these family members may have truly been involved in criminal activity, the frequency of their arrests demonstrate that by targeting an overwhelmingly poor extended family, southern masters used poverty as a predictor of deviancy.[14]

While stories like the Chastains' were relatively common in more rural plantation areas, the arrests of relatives en masse did not generally occur in Deep South cities. Indeed, as antebellum Americans became more geographically mobile, the idea of the intimate, face-to-face southern community was challenged, wreaking havoc on a social system long defined by personal honor. Parts of the region that housed larger towns, cities, or even new railroad stops increasingly became overrun with "strangers." Transient poor whites had no local kinfolk, no ties to the area's churches, and no real allegiance to the institution of slavery. Slaveholders, therefore, had no knowledge of which poor whites needed extra supervision – of who would help their slaves steal and drink, who would give birth to free black children, who would demoralize their work force, and who may try to lead their slaves into a bloody rebellion.

Predictably, it seems that the majority of vagrancy arrests occurred in large cities, where poor white anonymity was widespread. It was also impossible to keep the races separate in urban areas, as poor whites regularly came into contact with both slaves and free blacks in cities. Whites arrested for vagrancy tended to be in their late teens to early thirties, and they usually had some type of contact with blacks. Whether drinking, gambling, coupling, or trading with slaves in the underground economy, poor white men easily undermined masters' control over African Americans. But poor white women also posed a significant threat to the established racial hierarchy.

Slaveholders had a long history of incarcerating prostitutes and promiscuous poor white women on charges of vagrancy. They had good reason to regulate this section of the white population: interracial infants took on the legal status of their mothers, meaning that poor white women had the ability to produce an entire "race" of free blacks – a terrifying prospect for the southern gentry. Poor white women who acted in a sexually provocative manner, or had the economic need to sell their

[14] Anderson District, Vagrancy trials, 1829–1860, SCDAH; Seventh Census of the United States, 1850: Anderson District, South Carolina.

bodies for money, had the reproductive power to greatly disrupt America's racial hierarchy. Masters had multiple reasons to monitor the sexual behavior of white women, especially the poor ones. Many times, prostitutes and "immoral" women would be charged with vagrancy, as they did not have to be caught in the act. Instead of having to produce proof of prostitution, fornication, adultery, or lewd behavior, masters simply jailed poor white women for vagrancy.

This sexual nature of many arrests is evident in the few pieces of trial testimony that still exist. Mary Starns was accused of vagrancy in rural South Carolina in 1846. During her trial, a witness purported that Starns, a recent transplant from Franklin County, Georgia, had fled her native state after being charged with robbery and "house burning." The bigger scandal, however, had to do with Starns's living arrangements in her new residence. Accused of keeping a "disorderly house" (a house of prostitution), Mary Starns was apparently also living "in adultery with another woman's husband." James Burris, the man in question, had been financially supporting Starns, and District's slaveholders refused to turn a blind eye to the situation. By charging Starns with vagrancy, the State had very little to prove. Hearsay about morality and sexuality left her helpless in the face of southern vagrancy laws.[15]

Yet Starns's story is just one of many. Catherine Rhinehart and her daughter, Sabrina Dobson, were also arrested for the offense. As with Starns, Rhinehart and Dobson's court date began with classifying them as transient migrants with criminal pasts. Jeremiah Satterfield testified that Sabrina "acknowledged to me that [there was] evidence against her mother in North Carolina for murdering her one child." He claimed that Catherine was sentenced to be hanged until she was saved by a Governor's pardon. These accusations, based completely on hearsay, were never supported by actual evidence. But no evidence was needed. The die had been cast.

The impoverished mother-daughter duo, portrayed as lewd, sexually promiscuous women who loved to drink, fight, and generally raise hell, were said to have had a "Continual row all night long, almost every night firing guns, cursing, swearing, and hollowing." But the real bombshell – the one that surely gripped the attention of the entire courtroom – was that the two women were possibly selling their bodies to black men. One witness claimed that he noticed "several negroes around the house,"

[15] Anderson District, Vagrancy trials, 1829–1860, SCDAH.

salaciously adding that he believed the black men "are familiar with the women." Elijah McColister testified that he talked to "a negro boy of Blasingame's" near the women's residence one evening. The man he referred to apparently "had a bottle of spirits," and "said he was after Sabrina and not the old woman." McColister obviously concluded that "the negroes was familiar with the women and that the women was trading with them also." Perhaps the final setback in the women's case came from a relative of Elijah's, Andrew McColister. He claimed that one "Saturday evening 3 or 4 weeks ago between sundown and dark I saw 3 negro fellows at Miss Rhinehart's. Their business I did not learn others were hanging around and about there she went out shortly after I got there and did not return while I staid." Sabrina Dobson and Catherine Rhinehart were thus charged with vagrancy for a very specific reason, a reason that had absolutely nothing to do with the law's stated purpose. The Deep South's slaveholders wrote the laws, interpreted the laws, and enforced the laws. Vagrancy charges served the slave owners by keeping poor whites and blacks separated, especially sexually.[16]

When Sarah Wynn, also known as Sarah Clem, was formally charged with vagrancy in Columbus, Georgia in 1860, she had already spent several years in and out of the local jail for public drunkenness. Wynn was in her late 30s and had a rather difficult past. Census records reveal that she was living with her parents and brother, the Clems, in 1850 when she was in her late 20s. Although Wynn herself was destitute, her parents were better off, qualifying as small farmers with $1100 worth of personal property and real estate. Because of her last name, it is apparent that Wynn had been married and was either widowed, divorced, or abandoned.[17]

William Brown, the first man to testify against Wynn, was a 60-year-old planter from New York. An extremely wealthy widower with at least twenty slaves, Brown reported that he saw Wynn "frequently drunk in the streets," he had never known her to work, and that she often used "immoral obscene and profane language." A county marshal added scandalously that Wynn frequently appeared drunk in public places "with her clothes nearly torn off of her." Finally, Davenport P. Ellis, a well-off merchant in his mid-40s, was called as the State's last witness. Ellis brought up new information about the defendant: in recent months, he

[16] *Ibid.*, Sixth Census of the United States, 1840: Greenville County, South Carolina.
[17] Muscogee County, Superior Court Minutes, 1859–63, GDAH; Seventh and Eighth Censuses of the United States, 1850 and 1860: Muscogee County, Georgia.

had seen Wynn at Colonel Osborn's house, "drunk and noisy and threatening persons." Osborn, a "man of weak intellect and very imbecile," had a legal guardian to care for him and his rather large estate. Apparently Osborn, despite being listed in census records as "insane," was extremely wealthy. In addition to land and property, he also owned thirty-two slaves. According to Ellis, after Sarah Wynn accused Osborn of "staying with other women," Osborn ordered her off the premises. Osborn said that she "annoyed him greatly … and that he could not get rid of her."[18]

The two witnesses for the defense, however, told a very different story. Wynn's mother, Jane Clem, took the stand first. By the time of the trial, Clem was a 65-year-old widow whose circumstances had degenerated considerably, as the 1860 census showed her living with several other jobless "paupers." She admitted that while her daughter used to be "very bad," she had "reformed within the past eight months." Wynn was now employed by Colonel Osborn. She stayed "there night and day waiting on and sewing for" him, and she earned $10 a month. Several times, according to Clem, Osborn even sent his "Rockaway [carriage] and boy" to pick up Wynn. The final witness, a fiftyish woman who resided with Jane Clem, corroborated the story completely. Wynn "was behaving herself very well while at Osborn's." Census records from 1860 confirm the women's testimonies. Wynn, then 38 years old, lived with William Osborn, a 65-year-old, widowed planter with $2,500 worth of real estate, $10,000 worth of personal property, and more than thirty slaves. Although it is not quite clear from the evidence what kind of relationship Wynn and Osborn maintained, a poor white woman living with a wealthy, mentally deficient slave owner must have raised some moral concern within the community.[19]

Furthermore, Wynn's wild and erratic behavior, coupled with her alcohol problems, probably caused many slaveholders alarm. The suggestive comment about Wynn's clothing was particularly noteworthy, for Sarah Wynn's wanton sexuality and her proximity to Osborn's slaves was a combination with the potential to disrupt the local hierarchy. Because Wynn had acted outside of socially acceptable gender and class roles, she

[18] *Ibid.*; U.S. Bureau of the Census. Slave Schedules, Eighth Census, 1860: Muscogee County, Georgia.
[19] Jane Clem and Mrs. Maugham: Eighth Census of the United States, 1860: Muscogee County, Georgia. Both women were listed as paupers with no occupation. William Osborn: *Ibid.*; Eighth Census of the United States, 1860, Slave Schedule: Muscogee County, Georgia.

was sentenced to three years in the state penitentiary. She served all but three months of her term. Unfortunately, Sarah Wynn never seemed to improve her lot in life. In 1870, she was living in Muscogee's poor asylum.[20]

Although white women made up a decent percentage of southern vagrants, poor, able-bodied young men comprised the largest group by far. While some of these men had wives and children, many of them at least appeared to be single in census records. With the transience of the poor white population, however, it is possible that many of these men simply lived apart from their families for the majority of the year, working short-term jobs or searching for work. A prime example of poor white men leading a nomadic existence was Edward Isham, who moved every year or two, leaving behind a string of "wives," lovers, and illegitimate children. Victoria Bynum wrote that the women in Isham's life often kept him from self-destruction, but they also enabled him to live outside both state and moral law. With completely absent fathers such as Edward Isham, it is not surprising that many of the poor white vagrants found in census records seemingly grew up in female-headed households. Radford White, an 18-year-old charged in Bibb County in 1855, resided with his jobless mother. William Holt, a 20-year-old laborer from Macon, also grew up without a father figure. And Ezekiel Ward, charged with vagrancy in Morgan County in 1858, seemed to have been raised by a destitute mother and was supported financially by older brothers who worked as laborers.[21]

The fractured family lives of poor whites often caused these wandering men to be viewed with suspicion. As Lawrence Friedman wrote, nineteenth-century America was a "society based on mobility and immigration," but it "was also a society suspicious of immigrants and strangers, especially those who were detached and alone, without community or social circle or family, without fixed setting." Trials frequently mentioned the defendant's recent move to the area as a reason for suspicion; rumors abounded about these men's reasons for leaving home. Even

[20] Sarah Wynn: State of Georgia Board of Corrections, Inmate Administration Division: Central Registration of Convicts, 1817–85, GDAH; Ninth Census of the United States, 1870: Muscogee County, Georgia.

[21] Bolton, *The Confessions of Edward Isham*, 1–18; also see Chapter 6. Radford White: Bibb County, Superior Court Minutes, 1852–56, GDAH. William Holt: *Ibid.*; Seventh Census of the United States, 1850: Bibb County, Georgia. Ezekiel Ward: Morgan County, Superior Court Minutes, 1820–65, GDAH; Seventh Census of the United States, 1850: Morgan County, Georgia.

if a poor white was from the next town over, that alone was enough to cause some distrust. In 1845, William Avery was charged with vagrancy in South Carolina's Anderson District, essentially for stealing foodstuffs – mainly in the form of corn – from seven or eight of his neighbors. Described as "a drunken, dishonest man," Avery supposedly had been run out of Greenville for stealing corn as well. This damning trial "evidence" was once again hearsay; trusted members of the community were allowed to present rumors as facts inside the courtroom. Yet for slaveholding locals, hearsay *should have* functioned as fact. Because they lacked any knowledge about Avery's ancestry, family connections, respectability, and background, they had no choice but to believe what esteemed men within their communities said about the situation. Their property – and indeed, their safety – was at stake if they did not.[22]

Still, southern-born poor whites were not held to the same exacting standards reserved for Northerners and Europeans residing within the region. As Edward Ayers found, the foreign-born population was less than 3 percent of whites in the 1850s South. Yet they comprised between 8 and 37 percent of the region's prisoners. People who emigrated into the slave states from free areas arrived with their own beliefs, ideas, and political agendas. In a slave society, this knowledge of the outside world worried masters greatly. They certainly did not want their slaves to hear talk of abolition or to know that blacks were free in other parts of the world, and to accomplish this task they needed to keep other poor whites ignorant of those facts as well. While all European immigrants endured additional scrutiny, Irish immigrants were clearly some of southern judicial system's primary targets. It was no coincidence that the Irish Famine began in 1845, and by the next year, southern papers were complaining of "frequent conflagrations" in Charleston and Savannah. "The number of vagrants and vagabonds hurrying from village to village and from city to city," the editor opined, was never "so numerous in the Southern States as at the present moment."[23]

To put this fear of immigrants into perspective, about two-thirds of the people sent to Georgia's prison for vagrancy were born outside of the state or country, and at least two out of the nine women were from Ireland. A list of people charged with vagrancy in Kershaw District, South Carolina, reveals that Irish immigrants (and occasionally Germans) were

---

[22] Friedman, *Crime and Punishment*, 102; 103; Anderson District, Vagrancy trials, 1829–1860, SCDAH.
[23] "Fires in Savannah and Charleston," *Columbus Enquirer*, March 18, 1846, 2.

still being arrested at significantly higher rates than southern-born poor whites, well into the mid-1850s. Patrick Haffie, James Dawson, James Sullivan, Daniel McBright, John Bowen, Joseph E. McCauney, John Kennedy, Condy McHughs, and Edward Fraal were all deemed "persons of suspicious character." The Irish appear repeatedly in arrest records, especially in port cities like Savannah, where John Harper was arrested twice for vagrancy in 1845. A 25-year-old illiterate laborer from Ireland, Harper was finally discharged after swearing to his inability to pay jail fees. Likewise, John Casey, an Irishman in his 20s, was jailed twice for the crime in 1856 and 1857. But Irish *men* were not the only immigrants who cycled in and out of the Deep South's jails. In fact, Irish women were frequently detained and convicted of the crime at higher rates than men. One of Savannah's most notorious vagrants, Betty C. McLiam, spent years in and out of the city jail before her conviction in 1861. At 30 years old, McLiam, a prostitute from Kilkenny, Ireland, was sentenced to three years of hard labor in Milledgeville. She served all but three months of her sentence. Additionally, Catherine Ryan, the 22-year-old wife of an Irish painter, Anna Clark, a 34-year-old illiterate domestic worker, and Mary Powers, a 17-year-old prostitute, all spent time in the Savannah jail for vagrancy in the few years right before the Civil War.[24]

Irish immigrants helped swell the already growing poor white population in the Deep South, adding thousands of young, single, impoverished people to an already dispossessed population. As the numbers of able-bodied, fighting-age men increased, slave owners obviously had cause for some concern. With memories of the Vicksburg Gamblers, Nat Turner, Denmark Vesey, and many other smaller revolts, slaveholders were undoubtedly apprehensive. Essentially masterless men, poor whites had no one to answer to, no family name to uphold, and thus possessed a unique form of personal freedom. To the master class it seemed that these men had no responsibilities, that they traded the duties of men for the

[24] State of Georgia, Central Registration of Convicts, GDAH; Kershaw District, Court of Magistrates and Freeholders, Trial papers, 1802–1861, SCDAH. John Harper: Chatham County, Superior Court Minutes, 1841–45, GDAH; Seventh Census of the United States, 1850: Chatham County, Georgia. John Casey: Chatham County, Superior Court Minutes, 1841–45, GDAH; Eighth Census of the United States, 1860: Chatham County, Georgia. Betty C. McLiam: *Ibid.*, State of Georgia Board of Corrections, Inmate Administration Division: Central Registration of Convicts, 1817–85, GDAH. Catherine Ryan: Chatham County, Superior Court Minutes, 1859–65, GDAH; Ninth Census of the United States, 1870: Bibb County, Georgia. Anna Clark: Savannah Jail Records, 1855–63, GDAH; Eighth Census of the United States, 1860: Chatham County, Georgia. Mary Powers: *Ibid.*

pleasures of boys, whether drinking to great excess, gambling, fighting, or cavorting with loose women and prostitutes. One Georgia vagrant was jailed after reports and complaints of his being a "turbulent individual." This "turbulence," the propensity for violence, and the disaffection and anger that often accompany poverty, formed a potentially explosive combination. When a human being is poor enough to feel as though he has nothing to lose, and has no real hope for tomorrow, he is often not disposed to think beyond fulfilling immediate, short-term survival needs. Perhaps this focus on the present is part of the reason that poor whites never truly organized to do anything about their larger plight – even though they surely understood *why* they were in that economic position in the first place. But this focus on immediate desires also encouraged an individual to exist outside of the law; to break social and moral codes without truly considering the stark reality of the eventual consequences. Slaveholders quickly realized the potentially subversive consequences of the freedom inherent in poor whites simply not giving a damn. And in many cases masters seemed to view the poverty-to-crime path as a slippery slope: petty theft could lead to trading with slaves, which could then lead to personal relationships between the two groups, which may then lead to revolts or rebellions. All in all, slaveholders believed they had a legitimate reason to worry.[25]

Worry was, of course, the consequence of maintaining such a large poor population. Slaveholder anxiety would become even more intensified as hunger and abject poverty became widespread problems in the later antebellum period. After his arrest for vagrancy in 1841, James Browning was accused by several of his upcountry South Carolina neighbors of stealing corn. His children apparently often pilfered and even broke into a nearby house, ostensibly searching for food. Browning's wife was overheard saying that "it was hard to live on bread and sometimes [there was] not enough of that." In a final statement that completely eviscerated his masculinity, Mrs. Browning asserted that she "could do better with[out] him than with him." The extent of the Browning's poverty meant that a poor white man like James could not even function as a master of his own home. Frequently physically absent and otherwise unable to financially provide for their families, many poor whites must have felt like failures as men.[26]

[25] "Untitled," *Columbus Enquirer* (GA), May 13, 1846, 3; Anderson District, Vagrancy trials, 1829–1860, SCDAH.
[26] "James Browning – Vagrancy," *Ibid.*

Even in the Appalachian foothills and mountainous regions where slaves comprised small percentages of the population, poor whites were arrested for vagrancy with relative frequency. Although the juries in these areas were generally composed of more slaveholding yeomen than large slaveholders, the fact remains that local officials made a point of jailing their county's poor whites for vagrancy. Several other cases out of Anderson, South Carolina, prove that these arrests depended on the accused's character, associates, and propensity to commit other crimes. As previously mentioned, William Avery was charged with vagrancy, and his trial echoed many of the concerns that southern citizens had about James Browning. Accused of pilfering a grindstone from a neighbor, corn and geese from another, and various food items from at least four or five others, Avery's guilt seemed quite evident. But instead of multiple counts of larceny, local officials charged him with vagrancy, likely due to the burden of proof being so low and the penalties being so severe. These few cases from the upcountry reveal that while vagrancy arrests in lower-slave areas occurred with less frequency, the people charged were often on trial for similar reasons as poor whites in the plantation belt.[27]

Edmond Thacker, an illiterate farm laborer who had been recently widowed, led a hard, miserable life. Owning no property or real estate, Thacker had four young children to support by himself in rural South Carolina. Charged with vagrancy in March 1852, Thacker was basically on trial for his shortcomings as a financial provider, coupled with his propensity for hard drinking.[28]

The prosecution built their case around the fact that Edmund Thacker had been offered several short-term job opportunities but turned them all down. Whenever Thacker deemed work too dangerous, or wages too low, he refrained from accepting the employment. Thacker's inability to economically support his family led to his children begging for food and help from neighbors. The poor, motherless children "were generally by themselves," reported neighbor John Hembree, and "they generally complained of having nothing to eat – they often asked [me] for to giving them something to eat, sometimes [I] gave them some." The most distressing part of this story, Hembree asserted, was that Thacker *could* have

---

[27] "William Avery – Vagrancy," Anderson District, Vagrancy trials, SCDAH.

[28] "Edmond Thacker – Vagrancy," *Ibid.* (note: his name is spelled "Edmond" on the document title but "Edmund" within the trial papers); Seventh Census of the United States, 1850: Anderson District, South Carolina; Eighth Census of the United States, 1860: Anderson District, South Carolina; "Edmond Thacker – Vagrancy," Anderson District, Vagrancy trials, 1829–1860, SCDAH.

provided for his family "if he had not spent his money on liquor." Thacker had apparently been drinking frequently, especially "since his wife died." Hembree further claimed that the accused "had not worked much at any one place, but from place to place, not long at any one place." While most poor white men were in the same employment predicament, Hembree piled on more injurious testimony, claiming he had "once tried" to get Thacker to work for him and earn "provisions," as "his children were badly clothed just enough to hide their nakedness." Yet even with hungry, ill-clad children, Edmund Thacker refused to work.[29]

The second witness, John Hise, had a slightly more sympathetic view of Thacker, commenting that "his children was clothed as well as poor children generally are." Hise even saw the accused "plowing in wheat for Cassa Gentry last fall." But he had the same problem with Thacker that John Hembree did. Hise had offered Thacker a job, but he refused to take it. While seemingly a lazy, obstinate move by Thacker, the reality of the situation was more complicated. Hise had offered Thacker 37.5 cents per day – plus board – to work. Real wages in the South had begun to fall in the late 1840s, and they continued their plummet downward throughout the 1850s. Robert Fogel famously characterized this period as a "hidden depression" for free labor. But Thacker was used to earning more for his labor and held out for a better price. Trying to negotiate with his potential employer, Thacker attempted to convince Hise that his labor was worth more than the offered amount. He had worked for Henry Jury for 40 cents a day, he pleaded, and did not need board anyway. Yet when Hise refused to budge at all on the wage issue, Thacker refused the work. Unfortunately for Edmund Thacker, slavery had rendered his bargaining power obsolete. He only had two choices: to take the wages offered or give up the chance to earn anything. Men who chose the latter option were always liable to be charged with vagrancy.[30]

The testimony of John W.B. Skelton exposed Edmund Thacker's third refusal to work. Once again, a neighbor had offered Thacker a job, and once again he refused it. Of course, Thacker claimed to have another legitimate reason for rejecting the opportunity. Skelton wanted him to ditch, a job deemed too risky for valuable slave labor. Thacker "did not do it, alleging his health was not good and ditching injured him."

---

[29] *Ibid.*
[30] *Ibid.*; Margo, *Wages and Labor Markets*, 144; "Edmund Thacker – Vagrancy," Anderson District, Vagrancy trials, 1829–1860, SCDAH.

Thacker, therefore, turned down work three times, while his children simultaneously "complained that they had nothing to eat." For each abandoned opportunity, Thacker had a different reason for forgoing the job. If southern vagrancy arrests had really been about labor, Thacker would have been convicted. Yet the final few witnesses in his trial likely saved him from years in jail, massive debt, and perhaps corporal punishment. As a recent widower, they claimed, Thacker had to spend most of his time at or near his home, tending to his very young children. And despite his rejection of employment offers, Thacker apparently still had enough money to occasionally purchase food for his family during the most dire times. Witnesses testified that when they gave Thacker corn or meat, he paid for it. Repeatedly, people commented that it was "difficult to get provisions." Although Thacker "is in a bad fix," one man opined, he "has never been accounted a lazy man." Thacker's saving grace was the fact that vagrancy law had little to do with labor. Even though he drank to excess, his other behaviors seemed relatively tame – he was not frequenting whore houses, gambling and fighting, or cavorting with slaves. Furthermore, it was much easier for the local government to acquit Thacker so that his children remained in his care. The district did not want the burden of four more young orphans.[31]

Thus, while there were certainly times the accused's poverty was the only reason for a vagrancy charge, records generally show that poor white male vagrants were ascribed a combination of stereotypical traits: they were considered idle and lazy, they loved to drink to great excess, they had personal contact with slaves and free blacks, they fought, they gambled, and they were generally promiscuous. Jacob Waddel's case is a good example, as he was convicted of vagrancy based on his drunken and immoral behavior. The court based its decision on the everyday actions of Waddel – not on one particular event or "act" of vagrancy. Waddel's case was not substantively different from those of other vagrants, yet somehow he had the resources to petition the county court's ruling, offering interesting insight into the life of a poor white vagrant. The first witness for the prosecution, Joseph Caswell, claimed that Waddel had "worked on a house" for him two years prior to the arrest, and had "heard that defendant built a room last year for William Walker." Still, he swore that he did not know what Waddel did for a living; he only knew that the defendant had four or five children and that he had not seen him in the past year. During

[31] *Ibid.*

cross-examination, Waddel's lawyer asserted that Waddel worked as a carpenter, and thus had "to go about frequently to get work."[32]

James Wadsworth lived only half a mile from Waddel, and "saw him oftener in the road than elsewhere." He knew that Waddel had planted some potatoes that year, but saw no other "signs of cultivation" or "crop about the house." Wadsworth described Waddel's home as a "log cabin," and reported that Waddel had also come to him looking for meat, although he offered to pay for it. Agreeing with other witnesses, Wadsworth stated that several times he had seen Waddel drunk at Doolittle's Grocery, although not within the past two years. During cross-examination, Waddel's lawyer once again stressed that the defendant worked as a mechanic, and "mechanics work about." Wadsworth replied that he did not know whether Waddel worked or "idle[d] his time."

Although Waddel ultimately lost his appeal, he does not show up in the penitentiary records. He may have simply served his time in the Marion County jail. Clearly, however, Waddel improved his financial situation in the years following his conviction, although some of his prosperity was doubtless attributable to the complete economic upheaval of the Civil War. By 1870, Waddel owned $150 worth of real estate and $300 worth of personal property – significantly more than the $10 worth of furniture he owned in 1858. His case nicely illustrates several points about the lives of poor whites. First, it highlights the exclusion of poor whites from the southern labor system. Waddel's lawyer clearly expected the court to realize that, as a mechanic, Waddel frequently had to be away from home to search for whatever scattered work he could find. Furthermore, like many other poor whites, Jacob Waddel obviously had a serious drinking problem. Finally, his inability to find work near his home, combined with his frequent drunkenness, ultimately led to a very fractured, unstable, poverty-ridden life for his wife and children.[33]

William Melvin McDaniel was also charged with vagrancy in the late 1850s. McDaniel, a 17-year-old from Muscogee County, Georgia, undoubtedly led an "immoral" life. His trial made it clear that he was being condemned for his general lifestyle, not any one specific action. Like almost all white vagrants, McDaniel came from a less fortunate

---

[32] *Waddel vs. Georgia; Jacob Waddel vs. The State*, Brief of Evidence, filing 9/16/1858, judgment 2/4/1859. Case A-2666, GDAH.

[33] John Kemp and James Wadsworth: Eighth Census of the United States, 1860: Marion County, Georgia. Jacob Waddel: *Ibid.*: Chattahoochee County, Georgia. Waddel was listed as a forty-five year old farmer who lived with his wife and three children.

background. The 1850 census showed that his father, an illiterate laborer from South Carolina, owned no land and only $200 worth of personal property, and had six children to feed. Like many young men who felt completely disengaged from society, McDaniel began acting in a self-destructive, often lawless manner.[34]

The first witness at McDaniel's trial, the local marshal James Hughes, reported knowing the defendant for five or six years, in which time he had "seen him do nothing for a livelihood." Instead, McDaniel was "a young man of bad character" who spent time at whorehouses in "a bad part of town." He was also known to drink "whenever he can get liquor." Hughes recalled that McDaniel had been locked in the guardhouse several times during the present year – he even broke jail once. The next witness, another county marshal, stated that he had known McDaniel for four years, and that he had seldom seen him sober. Thus, McDaniel began drinking to extreme excess at the tender age of 12 or 13 years old. The marshal confirmed that McDaniel frequented houses of ill-repute and that he had "no visible means of support." A final witness further corroborated that McDaniel, who "frolicked around whorehouses and drank liquor," had been locked in the guardhouse for the past month.[35]

Henry Johnson, an illiterate poor man, was the first witness for the defense. Johnson told the jury that McDaniel had "worked sometime" on a river dam "opposite Columbus." On cross-examination, however, Johnson admitted to seeing McDaniel "pretty drunk ... some two or three times about Christmas," and he also knew of at least two fights in which the defendant had participated. Witnesses Garland B. Terry and John Allen had both previously employed McDaniel. A master carpenter in his 50s, Terry hired McDaniel to work on a bridge for five days, and then to work on a racetrack in LaGrange for five or six weeks. Although Terry admitted that the defendant had a "reputation of being a rowdy," he had never seen him drunk. Allen, also a carpenter in his 50s, had a very different experience. He hired McDaniel to cut wood, but after a few days the defendant quit. Allen "could not prevail upon him to continue work." Instead, McDaniel "strolled about town drinking."[36]

---

[34] Muscogee County, Superior Court Minutes, 1858–9, GDAH; Seventh Census of the United States, 1850: Gwinnett County, Georgia. McDaniel was 8 years old. He does not appear in the 1860 census.

[35] Muscogee County, Superior Court Minutes, 1858–9, GDAH.

[36] Henry Johnson: Eighth Census of the United States, 1860: Muscogee County, Georgia. Johnson had $100 of personal property and no real estate. Garland B. Terry: *Ibid.*: Quitman County, Georgia. John Allen: *Ibid.*: Muscogee County, Georgia.

The jury obviously took all of the testimonies about McDaniel's wayward character seriously. They condemned McDaniel to two years in the state penitentiary, where he served the majority of his sentence working as a carpenter. Whether because of prison, or personal maturity, or the War, by 1870 McDaniel had reformed his untamed ways. He was listed in the census as a 27–year-old farm laborer with a wife and young son.[37]

Perhaps the most interesting testimony in McDaniel's case provided insight into what many poor white men were probably feeling. Henry Johnson, undoubtedly the poorest witness, admitted to the court that McDaniel had once professed "that he had as soon be in the penitentiary [as] anywhere else, and didn't care a damn." McDaniel's depression-fueled apathy about his future deserves closer analysis. In *Roll, Jordan, Roll*, Eugene Genovese reinterpreted what was considered fatalism among slaves, demonstrating that many forms of slave resistance actually resulted from submerged anger and resentment. Slaves feigned illness, broke tools, and ran away; poor whites got too drunk to work, broke tools, and bought stolen goods from slaves. Shirking, drinking, whoring, stealing, and fighting were all ways that southern poor whites could simultaneously escape and buck a system in which they had no stake. The harsh realities of the daily lives of poor whites – such as McDaniel, or Thacker, or Waddell – make it easy to understand *why* these people might have felt isolated within the southern society. By throttling the opportunities of free laborers, slavery and slaveholding interests stripped poor white males of their jobs, drove down their wages, and crushed their sense of self-worth, their honor, and even their most sacred trait: their "whiteness."[38]

And while it seems logical that masters would be more concerned about sexual relationships between white women and black men, several vagrancy cases involving poor white men and black women seem to indicate otherwise. Because all children born to slave women increased the wealth and workforce of the South's slaveholders, masters probably did not worry much about white male/enslaved female affairs. But perhaps it was poor white men's commingling with free black women that bothered slave owners, as the offspring of these relationships would also add to the free black population.

---

[37] William McDaniel: Muscogee County, Superior Court Minutes, 1858–9, GDAH; Ninth Census of the United States, 1870: Harris County, Georgia; State of Georgia Board of Corrections, Inmate Administration Division: Central Registration of Convicts, 1817–85, GDAH.

[38] Genovese, *Roll, Jordan, Roll*.

Census records help corroborate this theory. For example, Washington Allen, arrested for vagrancy in 1844, was in his 20s and employed in manufacturing. He lived with one older white woman who was most likely his mother, as she was between 60 and 70 years old. However, Allen also resided with two "free colored" females – one between 10 and 24 years, and one younger than 10 years old. It is very probable that these free blacks were Allen's lover and daughter. Allen was convicted the year after his arrest, although it is unclear what his sentence entailed.[39]

Likewise, John Mitchell, a 62–year-old seaman from Virginia, was arrested in Chatham County, Georgia. Mitchell lived in Savannah with two free black men, three free black women, and three female slaves. It seems very plausible that he was involved in a sexual relationship with an African American woman. Lewis Gregory was also accused of vagrancy, also likely due to his fraternization with free black women. Gregory was in his 60s and employed in manufacturing. He lived with one white female and two free black females. Given their ages, in all likelihood these three women were Gregory's lover and daughters – perhaps one daughter was white enough to "pass," or maybe both he and his partner had children from previous relationships. Gregory's bond was set at an exorbitant $500 and could be "voided ... [on] the condition that the said defendant was industrious and orderly for the space of one year." The convictions of these three men probably served as warnings to other poor white men who cohabitated or cavorted with free black women.[40]

Indeed, as Timothy Lockley claimed, during the 1840s and 1850s the Deep South's slaveholders "became increasingly concerned" about the interactions between poor whites and slaves. One Georgia planter condemned "vagrants, traveling as organ-grinders and show-masters, having frequently clandestine intercourse with our slaves, and infusing dangerous notions, telling them, among other things, that they ought to be free." In 1855, Henry Tie was arrested for vagrancy in Kershaw, South Carolina, likely because of his interactions with blacks and other "low associates." One witness claimed to have seen Tie "with a jug of whiskey conducting negroes out of town." While admitting that he had "conducted illicit

[39] Morgan County, Superior Court Minutes, 1840–51, GDAH; Sixth Census of the United States, 1840: Gwinnett County, Georgia.

[40] John Mitchell: State of Georgia Board of Corrections, Inmate Administration Division: Central Registration of Convicts, 1817–85, GDAH; Sixth Census of the United States, 1840: Baldwin County, Georgia. Lewis H. Gregory: Richmond County, Superior Court Minutes, 1820–1900, GDAH; Fourth Census of the United States, 1820: Richmond County, Georgia; Fifth Census of the United States, 1830: Bibb County, Georgia.

traffic with slaves 18 years ago," Tie swore that he had been a law-abiding citizen since that time. Similarly, officials in Columbus Georgia, arrested Ann Willis for vagrancy after she supplied a slave with a half pint of liquor, "without the knowledge and consent of the owner, overseer, or employer." The sharing of intoxicating spirits between a blacks and whites could certainly preface a range of interactions, from those of a sexual nature to those of a criminal nature. Liquor always functioned as a social conduit between the races.[41]

Masters, of course, worried about any kind of conviviality between African Americans and poor whites. And from rebellion to miscegenation to the underground economy, alcohol was central to much of the mayhem created by the South's poor. But they also had other reasons to oppose the widespread use of liquor. Drunkenness and alcoholism were very serious problems in antebellum America; few people today can fully grasp the culture of abuse, death, and destruction created by the misuse of the drug. Indeed, alcohol was central to the vast majority of southern fights and affrays, just as it was to poor whites' other vices of prostitution, petty criminal activities, and gambling. Whether rolling the dice, playing cards, or spinning the faro wheel, games like chuck-a-luck and seven up allowed the upper classes to arrest poorer whites who were simply seeking a few hours of entertainment. Yet the reason for their relatively frequent imprisonment was clear: gambling often included slaves and free blacks.[42]

Drinking to excess became such a problem in antebellum America that temperance societies began forming in the 1820s and 1830s. Leaders of this movement were quick to point out the connection between poverty and intemperance. "People in the antebellum United States consumed extraordinary amounts of alcohol," Forret explained. "Generally speaking, men outdrank women, lower classes out-consumed upper classes, and unskilled laborers imbibed more than skilled employees. By these criteria, poor white men must have consumed more alcohol than any other group of whites." J.R. Gillmore, writing for *Harper's Magazine* in June of 1864, estimated that "half a million" southern poor whites were predisposed to becoming addicts, as they were especially "given to whisky-drinking, snuff-dipping, clay-eating, and all manner of social vices." While historians may never know exactly how prevalent alcoholism and drunkenness actually were, sources ranging from coroners'

---

[41] Lockley, *Lines in the Sand*, 129; Kershaw District, Vagrancy trials, 1821–1855, SCDAH; Muscogee County, Superior Court Records, 1858–9, GDAH.
[42] Ely, "Few Subjects," 851.

reports to newspapers to criminal trials indicate that a large percentage of poor white men, and a significant number of poor white women, frequently engaged in heavy drinking benders. Furthermore, hundreds of Southerners died from alcoholism or alcohol poisoning each year.[43]

Both the affluent and the upper-middling classes drank at licensed taverns. These were "respectable" places, usually serving food and sometimes boarding patrons. Taverns, of course, were not the target of temperance activists. They primarily concerned themselves with controlling the actions of poor whites, who typically purchased their liquor from illegal dram shops or groggeries. Sometimes grocery stores would sell liquor on the side, but other grog shops operated out of individual homes or makeshift roadside stands. One Macon, Georgia, paper estimated that by 1835, Bibb County had "not less than fifty licensed dram shops, and some eight or ten not licensed," which were blamed as the "fruitful source of nearly all the criminal prosecutions" in the locality. But slaveholders did not have much success in stopping the proliferation of groggeries. By the late 1840s, another article guessed there were 500 grog shops throughout the state.[44]

As W.J. Rorabaugh wrote in *Alcoholic Republic*, antebellum America was, in fact, a nation of heavy drinkers. During the first third of the nineteenth century, consumption of distilled liquors continued to increase until it exceeded five gallons per person per year, "a rate nearly triple that of today's consumption." Throughout the antebellum period, alcohol was a central part of many people's lives. Many young boys were taught to drink small amounts of diluted alcohol as toddlers. But women were no strangers to the drink, either. They consumed between one-eighth and one-quarter of the nation's liquor. Even slaves partook in this national pastime, Rorabaugh noted, as masters generally used watered-down alcohol as a work incentive during harvest time, "and many allowed their bondsmen a three-day spree at Christmas."

By the 1830s, the custom of drinking small amounts of liquor all day long was declining, but binge drinking was on the rise. While this shift surely resulted from several factors, it is likely that as settlers pushed westward and people lived in more rural, desolate places, they used

[43] Forret, *Race Relations*, 52–3; J.R. Gillmore, "The Poor Whites of the South," *Harper's New Monthly Magazine*, Vol. 21, No. 48 (June 1864): 115, accessed in the Alfred H. Stone Collection, MDAH

[44] "Presentments," *Georgia Telegraph* (Macon), Jan. 29, 1835, 3; "Usury Laws & c.," *Ibid.*, Nov. 2, 1847, 3.

alcohol to relieve feelings of loneliness and anxiety. "When he was sober, his inability to realize his aspirations engendered an acute sense of frustration that increased during long periods of abstinence," Rorabaugh wrote. "A drunken spree enabled him to turn his thoughts away from the failure of his own life, to perpetuate his illusory hopes, to deny the contradictions between his ideals and reality." For many poor whites, who lived hard, haggard lives with no real hope for a better future, getting drunk was a conscious choice, he concluded, "an act of self-will by which a man altered his feelings, escaped his burdens, and sought perfection in his surroundings. Because drinking was a matter of choice, it increased a man's sense of autonomy. To be drunk was to be free."[45]

This freedom, however, had consequences. Part of this effort to restrict consumption stemmed from the fact that liquor undoubtedly disrupted the labor market, rendering the drunkard unsuitable for work, less productive, or even dangerous. Vagrancy trials often focused on how frequently the accused chose to drink and carouse instead of search for work. Furthermore, it was no accident that employers generally paid wages on Saturday nights; they knew that many workers would be too drunk or hungover to perform their jobs the next day. Perhaps this culture of alcoholism helped produce the so-called "Blue Laws" in the Deep South that banned the sale of alcohol on Sundays, as slaveholders would have recognized the obvious benefit of prohibiting the liquor trade during the only day that slaves and other laborers had time off from work. If sales were limited on Sundays, masters and employers would have more-productive workforces on Monday morning. The most addicted drunks often worked infrequently, often only enough to buy a little food and a lot more alcohol. County court records reveal that one- or two-month benders were not uncommon; after the drunkard "dried out" for a few days he would work several small jobs to earn enough provisions for the next bender.

Furthermore, newspapers were peppered with reports of assaults, murders, and affrays committed by drunken poor whites. One article in Macon, Georgia, reported the escape of John and Daniel Jackson, a father and son duo "guilty of corrupt and willful perjury, and ... assault with intent to murder. Both ... are hardened scoundrels, fond of the dram shop, prone to broils, ready to contract debts without intending to pay, and a burthen and pest to any neighborhood in which they reside."

---

[45] Rorabaugh, *The Alcoholic Republic*, 8; 14; 12; 13; 169; 161; 151.

Suspecting the Jacksons had absconded to Pike County, Alabama, the paper offered a $25 reward for their apprehension. Another Georgia paper, the *Federal Union*, described two different drunken affrays over one weekend. Both involved multiple stab wounds, and at least one resulted in death: "Both of these affrays were instigated by whiskey. One if not both quarrels originated in a groggery – those pestiferious sinks of inequity that breed pauperism, vagabondism, and crime by the wholesale." Grog shops, the paper purported, "are filling the land with mourning, and our prison houses with victims." When drinking to great excess, poor whites often lost their self-control, and this loss of restraint could lead to proving one's self-worth through violent means. "Fatal affrays" were common occurrences; and intoxication contributed to the deaths of many poor white Southerners.[46]

Alcohol, therefore, did much more damage than just encouraging criminal activity among the white lower class. Poor house records, coroner's reports, and newspaper obituaries reveal just how deadly alcohol was in the antebellum period. Some fatalities were suicides, some were accidents, and some resulted from years and years of abusing the substance. "Delirium tremens," more commonly known as the "DTs," or the "shakes," resulted from alcohol withdrawal. It produced intense irritation and anxiety, culminating in muscle spasms that could cause the entire body to tremble. Delirium tremens was often listed as the cause of death for alcoholics. In 1857, a painter from Macon, Georgia "committed suicide by jumping down a well. ... He had been drinking freely, and was doubtless laboring under delirium tremens. A Coroner's Inquest was held over his body, and rendered a verdict to that effect."[47]

While drink-fueled suicides often involved other instruments of death, like pistols or rope, at times people literally drank themselves to death, perishing from alcohol poisoning. These types of deaths were overwhelmingly accidents, but there were a few cases with intent. In Walton County, Georgia, a "tailor by trade and a drunkard in habit" reportedly "deliberately committed suicide, by swallowing three or four half pints of raw whiskey, one after another! A few minutes previous to his death, he was heard making use of the most horrid imprecations, hurrahing for the d— and saying he was bound for h–!" While not all drunks extinguished their

---

[46] "Petition for Prohibiting the Sale of Liquor," Folder "Temperance," Petitions, 1817–1908, Mississippi Legislature, MDAH; "Look out for the Villians!!," *Macon Telegraph*, May 7, 1831, 4; "Serious Affrays," *Federal Union*, Jan. 18, 1853, 2.

[47] Rorabaugh, *Alcoholic Republic*, 169; "Untitled," *Southern Recorder*, July 14, 1857, 3.

lives with such dramatic flair, thousands of southern deaths could share the verdict of his coroner's inquest: "premeditated death by whiskey."[48]

Out of the accidental cases, the wretched life of James P. Young, who died in 1841, revealed the toll alcohol could take on one man. As a poor laborer, Young had boarded in a room with other men. One of his roommates testified that "he heard him often in the night groaning but that was customary with him when he was drinking, and that he had been drinking on yesterday." He did not even notice Young had died until a "negro man told him." Samuel Gilmer, Young's employer, said that the deceased had "commenced drinking" about *seven weeks* prior to his death, "and does not think that he has been sober more than four days since." Gilmer realized that Young "was trembling on Saturday morning and requested for me to send for some whiskey to cool off on." Gilmer complied with Young's wishes, but the poor addict "took one drink and in a very short time threw it up; he said that lately it served him that way when he took it in the morning." Still, somehow, Young "went on and did a pretty good days work ... after a spell of drinking last year he had something of a fit." Variations of Young's story appear in every single southern county coroner's reports or death records. These poor white men needed to de-stress and unwind, and had a number of legitimate reasons to want to escape their current realities. They could not, with any sense of self-awareness, waste time dreaming of the future; they needed something more immediate, something that lightened their present. Simply stated, poor whites needed to escape psychologically from the drudgery of their daily lives.[49]

Aside from the death of the drinker, alcohol was also partially responsible for the loss of thousands of other lives. Whether liquor helped cause a fight, or intensified domestic violence, it played a part in many antebellum disturbances. James Martin stabbed Daniel Dougherty to death in "the vicinity of the drinking saloon adjoining the Holland House" in Atlanta. In Augusta, Samuel Wilson, a painter, "was shot down and instantly killed in the streets on Saturday night" by a drunkard "who was currently lodged in the county jail." Another nearby man was killed during a drunken affray "by a blow on the head from a brick." Both these homicides, the local newspaper lamented, were "Rum's Doings." And in February of 1860, a 30-year-old farm laborer named John Saunders lost

[48] "A Drunkard's End!," *Macon Telegraph*, Jan. 28, 1828, 2.
[49] "August 22, 1841," Abbeville County, Coroner's inquisition books, 1840–1849, SCDAH.

his life after drunkenly insulting Addison Attaway at a groggery in Hancock County, Georgia. The two men had both been drinking at A. Quill's grocery, and by all accounts appeared friendly at first. After the men became inebriated, however, a fight quickly ensued. Saunders called Attaway a "God damn shit ass." Attaway called him a liar, and Saunders immediately attacked him. Attaway retaliated by grabbing the nearest whiskey decanter and whacking Saunders across the skull, prematurely ending his life over a trifling, drunken insult.[50]

Slave owners, therefore, had many reasons to keep poor whites away from alcohol, but the maintenance of the slave system was obviously of great importance. Regardless of the law, wealthy Southerners could buy alcohol whenever they wanted – only poor whites were charged with crimes involving drunkenness or the liquor trade. As these frequent arrests prove, much of the poor population, whether black or white, had easy and continual access to alcohol in the underground economy. With liquor averaging 40 cents a gallon, a pint only cost a nickel throughout much of the antebellum South. Even the poorest whites and slaves could afford to purchase this inexpensive commodity. More commonly, though, the South's two underclasses used liquor itself as currency. Masters knew that runaways could usually spend a night or two with a poor white in exchange for alcohol. Indeed, spirituous liquor seemed to be the driving force behind many of the region's crimes, especially larceny.[51]

Avery Craven summarized the importance of alcohol in black-poor white interactions: "Sometimes the Negro slipped away to labor at night in the fields of a less energetic white in return for his liquor; sometimes a system of theft was perfected by which plantation equipment and supplies passed in payments; sometimes the black economized his own rations that he might secretly exchange his surplus for the means of a spree." Traveler Daniel Hundley also noticed the effect of alcohol on black/poor white interactions. He proposed that abolitionists focus their attention on the South's white groggery-shop keepers, as "they can tell you who are the most reckless, daring, villainous, and discontented of negro men." He wondered why abolitionists did not "initiate" these liquor-dealing

---

[50] "Homicide," *Atlanta Weekly Intelligencer*, April 19, 1855, 2; "Two Men Killed in Two Days," *Atlanta Weekly Intelligencer*, Dec. 30, 1857, 2; "John H. Saunders," Hancock County, Superior Court, Proceedings of Coroners Inquests, GDAH; Eighth Census of the United States, 1860: Hancock County, Georgia.

[51] Genovese, *Roll, Jordan, Roll*, 641–2.

lower-class whites into their "secret plots for fostering negro insurrections, for poisoning, maiming, and murdering the white families of the South."[52]

Furthermore, because both cities and rural areas housed brothels and "disorderly houses," liquor was often assumed to play a part in black men's "improper association" with white women, especially prostitutes. Alcohol clearly enabled – and even encouraged – personal relationships between the races, and for that reason alone slaveholders needed to tightly regulate the liquor trade. The Grand Jury of Marion County, Georgia, linked the two practices together:

> We sincerely deplore the alarming prevalence of crime and immoral practices in the community ... they are to be ascribed in almost every instance to the use and sale of intoxicating liquors ... trading with and furnishing ardent spirits to our negroes prevail to a considerable extent in our midst is very generally believed. ... We hope all good citizens will use more than ordinary diligence to ascertain who these violators of the law are, and prosecute them to the fullest extent of it.

Likewise, in Mississippi, a "Petition for Prohibiting the Sale of Liquor" from the 1850s called for the end of the alcohol trade, as "illegal and clandestine traffic is continually kept up by corrupt men with our slaves, by which they are rendered disobedient and tempted to dishonesty."[53]

Masters had long suspected white men involved in the liquor trade of being abolitionists. According to their logic, anyone who served slaves liquor knew that he was putting the safety of the white population in jeopardy. Most American slave revolts involved spirituous liquors, and this fact continued to haunt the Deep South's slaveholders, who genuinely feared the emboldening qualities of the drug. As Hundley noted, "Whenever two criminals have the same terrible secret to keep, there is sure to spring up a sympathy betwixt them; hence, there is a real sympathy between the slaves and the groggery keepers, and this is why the latter are sometimes abolitionists." Thus, simply because poor whites and slaves were illegally trading together, they were united against a common foe: the slave owner.[54]

Judge I.L. Harris warned the people in his Georgia County about the trouble that accompanied alcohol sales in the underground economy.

---

[52] Craven, "Poor Whites and Negroes," 18–20; Hundley, *Social Relations*, 231.

[53] Bolton, *Poor Whites*, 50; "Georgia, Marion County, General Presentments of the Grand Jury, Panel No. 1, March Term 1858," *Columbus Enquirer*, March 16, 1858, 3; "Petition for Prohibiting the Sale of Liquor," MDAH.

[54] Quoted in Edward L. Ayers, *Vengeance and Justice: Crime and Punishment in the 19th Century American South* (New York: Oxford University Press, 1984), 130–1.

"Selling liquor to slaves is very common in our midst," he lamented, and "The law is violated by the hour. ... Much of this liquor is doubtlessly purchased through the instrumentality of trifling white boys and vagrant white men." Because of the interaction between these two groups, slaveholders had real reasons to worry. Judge Harris admonished his peers, brashly stating, "You may talk of abolition incendiaries, exciting our slaves to insurrection, while he, who supplies them with liquor, is doing them more damage." Masters clearly recognized the precariousness of the situation, and in the few years before secession they used every resource available to end the liquor trade between poor whites and blacks. Regardless of the stringency of their efforts, however, they largely failed. For people who had little prospect for a better future, and every reason in the world to escape the present, the threat of jail time had little bearing in their decision to imbibe. Whether black or poor white, liquor offered unfree and nominally free people a chance to experience freedom, if for but a brief moment.[55]

Aside from the alcohol trade, however, the bartering of foodstuffs and "provisions" made up a sizable percentage of transactions in the underground economy. Ex-slaves often recounted times of stealing from their owners for their own consumption. But they also frequently added that poor whites had some influence over their pilfering. Octavia George believed that "poor white folk are to blame for the Negroes stealing because they would get the Negroes to steal their master's corn, hogs, chickens and many other things and sell it to them for practically nothing." Another woman similarly recalled that "other niggers off other places would steal from the masters and sell to po' white folks, and they would give them things for it. That's how they did on my place." The underground economy had become so disruptive in the Deep South that, by the 1840s, county officials began cracking down on peddling licenses in an effort to curb illegal trading.[56]

Just as agricultural workers had appropriated certain goods from landowners for centuries, slaves often felt they had a moral right to the fruits of their own labor. Slaveholders began to worry in earnest, however, when slaves began selling and trading those goods with non-slaveholders. As Alex Lichtenstein wrote, the hegemony of masters was threatened when African Americans moved from the "moral economy to

---

[55] "Judge Harris' Charge to the Grand Jury," *Southern Recorder*, March 6, 1860, 3.
[56] Octavia George, *American Slave*, Vol. 13 (OK), 111–2; "When It's Right to Steal From Your Master," *Ibid.*, Vol. 18 (Fisk), 36.

the actual economy." Kathleen Hilliard studied the purchases of slaves in the legal marketplace, finding that nearly 65 percent of their purchases were related to cloth and clothing, while food and drink comprised less than 15 percent. This pattern of consumption strongly suggests that slaves had other alternatives when procuring additional rations and alcohol. Of course, some masters allowed slaves to raise their own crops on small plots of land. Still, most alcohol, as well as some food, was surely acquired via the underground economy. For trading with and selling goods to slaves, poor whites earned their place as the pariahs of the region's political economy. One traveler's observation in 1854 was echoed repeatedly throughout the late antebellum South: "I have hardly visited a single planter ... who did not complain of the annoyance which the vagrant and dishonest habits of some of his poor neighbors gave him."[57]

Thus, the interracial trading network clearly concerned the slaveholding class, who realized that the interaction of free blacks, slaves, and poor whites meant a majority of Southerners were already colluding in open defiance of them. J.J. Rainwater, a poor white from Mississippi, skipped town to avoid arrest for "unlawfully receiving a side of bacon from a slave." Also accused of accepting stolen cash from the same slave, Rainwater had been smart to abscond, as the local justice of the peace determined a "palpable ... case of guilt." Rainwater's indiscretions ultimately earned him "the condemnation of the public as a *dangerous man in a slave community.*" Indeed, frequent contact between the underclasses supposedly laid the groundwork for revolt and rebellion. Masters knew they had to intensify their efforts at segregation, heavily policing the poorer segment of the white population.[58]

Both slave patrols and vigilance committees took on this task, monitoring, as Sally Hadden noted, "not only slaves, but the shadowy underworld inhabited by poor whites who traded forbidden liquor and stolen farm goods with them." Many areas in the Deep South called for stricter regulations by the patrols as the antebellum period wore on. One local Farmers' Club even implored the patrol to take action against poor

---

[57] Alex Lichtenstein, "'That Disposition to Theft, With Which They Have Been Branded': Moral Economy, Slave Management, and the Law," *Journal of Social History* 21 (spring 1998): 414–5; Kathleen M. Hilliard, *Masters, Slaves, and Exchange: Power's Purchase in the Old South* (New York: Cambridge University Press, 2014), 82–3; "The South," *New York Times*, Jan. 26, 1854.

[58] Mississippi Legislature, Petitions, 1817–1908, "Petition," Folder "Various Requests 1857," MDAH, italics added.

whites, encouraging their arrest and punishment: "There is a class of white men about here that a patrole would do good in [c]atching those Hunting Fishing & Ste[a]ling rascals ... they could take them up & prosecute them & this should be done." The increasing frequency of biracial interaction, especially in the underground economy, had slaveholders trying to eliminate traffickers' privileges of white citizenship in the 1850s. Attempting to restrict the Constitutional rights of poor whites, slave-owning lawmakers called for the "imposition of civil disabilities," essentially the denial of legal rights and privileges to people who had been convicted of crimes. These civil disabilities, of course, would permanently disenfranchise the convict. Simultaneously, masters proposed the admission of slave testimony to help convict poor whites of criminal activity. None of these measures were particularly surprising. As Hadden concluded, because poor whites "sometimes ran illicit meeting houses where insurrections were discussed, [they] posed too great a threat to the white social order" for the slaveholders to ignore.[59]

Unsurprisingly, in the slave South the criminal most "consistently punished to the extreme letter of the law" was the slave stealer. According to one scholar, a white person who dared to kidnap a slave was immediately branded "the anarchist of Southern serfdom," and was liable to be sentenced to death. Carrying away a black laborer actually elicited a much more serious punishment than did assault and even manslaughter or murder. This difference in penalties also stemmed from the fact that few antebellum Southerners held life itself in high esteem. Human brutality guided the southern system. Nevertheless, despite harsh sentences for the crime, white bandits across the region continued attempting to steal black Southerners. Following petty larceny, manslaughter, and grand larceny, "negro stealing" was the fourth leading cause of imprisonment in mid-1840s Mississippi.[60]

Most cases generally fell into one of two categories. The first scenario was literal – a poor white would simply kidnap a slave and flee the area,

[59] Hadden, *Slave Patrols*, 104; Harris, *Plain Folk and Gentry*, quoted on 68; Planitzer, "A Dangerous Class," 42; Hadden, *Slave Patrols*, 104.

[60] Jack Kenny Williams, *Vogues in Villany: Crime and Retribution in Ante-bellum South Carolina* (Columbia: University of South Carolina Press, 1959), 41; 42; 43; 35; 36: In many districts in South Carolina, far more than half the murders were committed with weapons other than firearms, suggesting "that among the common folk, at least, pistols and rifles were not widely owned."; Walker, *A Bachelor's Life*, 266, editor's footnote 184, also see Lyda Gordon Shivers, A History of the Mississippi Penitentiary, (MA Thesis, University of Mississippi, 1930), 9; 18: "In 1849 seventeen inmates had been convicted of Negro stealing."

either keeping the slave for himself or selling the slave at another location. Also known as "blackbirding," the practice was common enough to cause concern, as a stolen slave could mean a thousand dollar-plus hit for the slave owner. Andrew Simms, enslaved in northern Florida, recalled that "other whitefolks ... caused troubles." They would "Sneak around where there was lots of the black children on the plantation and steal them. Take them poor children off and sell them." The second type of slave stealing was done at the slave's behest. Sometimes a poor white would receive money for helping slaves out of the county and nearer to freedom, and sometimes they would simply carry away a lover or child or friend.[61]

Personal relationships between whites and blacks could possibly have been the predominant reason for slave stealing. In many instances, single, unattached men "kidnapped" young black women, as in the case of Bedford Head, charged with the offense in 1859 for stealing 16-year-old Harriet and 50-year-old Millie. While Head's crime was unremarkable for the time, slaveholders throughout the South sought both federal and local solutions to derail this aspect of the Underground Railroad. Bolton underscored the seriousness of the activity, finding that in 1856, almost one-tenth of Mississippi's state prisoners had been convicted of "negro stealing." Many of these whites were merely guilty of attempting to help slaves escape to freedom. Still, the actual number of men incarcerated throughout the Deep South for slave stealing will always be underestimated. Because county-level minute books and other legal documents lacked a system of standardization, different counties listed crimes under disparate headings. There are many instances in which charges for larceny – even "simple larceny" – were actually cases of slave stealing. Without any trial transcripts or notes, it is impossible to know how many Southerners were prosecuted for the offense.[62]

A case out of Muscogee County, Georgia, gives one scenario for how these "slave stealings" materialized. In November of 1859, just two years before secession, Simeon Perry, Ephraim Knowles, and Matthew Axam were tried for "taking" three slaves with "intent to steal." Several other poor white men were arrested and tried for more minor offenses in this case. The three slaves were owned by three different slaveholders. Sarah, 25 years old, Amey, a "copper colored" 30-year-old, and Buck, 40, were

---

[61] Andrew Simms, *American Slave*, Vol. 7 (OK), 296.
[62] Muscogee County, Superior Court Minutes, 1859–63, GDAH; Bolton, *Poor Whites*, 108–9.

valued by the court to be worth about $1000 each. The star witness happened to be at Simeon Perry's house when the men hatched the plans to steal the slaves. He claimed that Ephraim Knowles asked Simeon Perry to "come to Columbus to move a family that has just come on boat from Eufala," Alabama. When Perry responded that, "he did not have enough to support his family while he was gone, Mr. Knowles replied that he would give him fifty dollars for the trip," the witness continued. To sweeten the deal, Knowles then reached into his pocket and pulled out 13 dollars "in papers," extending his offering to Perry. Simeon Perry, who had three children to feed, ultimately decided to accept the cash, immediately handing the banknotes over to his wife. Several days later, Perry was arrested by the local law enforcement for hiding the three contraband slaves in a wagon. Although only disparate pieces of the story were recounted in the testimony, all of the accused were found guilty. Perry, Axam, and one other man were sentenced each to ten years hard labor in the penitentiary. Ephraim Knowles, who orchestrated the entire heist, was given six years. The severity of their punishments revealed that slaveholders took their crime very seriously.[63]

Just over a year later, on the actual day of South Carolina's secession, several men were tried for the murder of a reputed underground railroader in Edgefield County. James Reynolds, the 18-year-old son of a poor landless laborer, was ruthlessly killed by the heirs of a slaveholder for being "an abolitionist." The murderers, Joseph, Wade, and Musco Samuel, were the teenage sons of Musco Samuel, Sr., a farmer who owned twelve slaves in addition to $3,500 worth of real estate and personal property. Eye witnesses described the brothers berating Reynolds, incredulously asking "how he dared to insult" them, accusing Reynolds of telling "damned" lies. Joseph Musco, the eldest, "abused the deceased very much," labeling Reynolds an abolitionist who "had run negroes to free states and freed them." Further accusing the poor boy of taking money to the escaping slaves, the Musco brothers beat Reynolds mercilessly. Joseph even attempted to shoot the victim before being stopped by more level-headed bystanders. All the while James Reynolds reacted in a calm manner, saying very little "except that he never denied anything that he did." He made "no

---

[63] Muscogee County, Superior Court Minutes, 1859–63, GDAH; Simeon Perry: Eighth Census of the United States, 1860: Muscogee County, Georgia. In 1860 he was listed as a 45-year-old with three teenage children and a wife. No occupation is listed; instead it says "penitentiary – stealing." His family owned $100 of personal property but no land. Matthew Axam: *Ibid.*: Baldwin County, Georgia: Listed as an illiterate, common laborer, he was in the state penitentiary for "simple larceny."

show of fighting whatever and used no insulting language," yet he lost his life after a particularly powerful blow to the head. Joseph Musco had traded his gun for a stick, and literally beat the Underground Railroader to death. James Reynolds – a poor, white, non-slaveholding young man – ultimately sacrificed his life for his involvement in disrupting slavery.[64]

Not all slave stealers, of course, were abolitionists. In fact, the most well-known kidnapper, John A. Murrell, was the original American outlaw. An infamous southern "land pirate" who allegedly tried to ignite a massive slave uprising in 1835, Murrell's exploits have been recounted by historians like Walter Johnson. Similarly, the story of the Vicksburg Gamblers, a group of white men who were hung for purportedly inciting a slave rebellion, confirmed masters' worst fears. As lower-class white men were issued more political powers during the Jacksonian Era, upper-class leaders and middling class "strainers" were forced to make sure their worlds and their fortunes remained safe and untouched. The possibility of real revolt, whether class-based or bi-racial, always concerned slave-owning Southerners; their actions clearly attest to this fact. As the ante-bellum period wore into the 1840s and 1850s, slaveholders' fears peaked. Indeed, aside from the well-known rebellions and "unhatched plots," several recent historians have discovered evidence of smaller, generally inchoate, planned revolts. Although more research is needed on the topic, there were multiple conspiracies between slaves and poor whites to over-throw the prevailing hierarchy in the late antebellum period. Bolton uncovered one such plan from 1845 for insurrection in North Carolina. A letter, written by a slave, tells of at least two poor whites who were supposed to help with the revolt. William Taylor, a landless white farmer, and Eli Penry, a poor dram-shop keeper, were to serve as "captains." After freeing both blacks and poor whites from the county jail, the men planned to "tie all the whites" and shoot "every man that [won't] go with them." Eli Penry even offered all "his powder and shot for half the money." Penry's job made him an obvious leader; he could "make all the men drunk and ... [thus] make them do anything."[65]

---

[64] Edgefield County, Coroner's Inquisition Books, 1844–1902, SCDAH; James Reynolds: Eighth Census of the United States, 1860: Edgefield District, South Carolina. His father was a 52-year-old laborer with no land and $50 of personal property. Musco Samuel, *Ibid.*, Eighth Census of the United States, 1860, Slave Schedule: Edgefield District, South Carolina. Samuel was a farmer who lived with 13 "adult" or teenaged children. Sons were listed as "J.G." (Joseph) 21, "W.C." (Wade) 19, and "M" (Musco Jr.) 17.

[65] Walter Johnson, *River of Dark Dreams*; Augustus Q. Walton (AKA Virgil Stewart), *A History of the Detection, Conviction, Life and Designs of John A. Murrell, The Great*

While most scholars have held that slaveholders had little to worry about in reality, the very *possibility* of an uprising was enough to help solidify the growing culture of poor white "policing" and incarceration. Three years before secession, a Chatham County, Georgia jury tried William McGuire for "attempting to excite an insurrection and revolt of the slaves." Still another poor white, John Pool, heard about John Brown's Harper's Ferry raid and mindlessly told a Hancock County, Georgia overseer that he would "black himself" and join "the strong side" when war broke out. He was tried for "uttering abolitionist sentiments," but after being labeled a "poor, simple native," Pool was finally discharged with a stern lecture. Forret discovered an additional small rebellion that erupted in Alabama in 1860, instigated by "the low-down, or poor, whites of the country," who apparently banded with slaves to demand a redistribution of "land, mules, and money."[66]

All of these cases, all of these stories, show that the lives of poor whites were inextricably tied to the institution of slavery, and often the lives of the slaves themselves. As one son of a slaveholder stated, "Some non-slaveholders were always meddling in slaveholders' business. Such men were not thought of much by slaveholders – they were always trying to get slaves to do something wrong." With so little to lose, poor whites obviously gave slaveholders cause to worry, and these fears reached a fever pitch during the 1850s. Masters' most serious anxieties about poor whites concerned the prospect of bi-racial revolt, and it became more and more imperative to separate poor whites and blacks. Genovese believed that in the late antebellum period, slaveholders' panic "at the slightest hint of slave insurrection revealed what lay beneath their endless self-congratulations over the supposed docility, contentment, and loyalty of their slaves." The master class *did* have something to fear. In the decades leading up to the Civil War, poor white non-slaveholders were disrupting the hierarchical order of the South. Whether interacting with slaves and free blacks on very personal levels or subverting the notions of "decent" behavior, lower-class whites had the power to dismantle the structural order of society. Indeed, when the Savannah City Council met in 1859,

---

Western Land Pirate, (Cincinnati: s.n., 1835), MDAH; Joshua D. Rothman, *Flush Times and Fever Dreams: A Story of Capitalism and Slavery in the Age of Jackson* (Athens: University of Georgia Press, 2012); Bolton, *Poor Whites*, 109.

[66] Lockley, *Lines in the Sand*, 128; Harris, *Plain Folk and Gentry*, 64–5; Forret, *Race Relations*, 153.

their primary focus was on white people – poor non-slaveholders whose "alleged unsoundness in reference to our system of slavery" threatened the Deep South in a way no northern abolitionist could. Yet because slaveholders never achieved sufficient segregation between the two under-classes, they were forced to come up with other ways to control the potentially explosive population.[67]

---

[67] Elliot and Moxley, *Tennessee*, Vol. 6, 1842–3; Genovese, *Roll, Jordan, Roll*, 595; Lockley, *Lines in the Sand*, 129.

7

Poverty and Punishment

Slavery is a monstrous evil, when considered in all its bearings; it makes us poor; poverty makes us ignorant; ignorance makes us wretched; wretchedness makes us wicked, and wickedness leads to the devil!
— Hinton Helper[1]

Soon there comes a time in the history of a people that continue to enslave men, a time when there are in reality but two classes, masters and slaves. There may be a class that retain[s] the shadow of freedom, but their liberty is only nominal. They are used to further the interests of the masters, or driven from the country.
— Provincial Freeman[2]

On a clear spring day in 1846, a poor young man named Roderick was lead slowly up the courthouse steps in Kershaw, South Carolina. With his head down he ascended, one foot before the other, until he finally reached the top. Ordered to turn toward the crowd, Roderick followed orders – perhaps defiantly, filled with rage, or perhaps with a sense of despair, choking down feelings of utter humiliation. As the local sheriff began the proceedings to auction off Roderick to the highest bidder, the gravity of the situation unfolded. It was nearly impossible for any human being to be publicly degraded and sold without an immense loss of honor and self-worth. Indeed, as the sheriff started the bidding Roderick likely experienced one of the darkest moments of his life. He was no longer independent. He was no longer free.[3]

---

[1] Helper, *The Impending Crisis*, 82.
[2] "White and Black Slavery," *Provincial Freeman*, Dec. 29, 1855.
[3] Kershaw District, Court of Common Pleas, Capias ad Satisfaciendum executions, 1800–1859 (SCDAH).

Five years later and a few counties over in Laurens, South Carolina, another man portentously climbed that district's courthouse steps. James, who had stolen a horse, turned toward the crowd awaiting a different fate than Roderick's. James was about to receive twenty-five lashes – just one-fourth of his total punishment. Over the course of the next three Saturdays, James endured a public whipping three more times, until his back bore the scars of 100 lashes. He would spend the next four months incarcerated, hoping that his open wounds would heal despite languishing inside a hot, squalid cell. He likely suffered through periods of intense anxiety and deep depression, feelings that would probably continue to haunt him for the rest of his life.[4]

These types of accounts were unfortunately quite commonplace among African American slaves. But the two men from these stories were not slaves. They were not even black. Roderick McLeod and James Grigg were white men, United States citizens who were entitled to constitutional rights, and theoretically entitled to the privileges of whiteness in a racist society. While most scholars assert that the whipping and "selling" of white men and women ended during the Jacksonian period, these customs did, in fact, continue in the Deep South until the Civil War. Although the practice was not widespread, local judges occasionally ordered these methods as part of a person's punishment, generally for nonviolent property crimes, like Grigg's theft of a horse. Other times, these sentences were penance for unpaid court fees and small amounts of debt. Roderick McLeod, for example, fathered a child out of wedlock with a woman named Harriet Waters. Charged with bastardy in April 1846, he was ordered to pay $25 each year for twelve years to support his daughter through her adolescence. That amount of money, by itself, would have been possible (though rather difficult) for a poor laborer to pay. Nevertheless, McLeod also needed to enter a recognizance of $300, which meant he would have to show up to court and swear to make the scheduled payments. But it appears from district records that he never did so. "In the default thereof," the court warned, "on the sale day in May next," the sheriff was supposed to "hire the said Roderick McLeod out to service for any time not exceeding four years, and the proceeds of his labour shall be applied to" financially supporting his daughter. On the surface, this punishment makes logical sense, as the primary goal of the legal system should have been the material support and welfare of

---

[4] Laurens District, Court of General Sessions, Capias ad Satisfaciendum executions, 1826–1870 (SCDAH).

the little girl. The actual outcome of McLeod's sale, however, did not accomplish that objective. A simple, single sentence told of McLeod's fate: "Sold according to the within order to Angus McSween for $1." McSween, a 65-year-old farmer from Scotland, lived with his wife within the district. He owned $5,000 of real estate, as well as ten slaves. McLeod's "sales price" strongly suggests that the recorded sum was paid on a weekly or monthly basis, rather than for long-term arrangements. Essentially serving as indentured servants, therefore, poor white debtors and criminals were at times auctioned off for their services, with all the symbolism that conveyed. The punishment of other white convicts in such public, spectacle-like settings further sent a clear message to non-slaveholders. Masters must have felt the need periodically to remind poor whites that their freedom was conditional.[5]

While the poor were treated with disdain all throughout America, from the time of the early Republic slave states stipulated harsher punishments, even for nonviolent offenders. For example, since the eighteenth century, Massachusetts had only one capital crime, while South Carolina had *twenty*, including nonviolent property crimes like horse stealing, burglary, grand larceny, and forgery. Even with a strict set of punitive laws, southern policymakers also used other methods to deal with transient poor whites. By the 1840s, most counties had established poor houses or farms, institutions where the impoverished could find shelter, food, and at least a few days of respite. The justices in one North Carolina county noted that the poor "can be kept much cheaper there than in the county jail." Michel Foucault argued that institutionalized governmental projects – the prison, the poor house, and the hospital – all operated with the same end goal. Their main objective was the creation of a society governed through surveillance; therefore, discipline was paramount. And in the slave South, probably more so than anywhere else in the country, impoverished people endured official scrutiny in all places and at all times. With guards, marshals, constables, and sheriffs firmly established as fixtures in every community, with the growing numbers of uniformed police officers, and with the nightly rides of the slave patrols, poor Southerners – both white and black – lived under the constant watchful eyes of the slaveholders.[6]

[5] *Ibid.*; Kershaw, Capias ad Satisfaciendum executions; Seventh Census of the United States, 1850: Kershaw District, South Carolina; Seventh Census of the United States, 1850, Slave Schedule: Kershaw District, South Carolina.
[6] Ely, "'There are Few Subjects," 858–9; Hindus, *Prison and Plantation*, 93; Ely, "'There are Few Subjects," 856–7.

The heaviest periods of incarceration in the prewar South came in the 1840s and 1850s, just as the region began to industrialize. By this time, many poor white laborers were paid with wages, and property crimes dominated the local level criminal court dockets. Slaveholders were preoccupied with protecting their property rights; modern European laws were considerably less punitive. After all, much of Europeans' wealth came from landholdings, tangible assets that cannot be easily "stolen." Slave owners, on the other hand, held the majority of their wealth in slaves. And slaves could run away, be "inveigled," maimed, killed, or rendered economically worthless. Slave property demanded far more protection than any other possession. Slaveholders' aggressive protectiveness of their wealth, therefore, clearly added to the growing criminalization of poor white Southerners, who always posed a risk to their property. Poor white men, especially, began to be considered "dangerous" and violent individuals who were always looking for trouble. As Edward Ayers found, affluent Southerners likely feared poor white men more than they did slaves. The note of one physician contained sentiments that seemed to "have been widely shared." When traveling alone, the doctor admitted, "the sudden appearance of a white man generally excited some apprehension with regard to personal safety, but the sight of a black man was always cheering, and made him feel safe."[7]

Wealthy whites often did have legitimate reasons for alarm when encountering unknown poor whites in non-public settings. Much like the images and stories of the Wild West, the antebellum Deep South was often a lawless and frightening place characterized by violence. There were rag-tag gangs of unemployed men who earned livings through lives of crime. Likely feeling entitled to the bounty they stole from affluent slaveholders, these men often terrorized propertied Southerners. As the infamous bandit John Murrell supposedly reasoned, by plundering the masters of men, some sense of equity was restored, because "society will seldom venture to trifle with the powerful but it will trample on a beggar and distain to calculate the wrong." Whether ambushing travelers on remote stretches of highways, or simply pilfering from plantations, these loosely organized gangs helped alleviate some of the grievances of poor whites. At the same time, they added to the stereotypical image of the poor as dangerous criminals.[8]

---

[7] Ayers, *Vengeance and Justice*, 132.   [8] Quoted in Grimsted, *American Mobbing*, 151.

These "white victims of slavery," as Hinton Helper called them, lived in a constant state of *qualified* freedom: one legal misstep, one wrong acquaintance, one unpaid debt – could lead to an indefinite loss of liberty. As Richard Morris hypothesized, the relatively frequent imprisonment of poor white Southerners, combined with other methods of compelling them to work at low wages, set the precedent for the treatment of African Americans following the Thirteenth Amendment. White "bondage," according to Morris, "provided the necessary experience in the control of 'free' labor which served as the design for the emerging pattern of quasi-freedom cut to fit the emancipated Negro in the era of Reconstruction." Rarely have modern scholars realized the accuracy of Morris's convincing ideas about class and power in the slaveholding states. Still, a few have confirmed key pieces of his theory. Jack Kenny Williams, for example, contended that class largely dictated a southern criminal's sentence. Punishments for the affluent, he wrote, were nearly always fines, while poorer whites received public whippings and were incarcerated. Much of this variation in treatment was written off as a by-product of the accused's supposed intentions. If an affluent slaveholder committed a misdemeanor, local judges classified the criminal acts as "innocent amusement or understandable self-defense." But when poor whites made similar mistakes, their actions "were designated as crimes against the State."[9]

Grave disparities in both arrests and punishments confirm the importance of class among the Deep South's whites. Williams's seminal study of crime in South Carolina, *Vogues in Villainy*, blamed the "consistent severity of the penal codes" on the "low estate of the criminal group." Upper-class slaveholders realized that many of the accused would spend years funneled in and out of the justice system, often due to alcohol addiction or extreme poverty. Lancaster's *Ledger* reported in 1853 that four-fifths of all criminal charges were related to alcohol. Moreover, Williams found, the "bulk" of indicted criminals were not able to read or write. But illiteracy was not the accused's only hurdle in the courtroom: verbatim testimony strongly suggested that some of the alleged criminals "were hardly able to speak the English language in an understandable fashion." The prosecuted were seemingly so uneducated, and so cut off from the wider, capitalist society, that they demonstrated many traits of pre-modern agricultural peoples. In fact, many sessions court minutes contained the phrase, "The def[endant]s are poor," indicating the strong

[9] Helper, *The Impending Crisis*, 44; Morris, "White Bondage," 207; Williams, *Vogues in Villainy*, 134.

correlation between poverty and crime. This link had become so obvious by the late-antebellum period that William Gregg, the champion of southern industrialism, claimed in 1845 that "thousands" of poor whites were starving and thus turning to stealing as a result. Grand planter James Henry Hammond estimated that at least 50,000 whites were unemployed in South Carolina in 1850. These paupers were forced, he reasoned, "either to beg or steal in order to live." The chances for poor whites to rise out of poverty, it seemed, were dwindling in the lead up to secession. As poverty worsened, crime rates rose, mostly for crimes involving the property of the respectable upper-middling and upper classes. When poor whites were involved in disputes and bloody affrays with other poor whites, though, there was rarely intervention from the criminal justice system. As Williams concluded, more affluent Southerners likely "thanked God and took heart when one poor-white killed another."[10]

Nearly as infamous as southern election days, the region's "court days" were often hedonistic affairs filled with revelry. Held for a few weeks twice a year, court days likely ironically served as a safety valve for the less affluent classes of the community. Typically, these events drew every lower-middling and poor white into the town for a few days of entertainment and socialization, and of course, heavy drinking. Court days likely provided a sense of community among poorer whites, a difficult accomplishment in rural areas. As they shared gossip about friends and family, they probably also shared feelings of oppression and bitter resentment for the all-powerful slaveholders controlling the judicial system. The scattered remnants of witness testimonies in these local trials often indicated just how uneducated and illiterate many poor whites were, and they also revealed the apparent frequency of interracial interactions (and even interracial living arrangements) between blacks and lower-class whites.

While the make-up of antebellum southern juries has not been closely examined yet, it seems highly likely that most jurors were chosen from among the wealthiest, most respectable citizens of each county. Why would slaveholding lawmakers allow otherwise? To assure the safety of both their assets and their position in society, masters needed like-minded individuals deciding who posed a serious threat to the peculiar institution. There were two types of juries in southern courtrooms: the grand jury decided whether or not there was enough evidence for the accused to

---

[10] Williams, *Vogues in Villainy*, 134, 23; 7; 24; 25; 23.

stand trial. Then the petit jury heard evidence and testimony, determining guilt. As one slave owner declared, men who served on southern grand juries were generally chosen for their "superior intelligence, wealth, and purity of character." From a cursory study of a few juries in two Georgia counties, Edward Ayers determined that grand juries were filled with affluent slaveholders. Out of the twenty-four (two twelve-men panels) grand jurors in Greene County, Georgia's 1853 term, all but one man could be found in tax rolls or census records. Only one of twenty-three was landless, and only seven were non-slaveholders. They averaged fifteen slaves each, and owned an additional $9,000 of non-slave property. The county's median wealth was less than $4,000, indicating that these grand jurors were much, much wealthier than the bulk of the people who were being tried. Whitfield County's numbers were similar. Furthermore, in most places in the Old South, juries were drawn from tax registers, so many poor whites were not even on the rolls to be called for duty in the first place. Given the often transient lives of poor white men, and the fact that most of them did not have the luxury of stopping work for several days or weeks at the court's behest, they were probably precluded from becoming jurors by multiple factors. Poor men could never expect to have a jury of *their* peers deciding whether or not they faced a criminal trial.[11]

Unlike the very wealthy grand jurors, it seems that a different class of men may have served on petit juries. Based on two small samples, Ayers determined that petit jurors generally owned property slightly below county average rates, and some of the men were occasionally absent from tax lists and census records, indicating that they may have owned little, if any, property. Yeomen and other middling-class Southerners habitually grumbled about wasting time for jury duty, away from their farms and their work. Because so few men wanted to serve, court clerks and officers were often forced to get anyone they could to fill the jury box. A few scattered pieces of evidence confirm that some localities did have great trouble recruiting "respectable" men to hear cases. In 1858, one newspaper even tried to persuade Georgia's legislature to abolish the penitentiary, replacing it with whipping, branding, and hanging. But there was one caveat: that each county "provided honest and intelligent men sit upon criminal cases, and not vagabonds, as is too often the case now."[12]

It is, therefore, possible that poor white men served on petit juries. Yet just as at the ballot box, the most impoverished men were the likeliest to be

[11] Ayers, *Vengeance and Justice*, 113.   [12] *Ibid.*, 113.

"bought" or won over by the local elite, who controlled their employment and credit options. Outside of large towns and cities, southern juries were surely influenced by local connections and family ties. It was incredibly hard to find "disinterested" jurors in rural areas, where kinship ties were strong and gossip traveled quickly. The importance of personal connections in the Deep South was not limited to juries; family relationships, friendships, and the all-powerful dollar pervaded every branch of the criminal justice system. Charged with grand larceny in Spartanburg, South Carolina, one lucky man received executive mercy due to "his family connections." A Mississippi paper reported in 1854 that "even the bloodiest murderer has no fears of the Penitentiary, *provided* he has either money or friends."[13]

Still, in southern courtrooms, the grand jury reigned supreme – the power over the accused's fate rested firmly in their hands. They met for a couple of weeks twice a year, discussed the state of affairs in the county, and made recommendations to local politicians. Then, they decided the fate of all those imprisoned within the last six months. In all Deep South states, the act of arrest and immediate incarceration seemed far more significant than actually prosecuting the case. Indeed, grand juries had a high rate of returning a verdict of "no bill," essentially dropping the charges, whether due to a lack of evidence to proceed to trial or because of the economic status and personal connections of the accused.

Michael Hindus examined the penal systems of both nineteenth century Massachusetts and South Carolina, comparing crime and conviction rates, sentences, and the overall judicial system. While only 16.5 percent of Massachusetts's cases ended in no bills, a large proportion of South Carolina's did, strongly indicating that grand juries used the no bill as a pardon or early acquittal. First, approximately 20 percent of the state's assault cases were dropped after the defendant paid his arrest and jail costs. Then, out of the cases that made it to a grand jury, *two-thirds* ended in a no bill, and the charges were dropped. South Carolina's high arrest rate affirmed "a high level of frivolous prosecutions" throughout the region. Hindus's findings align with those of Williams, who determined that the state's antebellum grand juries returned true bills in 63 percent of indictments, leaving about 37 percent of cases with no bills. Yet neither scholar clearly articulated the significance of their findings. If South Carolina and other Deep South states were arresting large numbers of

---

[13] Ayers, *Vengeance and Justice*, 112; Williams, *Vogues in Villainy*, 24; quotes from Ayers, *Vengeance and Justice*, 112.

people who would never even stand trial, then the officials making arrests were doing so over insignificant indiscretions at best and baseless accusations – with no relevant evidence – at worst. It seems that in the slave South, the act of arrest and the period of confinement before arraignment were used as punishments themselves. Under this model, an individual could be incarcerated for weeks and months without ever being formally charged with a crime. For all intents and purposes, due process was nullified.[14]

To deal with the growing ranks of criminals, by the late antebellum period almost every Deep South county had some sort of jail or makeshift guardhouse, although very few records from these institutions have survived. The majority of these "Jail" or "Sheriff's" registers contain little more than a balancing of books and listings of financial transactions. Despite this fact, historians have been able to identify several important factors common to most of these institutions and the ways that they operated. In most jails and guardhouses, prisoners were housed together, regardless of race or sex. Savannah's jail, for instance, incarcerated whites, slaves, and free blacks of both sexes; generally, one-third to one-half of the prisoners were African American. The only trait that most of the inmates shared was class: whether black or white, man or woman, the people arrested were nearly always poor. In 1835, the Savannah jail committee reported that it usually housed "sailors and indolent people who are often intoxicated. ... These people are generally paupers." In some sections of the Upper South, like the central piedmont of North Carolina, fighting or assault and battery made up about one-half of the prosecuted crimes. Yet most other areas, especially those with high percentages of slaves, property crimes like theft were considered a grave threat to society. Thieves served much more punitive sentences than other criminals. In Georgia's low-country, assault crimes averaged three to three and a half years imprisonment, while manslaughter sentences lasted only six months longer. But thieves and burglars – non-violent offenders – served roughly four and a half years for crimes involving property. Killing a human being warranted less of a sentence than larceny.[15]

This preoccupation with materialism and affluence came to permeate the southern criminal justice system, from the governmental chambers to the courtroom. Slaveholding lawyers comprised a large percentage of

[14] Hindus, *Prison and Plantation*, 86; 92; 97; Williams, *Vogues in Villainy*, 80.
[15] Savannah Jail Records, 1855–63, GDAH; Lockley, *Lines in the Sand*, 127; 126; Bolton, *Poor Whites*, 59; Lockley, *Lines in the Sand*, 98.

state legislators, and – in addition to the fame and respect that came with holding office – they often made sizable fortunes. The interconnectedness between the legal system and extremely affluent individuals was self-evident. Criminals who owned property posted bond, bailed themselves out, and paid off their fines while rarely having to go to jail. For those without property, the situation was completely different. As economic inequality continued to grow throughout the 1850s, the cotton boom made the rich richer, and left the poor to fend for themselves, especially after the financial panic of 1857. For whites who were already struggling economically, the subsequent years did not herald much of a financial recovery. Not surprisingly, this period coincided with a dramatic increase in "criminals" in the Deep South. Chatham County, Georgia, for example, prosecuted more people for property crimes in 1858 and 1860 than in any other years of the decade.[16]

Like poor whites, free blacks were arrested frequently, for a variety of offenses. Most slaves, on the other hand, spent time in jails only after running away and getting caught, or if they had committed an extremely violent crime. In the fall of 1859, for instance, in Kershaw, South Carolina, twenty-five individuals were incarcerated in the local jail. Out of the twenty-five prisoners, there were eleven black men: two free men of color had been arrested for burglary, two slaves for assault and battery, and seven slaves for attempting to escape to freedom. In the case of runaway slaves, the local jail would house them until the owner made arrangements to pick them up. For all other slaves, it made little economic sense to pay jail costs for the ones who stole or misbehaved. More importantly, slaveholders still needed the offending slaves' labor and thus relied on whipping as the primary form of punishment. Masters could – and did – force slaves to work mere days or even hours after they received savage beatings. But to preserve their wealth, slaveholders also had to restrain themselves in meting out these punishments; if they went over-board, they could deprive themselves of capable, energetic labor. Severe castigation of poor whites, by contrast, cost slave owners nothing.[17]

Most slaves considered jails "white" institutions. Freedmen and women recalled repeatedly that jails were built primarily to incarcerate whites. Ruben Fox declared "There weren't no such things as jails for colored folks. There were jails all right enough, but only white folks were

---

[16] Ayers, *Vengeance and Justice*, 31; 55; 97; 91.
[17] Kershaw District, Court of General Sessions, Sheriff's returns of prisoners in jail, 1803–1888, SCDAH.

put in them." Elisha Doc Garey concurred, saying that "White folks used to get locked up in them but I never did see no Niggers in one of them little jailhouses." One freedman from Georgia even juxtaposed the plight of black and white troublemakers: slaves who reacted negatively to cruel punishments were "quickly gotten rid of. Many were sent to Mississippi or Texas. White offenders were sent to chain gangs, but there were no gangs for slaves." Still another man claimed that the infamous "nigger dogs" were sent after "white folks too." The region's antebellum legal system, it seemed, *was* primarily structured around incarcerating poor whites. The guardhouses and jails scattered throughout every county seat, town, and city, were built with a main purpose – to deprive troublesome or suspicious poor whites of their liberty. Enslaved as a child in Mississippi, Dempsey Pitts confirmed this class element of the legal system: "There weren't no jails, except for the poor whites," he recalled.[18]

Poor whites were undoubtedly targeted by the legal system, and their punishments often helped blur the line between slavery and freedom. William Barney wrote that "Common laborers, as a group, faced a host of coercive mechanisms. Indentured servitude, involuntary apprenticeship, compulsory labor for debtors, vagrants, the unemployed, and seamen were some of the devices by which" the poor became unfree. In Panola County, Mississippi, for example, nearly every single person charged with a criminal offense in the 1850s was listed as a "laborer." Not only were poor whites more commonly prosecuted for crimes, but their sentences were generally much harsher than they were for the more affluent. Studying homicide conviction memorials and petitions to North Carolina governors in 1850s, Scott Culclasure concluded that "the combination of violence, transience, and poverty assured these poor white Southerners of sterner treatment when they came before the courtroom bar."[19]

On the other side of this class divide, Ralph Wooster established that the separation of powers was nearly non-existent in local government, where a small handful of propertied slave owners controlled nearly everything. Whether called the board of commissioners, the county court, or

---

[18] Ruben Fox, *American Slave*, Vol. 6 (MS), Supplement, Series 1, Part 2, 776; Elisha Doc Garey, *Ibid.*, Vol. 12 (GA), Part 2, 4; Milton Hammond, *Ibid.*, Vol. 12 (GA), Part 2, 94; Abe Kelley, *Ibid.*, Vol. 6 (MS), Supplement, Series 1, Part 3, 1270; Dempsey Pitts, *Ibid.*, Vol. 9 (MS), Supplement, Series 1, Part 4, 1712-3.

[19] Barney, *The Secessionist Impulse*, 41; Panola County, Circuit Court Minutes, 1850–57, MDAH; Scott P. Culclasure, "Edward Isham and Criminal Justice for the Poor White in the Antebellum South," in Bolton, *The Confessions of Edward Isham*, 72.

the police jury, these politicians were in charge of such diverse tasks as "supervising elections, establishing ferries, laying out roads, building bridges, appointing and maintaining slave patrols, caring for the poor, maintaining public buildings licensing liquor retailers, levying the county tax, regulating taverns and houses of entertainment, and establishing quarantine and health regulations." As one of the most powerful and important local officials, the sheriff enforced ordinances, regulations, and laws. He also managed the jail or guardhouse, executed warrants, and sometimes helped supervise elections. Local magistrates wielded incredible authority as well – especially in between court sessions. Magistrates were especially prone to abuse their positions of authority, however, because their pay depended on fees. Quite commonly, grand juries complained that magistrates brought groundless claims against individuals in an effort to collect more money. Many of these cases were never formally prosecuted, while others were rejected by juries altogether.[20]

As poor whites continued filling jail cells across the Deep South, many of the largest cities began establishing professional, uniformed police forces. By the mid-1840s New Orleans, Savannah, and Charleston used police to impose social and racial conformity, jailing individuals for the most benign behavioral infractions. Indeed, the rise of professional law enforcement changed the entire system of criminal justice. Private citizens, "free" white men, were now under regular surveillance. Not content with punishing people who had committed particularly heinous crimes, police locked up gamblers, vagrants, and drunkards, sometimes long before they actually did anything of a criminal nature. Of course, the cyclical nature of jailing people for insignificant reasons often became self-perpetuating. Poverty's link to recidivism has always been strong, especially when recently released convicts lacked immediate access to food and shelter.[21]

Not all poor whites found enough incentive in food and shelter to remain incarcerated, however. For the imprisoned, whether awaiting formal charges or serving out a sentence, their plight often centered on survival. Most of the incarcerated complained of hunger, as standard fare throughout most of South Carolina consisted of a small loaf of old bread and a pint of watery, "repulsive" soup. Even given the horrible conditions of confinement, however, southern crime rates rose in the 1840s and 1850s as localities began experiencing serious problems with burglary.[22]

[20] Wooster, *People in Power*, 84; 83; Hindus, *Prison and Plantation*, 29–30.
[21] Ayers, *Vengeance and Justice*, 82–3; 90; Lockley, *Lines in the Sand*, 128.
[22] Williams, *Vogues in Villainy*, 114; 117.

Incarcerated individuals escaped from local jails with relative frequency. In 1858, South Carolina's Governor R.F.W. Allston admitted that "Escapes have been more frequent the past year than I am willing to enumerate." Indeed, throughout the antebellum period, guardhouses and jail buildings were generally not structurally sound enough to prevent enterprising, able-bodied prisoners from figuring a way out. One summer James E. Robbins "broke the jail at Sandersville, Georgia." He escaped with Andrew J. Newsome, imprisoned for slave stealing, "by boring through the ceiling with an auger, furnished him, it is supposed, but some mean white man."[23]

Attempted escapes from prison were much rarer than jail escapes. Generally, convicts had to work together to ensure that the prison-break had a chance at success. In 1843, a group of men tried to escape the penitentiary at Milledgeville. The *Georgia Journal* reported that their "conspiracy" originally included seventy convicts who promised to flee the prison together. When the men heard "a given signal, a rush was made to the gate, by a large number concerned, but only eleven succeeded in getting out." One of the men, named Nichols, "was badly wounded, though not captured" after being shot by a guard. All but one of the convicts initially succeeded in their escape, but five of them were recaptured in the following days, and one man died. Prison escapes were clearly much more dangerous and prone to failure than jail breaks.[24]

Escape, however, was not the only way that white prisoners expressed their disgust with the judicial system – they also destroyed the structures that were built to imprison them. One of the main reasons few antebellum jail records exist today is the historic prevalence of fires. While these fires were sometimes set by poor whites who were attempting to escape, others were started by recently freed prisoners or even sympathetic friends and family members. For instance, in less than four months during the mid-1850s, the *Atlanta Weekly Intelligencer* reported at least three intentional jail fires. In Blairsville, a small town in northern Georgia, a prisoner named Jason Cladden started a fire "in order to make his escape." Unfortunately for Cladden, who was only "serving out a few months imprisonment," the blaze consumed him before he could free himself. A few months later, just after the citizens of another Georgia county spent $3,500 constructing a new jail, the building was burned to the ground one Sunday morning. The paper reported that "it was beyond all doubt set a

[23] Quoted in *Ibid.*, 120; "Alden at Large," *The Intelligencer* (SC), Aug. 28, 1860, 4.
[24] "Escape of Convicts from the Penitentiary," *Georgia Journal*, June 6, 1843, 3.

fire by some incendiary." And in South Carolina, local papers lamented the fiery destruction of both the Camden jail by an inmate, and the Sumter courthouse by "a person unknown." White Southerners, it seemed, were becoming quite bold in their opposition to the perceived injustices of the criminal system.[25]

Edward Isham, the infamous poor white who murdered a former employer a few years before the Civil War, bragged that during the heyday of his criminal activities, "Everybody was afraid of me and no officer would attempt to take me." His statement is telling. Isham's pride in his own little reign of terror doubtless reflected a newfound, albeit primitive, sense of masculine honor. He may not have been smart enough or industrious enough to improve his economic station in life, but for a time he was tough enough to instill fear in slaveholders and powerful local officials. In a world where physical dominance and brutality allowed slave owners to remain masters, slaveless poor whites received daily lessons in the efficacy of violence. Slaveholders frequently used cruelty and brutality to their own advantage; it made logical sense for the lower classes to expect similar results. Lacking wealth and privilege, poor white men attempted to prove their self-worth through violent and destructive means. If the people in power refused to recognize lower-class men's honor and autonomy, poor whites could create their own hierarchy of honor by acting out against the establishment – by being the meanest, most impulsive, most lawless man in the locality. Lacking the resources to have a voice in society, these men demanded to be heard the only way they knew how. To be taken seriously by the southern gentry, poor whites began relying on the most primal type of honor, one that depends on strength, physical prowess, and a type of existential freedom based on living in the moment.[26]

Throughout the late antebellum period, therefore, masters tried to control lower-class whites in innumerable ways. Poor whites responded to their attempts to secure hegemony by bucking the system, fighting authority, and damaging or stealing the property of the wealthy and powerful. In whatever small way they could, poor white men expressed their anger over their position in society by becoming as "free" as possible. As white men, they likely balked at the prospect of other white men ordering them around, manipulating both their lives and their livelihoods.

---

[25] "Jail Burnt," *Atlanta Weekly Intelligencer*, Dec. 16, 1854, 2; "Untitled," *Ibid.*, March 8, 1855, 1; Williams, *Vogues in Villainy*, 45.
[26] Bolton, *The Confessions of Edward Isham*, 3.

Whether drinking to excess, dropping out of society, or committing more serious crimes, poor white Southerners attempted to assuage the pain of powerlessness. Becoming either destructive and/or self-destructive, these "criminals" were seeking some semblance of control over their own destinies. Yet with the rise of the penitentiary and the carceral state, the quest for autonomy was typically fleeting.

In America, early penitentiaries certainly seemed to fit Michel Foucault's characterization as places of surveillance and punishment, rather than houses of reform. First appearing in the United States in 1790 with Philadelphia's Walnut House, prisons were built rapidly in the 1820s and early 1830s. In the slave South, intense debates over whether or not to build penitentiaries arose in most states. Interestingly, despite white Southerners' familiar disdain for tax-funded governmental projects, their states built the same types of prisons, at the same rate, as the industrializing North. Georgia originally constructed a penitentiary in 1817, and Tennessee finished building in 1831. By 1837, Louisiana had established a prison; in 1840, Mississippi followed suit, as did Alabama in 1850. Only sparsely populated Florida and the Carolinas remained without penitentiaries before the Civil War. Instead, the Carolinas relied on local jails and corporal punishment. Yet while North Carolinians, especially, continued debating the benefits and drawbacks of a penal institution, South Carolinian legislators were against the idea from the beginning. After the Nullification Crisis, the leaders of South Carolina began to "define themselves in conscious opposition to the values of 'progress.'" Because a slaveholder-dominated legislature appointed the governor, there was simply no two-party system to debate things such as penal reform. As Lawrence Friedman quipped, "more 'primitive' punishments" thrived in "this more primitive section of the country," where humiliation, shame, and corporal punishment remained "downright indispensable."[27]

Before the penitentiary formally existed in America, criminal sentences consisted of confinement in local jails, generally coupled with expensive fines. Punishments also included branding, whipping, cropping, and death. Once a state built a prison, however, much of the violence used to punish the convict disappeared from public sight. In general, whippings were no longer administered on the steps of the local courthouse; instead,

---

[27] Ayers, *Vengeance and Justice*, 34; Friedman, *Crime and Punishment*, 78; 79; 81; Wallenstein, *From Slave South to New South*, 81; Ayers, *Vengeance and Justice*, 35; Bolton, *Poor Whites*, 110; Ayers, *Vengeance and Justice*, 58; Friedman, *Crime and Punishment*, 81; 82.

lashings became private affairs, taking place behind prison walls. Likely influenced by the social mores of the Jacksonian era, violent retribution against criminals became increasingly unpopular. By the late antebellum period, public displays of violence against criminals had all but ceased in many areas of the country, especially the urbanized North, where a combination of humanism and religious awakening had rendered the practices barbaric. According to Friedman, public punishments of "stigma and shame" naturally fell out of favor in "an age of rapid growth, impersonal cities, and rootless populations." Occasional hangings still took place for the most heinous criminals, but free-state governments stopped using the more cruel forms of torturous body mutilation by the 1830s.[28]

In the Deep South, however, where the system of slavery was predicated on viciousness, public violence against individuals – both black *and* white – continued to play an important role in the maintenance of society. The southern legislators who supported building penitentiaries tended to be the wealthiest men in their counties, and thus had more investment in the southern hierarchy. These affluent planters still resorted to public spectacles of violence when they deemed it necessary, but they simultaneously privatized most of the violence against white convicts. For instance, Alabama's prison employed punishments such as straight-jackets, solitary confinement, a diet of bread and water, and a form of water torture where the head is gradually immersed in ice cold liquid. Yet one particular punishment invoked the overwhelming indignation of white convicts – whipping. Historically associated with controlling and punishing slave behavior, white prisoners found flogging incredibly humiliating. One penitentiary report even endorsed the efficacy of this cruelty: "Immaterial how degraded a convict may be ... being placed under the lash is the most degrading of all imaginable positions."[29]

In the Deep South, these "degraded" convicts were almost all poor white men. After 1818, Louisiana was the only southern state consistently to admit slaves into the penitentiary, as an alternative to hanging. Although free people of color made up a large percentage of the Upper South's prisoners, the Deep South's institutions of corrections rarely housed any. Comprising one out of every three of Virginia's prisoners and one of every two of Maryland's convicts, free blacks made up less than 1 percent of Alabama and Mississippi's populations in the 1850s,

---

[28] *Ibid.*, 77.   [29] Ayers, *Vengeance and Justice*, 42; 53; 70.

while there were no free blacks in Georgia's prison. The Deep South's penitentiaries, therefore, almost exclusively housed whites. Out of these convicted whites, high proportions of them were immigrants (especially the "Famine Irish") and city dwellers. Most were impoverished, and many were nonviolent offenders. The majority of inmates were not incarcerated for murder, rape, or even assault; instead, about one-half of them spent years laboring under the lash for insignificant property crimes like petit larceny and burglary.[30]

Mississippi's penitentiary was constructed in 1840 in Jackson. According to Charles Bolton, state politicians sold the idea to the public by claiming that a prison would "provide for the humane treatment of criminals and to free them from such 'barbarous punishments' as whipping and branding ... physical forms of discipline [that] were generally associated with slavery." There were likely two main reasons for this privatization of violence. First, the timing coincided with a rise in poor white discontent following the Panic of 1837. Perhaps masters were attempting to assuage some of non-slaveholders' ill will following the great consolidation of wealth and landholdings. Second, and much more significantly, beating a white person in front of a slave could help destroy the "established boundary" between slavery and freedom. But as southern states turned to imprisonment, the only change in lawful white corporal punishment was that it now happened overwhelmingly in private – within the prison bounds – instead of in public, where slaves and non-slaveholding whites could witness it. Mississippi's prisoners, "almost exclusively" poor whites, were primarily incarcerated for property crimes, with two-thirds of them serving time for theft.[31]

Not surprisingly, in a region completely dependent on forced labor, it was not long before the Deep South's prisons resembled plantations or factories. Convicts were made to work long hours in ungodly conditions, and if they faltered in their labor, they immediately suffered under the crack of the whip. Throughout the later antebellum years, prisoners produced a wide array of goods, from wagons to slave shoes to pails to bricks. But some of these projects came to a halt when working men all across the region began complaining about competition with prison labor. Mississippi's prison, like those of the other southern states, was supposed eventually to become a self-sustaining enterprise; the gentry certainly did not want to have to support it with tax dollars. Originally,

---

[30] *Ibid.*, 61; 75.   [31] Bolton, *Poor Whites*, 110; 111.

the superintendent worked prisoners in various trades, turning a profit as early as 1843. To achieve this result, however, the prison wardens needed to command complete control and obedience from the incarcerated – not just as prisoners, but also as laborers.[32]

C.M. Hart, the superintendent of Mississippi's penitentiary in the 1840s, started his job with only $500 in funding from the state. Using this money, as well as forced convict labor, he erected a blacksmith's shop, a coal house, and a stable, reporting that "articles manufactured by the convicts" were being "sold for cash." His plans for the future including using convict labor to manufacture bricks for the growing city of Jackson. Hart even asked the state to furnish him with five black slaves to cut and haul wood for the kilns, and to tend to the kilns at night, "when convicts cannot be employed." Access to these two types of unfree labor made Hart so sure of the brick factory's success that he predicted "a revenue to the state" within three years of operation. Over the next few years, however, Jackson's artisans and mechanics began protesting that they could not compete with unpaid prison labor. Deciding to head off any further problems from non-slaveholding working men, Mississippi's politicians turned the prison into a cotton factory in 1849 and it stayed that way for over a decade, producing profits of about $20,000 a year. When the Civil War began, the state converted the penitentiary into a munitions factory.[33]

Cruel and barbarous treatment of these laborers could be detected from the earliest days of the institution, but actual accounts of the violence demonstrate just how frequently these mostly nonviolent criminals were viciously abused. The superintendent's report from 1840 began by listing each convict as a number – without a name – a method that slaveholders and bureaucrats sometimes used to enumerate slaves. Beside each number, Superintendent Hart recorded a brief description, and many of them related to work ethic and labor: Number 20 "works indifferently," and Number 28 "works badly, is very deceptive, and required very close watching." While "Nothing but fear" made convict Number 23 work, Number 12 held the title of the "laziest and most stubborn of all the convicts. All moderate punishments have no effect upon him. Nothing but stripes will make him work, and observe the rules of the prison." Prisoner Number 2, however, suffered the cruelest fate. Apparently

[32] Ayers, *Vengeance and Justice*, 75; "Mississippi Penitentiary Superintendent's Report," Folder 1840, MDAH.
[33] *Ibid.*; Ayers, *Vengeance and Justice*, 66–7; Bolton, *Poor Whites*, 111.

stubborn, disobedient, and refusing to work, he was put on bread and water and isolated from the other convicts. When those punishments seemed to have little effect on Number 2's behavior, the superintendent whipped him with a leather strap, claiming to have given him less than eight stripes. Following the savage whipping, however, Number 2 kept complaining that he felt sick. Yet since he had "feigned sickness before," the superintendent refused to believe him and continued forcing him to work. A week later prisoner Number 2 died. Hart was, of course, never held liable for the convict's brutal death. Instead, it seemed as if the superintendent became even more confident and bold in his methods. Although he never hesitated to use violence to make the convicts labor, Hart also took great care to ensure that the corporal punishments he issued would not affect the prison's profit margin by keeping a convict from working. Sounding very much like a slaveholder, the superintendent rather proudly concluded that the "strap, or paddle, which while it produces instantaneous pain, has the desired effect, does not wound or mutilate, or cut the body, and admits of little or no interruption in the labor of the day."[34]

Georgia's penitentiary was, in many ways, similar to Mississippi's penitentiary. Originally erected in Milledgeville, the antebellum capital of the state, politicians expected it to become self-supporting immediately (although in the early years that never happened). After the prison was destroyed by a fire in 1831, the legislature considered abolishing the institution altogether, returning to the pre-penitentiary system of corporal punishment. Yet more progressive forces prevailed and the following year the prison was rebuilt. Because the prison did not produce a profit over the next few years, in 1843 the state senate passed a bill to hire out convicts, but the House postponed the bill indefinitely, effectively killing it. Instead, as the *Columbus Enquirer* reported, to raise money "All articles manufactured" at the penitentiary would "be sold (at low cash prices) in six or twelve months' time." Georgia's convicts were worked harder and longer to try to meet these budgetary restraints, as a journalist from Athens reported a year later. The Warden, Charles H. Nelson, apparently embodied "an inhumanity and cruelty that would have disgraced a brute." Despite Nelson's critics, he continued working the convicts like slaves. By the 1850s, Georgia's prisoners had built 371 cars for the Western and Atlantic Railroad, finally paying off the penitentiary's

---

[34] "Mississippi Penitentiary Superintendent's Report."

construction debt in the process. Much like Mississippi's Superintendent, Georgia's Warden knew how to effectively use violence to optimize labor output. Indeed, these two men had learned from slaveholders how to successfully exploit unfree laborers. Southern prisons proved that whites – like blacks – could be deprived of their liberty and forced to work at the command of the lash. Perhaps most importantly, the antebellum prison experience proved that, properly coerced, unfree white labor could successfully produce a profit.[35]

Profits, however, were not the only financial concern of the Deep South's judicial system. As previously discussed, antebellum courts functioned on a fee system. From a sheriff's fee for the actual arrest itself, to accrued daily jail fees, to the payment of the solicitor general, the courts depended on the accused for reimbursement of their own legal costs. These fees, especially when combined with the fines imposed for most criminal convictions, could vary widely, from 5 or 10 dollars to hundreds of dollars for more serious offenses. And while every state laid out statutory guidelines on what each step of the legal process should cost, local courts were able to tack on additional charges at will, knowing the defendants had no recourse to challenge these costs. Aside from civil cases, it is relatively rare to find explicit monetary details concerning fines and fees in antebellum southern minute books, and when numbers do appear, they vary greatly. In most states, completely indigent people supposedly had the option of taking an oath of insolvency, and then local taxes would be used to compensate the court. In practice, however, it is unclear how often this actually happened.

In Savannah, for example, each night accused criminals were arrested and lodged in jail. The next morning they generally received a cursory hearing in the Mayor's Court. While some of the accused were fined and released, others were returned to jail, either to await the next session of the Superior Court, or simply because they could not pay their fines. And because court sessions were only held twice a year, some people were lodged in jail for six months before even having the chance to be fully arraigned. Regardless of the amount of fines and fees, though, most poor whites would have had trouble trying to pay them. With rare access to actual cash, poor white suspects faced two realities: remaining imprisoned for lengthy periods of time, or getting a benefactor to pay the fees or post bond. Whenever this scenario did arise, it undoubtedly strengthened the

---

[35] Wallenstein, *From Slave South*, 81; 82; "Penitentiary, Georgia," *Columbus Enquirer*, Oct. 4, 1843, 3; Ayers, *Vengeance and Justice*, 52; 66.

culture of paternalism. Having a well-known, affluent member of the community vouch for the future behaviors of a poor white could be likened to having a patron taking responsibility for the actions of a free black.[36]

Yet for the vast majority of poor whites, there was no benefactor posting bonds. Most historians purport that the widespread jailing of debtors ended in the Jacksonian period. But this was not the case in the Deep South, where the practice thrived in many localities throughout the late antebellum period. Originally, Old English law separated debtors into two separate classes: the rich and "respectable" middle classes had one set of laws, and the poor had another. Bankruptcy law, as John Fabian Witt wrote, had always been as much about the "interests of creditors as it had been about providing fresh starts to debtors." As part of the legal code reserved for the (formerly) affluent, bankruptcy was, especially in the nineteenth century, a "commitment to social provision for middle-class risks." For the truly indigent, there was no legal recourse, and being in debt easily landed a person in jail. As dire as the circumstances were for debtors in England, however in America, "comparatively harsh rules" shaped both the law of torts and poor laws. Southern states in particular had little incentive to help lift poor whites out of poverty; thus the poor never enjoyed the forgiveness of debts or the clean slate of bankruptcy. Instead, poor whites were left to sink deeper and deeper into debt, racking up excessive court and jail fees as they attempted to navigate the legal system – falling into the endless, cyclic abyss of owing the court money they were unable to earn. Poor law and criminal law were deeply historically intertwined. The fact that poor white southern debtors were still deprived of liberty in the 1840s and 1850s is hardly surprising.[37]

Colonial American jails "housed debtors" but did not usually confine them to cells. Generally allowed to work within the prison bounds during the days, the debtors would return to the jail to sleep at nights. There were also workhouses and "houses of correction," institutions that boarded vagrants, idlers, and paupers, functioning as something between a poor house and a guard house. By the 1820s, one historian wrote, only those debtors owing large sums of money spent more than a month in jail, usually with the added privilege of roaming the prison bounds. In general, most legal scholars have held that imprisonment for debt ended by the

[36] *Ibid.*, 74.
[37] John Fabian Witt, "Review Essay: Narrating Bankruptcy/Narrating Risk," *Northwestern University Law Review*, 98, No. 1 (2003): 327; 305.

mid-1830s. Although true for much of America, historians have uncovered recently a different reality in the Deep South. While many Upper South states had changed their laws by the later antebellum period, states with larger percentages of slaves lagged behind. North Carolina, for example, had an Insolvent Debtors Law which "provided for the release of any debtors imprisoned for more than twenty days once they took an oath that they did not have property worth more than $10 other than property exempt from execution." The law was not like bankruptcy – the impoverished debtor was still responsible for his debt. Still, North Carolina's laws were much more humane than South Carolina's, where incarceration for debt was not abolished until Reconstruction. As Witt confirmed, "Imprisonment for debt persisted into the 1830s and 1840s; in some Southern states it was not formally abolished until the early 1870s."[38]

Originally, debt imprisonment in the antebellum South was largely the result of the adoption of an early English law, capias ad satisfaciendum, popularly referred to as "ca. sa." As "the creditor's ultimate weapon," Peter Coleman stated, ca. sa. "was the right to imprison his defaulting debtor until the obligation had been paid." The local sheriff, by writ of execution, would arrest and jail the debtor until the court date, unless, of course, the debtor had enough money to purchase his own release. The creditor then had the option of proceeding "in one of two ways. By the first method he filed suit to recover the overdue debt. If the trial court upheld the demand it issued a final judgment providing for the assignment and sale of the debtor's assets, personal property first, then real property." Thus, for the accused who still owned wealth, the sole punishment was the repossession of enough property to pay off the original debt. But the truly indigent people who could not satisfy the loan were forced to remain in jail, paradoxically, until they *could* repay the loan. This legal practice, also known as the mesne process, was quick, easy, and inexpensive. The plaintiff merely had to appear before a court official and swear that a debtor was hiding assets, or simply that a debt was overdue. By that point, the debtor's fate was sealed: the inability to make a payment on a loan meant the end of freedom.[39]

[38] Friedman, *Crime and Punishment*, 49; Peter J. Coleman, *Debtors and Creditors in America: Insolvency, Imprisonment for Debt, and Bankruptcy, 1607–1900* (Washington, D.C.: Beard Books, 1999), 254; 257; Bolton, *Poor Whites*, 26; see Morris, "White Bondage," 202, Footnote 55: In South Carolina, "Imprisonment for debt was not abolished until 1868."; Witt, "Review Essay," 308.

[39] Coleman, *Debtors and Creditors*, 3–5.

One of Georgia's original statutes concerning insolvent debtors, adopted in 1801, changed very little over the next sixty-plus years, at least for the truly impoverished. Perhaps one of the most concerning aspects of the law required the jailing of all debtors who "shall not be able to satisfy and pay his ordinary person fees, [when] such fees shall be paid by the person at whose insistence such insolvent person may be confined." The creditor, therefore, was all-powerful in deciding whether or not the debtor would become incarcerated. As long as the creditor agreed to pay jail fees, the county would imprison the debtor, regardless of how insignificant of a sum he owed, and regardless of time. But for those "debtors" who somehow had enough wealth to post bond, an 1820 act permitted them "the privilege of the jail yard," a ten acre circumference around the jail that would be expanded to a hundred acres in 1840. Not until 1850 did state legislators amend the wording of the law to include "the privilege of prison bounds" to all debtors, notwithstanding their inability to post bond. For the most part, however, the state's capias ad satisfaciendum laws remained unchanged from the very beginning of the nineteenth century, despite efforts to amend or abolish them. In 1845, for example, one Georgia legislator introduced a bill "to prevent the issue of a 'capi[a]s ad satisfaciendum' against defendants, until the plaintiff swears that he believes the defendant has property or money fraudulently concealed." But slaveholders, who comprised 70 percent of the state's legislature, immediately rejected this reasonable amendment, suggesting that the primary goal of the law *was* to jail debtors, not to recover overdue debts.[40]

Slave owners regularly enforced these laws, as the 1859 statue book included "An act to authorize the Justices of the Inferior Court of this State, to discharge Insolvent Debtors confined by process." According to the act, local jails were overcrowded with both debtors and criminals, necessitating the intervention of lower court judges to continually release some of the incarcerated. It is unclear what became of the debts of the freed prisoners; in all likelihood, they were listed as insolvent, with the

---

[40] Howell Cobb, *Analysis of the Statutes of Georgia, in General Use, with the Forms and Precedents Necessary to Their Practical Operation, and an Appendix, Containing the Declaration of Independence; the Articles of Confederation; the Constitution of the United States; the Constitution of the State of Georgia; General Washington's Farewell Address, and the Naturalization Laws Passed by Congress.* New York, 1846. *The Making of Modern Law: Primary Sources*, Web. August 15. 2013, 631; Coleman, *Debtors and Creditors*, 235; "Georgia Legislature," *Albany Patriot*, Dec. 3, 1845, 2; Wooster, *The People in Power*, 41.

state absorbing their public debts. Perhaps this excess of prisoners helped push Georgia to outlaw the practice of jailing females for ca. sa in 1847, with Alabama following suit in 1852. Other Deep South states, however, made no distinction as to the sex of the debtor – any individual who owed even a small sum of money was at risk of losing their liberty.[41]

And for those unlucky individuals who did lose their freedom over debts, the waiting time before formal charges or trials varied widely. It seems likely that many of the debtors in the later antebellum period experienced lengthy periods of incarceration, sometimes in between the initial arrest and actual trial, and sometimes while awaiting formal charges. Georgia's 1859 code advocated the release of debtors who had been languishing in jails with no semblance of due process, explaining that "It often happens that prisoners, debtors and criminals, are committed and sent to jails in other counties than those to which they belong," and "are frequently left there without prosecution." In Hinds County, Mississippi, sheriffs were often commanded to arrest small-time debtors, even in cases where the prisoners would have to wait until the next court term for a hearing, which could sometimes take as long as six months. Furthermore, these arrests were still prevalent in the years leading up to the Civil War, as evidenced by the number of southern newspapers offering various forms related to capias ad satisfaciendum. Indeed, as late as 1857 Mississippi's legislature ordered $1.50 to be paid to sheriffs for "Serving ca. sa. on each defendant." Two years later, Georgia declared that jailers should get sixty cents for receiving any "prisoner or debtor," while a justice of the peace was entitled to thirty-five cents for each capias ad satisfaciendum execution.[42]

Due mainly to overcrowding, by the later antebellum period most Deep South states allowed debtors the privileges of prison bounds, a specified area surrounding the jail. Convicts would ostensibly try to find

---

[41] Howell Cobb, *A Compilation of the General and Public Statutes of the State of Georgia; with the Forms and Precedents Necessary to Their Practical Use. and an Appendix. Containing the Naturalization Laws; the Constitutions of the United States and of Georgia, and the Rules of Practice.* New York, 1859. *The Making of Modern Law: Primary Sources*, Web, August 15. 2013, 335; 334; Coleman, *Debtors and Creditors*, 235; John J. Ormond, *The Code of Alabama.* Montgomery, 1852. *The Making of Modern Law: Primary Sources*, Web, August 15. 2013, 448.

[42] Cobb, *A Compilation*, 334; Hinds County, Circuit Court Minutes, 1859–62, MDAH; "List of Blanks," *Albany Patriot* (GA), May 4, 1855, 4; William Lewis Sharkey, *The Revised Code of the Statute Laws of the State of Mississippi.* Jackson, Mississippi, 1857. *The Making of Modern Law: Primary Sources* Web, August 15, 2013, 145; also see 535–7; Howell Cobb, *A Compilation*, 435.

work within the prison bounds during the day, and return to jail at night to sleep. Even in the punitive state of South Carolina, by the early 1830s many debtors who were sentenced to both a fine and imprisonment were given the privilege during the day so that they could try to pay off their fines. Arrests for debt remained frequent throughout the 1840s and 1850s. Fairfield District, South Carolina's "prison bounds bonds" record book literally contains several hundred standardized, (blank) fill-in-the-blank forms for people charged with ca.sa. Several cases from Anderson District provide examples of how capias ad satisfaciendum operated in practice. In 1847, the local sheriff lodged James H. Taylor in jail "for $159.50 and costs," while in 1855 William Browning was imprisoned for a mere $17.00. Four years later the sheriff searched for Norman Bronson, who apparently owed William Way and Company $223.89. But Bronson absconded before he could be arrested. The sheriff noted, "I have made search and have not been able to find this defendant in my district," a statement that likely functioned as a refrain throughout the southern states. Imprisonment for debt was yet another incentive for less affluent whites to stay constantly on the move.[43]

Perhaps one of the most striking practices of local southern courts was the "auctioning off" of paupers, debtors, and criminals. Poor white children had been bound out as cheap laborers for decades, but "selling" adults for their labor meant that some white Americans were essentially working as indentured servants throughout the late antebellum period. Whether to save money on poor houses or incarceration costs, poor white debtors and criminals were auctioned off for their services, with all the allegory that practice entailed. Put simply, the bidders agreed to take the prisoners off the county's hands to have their labor to exploit. The entire practice likely originated with the auctioning off of paupers, usually as a group. In these types of cases, rather than putting their own money down, bidders were actually competing to show how little assistance they would require from the county for the paupers' upkeep. As the courts began ordering debtors and convicts to be auctioned off, however, the transactional part of the process changed. It seems that when these whites were "sold," they were auctioned off to the highest bidder, and the proceeds from the sale would be applied to the convict's court fines and fees. Both of these methods saved county governments money while further

[43] Williams, *Vogues in Villainy*, 118; Fairfield District, Court of Common Pleas, Prison bounds bonds, 1829–1861, SCDAH; Anderson District, Court of Common Pleas, Capias ad satisfaciendum executions, 1828–1859, SCDAH.

privatizing the responsibilities of localities. In either scenario, the winning bidders, of course, were grateful for the chance to purchase such cheap labor, and the minimal amount of care they were required to provide for the poor only added to their profits.[44]

As for the Deep South's criminals, those "auctioned off" were usually men who had been convicted of vagrancy, livestock theft, or bastardy. In South Carolina vagrants could be publicly sold for terms of six months to a year and a day. If no one was willing to purchase the vagrant's labor, "the sessions court ordered that he be whipped anywhere from five to thirty-nine lashes." One Civil War veteran, George Brown, remembered seeing white men for "sale" in Tennessee as a boy. He described a vagrant as being sold for an incredibly insignificant amount of money, further suggesting that these auction rates were likely daily or weekly rates. "The men who idled were arrested under the Vagabond Act and made to work. I knew one man, John Henderson, who was bid off at 6 ½ c. and put to work by the buyer," until "he bought his freedom."[45]

Richard Morris purported that South Carolina's laws authorizing the "sale" of vagrants and "putative fathers … stemmed from the archaic debt laws still in existence" on the eve of secession. As for the crime of bastardy, during the late antebellum period many upper- and middling-class Southerners were concerned about sexual relationships among poor whites, who often eschewed the institution of marriage. Grand juries all across the region complained about the poor living in "open adultery." Up until 1847, white men convicted of bastardy in South Carolina could be sold into servitude for four years. However, according to Jack Kenny Williams, the restrictions under this statute were "repeatedly ignored," as some men served much longer sentences. Morris's findings confirm this fact. If the putative father defaulted on payments of $25 a year until the illegitimate child turned twelve, he was liable to be sold for his labor to the highest bidder. The proceeds of this sale "were applied to the child's upkeep." Occasionally southern courts sold these alleged fathers for shorter periods of time, but sometimes their sentences far exceeded what the law allowed, as in 1843 when the Barnwell sessions court sold Bryant Weathersbee for *ten years*.[46]

[44] Ely, "Few Subjects," 858; Lockley, *Welfare and Charity*, 22.
[45] Morris, "White Bondage," 199; Elliot and Moxley, *Tennessee*, Vol. 1, 388–9.
[46] Morris, "White Bondage," 202; Williams, *Vogues in Villainy*, 57; 55; Morris, "White Bondage," 200; also see 224–5.

This type of forced labor obviously blurred the lines between slaves and free white citizens. But so did the public corporal punishment of poor whites – generally by means of whipping – which occurred in almost every Deep South state. While scholars who have worked extensively with local southern legal records know that these lashings occurred, the larger narrative of American history often obscures this important fact. Indeed, one of the most revered scholars of American crime and punishment, Lawrence Friedman, held that most corporal punishment, including whipping, had ended by the close of the Jacksonian period. Citing the prison as "the centerpiece of correctional theory," he declared that "whipping ... fell into disrepute. In an age of rapid growth, impersonal cities, and rootless populations, public punishments (punishments of stigma and shame) seemed to lose their power. These tools worked best in small, closed communities." While Friedman's theory was certainly true for the rapidly industrializing North, his description of "small, closed communities" still applied to areas of the late antebellum Deep South. The public, violent punishment of black Americans was a common sight in these regions. For white Americans, state-sanctioned corporal punishments were much rarer, but they did, in fact, occur. Poor white debtors and criminals were publicly beaten and whipped throughout the late antebellum and Civil War eras. While the vast majority of the lashings were committed by mobs, vigilantes, and individual slaveholders, some floggings were sanctioned by state and local officials. Growing up in Lauderdale, Alabama, Benjamin Derby remembered "a few loafers in the country that would steal and we had the whip law and run them out. ... They had to work and did work and made a good living or they had to leave the country. I saw my father and other men whip one man and make him leave." Former slaves also confirmed that white men were still being whipped in the years leading to secession. Betty Chessier recalled, "The only person I ever seen whipped at that whipping post was a white man." Charles Crawley concurred, saying, "Yes the poor white man had some dark and tough days, like us poor niggers; I mean [they] were lashed and treated, some of them just as pitiful and unmerciful."[47]

In the slave South, violence was not only an accepted part of daily life, it was also a fundamental necessity. So even with the rise of the

---

[47] Friedman, *Crime and Punishment*, 49; Ayers, *Vengeance and Justice*, 102; Elliot and Moxley, *Tennessee*, Vol. 2, 632–3; Betty Foreman Chessier, *American Slave*, Vol. 13 (OK), 31; Charles Crawley, *Ibid.*, XVII (VA), 9–10.

penitentiary and the privatization of most corporal punishment, slave-holders still employed public spectacle whenever they needed to reassert their power over slaves, free blacks, and even poor whites. Masters made sure to preserve their legal right to whip and publicly humiliate other white men, codifying bodily harm as a just punishment for several seemingly benign crimes. Poor whites convicted of trading with slaves were liable to be whipped in most southern states, and larceny charges from livestock stealing to petty theft warranted similar treatment. Georgia, the only Deep South state officially to abolish whipping and torture, still entertained notions of reintroducing corporal punishment throughout the 1840s and 1850s. As Bolton found in North Carolina, a state that "mandated corporal punishment for a variety of crimes ranging from theft to fighting ... poor whites convicted of theft usually involved a fine for women but a public whipping for men." And South Carolinian officials, according to Forret, "inflicted as many as thirty-nine stripes on whites – men only – caught gambling with slaves or free blacks, in addition to fines and imprisonment that both men and women faced." The Palmetto State's legal code also allowed whipping for petit larceny, receiving stolen goods, and perjury, and the offense of horse stealing warranted between fifty and two hundred lashes. And while the practice began engendering some public backlash in the 1850s, South Carolina's legislature did not seem too affected by the sentiment. As late as 1857 they passed a law requiring whipping as part of the punishment for white males who had been convicted of trading with slaves more than once.[48]

Both Alabama and Mississippi required every county to build a "jail or county prison, well secured with iron bars, bolts and locks; and also, one pillory, whipping-post, and stocks; and every jail so to be erected, shall consist of three apartments at least; one of which shall be appropriated to the reception of debtors." These laws were still in effect at the time of the Civil War, and from all indications, they were still used, if sparingly. In Alabama, stealing was generally punishable by "fine and imprisonment, or whipping, as the court shall think to inflict." Even vagrancy warranted very harsh penalties for repeat offenders, whether male or female. If a second arrest occurred less than twenty days after a vagrant was released from jail for a first offense, the accused was incarcerated for one month,

---

[48] Planitzer, "A Dangerous Class of Men, 40; Wallenstein, *From Slave South*, 83; Bolton, *Poor Whites*, 60; Forret, *Race Relations*, 60; *The Statutes At Large Of South Carolina*, Columbia, 1841. 10 vols. *The Making of Modern Law: Primary Sources*, Web, August 15, 2013, 297; 286; Forret, *Race Relations*, 106.

"with all costs accruing thereon; which if he or she neglect or refuse to pay, he or she may be continued in prison until the next county court." If the defendant was then found guilty, the "court may proceed to hire the offender for any term not exceeding six months, to make satisfaction for all costs." However, the law stipulated an important caveat: if the vagrant "be of noted ill fame" and thus no one would hire them, thirty-nine lashes on "his or her bare back" would suffice as justifiable punishment. South Carolina also recommended selling off the "services" of the vagrant for one full year "at auction." Just as in Alabama, if "no purchaser" was found, the offender would be whipped and then given three days to leave the district.[49]

Aside from vagrancy, there were a number of other crimes that warranted the lash in the antebellum South. From the perspective of corporal punishment against whites, South Carolina had the most punitive legal code in the region, probably due to several factors. Aside from the obvious problem of not having a state penitentiary, its leaders seemed less concerned than other Deep South states over poor white discontent. Much of their apathy likely stemmed from the fact that South Carolina had higher rates of slaveholders than did its neighbors, making its poor white population proportionally less significant. States with a more economically stratified white population showed a little more restraint in the meting out of punishments for white convicts. Unfortunately, the vast majority of legal records from this period lack sentencing information, so it is difficult to ascertain how frequently white people were publicly whipped in the late antebellum period. Still, public whippings of white people *did* take place, and the spectacle of it all further blurred the lines between slavery and freedom, black and white.[50]

Jack Kenny Williams attempted to categorize the antebellum punishments of South Carolina's convicts. Local judges sentenced about 10 percent of the state's felons to death, and out of the 90 percent remaining, 50 percent were fined, 20 percent were jailed, and an astonishing 30 percent were sentenced to whipping, the pillory, or branding. Oftentimes

[49] Sharkey, *The Revised Code*, 703; Clement Comer Clay, *Digest of the Laws of Alabama: Containing all the Statutes of a Public and General Nature, in Force at the Close of the Session of The General Assembly, in February, 1843. To Which are Prefixed, the Declaration of Independence; the Constitution of the United States; the Act to Enable the People of Alabama to Form a Constitution and State Government, &c.; and the Constitution of the State of Alabama.* Tuscaloosa, 1843. *The Making of Modern Law: Primary Sources*, Web, August 15, 2013, 162; Clay, *Digest of the Laws*, 592.

[50] *The Statutes At Large Of South Carolina*, 1841, 582.

these punishments were paired with fines or jail time; the most common combination included a fine and a lashing. According to Williams, "the view of a pickpocket or a hog-stealer receiving his 'dorsal application' was a common one." Actual lashings were usually administered by the sheriff, and sometimes by jailors or deputies. Occasionally judges specified whether the lashings should be "moderately laid on" or "well laid on." Probably the most commonly ordered sentence was thirty-nine lashes, a number derived from the Biblical code of Moses, which stipulated penalties at "forty stripes save one." Sentences could range from as little as one, two, or three lashes up to 119 lashes. Two horse thieves, convicted in Columbia in 1852, were sentenced to 119 lashes, to be doled out in monthly installments of 39-20-20-20-20. The men were jailed between the whippings. Horse stealers received the most severe sentences; it was rare for them to receive less than fifty stripes. Yet no matter the number of lashes, a primary objective of whipping white people was to completely and utterly embarrass them, degrading them to the level of slaves. Governor John Means confirmed this point in 1852, stating that "when a white man once had" a public whipping, "he disappeared and never returned again." The shame and stigma associated with being punished like a slave was simply too much for most men to bear.[51]

At least in the case of South Carolina, the administration of public whippings changed over time. For one thing, in the early antebellum years, considerable numbers of white women were ordered to receive the brutal punishment. While most of these women were lashed less than eleven times, public sentiment began changing by the mid-antebellum period, causing the practice to become rare. When one woman was sentenced to a whipping in 1853, public anger became so intense that the governor pardoned her before the lashing. While vigilantes and other extra-legal groups continued to flog white women throughout the end of the Civil War, it seems that by the 1850s local judges stopped using whipping as a punishment for them. There was, therefore, a gendered distinction in punishment in the years leading up to secession. While poor white men still suffered under the lash of the law, poor white women were increasingly punished by an intensified policing of their sexuality. Physical punishments may have been restricted to men, but slaveholders gradually began regulating the bodies of poor white women.[52]

---

[51] Williams, *Vogues in Villainy*, 107; 106; 106; 108; 109; 108; 109.
[52] *Ibid.*, 109; 110. See Bynum, *Unruly Women*.

South Carolina's decision to stop flogging poor white women coincided with the legislature considering a number of bills in the early 1850s to either regulate or reform the whipping of whites. During these years, two of the state's governors tried to substitute hard labor for the practice; one even attempted to outlaw the public whipping of whites altogether. Although no bill ever became law, punitive sentences became much more infrequent in the years leading to secession. A great deal of the public's outrage, it seemed, stemmed from the fact that growing numbers of African Americans were watching the spectacles, leading both slaves and free blacks to question the racial divide by considering poor whites their social equals. In 1846, a grand jury out of Charleston complained about the "self-congratulation" among blacks over "the degradation of the white by the same punishment." Despite mounting criticism of the practice, the system did not change, and poor white men were publicly whipped in South Carolina up through the Civil War.[53]

Silas Bond, a severely impoverished laborer in Martin County, North Carolina, was whipped for stealing food in 1828. Born to poor parents, his three siblings were bound out as forced laborers. But Bond himself "was weak and ill grown," and thus "could not find a master willing to clothe and feed him for his services." Wandering from place to place with his mother, begging for food and shelter, he survived childhood living on the "verge of starvation." When at last Bond turned nineteen, his mother was finally able to hire him out. After several days of working and without having eaten a meal, Silas Bond pilfered "one joint of meat" from his employer. Bond's "master, vengeful," had the young man arrested for petit larceny. Upon Silas Bond's conviction, the local judge "passed sentence that he receive ten lashes lightly laid on. This conviction deprived him of the rights of citizenship." But Bond would not be the last North Carolinian whipped. In fact, by 1856 in Guilford County, North Carolina, the punishment for property crimes had gotten more punitive. When John Rogers pled guilty to burglary charges, the court sentenced him to thirty-nine lashes, "with a promise of thirty-nine more if he would appear here at the next Term of the Court." And Willis Hurley, convicted of stealing a horse in Randolph County in 1855, also received a two part sentence: thirty-nine lashes, and thirty more in four months' time. In all likelihood, few people stuck around to receive the delayed parts of their sentences.[54]

---

[53] Hindus, *Prison and Plantation*, 101; Williams, *Vogues in Villainy*, 110; Hindus, *Prison and Plantation*, 101; 102.

[54] Johnson, *Ante-Bellum North Carolina*, 71, Web.; Bolton, *Poor Whites*, 64–5.

In Laurens, South Carolina, several men charged with capias ad satisfaciendum for fines and court fees were also sentenced to public whippings. In 1844, William Hazel was "sentenced to receive twenty lashes on the bare back on the first Monday of April next." Originally charged for the relatively benign crime of petit larceny, Hazel apparently still owed the court $22.08. Listed in the 1850 census as a 30-year-old illiterate, landless, propertyless farmer, Hazel was obviously too destitute to pay that sum to the court. Yet because of his poverty, he was punished like a slave – with the crack of a whip. John Snow endured the same ordeal in 1851. Owing the court $31.80 for jail and trial fees stemming from a grand larceny conviction, Snow was further "sentenced to whipping and imprisonment." Like William Hazel, the prior year's census listed John Snow as a landless, illiterate, propertyless farmer. Again in 1859, a Laurens judge sentenced another man convicted of larceny to ten lashes for owing less than 25 dollars to the court.[55]

A few districts over in Kershaw, South Carolina, poor white men were being publicly whipped for similar crimes. In November 1848, the local court sentenced Harvey Smith to a year in jail for larceny. He was also ordered "to receive on [the] first Monday in January 15 stripes and on [the] first Monday in May 15 stripes." Less than a year later Norman Gillis, a landless farm laborer in his mid-40s, was convicted of stealing a sheep. The local court used Gillis to teach poor whites a lesson: respect the sanctity of their property (ALL of their property), or suffer through an incredibly vicious punishment. According to the sheriff's records, Norman Gillis's penance was harsh:

On the first Monday in July 1849 my deputy inflicted ten stripes upon the bare back of the defendant he having failed to comply with the sentence of the court. Which was repeated by him on the first Monday in August following on the first Monday in September following I inflicted upon the bare back of the defendant ten stripes. And on the first Monday in October following nine stripes.

In Greenville, South Carolina, Murrell Massey, along with several other poor white men, had been gambling with a slave when a disagreement broke out. Massey apparently beat and stabbed the slave "with a dirk in the back." The slave ultimately lived, but Massey was sentenced to "a $20 fine, two weeks in jail, and twenty lashes."[56]

[55] Laurens, Capias ad satisfaciendum executions; Seventh Census, 1850: Laurens District, South Carolina; Laurens, Capias ad satisfaciendum executions; Seventh Census, 1850: Laurens District, South Carolina.
[56] Kershaw, Capias ad satisfaciendum executions; Seventh Census, 1850, Kershaw District, South Carolina; Forret, *Race Relations*, 170–1.

Given all of these stories together, even if the public whippings of poor whites did not occur with great frequency, they *did*, in fact, happen. And every time a white person was publicly flogged, poor whites and other non-slaveholders were reminded in a very meaningful way that they had better support the established social order. As Forret wrote, "For at least a brief moment, flogging degraded the white man, reducing him to the level of slaves and temporarily suspending his membership in white society." Anyone who dared to disrupt the southern hierarchy was in jeopardy of being publicly humiliated and savagely beaten, subsequently robbed of almost every last vestige of white privilege.[57]

Masters used a variety of different means to keep poor whites and blacks separate, and sought above all else to protect their wealth and property. They simply had little use for poor whites. Incarceration, coupled with the threat of legally sanctioned public corporal punishments, helped keep these "masterless men" from disturbing the fragile southern social order. The slave South was violent and brutal, but also intensely capitalistic, and in some ways – particularly its criminal justice system – strangely modern. Crime and punishment had little to do with each other. As Foucault argued, the relationship between the two concepts was never based upon retaliation, vengeance, or rehabilitation. Instead, he concluded, there existed "a certain mechanism of power" within the rites of punishment: "of a power that not only ... exert[ed] itself directly on bodies, but was exalted and strengthened by its visible manifestations ... of a power for which disobedience was an act of hostility." The slave South *did* need a highly mobilized system of surveillance, as well as a violent, humiliating system of punishment *for whites* in order to protect the institution of *black* slavery. This heightened state of policing and discipline not only revealed that slaveholders were increasingly living in fear of disruption to the southern hierarchy; it also indicated that their position of power was becoming ever more precarious in the years leading up to secession.[58]

For decades scholars have wondered why a biracial coalition of the South's lower classes never emerged. Poor whites and blacks certainly realized that their respective oppressors were the same people. Whether trading together in the underground economy, drinking, gambling, or

---

[57] Forret, *Race Relations*, 105.
[58] See Ayers, *Vengeance and Justice*, Part 2; Michel Foucault, *Discipline and Punish: The Birth of the Prison*. Trans. by Alan Sheridan (1975; reprint, New York: Random House, 1995).

sleeping together, or helping each other escape imprisonment or slavery, the two races collectively undermined slaveholders' control in numerous ways. In its more direct forms, their animosity manifested itself in the destruction of affluent whites' property, the prevalence of violence, and the occasional plotted or attempted revolt. As Eugene Genovese found, "the slaves had some sense of being an exploited class, not merely an oppressed race." Poor whites experienced a variation of Genovese's theory. They recognized themselves as a distinct class because they were excluded from many of the privileges of whiteness. They had few tangible reasons to consider themselves as part of the ruling race.[59]

Certainly impoverished whites had few chances to challenge the established southern hierarchy. Wealthy slaveholders assured the region remained veiled in ignorance. Non-slaveholders were indebted to and financially dependent on them. The master class had created a legal system that allowed them to imprison, brutalize, and murder anyone who challenged the slave-based hierarchy. They constantly reminded poor whites and other non-slaveholders of their power – and that people who tried to disrupt their carefully crafted society were just one step away from slavery. Rising levels of incarceration, the "selling" of convicts and debtors, and the spectacle of public corporal punishment forced poor white men to reflect upon the status of their rights as white citizens within the slaveholding South, and the results of this reflection did not bode well for their future. The vitriol against the slaveholders was growing. Discussing the fate of poor whites, the Louisiana paper *True Delta* reported, "There never was a people so enslaved by stupid laws, so degraded by class legislation. Everything ... tended to one end, the aggrandizement of a small, narrow minded, selfish, ignorant and domineering class." By the middle of the 1850s, the cracks that had always been present within the façade of white racial solidarity finally turned into deep fissures. When the Panic of 1857 hit and wealth inequality continued to deepen, slaveholders realized that they had to be proactive in the defense of their property and power.[60]

After the Civil War, of course, white men were no longer the southern gentry's main legal targets. As soon as the slaves became free, the social structure of southern society changed dramatically. Emancipation actually heralded the end of the imprisonment of thousands of poor southern whites who had defied the slaveholders' social hierarchy. Former masters

[59] Genovese, *Roll, Jordan, Roll*, 597–660; 305.
[60] Quoted in Shugg, *Origins of Class Struggle*, 121.

no longer needed to protect slave property. Instead, they began using the criminal justice system to target freedmen and freedwomen, returning them to a state of quasi-slavery. This sudden transformation in the race of the southern "criminal" – overwhelmingly white during slavery, over-whelmingly black after the Thirteenth Amendment – confirms that the maintenance of slavery greatly exacerbated class tensions between whites in the antebellum period. Slaveholders used a variety of different means to keep poor whites and blacks separate, and the incarceration of dangerous whites and masterless men helped the owners of flesh reach this end goal. As slavery's existence continued to cripple economically a large percent-age of white Southerners, it caused many of them to disengage completely from society. Almost 100 years after slavery's end, Martin Luther King, Jr. explained this alienation, an alienation that has plagued the impover-ished underclasses of every civilization: "There is nothing more dangerous than to build a society, with a large segment of people in that society, who feel that they have no stake in it; who feel that they have nothing to lose. People who have a stake in their society, protect that society, but when they don't have it, they unconsciously want to destroy it."[61]

---

[61] See Ayers, *Vengeance and Justice*, Part 2; Martin Luther King Jr., interview in Henry Hampton, *Eyes on the Prize* (PBS/Blackside Inc., 1987).

8

Race, Republicans, and Vigilante Violence

A free press is an institution almost unknown at the South. Free speech is considered as treason against slavery: and when people dare neither speak nor print their thoughts, free thought itself is well nigh extinguished. All that can be said in defence of human bondage, may be spoken freely; but question either its morality or its policy, and the terrors of lynch law are at once invoked to put down the pestilent heresy.

– Hinton Helper[1]

Slavery suppresses the liberty of the poor white man of the South, as it does that of the black man, if not in the same degree, yet in the same manner and for the same purpose. It tolerates no independence of thought or discussion. Thousands, who, in heart rebel against its monstrous pretensions, have realized ... they cannot act out their honest convictions, their lips are padlocked; to demand a hearing for the truths of the Declaration of Independence, or the Sermon on the Mount, on their part, would be as hazardous as the demand of the slaves themselves for freedom.

– The National Era[2]

In Wetumpka, Alabama, just one year prior to secession, an illiterate poor white named Franklin Veitch "was dragged down to the margin of the river, laid across a log, and whipped by a throng of blackguards." Not content with using their slaves to humiliate and punish the impoverished white, the local vigilance committee – led by the most affluent slaveholders in town – ordered that Veitch be stripped naked, and ridden on a rail. "From the lintel of his own door he was repeatedly hanged until he

---

[1] Helper, *The Impending Crisis*, 409.
[2] "Settling the Slave Question," *National Era*, March 28, 1850.

was black in the face," a source reported, making the fact that Veitch survived the ordeal nearly unbelievable. While the local master class had once charged the poor man with "being a negro, and, afterwards, with associating with negroes," his particular offence this time was one of the most common charges throughout the Deep South. The owners of flesh ordered and executed the torturous violence, the vicious beating, and the savage lynching, all due to the unfounded allegation that Veitch "sold liquor to negroes."[3]

The vast majority of poor white assault victims were never in a position to exact revenge upon their torturers, but Veitch's case was taken up by a local lawyer, Robert Tharin. Tharin had been born into a wealthy slave-holding family but eventually became an abolitionist, largely because he realized how many southern whites were affected detrimentally by slavery. After securing Veitch's "mark," Tharin sued the impoverished man's abusers, attempting to achieve some small semblance of justice. Yet he soon realized that not only was the legal system completely rigged to favor slaveholders, but that the system itself could be relatively impotent in a region ruled by lawless violence and vigilante "justice" designed to perpetuate slavery. "The parties sued became more than ever unmerciful to Veitch," Tharin lamented, and "threatened to kill him, if he did not leave." The other local poor whites "secretly encouraged" Veitch to remain, but soon the abused man disappeared. "This non-slaveholder had yielded his rights through fear, and allowed himself to be taken out of the town," Tharin reported. Meanwhile, the anti-slavery lawyer "became the most unpopular man in Wetumpka." Simply because he defended the legal rights of the poor tortured man, Tharin became the new target of the slaveholding class. Eventually they would lynch and banish him, too, but not before he had seen enough vigilante violence to expose the designs of the master class to the rest of the world. Tharin truly felt a moral obligation to help rid the Deep South of what he deemed a cruel oligarchy, which had long violently lorded over not just blacks, but poor whites as well. Indeed, he resolved, "the class to which Veitch belonged had been growing more and more degraded, more 'defenseless' and more 'oppressed,' ever since I could remember." Yet slaveholders had created such an amazingly effective system of social control – replete with private, legal, and extralegal surveillance and violence – that the

[3] R.S. Tharin, *Arbitrary Arrests in the South; or, Scenes from the Experience of an Alabama Unionist* (New York: John Bradburn, 1863), 52.

underclasses truly risked their lives if they attempted to challenge the master class's power in any small way.[4]

Complicating their ability to control the region, and evident in Veitch's case, was the fact that slaveholders had to increasingly grapple with trying to achieve segregation. This task proved impracticable, and the racial ambiguity of growing numbers of Southerners only exacerbated the situation. Certainly by the 1840s and 1850s, the master class had trouble distinguishing lighter-skinned African Americans from poorer whites, whose skin often appeared darkened from laboring outside. White and black Southerners, sexually intimate with each other for centuries, had become so racially intermixed by the mid-antebellum period that slave owners truly did not know what to do. American slavery had always been based on race, but as a litany of various factors suggest, the notion of racial slavery itself was being challenged in the final decades before the Civil War. Questioning a white person's racial purity had long been a staple of both southern humor and personal ridicule. A well-known antebellum lawyer's trick was to accuse an opposing witness of being mixed-race. Even if there was no substance to the claim, it was an incredibly embarrassing ordeal for the person testifying.

Local courts began to preside over hundreds of cases determining whether certain slaves were white or black, whether certain free blacks should be considered white, and whether certain whites should be demoted to the status of free blacks. Simultaneously, newspaper advertisements for runaway "white slaves" began appearing. By the close of the 1850s, slaveholders passed laws virtually re-enslaving free blacks, while pro-slavery beliefs became more abstract, with some of the most vocal adherents advocating slavery for all poor laborers, regardless of race. With everything in the Deep South in such a constant state of flux, one point remained perfectly clear: masters needed a terroristic system of policing, surveilling, and torturing the poor (both white and black) to preserve their cherished institution. This vigilante system would ultimately help prevent impoverished whites from flocking to the Republican Party, or worse – from becoming vocal abolitionists.

While poor whites were certainly not black like slaves, they did not live, nor act, nor look like wealthier whites. Instead, they occupied a tenuous middle ground – slaveholders accorded them certain rights because of the color of their skin, but their actions and poverty surely disbarred them from

---

[4] *Ibid.*, 55; 56.

the unfettered privileges of whiteness. According to sociologist Matt Wray, the master class had long distinguished the poor as racially non-white, or "not quite white." In fact, impoverished whites' lack of whiteness was mentioned by both travelers to and residents of the Deep South. Olmsted declared that poor whites' "skin is just the color of the sand-hills they live on," Daniel Hundley said they were the "color of yellow parchment," and Fanny Kemble wrote several times about their "yellow mud complexion." Years later, scientists would learn that a substantial lack of nutritional iron led to dirt eating, otherwise known as the "poor man's malady." Dirt eating caused some poor whites to catch hookworm, while others contracted it by walking around barefoot. Hookworm often causes people to look pale and yellow. Others probably appeared jaundiced from alcohol abuse. Regardless of the causes, though, by categorizing poor whites as *not* white, slaveholders could classify the poor as racially inferior.[5]

Conceivably, to the master class, poor whites' "yellowness" racially classified them near yellow mulattoes, or perhaps somewhere near yellow Native Americans – a frequent comparison. Olmsted commented that poor whites' "habits are very much like those of the old Indians" because they "are quite incapable of applying themselves to any steady labor." Poor whites, like most southern Native American tribes, largely survived by hunting and fishing and also maintaining small subsistence gardens or farms. Supposedly, neither group exhibited signs of a capitalist work ethic; they worked to live and spent their time off doing what they pleased. A *National Era* article described the South's impoverished whites as

marked in any crowd ... having no blood in their cheeks, their eyes black, and their hair lank, they are as distinct a race as the Indian. In some respects they are not unlike them. They love to roam the woods, and be free there; to get together for frolic or fun; to fish and hunt; to chase wild cattle.

Poor whites, therefore, were generally considered different and separate from all other whites. Perhaps for this reason, throughout much of antebellum literature, poor southern white men were described as "dark and swarthy" ruffians, who served as a constant threat to the plantation system. They fit in nowhere. Instead, their mere presence indicated trouble for the master class.[6]

---

[5] Wray, *Not Quite White*; Hundley, *Social Relations*, 271; Kemble, *Journal*; Buck, "The Poor Whites," 45; Flynt, *Dixie's Forgotten People*, 34.

[6] Olmsted, *Journey*, 452; "The South," *National Era*, Nov. 25, 1847; Susan J. Tracy, *In the Master's Eye: Representations of Women, Blacks, and Poor Whites in Antebellum Southern Literature* (Amherst: University of Massachusetts Press, 1995), 185.

As race became more difficult for slaveholders to immediately classify, southern laws placed increasingly strict racial regulations on sex, drinking, gambling, and other interactions, further monitoring poor whites and blacks in an attempt to keep them separated. These tighter controls ultimately culminated in the free black "self-enslavement" laws of the 1850s. Simply put, the Deep South's legislatures ordered free blacks to move out of their states. If they failed to flee by a certain time, they would be forced to choose a master, effectively re-enslaving themselves. Slaveholders were trying desperately to restructure their society into white and black, free and slave, but strict racial dichotomies were no longer applicable in an increasingly racially mixed world. The master class desperately needed these divisions to order southern society, but by the late antebellum period, the region had changed so much that a simple demarcation was no longer possible. All of this racial uncertainty – non-slave black people, not fully free white people, and growing proportions of interracial people – continued to weaken the once heavily stratified southern hierarchy. Cases "deciding" an individual's race began peppering southern dockets. Walter Johnson estimated that judges were asked "hundreds of times to stabilize the visible confusion of a hybrid reality into the stable degrees of difference demanded by a ruling class that wanted to see the world in black and white."[7]

The mere presence of free blacks did, of course, challenge the entire notion of racial slavery. While in general free blacks only made up a small minority of people in the Deep South (only about 1 percent), they had a stronger presence in some states like South Carolina and Louisiana. Many of them lived in the large port cities, and others lived in smaller cities and towns. As Marina Wikrimanayake has shown, the increase in the region's free black population began slowing down in the 1820s and 1830s, so much so that by the 1840s the only increase was due to births within the free black community. Thus, slaveholders were emancipating fewer and fewer slaves, and prohibiting others from purchasing their freedom. "The bridge by which the slave might graduate to free status," she sadly wrote, "had been effectively destroyed."[8]

---

[7] Williams, *Vogues in Villany*, 96; Walter Johnson, "The Slave Trader, the White Slave, and the Politics of Racial Determination in the 1850s," *Journal of American History* 87, No. 1 (June 2000): 13; 14; 21; 20; 21; 23.

[8] Marina Wikrimanayake, *A World in Shadow: The Free Black in Antebellum South Carolina* (Columbia: South Carolina, 1973), 45–6.

It is also important to note that the Deep South's free black population was heavily interracial. In South Carolina, nearly half of the state's 8,960 free blacks were listed as mulatto in the 1850 census. A certain percentage of the free community were the sons and daughters (and sometimes, sexual partners) of slave owners who eventually afforded them freedom. These men and women tended to comprise the upper economic tier of free blacks, as many times masters trained their own enslaved children in skilled trades before granting them their freedom in adulthood. Conversely, the poorest mixed-race free blacks, especially common laborers and farmhands, were likely the children of poor white mothers and enslaved or free black fathers. Regardless of their ancestry, however, free blacks truly undercut the master class's carefully crafted society. Like poor whites, free blacks really did not have a place in South – they fit in nowhere and their mere existence challenged the premises upon which racial slavery was founded. Due to these facts, slaveholders not only stopped emancipating their slaves by the 1840s and 1850s, but they also began passing laws restricting many of the avenues to freedom. As free blacks witnessed more and more of their civil rights being legislated away, they were essentially left with two possibilities: flee the region and attempt to start over in a free state or territory, or stay put and pick a master. The poorer free blacks, of course, had little choice. The latter was their only option.[9]

Much like poor whites, free blacks were frequently targeted by agents of the criminal justice system, as well as members of other vigilante groups. Always at risk of "arrest, interrogation, and capital punishment by stray patrolmen," Wikrimanayake found, free blacks had to very carefully navigate their worlds, as any minor infraction could result in the permanent loss of their free status. Thus, free blacks' "enjoyment of natural rights ... is highly questionable. There was no right the black enjoyed that was not defined as forfeitable," she wrote. "His life, his liberty, indeed his very presence in the state were subject to the whims and vagaries of the state legislature and to the willingness of white citizens to tolerate an anomaly in their society." Georgia had required all free blacks to acquire white guardians as far back as 1810, and Louisiana and Tennessee quickly followed suit. Many other southern states adopted similar statues in the decade before secession. Although they were referred to as "free," therefore, free blacks were truly far from it. With their de

[9] *Ibid.*, 13.

facto masters vouching for them before the legal system, making decisions for them, and often "employing" them, most free blacks still had to bow and scrape for affluent whites. And when rumors over black insurrection swept throughout the Deep South in the 1850s, the situation became particularly dire for free people of color, as vigilante and mob violence engulfed the region. To an even greater extent than poor and immigrant whites, "free blacks were questioned, lynched and hanged," Wikrimanayake reported, and "those who survived lost their freedom in most Southern States."[10]

Several different stories concerning the re-enslavement of free blacks highlights the important intersection of class and race. Governor Whitemarsh Seabrook of South Carolina advocated the expulsion of "all free blacks who owned no real estate or slave property." The master class was astute enough to realize that property-holding free blacks – many of them sons and daughters of planters and wealthy yeomen – would politically support the slaveholders' cause out of their own economic interests. Less than a decade later, an entirely different proposal was discussed in regards to free black babies born to white mothers. The 1859 Grand Jury Presentment in Edgefield District "proposed that all mulattoes born of white women should be sold at public auction, a measure it hoped would constitute 'a remedy for the wrongs of the South.'" Some slaveholding politicians even warned that the status of free blacks exacerbated tensions between different classes of whites, because free blacks were often wealthier and enjoyed a higher social status than poor whites. One legislator from Athens, Georgia claimed that free blacks "are exerting an influence still more appalling" than abolitionism: "the degradation of the whites." Because free blacks owned "much more property, and dress[ed] much finer than many of our degraded poor white citizens," he continued, "they are looked up to them as their equals, and in numerous instances are their associates." *Both* poor whites and free blacks, it seemed, challenged the legitimacy – and the longevity – of a well-ordered plantation system.[11]

Impoverished whites' ambiguous racial classification was institutionalized within the criminal justice system in several ways. Interestingly, multiple southern prisons list white inmates' skin "color" (shade or

---

[10] *Ibid.*, 63; 70; 161; 168–9: "In Maryland, Tennessee, Virginia, Louisiana, Texas and Arkansas legislation either facilitated voluntary enslavement or provided the free blacks with a Hobson's choice between exile and enslavement."

[11] *Ibid.*, 169; quoted on 70; "Speech of Mr. Moore, of Clark," *Southern Watchman*, Nov. 18, 1858, 2.

complexion) in addition to age, occupation, hair and eye color, and place of birth. For whites alone, entries varied from fair, light, and medium to sallow, tawny, and dark. Many county court and local jail records classified whites in the same manner. The descriptions are strikingly similar to planters' slave lists, where "chattle" descriptions included designations like black, tan, mulatto, bright mulatto, yellow, and ginger-cake. Moreover, Wikrimanayake noted that courts "sometimes unwittingly added to the free colored population by consigning white persons of dubious origin to the degraded class of free blacks ... court decisions were often erratic." Clearly, race was no longer an absolute determinate of freedom, but neither was freedom a determinate of race. As Union General Joshua Chamberlain recalled in his memoir about the Civil War, after the fighting had ceased, he was surrounded by "wild-looking men in homespun gray, standing sulkily by, or speaking only to insist that they are civilians and not soldiers." At times, he continued, these were "white men, or what seem to be, declaring that they are not white, but colored; – a claim not often set up in that part of the Republic, though there may be some truth in it for all that; for there was in those days a whimsical variance between law and fact, – between being *actually white* and *legally white*."[12]

Given that race had become so indistinguishable in the Deep South, slaveholders needed some type of standardization to determine whether an individual was black or white, slave or free. The courts provided the most obvious means of uncovering a person's ancestry or reaching a consensus about their physical attributes. Throughout the region, hundreds (if not thousands) of cases of racial determination peppered the dockets. This method allowed and even encouraged members of the master class to assert their power over poor whites once again. They employed a variety of different methods to accuse impoverished whites of not "being white." These southern court cases very obviously foreshadowed the spate of litigation concerning racial determination in the Jim Crow Era. As Helen Catterall explained, "The issue of color usually arose in three classes of cases – prohibition against inferior courts or the tax collector, objections to witnesses testifying in the superior courts, and actions of slander for words charging the plaintiff with being a mulatto." Many Deep South states had legal definitions of how to classify a person's

[12] Central Registration of Convicts, 1817–68, GDAH; Wikrimanayake, *A World in Shadow*, 14; Joshua Lawrence Chamberlain, *The Passing of the Armies* (New York: Putnam, 1915), 158, italics mine.

race based upon ancestry (hypodescent rules), with many laws listing one-quarter or one-eighth "negro blood" as the qualification between white and black. A few states, such as Arkansas, had no legal definition of race, while South Carolina's statues did not use blood quantum at all. Regardless of the laws, however, the entire legal process of determining an individual's race was inconsistent, often chaotic, and completely subject to the whims and prejudices of both judges and juries. In an 1835 South Carolina decision, the state Supreme Court fully admitted that neither the constitution nor statutes defined "mulattos or persons of color." Thus, wrote the justices, "We cannot say what admixture ... will make a colored person," but "The condition ... is not to be determined solely by ... visible mixture." Instead, they suggested, the courts should rely on reputation, making it "proper, that a man of worth ... should have the rank of a white man, while a vagabond of the same degree of blood should be confined to the inferior caste." With one chilling sentence, the highest court in the Palmetto State affirmed that propertied men should be considered white. Poor whites, conversely, did not deserve the benefit of the doubt. Their poverty could be used to render them black.[13]

Scores of antebellum southern trials focused on the race of steamboat and railroad passengers. In one Alabama case, a slaveholder sued the owners of a steamboat, claiming that they knowingly allowed an escaping slave to flee on the vessel. The defendants held the man was white in "every appearance" and had been hired as a laborer. Although a local court had ruled in favor of the master, the appellate court reversed the judgement, holding that the owners of steamboats could not be required to look for proof of freedom from everyone. Because the passenger appeared white, there was no reason to question whether or not he was a slave. Likewise, in a Georgia case, Sam Wallace, supposedly white, was accused of being black and riding in a whites-only railroad car. Again, appellate judges ruled in favor of the superintendent of the railroad, who had no cause to question Wallace's racial classification. As the judges noted, the passenger appeared white – his "complexion was light, his hair straight" – and thus no further proof was needed.[14]

---

[13] See Catterall, *Judicial Cases*, Vol. II, 317, 346–7, 359, 491; Ariela J. Gross, "Litigating Whiteness: Trials of Racial Determination in the 1850s," *Yale Law Journal* 108 (Oct. 1998): 188, footnote 22: "After the Civil War, many states passed laws enlarging the definition of 'negro' to include everyone with any African ancestry—what is known as a 'one-drop' rule."; *State v. Cantey*, 1835 (358), in Catterall, *Judicial Cases*, Vol. II, 269.

[14] *Bell v. Chambers*, 38 Ala. 660, Jan. 1863, in *Ibid.*, Vol. III, 257; *Wallace and Wallace v. Spullock*, 32 Ga. 488, March 1861, in *Ibid.*, Vol. III, 83.

Other cases challenged the racial classification of individuals in determining tax status. In an 1843 case out of North Carolina, "tax execution ... was about to be enforced ... against the relators, as free mulattoes." Of course, the men in question claimed to be white. Henry Johnson, "the darkest," worked as an overseer, which at least bound his economic interests to the interests of the master class. His sister reportedly looked like "a quadroon," but the other two brothers, Thomas and John, were "very passable white men." Thomas had "light or sandy hair, and a sunburnt complexion." Apparently, their maternal grandfather had been considered a "Dutchman," but occasionally he had been referred to as "a colored man." Still, their "white" father was a Methodist preacher, and the family was respected within the local community. All members of the Johnson family "proved excellent characters. ... They associated with white persons," one witness added, "but never without question." Indeed, the three brothers had been expelled from the militia because they were regarded "as colored." Another witness claimed Thomas once voted for sheriff, but then the election supervisor "took his vote out of the box, and scratched his name off the list." The judge instructed the jury that "when men had been acknowledged as white men, and allowed all their privileges, it was bad policy to degrade them to the condition of free negroes." Finding the Johnson brothers to "be free white men," the local jury made a proper decision, the appellate judges argued, so a "New trial [was] refused."[15]

Countless analogous cases, in which the race of the accused or the race of the witness was questioned, occurred in the 1830s, 1840s, and 1850s. In one South Carolina larceny case, for example, two principle witness for the prosecution were objected to by the defense on the grounds that they were not white. Allegedly, one grandfather was black, but had been treated as a white man and even "exercised political privileges as such." Additional witnesses said the men were "ordinarily fair" and "are respectable, have always been received into society." One had even served as a militia officer. With extremely interesting wording, the jury found the men "not persons of color." The motion for a new trial was dismissed by the appellate court, which held that – because there was no legal definition of race – it was entirely dependent upon the "popular sense" definition, essentially leaving these momentous decisions up to local juries. One of the most interesting instances of racial accusations occurred

[15] *Johnson v. Boon*, I Speers 223, May 1843, in *Ibid.*, Vol. II, 385–6.

in 1864, during a murder trial. Apparently, one particular witness was objected to by the prisoner, who claimed witness had "negro blood." As a rebuttal, the Solicitor charged right back "that the prisoner was also of negro blood." After interviewing people who knew the witness' parents, the court held that the witness "was competent," meaning white. Still, a new trial was ordered. The complexities of race and class were seemingly endless.[16]

Ariela Gross examined racial determination litigation in the antebellum South, and ultimately decided that "Whiteness meant virtue and honor – good conduct, industry, and so forth." For a female, then, whiteness and honor "lay in the purity of her sexuality, in stark contrast to the degraded sexuality of a black 'Jezebel.'" For males, whiteness and honor was public. It could be found in a man's "statesmanlike behavior toward superiors and inferiors, his adherence to the gentlemen's code of conduct, his mastery of slaves, and his exercise of citizenship," she wrote. Taken together, these "performances" of whiteness became "increasingly important to the determination of racial status," especially in the decade prior to the Civil War. Although Gross's research is certainly compelling, adding class analysis to her findings proves extremely interesting. Every time she referred to the "performance" of whiteness, she was clearly citing honors and duties exclusive to affluent white Southerners – particularly, slaveholders. The level of whiteness those people in question had to prove, therefore, was upper-class whiteness. Acting "white" was acting wealthy. It was owning slaves, performing civic duties, and participating politically. Many poor whites never had the chance to demonstrate these supposed traits of whiteness, making their own racial classification suspect. The truly impoverished certainly did not qualify as white given the legal precedents. Far from believing they may become slaveholders themselves someday, some poor whites were instead worried that they might slip down to the status of slaves.[17]

"In the South," penned one abolitionist, "the most contemptuous epithets applied to the laboring whites, are such as 'slave,' 'white slave,' 'white mule.'" Seemingly horrified by the inhumanity inherent in these designations, the writer attempted to gain the attention of northern wage laborers: "Not only have we heard the white laborers of the South called by the planters white slaves, but we have heard the white laborers, the

---

[16] *State v. Cantey*, 2 Hill 614, May 1835, in *Ibid.*, Vol. II, 358; *State v. Norton*, 1 Winston 303, June 1864, in *Ibid.*, Vol. II, 250–1.
[17] Gross, "Litigating Whiteness," 167; 157; 112–3.

farmer, the mechanic and the manufacturer of the North, spoken of in the same terms." His rhetoric was likely effective, as these descriptions were meant to make all white laborers take pause, and consider what life would be like as a slave. If the institution of slavery was no longer predicated on race, the argument ran, lower-class white workers were just a step away from bondage. The specter of the white slave loomed large, especially in the 1850s, as cases of enslaved whites made national headlines, and commanded widespread attention. Olmsted reported one particular battle in Louisiana. Violet Ludlow had been born in Pike County, Alabama to white parents. However, after traveling to Texas with a man in 1853, she was sold as a slave, and then resold again. Violet fled her bondage, but was caught and jailed as a runaway slave, thus causing her to begin "instituting legal proceedings for her freedom." But Violet Ludlow's story was not rare, Olmsted claimed, as "Some days since, a woman named Pelasgie was arrested as a fugitive slave, who has lived for more than twelve years in this city as a free woman. She was so nearly white that few could detect any traces of her African descent."[18]

The term "white slave," therefore, had become ubiquitous in the decade before secession, much like the appellation "white nigger." "Not only was the word *slave* used ... to indicate the performance of work in ways unbecoming to whites," argued David Roediger, "but new and negative phrases such as *white nigger* (that is, 'drudge') and *work like a nigger* (that is, 'to do hard drudging work') came into American English in the 1830s, at roughly the same time that the term *white slavery* became prominent." Furthermore, an influx of white immigrants to America in the late 1840s and 1850s added to concerns over race, labor, and freedom. The Irish, especially, faced comparisons with blacks. Long considered "not white" by the English, the "Red Irish" were soon known as the "Black Irish" in America. Popular political cartoons depicted them as apes, much in the way they portrayed blacks. White laborers – whether immigrant or native, northern or southern – all had something to fear in a country that thrived on slave labor. And because the late antebellum years saw a great decline in the standards of living for American-born white laborers, Roediger concluded, "the metaphor *white slavery* dramatically gave way." The term, while

---

[18] "Reformers – Conservatism," *Anti Slavery Bugle*, Dec. 18, 1846; Olmsted, *The Cotton Kingdom*, Vol. II, 210, Web.

relatively commonplace, still must have provoked anxiety among lower-class white workers.[19]

Furthermore, advertisements for runaway slaves increasingly pointed out their "white" features and skin, and often warned that they would attempt to pass as white. Some ads described the bondsmen and women as "very white," "a white negro," or "nearly white"; one even described an absconder as having "straight hair, and a complexion so nearly white that it is believed a stranger would suppose there was no African blood in him." Even in the most rigidly structured slave societies, racial categories were constantly in flux. And after so many decades of sexual relationships between whites and blacks, a strict definition of race became more and more useless, even as it became more and more important to the prevailing hierarchy.[20]

In 1849, C.F. Dandridge of Desoto County, Mississippi, ran an ad for his runaway "mulatto boy," who "is very white, has straight hair, and will probably attempt to pass for a white man or free mulatto." Georgia's *Southern Recorder* offered the sum of $100 for the return of a "yellow" man named William and his wife Martha, who could "readily pass for a white woman." And J.M. Tyson promised a fee of $50 to anyone apprehending his runaway slave Albert. As the *Savannah Republican* reported, Albert was "25 years of age, [and] very white, so much so that he would not be suspected of being a Negro. Has blue eyes and very light hair." Some of the enslaved had become so racially indistinguishable that slaveholders were scrambling to come up with new forms of social control. One abolitionist article entitled "White Slaves" pointed out how categories of race no longer helped determine whether or not someone was free. It further called on the white laborers of the North to consider these white slaves as their brethren. "In portions of the South," it began, particularly Virginia,

one-fourth of the slaves are of mixed blood half, quarter, eighth, sixteenth but the merest drop of the African consigns the wretched possessor to the guardianship of the tobacco-spitting crew called chivalry who are certainly the most undereducated set of men of any pretension in the world. The "democracy" of the North alone sustain these seventy thousand oligarchs because the Southern democracy alone could not keep them or their schemes for extending their institution in countenance. Mechanics and farmers of the North! Are you content to see your brother mechanics and farmers of the South, "very white," bought and sold, hunted by blood-hounds, and roasted alive all these things being part and parcel of the system?

---

[19] Roediger, *The Wages of Whiteness*, 68; 133–4; 81.   [20] Olmsted, *Journey*, 640–1.

The juggernaut of race was ironically weakening slaveholders' control over the region. As slave skin became lighter, the theoretical arguments promoting chattle racial slavery undoubtedly weakened.[21]

The mounting tensions over race and slavery continued to play out in the court system, as well as the national press. Of course, not many "white slaves" were fortunate enough to ever escape slavery, or sue for freedom. The vast majority simply lived out their lives as slaves, and functioned as a stark reminder of the vagaries of race – and of the illogic of connecting race to slavery. As *The Liberator* reported, "all complexional distinctions have ceased among the victims of the slave plantations, and white slaves are as readily purchased as black ones, and 'no questions asked.'" A traveler through Mississippi and Louisiana recalled that a particular slave girl was pointed out to him in the fields: "That one is pure white; you see her hair?," the master asked. Her hair, wrote the traveler, was straight and sandy. "It was not uncommon to see slaves as white as that," he mourned, "so white they could not be distinguished from pure blooded whites." One South Carolina judge ordered the execution of a white man after he assisted his partner and lover, "a white slave woman," in her escape from bondage. The abolitionist press, of course, gleefully used these stories to help engender anger toward the master class. As racial categories became more indistinguishable, so too did the qualifications of who could become a slave.[22]

For a very few white slaves, however, there was some hope of emancipation. Children – especially female children – and young women had the best chances of gaining sympathy, whether from a judge, jury, or the American media. In 1859, the *National Era* ran a story about a case in Alabama. Apparently, a poor young white woman and her infant daughter were abducted from neighboring Georgia and sold into slavery across state lines. Patience L. Hicks, a 17-year-old farm laborer, had been "decoyed from her house, under the promises of marriage," by a man named Wilson. Hicks's mother, Casey Ann, headed a large family of children, and they were "all destitute of means." Quite interestingly, Patience Hicks clearly understood that her poverty might affect her racial classification. She made a plea to the court based upon both her economic

---

[21] "Wanted – A White Slave," *Anti Slavery Bugle*, Dec. 15, 1849; "$100 Dollars Reward," *Southern Recorder* (GA), Dec. 15, 1857, 3; "White Slaves," *Anti Slavery Bugle*, Nov. 3, 1855 (reprinted from the *Savannah Republican*); "White Slaves," *Frederick Douglass' Paper*, Oct. 26, 1855.

[22] "A Final Reply to 'J.W.'," *The Liberator*, Sept. 27, 1861; "The South," *New York Times*, Nov. 26, 1853; "Oh!," *The Liberator*, July 24, 1846.

class *and* her skin color. Because of her family's indigence, Hicks pleaded, she had no other choice but to work on a plantation as a laborer. Due to her job, therefore, she "is considerably sunburnt, which makes her appear rather dark." Although the probate judge ruled in favor of Hicks – she and her child were "free white persons" – the slaveholder who purchased them was set free with no penalty except paying the court costs. These types of cases, no matter how rare, highlighted the failure of race as a physical basis for determining who was a slave, and who was liable to become a slave. "How many of the hundred thousand illiterate poor whites of Virginia have been thus disposed of in the Southern [slave] markets we are unable to say," one journalist lamented. But there were "doubtless a good many ... proof of freedom is thrown by the laws of Alabama, or by the practice of her courts, upon her poor whites." Impoverished whites, the paper tried to explain, now held the burden of proof in determining their own status as free people.[23]

In yet another case of an ostensibly white woman suing for her freedom, in 1855 Abby Guy brought suit against William Daniel in Arkansas. As described by Gross, Guy asserted that Daniel "held her and her children unfairly in slavery despite the fact that she was white." Much like Patience Hicks, Guy claimed that she had darkened skin from laboring in the hot sun. One slaveholding witness admitted "that he had seen white persons who worked in the fields become as dark as Guy and her mother, and he had seen white persons with hair as curly as theirs." Despite having darker skin, Guy still appealed to the jury on the grounds that she was white in appearance, and that her doctors believed her to be white. Her enslaver claimed that he could prove there was "negro blood" in Guy's ancestry, and that she was a slave since she had always lived as a slave. "Not only was there no consensus about whether Guy was white," Gross wrote, "but there was also no consensus about the conjunction between status and race – about whether she should be free if white or whether she must be enslaved if black." Guy ultimately won her freedom, although Daniel appealed to the Arkansas Supreme Court. During both trials, people "testified about Guy's appearance, her reception in society, her conduct, her self-presentation, and her inherited status," Gross

[23] "White Slavery in Alabama," *National Era*, Sept. 15, 1859; *Guilford v. Hicks*, 36 Ala. 95, Jan. 1860, in Catterall, *Judicial Cases*, Vol. III, 239; "White Slavery in Alabama," *National Era*, Sept. 15, 1859; also see Lawrence Tenzer, and A.D. Powell, "White Slavery, Maternal Descent, and the Politics of Slavery in the Antebellum United States," Paper presented at University of Nottingham Institute for the Study of Slavery, July/August 2004.

concluded, thus leaving "the question of 'race' for the jury to decide, because the jury represented the community consensus." Perhaps not surprisingly, all of the successful cases of white slaves suing for freedom involved young women. Once again, the privileges of whiteness were more likely to be applied to poor females due to their sexuality, while slaveholders were more likely to maltreat poor white males. As Walter Johnson put it, "By buying ever-whiter slaves, the prosperous slave-holders of the antebellum South bought themselves access to ever more luminous fantasies of their own distinction."[24]

Thus, by the time of the Civil War poor whites' race constituted privilege only in their dealings with blacks. As Stephen Berry wrote, "In a racist society the race card is not always played. It doesn't have to be, because it is always available to be played. ... Race is the elephant in the room, and it can blow its trumpet as soon as it's called upon." Berry was surely correct – in interracial dealings, race trumped *everything* else. But as the antebellum period continued, telling the races apart became more difficult, and many of the benefits of whiteness were not extended to a large percentage of poor, non-slaveholding, non-landowning whites. The race card did not, of course, protect poor whites from the dire conse-quences of economic and social inequality. They were certainly not slaves, but poor whites enjoyed relatively few privileges as *whites*. Instead, their class status doomed them to continuing cycles of poverty, and limited their civil rights as white American citizens.[25]

Placed in the context of this class tension between whites, it becomes easier to understand why the master class so feared the emerging Repub-lican Party. Founded on principles of free labor, agrarian reform, and a type of relatively egalitarian, small-scale capitalism, Republicans not only seemed like radicals to slaveholders – they were truly revolutionary, and not solely due to their stance on slavery. The new party clearly elucidated the staggering differences between the two sections of the country, and the comparison did not bode well for the South, where large-scale, unre-strained capitalism reigned supreme. The region's dependence on brutal-ized, enslaved labor rendered wage laborers superfluous, and white workers' pay fell as job opportunities continued to disappear. Slave owners thus created a pervasive criminal system to deal with the

---

[24] Gross, "Litigating Whiteness," 111; 134–5; 137; 111; Johnson, "The Slave Trader," 18.
[25] Stephen Berry, Review of *Race Relations at the Margins: Slaves and Poor Whites in the Antebellum Southern Countryside*, by Jeff Forret. *Reviews in American History* 35, No. 3 (Sept. 2007): 383.

impoverished, and employed a variety of vigilante tactics to reinforce the penal state. Conversely, Republicans argued, in the free labor North, artisans, craftsmen, small farmers, and middling-class entrepreneurs helped create a democratic society that was, in many ways, progressive and dynamic.[26]

Prior to the formation of the Republican Party, antebellum politics were in a relentless state of flux. Both Whigs and Democrats were constantly losing members to more radical third party offshoots, like the anti-immigrant Know-Nothings and the reformist Liberty Party. Quite judiciously, Free Soil Democrats immediately connected their anti-slavery notions to land reform, specifically a Homestead Act. As Jonathan Earle held, this "resulting union between radical Jacksonianism and the antislavery movement ... is far more important than historians have allowed." By openly courting less affluent voters with promises of economic ascension (which would hopefully result in economic independence), Free Soil Democrats added a powerful weapon to the arsenal against slavery. Originally, "free-soil" had begun as an agrarian mantra for land reform, but Earle contended that by the mid-1840s it "encompassed a hodge-podge of reinforcing ideas about patriarchal landownership and slavery restriction." George Henry Evans, the British-born radical reformer, represented the interests of the Party. Persuaded that the concentration of American wealth rested in large part on the land monopoly of a few extremely affluent individuals, he contended that their unfettered power was much more dangerous than any industry, bank, religion, or political party. Evans devoted his life to land reform. Although he died before its passage, many scholars consider Evans the father of the Homestead Act, overlooking Andrew Johnson entirely. But Evans had clearly learned much from the powerful invective of the poor white Tennessean. "I think Slavery is a disgrace to the republic, black slavery as well as *white*," Evans plainly wrote. "Let us set the slaveholders an example by emancipating the white laborer, *by restoring his natural right to the soil*."[27]

Yet as these new political divisions and realignments occurred, the South's master class became even more defensive and entrenched in their pro-slavery stance. In the two decades prior to Lincoln's election, the

---

[26] Eric Foner, *Free Soil, Free Labor, Free Men: The Ideology of the Republican Party before the Civil War* (1970; reprint, New York: Oxford, 1995), 316.

[27] Jonathan H. Earle, *Jacksonian Antislavery and the Politics of Free Soil, 1824–1854* (Chapel Hill: North Carolina, 2004), 5; 7; 27; quoted on 35.

discussion over preemption and homesteading had convinced the slave power that westward expansion would eventually lead to the abolishment of the peculiar institution altogether. One paper out of Columbus, Mississippi insisted that homesteaders would all become abolitionists. It would be "better for us that these territories should remain a waste, a howling wilderness, trod only by red hunters than be so settled," the article concluded. And Robert Hayne of South Carolina complained that homesteaders were nothing more than lazy "drones," completely unworthy "of protection in a country where every man goes ahead who has any strength of will, or any firmness, or any character."[28]

With the proposal and passage of the Kansas-Nebraska Act in 1854, Free Soilers finally dropped all association with the Democrats, who remained controlled by southern slaveholders and their Doughface northern allies. Instead, the antislavery Free Soilers joined with former Whigs to create the new Republican Party, whose platform addressed urban poverty – as well as landlessness among non-slaveholding Southerners – by promoting (once again) a Homestead Act. Considered a "safety-valve" measure to help poor landless Americans and newly arrived immigrants become economically self-sufficient, members of the emerging coalition realized the dual benefits of passing such a measure. Hoping to weaken the powerful master class, Foner wrote, many Republicans believed that settlements in free labor territories "would demonstrate the superiority of free to slave labor, arouse the latent anti-slavery feelings of the southern poor whites, and begin the process of overthrowing slavery." But slaveholding politicians continued to block the passage of the Homestead Act, and it did not become law until after secession. Still, the bill represented, in Avery Craven's words, "the culmination of America's greatest democratic effort." Due to this fact alone, the radicalism of the Republican platform terrified the master class, who realized that poor southern whites would undoubtedly find the bill attractive. As Charleston's *Mercury* reported in March of 1860, the Homestead Act was the "most dangerous abolition bill which has ever indirectly been pressed in Congress."[29]

The aversion of the master class to any discussion over land or labor reform surely played a role in the branding of Republicans as "Black." Although the derisive moniker obviously referred to the anti-slavery

---

[28] Avery O. Craven, "The Coming of the War between the States, An Interpretation," *Journal of Southern History* II (Feb.-Nov. 1936), 314–5; all quotes on 314–5.

[29] Foner, *Free Soil*, 27; 53; Craven, "The Coming of the War," 317; Earle, *Jacksonian Antislavery*, quoted on 36.

beliefs of some of the party's members, it is important to note that African Americans were rarely referred to as anything other than "negroes," "niggers," or "colored" in the antebellum era. The term "Black Republican," therefore, not only denigrated Republicans in regards to race, it also raised the specter of Europe's Red Republicans – the continent's most radical and progressive political parties, who generally advocated for workers' rights and agrarian land reform. As Andre Fleche found, as early as 1848 Democrats in Missouri were denouncing "the St. Louis Republicans' radical, European-style socialism that attacked property rights, economic privilege, and, by extension, slavery. Democrats began conflating 'Black and Red Republicans' and comparing the German unionist platform to the most radical ideologies of 'Mazzini, Kossuth, Ledru Rollin, and Louis Blanc.'"[30]

The comparisons were not limited to Germans. Several other sources linked American Republicans to their French counterparts, at times even referencing the sans-culottes (lower-class radicals) of the French Revolution. *The Liberator* reprinted "South Carolina['s] Petition to Congress against White Slavery," which opened by lambasting the hypocrisy of the free states, home to "white slaves" and "pauper labor." Then, it categorized the crisis over disunion as a "conflict between poverty on one side and wealth on the other." Ultimately, the petition concluded, class "conflict" had given rise to both the "Red Republicans of France and the Black Republicans of America." Similarly, the *National Era* reprinted a tract allegedly penned by a disaffected slaveholder who compared American Republicans to the most radical elements of France. To help engender a deep fear of socialism, harangues condemning Black Republicans often included anti-immigrant invectives, as well as accusations that native-born whites were unpatriotic traitors. Warning of unruly, riotous mobs comprised of poor laborers, these types of classist, racist tirades likely accomplished their intended objectives:

Those French desperadoes who design the destruction of life and property are called Red Republicans. Why should not the reckless advocates of abolition and disunion be called the Black Republicans? This nefarious clan was powerless for other mischief than to effect the escape of a few hundred slaves, and so to continue the exasperation between the people of the free and slave States. It was composed

---

[30] Andre M. Fleche, *The Revolution of 1861: The American Civil War in the Age of Nationalist Conflict* (Chapel Hill: North Carolina, 2012), 45. As far as I can tell, the association of "Black Republicans" with "Red Republicans" is the primary reason that Republican states are known as "red" states, even in the modern era.

chiefly of foreigners, and the descendants of Tories, who have never been reconciled to the Union, and who agitate for its disruption as an act of filial vengeance for some Cow-boy ancestor. ... This party are willing to unite with Bedini, to bring this Government under Papal influence, to submit to the rule of England for the aid of her money or arms, to divide their American heritage with the Hessians of the Rhine or the Helotes of the Liffey.

Indeed, the writer cautioned, Black Republicans were becoming "powerful" enough to overthrow the slaveholders' "Union, and extinguish all fraternity amongst those who support it." Not to be outdone, on the very eve of secession South Carolina Senator James Chestnut, Jr., charged that the Republican Party of the United States was "governed by the Red Republican principles of France." Yet by adding antislavery beliefs to an already radical platform, the Party had "changed its complexion" and "blackened its face."[31]

Agrarianism may have served as the primary link between European socialists and American Republicans, but ideologies concerning free labor and workers' rights revealed another continuity between these progressive parties. As Karl Marx and Friedrich Engels wrote during the first year of the United States's Civil War, "Labour cannot emancipate itself in the white skin, where in the black it is branded." Although Foner claimed that free labor was a minor point to abolitionists – morality, rather than economics, reigned supreme – it is important to remember that abolitionists made up only a minority percentage of the party. For most Republicans, especially the old Jacksonian Democrats, the defense of free labor was incredibly important. Free labor was the key to understanding their opposition to slavery, as "many of these ex-Democrats were more antisouthern than they were antislavery."[32]

Despite the negativity associated with southern-born white workers, Republicans still were taken aback by slaveholders' newest theoretical attack on free labor. The master class had formulated an insidious defense of the peculiar institution, likely in direct response to the rising popularity of the Republican Party. Slavery in the abstract, as Elizabeth Fox-

---

[31] "South Carolina Petition to Congress against White Slavery," *The Liberator*, Nov. 9, 1860; "The Black Republican Party," *National Era*, Aug. 30, 1855; Michael K. Curtis, "The 1859 Crisis over Hinton Helper's Book, the Impending Crisis: Free Speech, Slavery, and Some Light on the Meaning of the First Section of the Fourteenth Amendment," *Symposium on the Law of Slavery: Constitutional Law and Slavery*, 68 Chi. Kent. L. Rev. (1992): quoted on 1167.

[32] Fox-Genovese, *Slavery in White and Black*, quoted on 10; Foner, *Free Soil*, xxii; 149–50; 177.

Genovese and Eugene Genovese wrote, became the slaveholders' primary justification for keeping human beings in bondage, particularly in the few years prior to secession. This doctrine "declared slavery or a kindred system of personal servitude the best possible condition for all labor regardless of race. Proslavery logic cast enslavement, broadly defined, as necessary and proper for much of the white race, as well as for practically all of the black race." The theory had its roots in the 1820s, when slaveholders and affluent landholders began arguing that the South's social hierarchy depended on "the formal exclusion of the unpropertied laboring classes from the benefits of individualism," consigning them "to some form of personal dependency." Whether or not these wealthy men were nullifiers or secessionists, they agreed that personal servitude was the natural condition for all common laborers, regardless of race. As "the necessary foundation for a civilized social order," Fox-Genovese and Genovese penned, slavery in the abstract rapidly won support throughout the Deep South in the 1850s, particularly in South Carolina. The issue gained such widespread support among slaveholders that in 1856 the Republican Party distributed handbills cautioning working class whites of the designing and devious plans of the master class – plans that eventually included enslaving poorer whites.[33]

Published in 1856, one particular pamphlet, *The New 'Democratic' Doctrine: Slavery Not to be Confined to the Negro Race, But to Be Made the Universal Condition of the Laboring Classes of Society: The Supporters of This Doctrine Vote for Buchanan!*, clearly intended to grab the attention of working men, both North and South. As if the title was not outrageous enough, the Republican tract then reprinted a spate of articles from southern newspapers defending slavery in the abstract. One editorial from the *Richmond Examiner* argued, "Slavery is right, natural and necessary, and does not depend on difference of COMPLEXION. The laws of the Slave States *justify* the holding of WHITE MEN in *bondage*." Next, one of the leading papers in South Carolina purported that "Slavery is the natural and normal condition of the *laboring man*, whether WHITE or black. The great evil of Northern free society is, that it is burdened with a servile class of MECHANICS and LABORERS, unfit for self-government, and yet clothed with the attributes and powers of citizens." Amidst the rising chorus, Alabama's *Muscogee Herald* also clamored: "Free society! We sicken of the name. What is it but a conglomeration of

---

[33] Fox-Genovese, *Slavery in White and Black*, 1; 9; 24–5; 69.

GREASY MECHANICS, FILTHY OPERATIVES, SMALL FISTED
FARMERS, and moonstruck THEORISTS ... who are hardly fit for
association with a Southern gentleman's body servant." By the mid-
1850s, therefore, the push to broaden the boundaries of slavery was
growing ever stronger.[34]

The most well-known southern-born Republican was undoubtedly
Abraham Lincoln, who had been born in middle Kentucky into a class
only slightly above the most impoverished whites. With little formal
education, Lincoln was a tireless autodidact, mostly teaching himself
how to read and write. His self-motivation was staggering. Yet due to
the fact that Lincoln spent his childhood and teenage years laboring in the
outdoors, his skin became dark and wizened. During his political career,
affluent slaveholders ridiculed his appearance, sometimes even insinuat-
ing that his tanned skin evidenced African American ancestry. All too
often, however, Lincoln's legacy – as both a president and a Republican –
is divorced from his early life experiences as a poor white Southerner. His
views on slavery were especially tied to his childhood, and the experience
of escaping slave-ridden Kentucky so that his father could make a living in
a section of the country unmarred by enslaved labor. He fully realized
how slavery affected all aspects of society, and pervaded the lives of
people who would never profit from it. In a speech at the Wisconsin State
Agricultural Society about a year prior to secession, Lincoln passionately
argued for free labor, and all its attendant legacies, including universal
education. He alleged that pro-slavery men considered the laborer "a
blind horse upon a treadmill." The master class believed that educated
workers were "not only useless, but pernicious and dangerous. In fact, it
is, in some sort, deemed a misfortune that laborers should have heads at
all," Lincoln concluded. "Those same heads are regarded as explosive
materials, only to be safely kept in damp places, as far as possible from
that peculiar sort of fire which ignites them."[35]

Indeed, many slaveholders believed that non-slaveholding southern
laborers should remain in ignorance for the safety and maintenance of
the slave system. They would be protected from notions of agrarianism,
workers' rights, and – especially – abolitionism. Lower-class white

[34] The Young Men's Fremont and Dayton Central Union, *The New 'Democratic' Doctrine*,
first two quotes on 1; third quote on 2; Web. All italics and capitalizations appear in the
original document.

[35] Abraham Lincoln, "Address before the Wisconsin State Agricultural Society, Milwaukee,
Wisconsin September 30, 1859," in Roy P. Basler, ed., *The Collected Works of Abraham
Lincoln*, Vol. III (New Brunswick: Rutgers, 1953), 479.

Southerners, of course, recognized their own obvious oppression, and as the antebellum period wore on, they became more and more overtly resentful of slaveholders. Class tensions between whites in the Deep South undoubtedly added to the causes of the Civil War. Pro-slavery men were already defending the peculiar institution from attacks by northern abolitionists and by the slaves themselves. When poor whites created a three-front battleground in the 1840s and 1850s, slaveholders had few viable alternatives other than secession to protect their main source of wealth and revenue. As one Southerner wrote in 1849, "a respectable number of men in the slave states, not daring to voice abolition sentiments, attacked slavery indirectly by supporting universal education, popular elections, and repeal of the law allowing slaveholders to count slaves in political representation." But for the poorest whites, involvement in the political process was limited. Without other methods to formally address their grievances, they often reacted in more direct ways. Whether blatantly challenging the primacy of the master class' power, making antislavery remarks, or simply interacting with blacks, impoverished whites made formidable foes. They had little to lose.[36]

A highly functional culture of vigilante violence had long existed in the South. It was even more entrenched in the Deep South, where large percentages of slaves and greater economic inequality between whites intensified social tensions. A journalist for the London *Times* reported during the secession crisis that while most masters denied living in fear of their slaves, the "curfew and the night patrol in the streets, the prisons and the watchhouses, and the police regulations, prove that strict supervision, at all events, is needed and necessary." This constant surveillance and policing – of both blacks and poor whites – verified the anxious state of slaveholders. Indeed, the master class needed to be kept alert. Prior to 1830, more than 100 of the United States's 130 abolitionist societies were located in the South. "Free speech is considered as treason against slavery," Helper clearly understood, "and when people dare neither speak nor print their thoughts, free thought itself is well nigh extinguished."[37]

The suppression of abolitionist ideas began in earnest during the 1830s, with slaveholders going after anyone – including postmasters – who distributed material that even mentioned antislavery sentiments.

---

[36] Nye, *Fettered Freedom*, quoted on 35.
[37] Eaton, *The Freedom of Thought Struggle*, quoted on 112; Williams, *Bitterly Divided*, 18; Helper, *The Impending Crisis*, 409.

Perhaps not surprisingly, masters became even more rigorous about enforcing these laws in the 1850s. Once Helper's book was published, slave owners' growing concerns reached a fever pitch, and they frequently resorted to both legal and extralegal violence to control the spread of *The Impending Crisis*. Senator Alfred Iverson of Georgia declared that slaveholders should "hang every man who has approved or endorsed" the book. In Greenville, South Carolina, Harold Wyllys was sentenced to a year in jail for giving a copy away. Daniel Worth, a North Carolina minister, was also arrested for distributing Helper's book in 1859. The statute outlawing the circulation of antislavery literature had been updated just five years prior, and the new punishments for the crime were particularly harsh. For a first offense, the accused would be whipped, and the second offense resulted in death. Given Reverend Worth's respectable career, the court mercifully excused him from the whipping, but did imprison him for a year. By 1860, it was evident that slaveholders had even more at stake. North Carolina, Helper's birthplace and home, amended their censorship laws yet again. This time, the punishment for a first offense was death. That same year the state's Supreme Court upheld the right of slaveholding politicians to censor *all* incendiary statements concerning the peculiar institution, regardless of whether or not those sentiments were aimed at (or heard by) African Americans.[38]

The Impending Crisis, of course, was only one of the targeted publications. All written materials were subject to search and seizure, and every word was carefully monitored. There was simply no freedom of speech in the slave South. "We should literally have no room for anything else if we were to publish all the details of whippings, tar-and-featherings, and hangings, for the utterance of Anti-Slavery opinions in the South," reported the *National Era*. When John Abbott traveled through the region in the few years before secession, he characterized nonslaveholders as "paralyzed by those laws, framed exclusively for the benefit of the slaveholder. Slavery seems almost more dreadful in its infliction upon them, then upon the blacks." Abbott thus realized why

the determined slaveholder is so very anxious to prevent these poor whites from learning how grievously they are defrauded. I do not wonder that, bowie-knife in hand, he watches the lips of the minister in the pulpit; that he tells the editor what he may say, and what he may not say; that he examines every book before he will allow it to pass into the non-slaveholder's house; that he examines his list of

---

[38] Curtis, "The 1859 Crisis," 1133; quoted on 1145; Brown, *Southern Outcast*, 146; Curtis, "The 1859 Crisis," 1164–5.

newspapers and periodicals, and decides what he may take; and that he ransacks the mail ... lest his defrauded white brother should receive some chance pamphlet, which might pour upon his darkened vision some rays of the sun of liberty.

The situation continued to grow ominous. Throughout the Deep South, poor whites and non-slaveholders were assumed to be enemies of slavery. Every utterance was scrutinized, every thought policed. As the future-Vice President of the Confederacy Alexander Stephens wrote, "I have no objection to the liberty of speech, when the liberty of the cudgel is left free to combat it."[39]

Instance after instance of the master class's heavy-handed censorship abound. One article announced that in South Carolina, "They now have a man in jail, and hope to accomplish his death, because he has dared to come between the white slaves of the South and their masters – his only crime being the circulation of an address to poor white folks, showing them their rights, and how to get them." In North Carolina, Adam Crooks and Jesse McBride, two antislavery northern preachers, were tried for the "circulation of incendiary publications." McBride had given a pamphlet to a little girl that contained some abolitionist language, and thus was sentenced to "prison for one year, to stand in the pillory for one hour, and to be whipped with twenty lashes." A similar situation occurred in Augusta, Georgia, when New Yorker James Cranagle was accused of "talking abolition when drunk." He was subsequently jailed, tarred, and feathered. Just across the Savannah River in Hamburg, South Carolina, Tom Burch, an Irish-born bricklayer and plasterer, apparently used "seditious" language among slaves. The local minutemen severely whipped him, shaved half of his head, and drove him out of the state. And in Oxford, Mississippi, after a man was acquitted in a court of law for "fomenting insurrection," the local vigilance committee remedied the alleged legal error. The poor man was publicly whipped and then driven out of town.[40]

Very closely related to these strict censorship codes, then, was the vigilante violence slaveholders used to curtail any challenge to their ubiquitous powers. Indeed, the maintenance of the Deep South's slave societies required unceasing surveillance, as well as the constant threat of

[39] Curtis, "The 1859 Crisis," quoted on 1159–1160; Abbott, *South and North*, 142–3; Grimsted, *American Mobbing*, quoted on 246.
[40] "Non-slaveholders of the Slave States," *Anti Slavery Bugle*, Dec. 1, 1849; Eaton, *The Freedom of Thought Struggle*, 139; Grimsted, *American Mobbing*, 120–1; Burton, *In My Father's House*, 146; Nye, *Fettered Freedom*, 189.

bloodshed. Policing both blacks and poor whites, slaveholders set up a three-tier "punishment" system that effectively prevented riot and rebellion. First, as independent, individual citizens, masters and overseers privately whipped the underclasses. Slaveholders also used the criminal justice system to incarcerate and brutalize individuals for debt and nonviolent behaviors they deemed illegal. Finally, affluent whites established an intricate system of vigilante brutality – complete with vigilance committees and minute men groups – to buttress the other systems and ensure that the masses were rendered either powerless or terrified. To truly understand southern social control, therefore, scholars need to stop focusing solely on the legal system, and instead recognize that these three methods of violence were all interrelated. Slaveholders so nearly perfected this system that even after emancipation they employed this triumvirate of violence again to reestablish control over the region. As one historian has argued, "Through it all the oligarchy of slaveholders in the south had become drunk with power and their hopes and ambitions knew no bounds." Their thirst for wealth was endless. But to maintain such an economically stratified society, the threat of violent reprisals had to be constant. The masters of flesh, recalled one Union soldier, "were haughty, improvident, intemperate and full of hate to the poor whites and blacks." Their actions, whether private, public, or vigilante, demonstrated just how accurate the young soldier had been in his characterization.[41]

Slaveholders unquestionably realized that they were losing the support of lower-middling and lower-class whites. Formerly apathetic nonslaveholders were growing more militant, and the underground economy flourished as slaves and the poorest whites interacted on a daily basis. Masters began forming quasi-military organizations in an effort to force the population into acquiescence. Vigilance committees, existing in the Deep South as early as the mid-1830s, began rapidly springing up throughout the region in the 1850s. These committees were essentially bands of slave- and property-holders who monitored both the behaviors and beliefs of less affluent whites. Bolton described the targeted whites as those "whose poverty or indolence made them undesirable." Slaveless whites increasingly found themselves inhabiting a world in which they had to censor every utterance and defend every action. Although vigilance committees were extralegal, they were still a cut above mob law, as the groups tended to be both more respected and more restrained. Despite

---

[41] Boucher, "In re That Aggressive Slaveocracy," *Mississippi Valley Historical Review* VIII (June 1921): 14; Pepper, *Personal Recollections*, 270, Web.

these differences, however, both mob law and vigilante violence functioned similarly, with comparable means and ends. Both forms of brutality buttressed the legal system, and all of these modes of violence – private, public, and vigilante – helped maintain the social stability of the South, and ultimately prevented an uprising of the underclasses.[42]

Whether mob or vigilante violence, the goal was the same: preserve the slave system, and protect the Deep South's hierarchical status quo. Jack Kenny Williams found that by 1854, all of South Carolina's larger communities had formally organized vigilance committees, who often advertised their meetings in newspapers. Even the rank and file of these groups were at least part of the slaveholding middling classes. Of course, only the most powerful planters dominated the leadership roles. Defenders of the groups proudly claimed that the committees were filled with affluent gentlemen, "to the manor born." Even the lowliest members, they bragged, were at least slave owners.[43]

In terms of economic class, then, there was quite a lot of overlap between members of vigilante groups and slave patrols. When the occasional non-slaveholder did join these terroristic groups, he generally owned land, and was likely on the cusp of slave ownership. Truly impoverished whites rarely if ever became members of these brutal gangs. Undoubtedly, vigilance committees and mob violence were to poor whites what slave patrols were to African Americans. But even as Sally Hadden has convincingly shown, slave patrols served a dual purpose: not only did they monitor and control the behaviors of slaves and free blacks, they also policed poor whites. According to one traveler, slaveholders knew that insurrectionist slaves could be "shot down," and this helped calm their fears of insurrection. "But should the poor whites ... begin to get their eyes open, and to claim their rights," he penned, "they could not so easily be disposed of." Hinton Helper had indeed "touched the sore."[44]

Especially during times of heightened worries over abolitionist revolts and slave riots, this extralegal structure of violence allowed slaveholders to intimidate poor whites and blacks, rendering them nearly powerless against a system with no rules and regulations, predicated upon baseless fears, unfounded gossip, and targeted innuendo. "It was a system grown of commitments to total mastery," one historian wrote, "and it was

---

[42] Steven A Channing, *Crisis of Fear: Secession in South Carolina* (New York: Norton, 1974), 25; 27; Bolton, 165.
[43] Williams, *Vogues in Villany*, 122; Channing, *Crisis of Fear*, 37.
[44] Bolton, *Poor Whites*, 45; Hadden, *Slave Patrols*; Abbott, *South and North*, 151.

accepted because it terrorized to silence almost all public doubts about the peculiar institution that fathered it." While historians will never know exactly how many people endured the horrors of southern mobs and vigilantes, it is quite clear that the bloodshed ratcheted up in the decade prior to the Civil War. There were at least 300 reported lynchings each year in the South alone. Furthermore, in the fall of 1856, a major insurrectionary scare swept through the region, primarily due to anxieties associated with the presidential election – and the newly formed Republican Party. Slaveholders blamed "white instigators" for the spate of violence that followed. As a wealthy planter from South Carolina's Beach Island Farmers Club put it in 1859, "There is a class of white men about here that a patrole would do good in katching[,] those Hunting Fishing & Steeling rascals."[45]

Stories of vigilance committees, minute men organizations, and local mobs lynching and killing poorer whites abounded in the late antebellum period. The majority of those brutalized were accused of abolitionism of some sort – whether they were distributing reading materials, talking to other non-slaveholders about worker's rights, or simply seemed too friendly with African Americans. A sizable percentage of the lynched were born outside of the South, and often outside of the United States, and most were employed in non-skilled wage labor. David Grimsted studied slightly more than 400 southern riots in the thirty-three years leading up to secession, and concluded that more than two-thirds of them fell into "three distinctively southern categories: mob punishment of alleged criminals (68); insurrection scare mobs (35); and mobs against those labeled abolitionist, although usually there was no evidence of abolition activity (162)." The riots against abolitionists peaked in the two years prior to the Civil War, with more than 115 instances of rioting-related violence recorded. Not only was vigilante violence becoming more frequent, the intensity and severity of the bloodshed was increasing. Most victims were whipped and then ordered out of the area, but increasing numbers of whites were murdered.[46]

Southern riots over criminal behavior were distinct from those of the North, because Southerners commonly used the whip to extract confessions and incriminations. While it is unknown exactly why, an

[45] Grimsted, *American Mobbing*, 113; Nye, *Fettered Freedom*, 182; Eaton, *The Freedom of Thought Struggle*, 99–100; Burton, *In My Father's House Are Many Mansions*, quoted on 77.

[46] Barney, *The Secessionist Impulse*, 168; Grimsted, *American Mobbing*, 101.

1835 Mississippi mob dragged a widow, Mary DuBose, into the woods and flogged her until she lost consciousness. When the elderly woman finally came to, half naked and bloodied, she admitted to a crime to avoid more torture. Ironically, her forced confession was later used in her *own* conviction before a court, for which she received thirty-nine more lashes on her bare back. "Such a case shows the commonly cooperative interplay of the South's judicial and extralegal systems," Grimsted concluded. At least as far back as the Jacksonian Era, vigilante violence not only coexisted with the southern criminal system, but the two methods of control actually bolstered each other, and were nearly mutually dependent. The same affluent men lorded over each system, and poor whites and blacks were left helpless to bore the brunt of the upper class's cruelty. Thus, southern mobs differed from northern mobs in another important way: they were more likely to be sadistic, violent, and even murderous. Things became so incredibly vicious throughout the region that newspapers reported horrifying statistics. In one week in 1835, eighteen whites were murdered in Arkansas. Likewise, fifteen white murders took place in Grand Gulf, Mississippi over the course of two months, and during one week in 1837, a dozen violent deaths were reported in New Orleans.[47]

The overwhelming majority of the victims of mob abuse had no legal recourse against their assailants. Whenever the brutalized did try to exact some sort of justice, they were often met with opprobrium from the larger community. In one case in Mississippi, sixty-seven petitioners requested the release of the vigilante William McMurty from jail. Claiming that he had merely gone along with the plans of the "most respectable citizens" in town by lynching Sam Hoague, the petition then argued that McMurty's actions were completely justified. Hoague was allegedly involved in a case of theft. But his real crime, for which he suffered under the torturous whip of the slaveholders, was "miscegenation." Even the local sheriff signed the petition, claiming that vigilante violence was so widespread that the "industrious mechanic" McMurty was simply acting "under mistaken notions of the law." It seems the master class employed extralegal violence not only to beat lower-class whites into submission, they also used it to turn poor whites against each other. By terrorizing the underclasses and turning them all into suspects, slaveholders created an environment in which the aspirational poor often turned on members of their own economic class. They became informants, policing their peers so that they,

[47] *Ibid.*, 101; 86.

at least, stayed in the good graces of the masters. The effectiveness of this type of terrorism seemed boundless. Mob and vigilante violence caused real fear among impoverished whites. Indeed, hundreds of lower-class South Carolinians signed nearly forty petitions to the legislature, pleading for increased restrictions on carrying deadly weapons, including "murderous Bowie kni[ves], Dirks, Pistols, Sword-Canes, etc." The petitioners desperately coveted protection from a "system of social bullying and intimidation."[48]

One particular Vicksburg mob gave four white men 1,000 lashes, loaded them onto a small, oarless boat, and then set them adrift the Mississippi River. The following year, the Magnolia State was further described as marred by social unrest: "there has lately been some lynching of some shopkeepers ... for selling whiskey to and harboring negroes. Each of the lynched received about one hundred lashes." In adjoining Arkansas, some fifty to seventy-five white gamblers were reportedly drowned by an angry mob. These vigilante actions undoubtedly added to the effectiveness of the criminal system; there was only a very fine line – at times indistinguishable – separating the two. Occasionally, vigilante committees and even mobs held "trials" for the accused, further blurring the categories of legal and extra-legal. During a six-year period in South Carolina, eight whites were convicted of abolitionism. But many, many others were dealt with by vigilantes. Violent reprisals kept increasing throughout the cotton boom of the 1850s. In one Louisiana town in 1859, for example, three white victims died "from the severity of the brutal whipping inflicted upon them." One man had been both shot and stabbed. Furthermore, "a number of other dead bodies ha[ve] been found in the prairies," and the local "Vigilance Committee ha[s] publically whipped nearly seventy citizens of their parishes ... without judge or jury, and have ordered them to leave the State in five days or suffer the penalty of death."[49]

This epidemic of extralegal violence became even more widespread – and more intensely vicious – from 1860 to 1861. Traveler John Abbott recalled the spectacle surrounding the punishment of one immigrant who dared to speak out against the powerful master class. "A poor Irish stone cutter, James Power, at work on the State House in Columbia,"

---

[48] *Ibid.*, 110; quoted on 97.
[49] *Ibid.*, 103; "Life in Mississippi," *Southern Recorder*, Aug. 16, 1836, 2; Grimsted, *American Mobbing*, 85; Sinha, *The Counterrevolution of Slavery*, 80; "The Louisiana Vigilance Committee" *Edgefield Advertiser*, Oct. 12, 1859, 1.

apparently remarked that he "thought Slavery objectionable, inasmuch as it caused the white laborers at the South to be regarded as an inferior and degraded man." For uttering such sentiments, Power was kidnapped by a twelve-man vigilance committee, who then ordered his public torture and humiliation. With a sadistic psychological twist, the slaveholder-dominated vigilance committee had two black men chain Power up, drag him through the mud, and then proceeded to parade him through town. A huge crowd of perhaps 3,000 people surrounded the lynching, and a "stout negro was ordered, with a cow-hide, to lay thirty-nine lashes on his bare back, which should draw blood with every stroke." After the poor man was mercilessly tarred and feathered, his open wounds weeping into the black tar, Power was "thrust into the negro-car, and sent out of the State." The master class had come to a resolute decision: it was time to remind poor whites – in no uncertain terms – that they were hardly a step away from assuming the status of blacks. Using black men to administer many of these brutal punishments was yet another reminder of this fact. Slave owners wanted to degrade poor and immigrant whites as much as possible, until they actually feared becoming slaves themselves. Whatever vestiges of white privilege the impoverished had formerly enjoyed, by the year of secession, all bets were off. All men who were not actively and vocally supporting secession and the Confederacy were considered traitors of the state, and were handled accordingly.[50]

A single edition of the Anderson, South Carolina's *The Intelligencer* referenced at least four separate instances of white men being lynched or killed for interacting with blacks. The September 11, 1860 issue very effectively warned white Southerners of impending bi-racial rebellions, and plots against slaveholders by a coalition of blacks and impoverished whites. In Texas, the first article stated, "A white man named Taylor, who had made negroes his only companions, had been ordered to get his traveling card immediately, or be hanged." Several buildings had already been burned down, and there were frequent threats of entire towns being razed. This frenzied fear of revolt caused yet another "white man implicated with the negroes" to be "hung near Ione." A second article recounted a plot to massacre slaveholders in Talladega, Alabama, apparently planned by a disaffected band of poor whites and blacks. "The concurrent testimony of the negroes examined, goes to show ... that the whole plot has been concocted and set on foot by white men," *The*

---

[50] Abbott, *South and North*, 102–3.

Intelligencer crowed. "Two white men, citizens of our county ... have been arrested and lodged in prison." Yet the dictates of vigilante violence would not allow these white men – traitors to their own race, slave owners claimed – to have the right to trial, or any other procedural right of due process, for that matter. Lem Paine, one of the alleged leaders of the plotted rebellion, was soon "forcibly taken from his prison...and hung from a large China tree." Still another article concerning anti-Confederate non-slaveholders focused on a story out of Adairsville, Georgia, a small rural town in the Appalachian foothills. A poor white man who recently had been "discharged from the penitentiary" was detained, not by the local legal authorities, but by the town's extralegal vigilance committee. The impoverished white "was detected in trying to instill wrong notions into the mind of a negro, who informed against him," the paper related, and thus received from the vigilance committee "thirty-nine lashes and a half shaven head."[51]

The holidays always proved particularly bloody in the slave South, where the specter of black rebellion increased whenever slaves were permitted days off from laboring in the fields. December of 1860, however, arriving on the heels of Lincoln's election, was likely the most violent Christmas season of the entire antebellum period. The *New York Times* reported that in Friar's Point, Mississippi, a vigilance committee hanged three white carpenters "for inciting the slaves to rebellion." Although these victims were migrants from northern states (as were many of the lynched), they still constituted part of the white laboring classes negatively impacted by slavery. Not content with simply ridding the locale of the traitorous carpenters, however, the town's slaveholders decided it best for "Other Northerners" to be shipped out of the region as well. Merely a few days later, both New Orleans and Mobile experienced bouts of vigilance violence, as Northerners and many immigrants were rounded up and ordered out of the slave South. Because these men were not born on southern soil, the slaveholders concluded, there was no evidence that they would not side with the Republicans, or worse, with abolitionists. "Any half-dozen ruffians, heated by the discussion of bad whisky and worse politics," one article ran, "have time and again constituted themselves a 'Vigilance Committee.'" The writer concluded that free speech simply did not exist in the South, where the master class quickly silenced

---

[51] "The Abolition Plot in Texas and Other States," *The Intelligencer*, Sept. 11, 1860, 4; "Excitement in Rome, Geo.," *Ibid.*, Sept. 11, 1860, 4.

every utterance about workers' rights and land reform, let alone notions of black freedom.[52]

The stories concerning vigilante violence – exacted by slaveholders on lower-class whites and all blacks, free and enslaved – abound throughout the late antebellum period and continue the entire duration of the Civil War. Always working in tandem with local criminal courts and police departments, the Deep South's vigilante groups were populated by the same men who ran local and state governments, who comprised the slave patrols, and who lorded over and brutalized slaves.

Thus, by the time of secession, poor whites had few options. Inhabiting a police state, with no economic standing and virtually no civil rights, they simply had no recourse for their many grievances. Short of an all-out rebellion, they had to either fight for the Confederacy or hide out from the military authorities for the duration of the war. "There is no doubt," believed Moncure Conway, "that the masses of the South required much forcing before they took up arms against the United States." As Georgian Robert Toombs bellowed on the floor of the U.S. Senate, "Gentlemen alone make revolutions; the lower classes are always the last to come into them." The Deep South's master class was one step closer to creating their own version of Babylon: a slaveholder-dominated republic devoted to exploiting and expanding slavery. Other forms of unfree labor – forms not exclusive to race – now ominously loomed on the horizon. Poor whites realized they had no place in the new Confederacy, except, perhaps, as soldiers. As one scholar determined, secessionists ultimately were successful "in discrediting the abolitionist as a radical and fanatic, and in enlisting the support of the non-slaveholder by threatening him with slave revolts and negro equality."[53]

Although slave owners' extensive use of violence to achieve secession has generally been overlooked by historians, it unquestionably existed. "The subsequent proceedings of the Southern leaders convinced all that there was a large element of Southern society which had been drawn into secession by force," Conway wrote, "and when to this was added the four millions of slaves, – held down by a power which had never asked 'the consent of those governed,' – it was recognized that the invasion of the South was really the liberation of its people. It will be seen, then, that every step of the South has been marked by perjury, treachery, and

---

[52] "Hanging by a Vigilance Committee," *New York Times*, Dec. 14, 1860; "The Crisis and Mob Law," *New York Times*, Dec. 17, 1860.

[53] Conway, *Testimonies*, 94; quoted on 94; Nye, *Fettered Freedom*, 38.

lawlessness." Secession certainly was not secured by a vote, nor popular will, nor by free choice, for that matter. The master class had long lorded over the region with police, slave patrols, vigilance committees, minute men societies, and mob brutality, and these instruments of surveillance and force all helped secure disunion. Therefore, "The lawlessness and violence of the secession movement" was completely consistent with the previous behaviors of slave owners, Conway argued. "Slavery is war in its chronic form. ... Its nightly patrols, its duels, its constant recourse to pistols and bowie knives, its suspension of all forms of law when an Abolitionist or an insubordinate slave is to be disposed of, its Lynch-law," he lamented, "all these things have long marked the life of that institution which war first created, and which, having always relied upon brute force as its central condition of existence, has, in bringing on a civil war, only resorted to its legitimate weapons." The violence borne by slavery had (and would continue to have) long-term consequences for all Southerners for generations to come. As Conway so elegantly concluded, "the worst kind of war is that of the strong against the weak."[54]

A year and a half into the horrific violence of the Civil War, the *Newbern Weekly Progress*, a North Carolina newspaper, attempted to explain that the masses of white Southerners never desired to leave the Union; that secession was designed and implemented by affluent slave-holders who cared nothing for poorer whites. "The great non-slaveholding masses of the South, who are, in every State, a vast majority of the citizens thereof, have hitherto been kept down and bound hand and foot, like a blind giant, by the negro-driving aristocratic minority," the paper began. Although impoverished white laborers knew that slave-holders considered them "floating capital," and realized that they "are kept in ignorance and degradation," they had few options in a region where the entire system was stacked against them. Instead, "the lords of the soil are assured that, otherwise – if educated and brought up to a standard of intelligence such as to enable them to understand their innate equal rights with other white men – they would rise up in peaceable and law-abiding insurrection at the ballot-box, and assert their dormant and intrinsic power, and break down the despotism that enthralls them." Yet because of their illiteracy, poor whites continued to be "chained down in the dungeon of ignorance," and thus unable to "overturn" and "revolutioniz[e]" the southern hierarchy. "KNOWLEDGE IS POWER," the

[54] Conway, *Testimonies*, 96; 97.

Progress proclaimed, "and it must be sequestered by the aristocracy, or the democracy will triumph."[55]

There was, however, one saving grace amidst all the death and destruction, the paper continued. The Civil War ultimately "opened up the pathway of deliverance from his bondage to the poor white man of the South," and it was "His liberation – not that specially of the negro, which is only secondary and incidental – his enfranchisement, and admission to an equality of rights with other men of the Caucasian stock" that formed "the great and manifest destiny which the revolution now in progress have developed and made plain." Perhaps, the journalist hoped, after suffering as second-class citizens for so long (and with their race always liable to be questioned), poor whites finally would become included in some of the privileges of whiteness.[56]

[55] "Fighting Unionism," *Newbern Weekly Progress* (NC), Oct. 25, 1862.　　[56] *Ibid.*

9

Class Crisis and the Civil War

They are now completely under the domination of the oligarchy, and it is madness to suppose that they will ever be able to rise to a position of true manhood, until after the slave power shall have been utterly overthrown.
— *Hinton Helper*[1]

They will have an Abolition party in the South, of Southern men. The contest for slavery will no longer be one between the North and the South. It will be in the South, between the people of the South.
— *The Charleston Mercury, 1860*[2]

In 1838, Ohio abolitionist Charles Olcott assailed the relationship between free white labor and black slave labor, charging that "a multitude of poor whites ... are ... by the monopoly of slave labour ... kept in the greatest poverty, want and ignorance. It is disgraceful in them to labour with slaves," he continued, "and if it were not the slaveholders will not hire them ... the poor whites in those states live, in a state of dependence bordering on pauperism." Because of the South's decided economic inequality between classes of white men, Olcott concluded that, "All of the evils of slavery are great evils; but one of the greatest is, *that it injures the free as well as the enslaved.*"[3]

---

[1] Helper, *The Impending Crisis*, 382.
[2] *The Charleston Mercury*, Oct. 11, 1860, quoted in Johnson, *Towards a Patriarchal Republic*, 44.
[3] Charles Olcott, *Two Lectures on the Subject of Slavery and Abolition* (Massillon, OH: "Printed for the Author," 1838), Vol. 11, No. 16, 54–5, MDAH.

In the two decades before the Civil War, poor whites became increasingly upset about their exclusion from the labor market, considering themselves an underprivileged class with few chances at upward mobility. And despite the fact that many of these people were uneducated, barely literate, or illiterate, they showed a fairly sophisticated understanding of the ways in which slavery oppressed them. As traveler James Redpath reported, all the poor whites he met "were conscious of the injurious influence that slavery was exerting on their social condition." Excluded from the benefits of whiteness in a world based on slavery, poor whites were essentially masterless men in a rigidly hierarchical world, and that fact deeply troubled the region's masters. This crisis, caused in large part by the "demoralization" of white laborers who were unable to earn a living wage, threatened the stability, and thus the safety, of southern slave owners, adding fuel to the secession flame.[4]

Several Confederate veterans spoke about this transformation in the two decades leading up to the war. Lee Billingsley, the son of a large slaveholder, admitted that "For ten or fifteen years just before the war the larger land and slave-owners did not regard manual labor as respectable for a gentleman." J.P. Dillehay, whose yeoman father owned only one slave, recalled a similar change, stating that "When I was a boy [slaveholders] did not think themselves better than one who did not have slaves, but just as the war broke out, they seemed to think themselves better than the ones who did not own any ... some of them would not speak to the men who did not own slaves." Thus, as the 1840s and 1850s rolled on, the socioeconomic plight of poor whites in the Deep South seemed to worsen. Slaveholders realized that they desperately needed to address this impending class crisis between whites – a predicament that was, ironically, a by-product of slavery. Instead of unifying all whites, black slavery had opened deep fissures in any semblance of racial solidarity.[5]

Governor James Adams of South Carolina observed "that free labor and slave labor w[ere] *necessarily* antagonistic to each other. The policy of teaching negroes the various trades, instead of putting them on the plantations, where they belong, tends to make the rich richer, and the poor poorer." Indeed, he continued, by bringing "slave labor into competition with white labor, and thus arraying capital against labor, (for the negro is capital) ... this will produce a spirit of antagonism between the rich and the poor." But Governor Adams was not acting out of

---

[4] Redpath, *The Roving Editor*, 88.
[5] Elliot and Moxley, *Tennessee*, Vol. 1, 317; Vol. 2, 691.

288 Class Crisis and the Civil War

progressive labor principles. Instead, he was reacting to the growing number of union associations and the increasing chorus of protests by white laborers demanding reform. Poor and lower-middling class whites held gatherings all across the Deep South, insisting on job segregation and wage protection.[6]

The same year that Governor Adams gave his speech on the perils of pitting white workers against slaves, 163 white laborers met in Charleston to pass resolutions against the "baneful evil" of slave hiring. This practice, they declared, hurt their own economic interests, and would eventually harm "the owner of the slave" as well. Two years later, Charleston's mechanics continued to petition the state of South Carolina for legal protections against black competition. All other trades benefitted from racial exclusion, their argument ran, so white mechanics deserved the same advantage. Although the legislature ultimately tabled a bill on restricting slaves from mechanical trades, the final sentence of the 1860 petition was portentous: "Is it wise to tax the loyalty of the working poor man, by such discriminations, to the institution which he is educated to defend, and in defense of which he is always the foremost?"[7]

In the six years before the Civil War, South Carolinian Mechanics Associations sent more than ten petitions and memorials to the state legislature, asking for non-competition laws for slaves, free blacks, and prisoners. Slaveholding politicians, of course, did nothing. A few states away, poor white workers in Jackson, Mississippi also called for "a permanent Mechanical Association and the suppression of the abuses committed by the owners of negro mechanics in 'permitting their slaves to go at large, trade as free men, [and] hire themselves out' ... to the ... direct injury of the mechanical classes in open violation of *social right*." R.H. Purdom, a master mechanic who addressed the Jackson meeting, issued a blatant warning to both slaveholders and slave hirers: an "early, decided course for the speedy suppression of the intolerable abuses" suffered by white laborers was necessary for the "permanent welfare of the institution of slavery itself." It seemed as if poorer whites were finally at their tipping point. They were willing – at least in theory – to threaten the institution of slavery in the interests of their own economic class.[8]

[6] "Negro Mechanics," *Federal Union*, July 6, 1858, 1–2; see Johnson, *Towards a Patriarchal Republic*, 46–52.
[7] Planitzer, "A Dangerous Class of Men," 74; 72.
[8] Takaki, "The Movement," 43; "Mechanical Association," *Mississippian State Gazette*, Dec. 29, 1858, 3.

Even some of the Deep South's most highly skilled laborers threw their support behind the demands of these new associations. The editors of a Milledgeville, Georgia paper eloquently defended poor white laborers, writing that "if the rich man's negro was placed in competition with us at the printer's case, and by lowering our wages, take[s] the bread from the mouths of our wife and children, a well of bitterness would spring up in our breasts against the negro and his master, that would render us the everlasting and uncompromising enemy of both." The editors then pointed out that men in their profession enjoyed legal protection against competition with slave labor. All whites, regardless of skill or economic status, were owed the same protections, they maintained. "Fortunately, however, the laws of the State protect printers against this humiliation and degradation," but "what the laws fail to do in this respect for other mechanics, a wholesome public opinion should effect for them." Urging legislators to do something about poor whites' predicament, the editors concluded that current conditions made "the poor mechanic of the South" both "the enemy of the negro and of the institution of slavery."[9]

A writer to the Mobile *Mercury* in Alabama echoed these sentiments. If slave owners stayed "deaf to the just claims of white laboring men," then the poor should "act in the manner and take measures for their own protection." Indeed, he argued, the integration of the southern labor force had destroyed the "rights and dignity of white men." What Southerner would "be willing to see his son working at the same bench with a set of buck negroes, and on equality with them?" One Georgian declared that "It is impossible to rally the working people of the country to dissolve the Union for the protection of the slaveholders." That same year, a meeting of mechanics and working men convened in Lexington, Kentucky. The members resolved that slavery "degraded labor, enervated industry, interfered with the occupations of free laborers, created a gulf between the rich and the poor, deprived the working classes of education, and tended to drive them out of the state." They provocatively concluded that "public and private right" required slavery's "ultimate extinction." Unsurprisingly, lower-class white laborers became some of the most outspoken foes of disunion.[10]

The threat of an angry, jobless mob caused some southern lawmakers to propose restricting slave labor to agriculture, hopefully ensuring poor whites' fidelity to slavery. Non-slaveholding workers were already

[9] "Negro Mechanics," *Federal Union*, July 6, 1858, 1–2.
[10] "Employment of Slaves," *Mobile Mercury*, quoted in Planitzer, "A Dangerous Class of Men," 80; Mandel, *Labor, Free and Slave*, quoted on 174; quoted on 21–2; 174.

pushing for some sort of division of labor. Their associations seemingly demanded nothing short of privileging white labor by excluding slaves and free blacks from certain types of work. One proposed solution seemed to gain favor incrementally as more states seceded from the Union. Judge H.F. Hopkins, of Mobile, Alabama, carefully explained the benefits of this plan. In an effort to preserve slavery, he wrote, "slaveholders should ... thorough legislative action ... confine the negro to the soil, thus to elevate and open up the mechanic trades to the non-slaveholding people around them." The Judge concluded that once blacks were limited to agricultural work, "the mechanic would be at once converted from an ... enemy of negro slavery into its finest advocate and supporter, because he would feel himself then lifted up in the solid scale of social responsibility, and maintained in that position by the subordinated negro, confined exclusively to menial services." This discussion over limiting slaves to agriculture revealed just how deep slaveholder fears ran.[11]

Industrialists used poor whites' growing labor unrest as an opportunity to try to position the factory as the simple solution in segregating the labor force. With new factories, boosters argued, jobs could be arranged in a hierarchical manner: blacks would work in the fields, in the "lowliest" of jobs with the hardest physical toil, while poor whites would work in industry. J.M. Wesson, a Mississippi industrialist, even proposed creating an economic stake in slavery for poor whites by employing them to manufacture clothes and shoes for slaves. Regardless of how segregation was pitched, the Deep South's slaveholders proposed similar plans in every state. In their pleas for implementing a racial division of the labor force, they often cited protecting the institution of slavery as their main purpose.[12]

Furthermore, by the eve of war, slave owners began trying to scare poor whites into supporting secession by warning of the dire consequences of black emancipation. First, they predicted that poor whites' wages would fall quickly and drastically – to the point of literal starvation. Second, they said that poor whites would suddenly be the social equals of the newly freed men. Finally, masters warned in most incendiary fashions that a bloody racial war between the two impoverished classes would undoubtedly follow freedom, and that poor whites would be slaughtered by the thousands. This type of fear-mongering should be

---

[11] "Negro Mechanics," *Southern Federal Union*, July 23, 1861, 1; Escott, *After Secession*, 29.

[12] Barney, *The Secessionist Impulse*, 42; DuBois, *Black Reconstruction in America*, 80.

recognized by historians as part of the lead-up to the fanatical violence of the Jim Crow era. In the few years before secession, southern slaveholders literally laid the foundation for the irrational, extremist, racist fear that would come to dominate the decades following the war.

In 1860, Georgia Governor Joseph Brown warned the region's poor whites that abolishing slavery meant that blacks would become their "equals, legally and socially." Slaves were accustomed to only earning basic food and clothing in exchange for their labor, he continued, and would require little more after freedom, rendering the possibility of emancipation terrifying for poor whites. Brown cautioned that

The poor white man would then go to the wealthy land-owner and say, I wish employment. Hire me to work. I have a wife and children who must have bread. The land-owner would offer probably twenty cents per day. The laborer would say, I cannot support my family on that sum. The landlord replies ... The black man who lives on my land has as strong an arm, and as heavy muscles as you have, and can do as much labor. He works for me at that rate, you must work for the same price, or I cannot employ you ... the poor, honest laborers of Georgia, can never consent to see slavery abolished, and submit to all the taxation, vassalage, low wages and downright degradation, which must follow. They will never take the negro's place; God forbid.

A year later the Governor continued on the same theme, claiming that "The negro would, when free, be placed nearer a state of equality with the white laborer, and ... would come into direct competition with the poor white laborer, and would soon under-bid him, and reduce the price of labor to as low a rate as would sustain life." Thus, nearly five months after the start of the Civil War, the leader of one of the largest slaveholding states was still trying to convince lower-class whites that slavery served their interests, too. Black emancipation, Brown warned, "would bring ruin on the poor white man, and degrade his family far below the present condition. ... In other words," the Governor further propagandized, "the rich and poor are alike interested in sustaining slavery and in sustaining the price of labor."[13]

Alfred Iverson, another Georgia politician, joined in the campaign to scare poor white laborers into supporting the peculiar institution. Slavery, Iverson argued, "elevates the character and condition of the poor white man ... he well understands that if slavery be abolished the value of his own labor will be diminished, his political and social condition lowered,

[13] "Letter from Gov. Brown, Milledgeville, Dec. 5, 1860," *Federal Union*, Dec. 11, 1860, 3; "Governor's Message," *Southern Recorder*, Nov. 12, 1861, 3.

and his personal safety itself greatly jeopardized. Set the negroes free, and the rich man ... can escape them by relocating to a Free State or some other safe and quiet place." However, Iverson cautioned, the poor white would not be able to afford the same luxury. Without the financial means to flee the South, "The poor man must remain upon the soil, to encounter the ravages of the 'black plague' ... [it] would sooner or later lead to a war between the races ... [and] The brunt of that war would necessarily be borne by the poorer classes of the white population – the effects would fall mainly upon them, and they would reap a rich harvest of all those tortuous evils which follow." By predicting that poor whites would be massacred by the "black plague," masters tried to scare white laborers into supporting the institution of slavery – regardless of what it did to their jobs or wages.[14]

Subsequently, the importance of racism – and race baiting – cannot be overstated. The success of the secessionist movement was entirely dependent upon it. Alabama Supreme Court Justice John D. Phelan remarked that if slavery were destroyed, the "poor and middling classes" would feel the toll most heavily, because "negro ... domination" and "amalgamation" would necessarily follow black freedom. The rhetoric became so inflamed that by 1860, Andrew Henry, the Irish-born editor of the *West Alabamian,* warned that Southerners should soon expect to "Submit to have our wives and daughters chose [sic] between death and gratifying the hellish lust of the negro!! Submit to have our children murdered, our dwellings burnt and our country desolated!!" When describing the consequences of abolition, slavery's vociferous defenders always envisioned a bloody, violent future for the South, where African Americans lorded over whites. "So awful was this prophecy, so extreme the language, that a modern observer is compelled to question the depth of fear that lay beneath it," wrote one historian. Still, "abolition was regarded as an unthinkable horror, attendant with boundless physical, economic, social, and political disasters."[15]

Poor whites had no personal or economic interest in the peculiar institution, but slaveholders desperately tried to convince them otherwise. The southern gentry had plenty to think about as they entered election season in 1860. Clearly, the loyalty and devotion of the region's poor whites was

---

[14] "Speech of Hon. Alfred Iverson, Delivered at Griffin, July 14, 1859," *Weekly Georgia Telegraph,* July 26, 1859, 1.
[15] Barney, *The Secessionist Impulse,* 229; quoted on 228–9; quoted on 228; Channing, *Crisis of Fear,* 58.

high on their minds. J. Henly Smith, the non-slaveholding political pro-
tégé of Alexander Stephens, expressed these concerns several times right
before the 1860 presidential election. If Republicans won, he wrote, they
will "have adherents and supporters all over the South – in every state. . . .
The non-slaveholders will very generally adhere to the new party, and
slavery will be crushed out forever." Indeed, the inevitable rise of a
southern Republican Party was one of the most compelling arguments
secessionists had for immediate action. The specter of Black Republicanism was omnipresent; secessionists tried their best to paint the party of
Lincoln as "a foreign menace which should be treated as if it were an
infectious disease." As Roger Shugg found in rural Louisiana, "a few men
were thrust into jail because 'they hurrahed for Lincoln' or revealed 'the
darkest Abolitionist proclivities.'" All over the Deep South slaveholders
scrambled to come up with a plan to preserve slavery, and to do that, they
had to blunt or redirect the anxiety of the white masses. The white
working class was under-worked, under-paid, and increasingly fed up
with the peculiar intuition. As one poor white laborer succinctly put it, "if
it came to a war over slavery, he was going to fight against it . . . perhaps
he could get better wages."[16]

But everything changed on October 16, 1859, when the abolitionist John
Brown, along with five black and fifteen white men, attacked the arsenal at
Harpers Ferry, Virginia, hoping to incite a massive slave rebellion. Slaveholders' worst fears were instantly realized. Slave rebellion was imminent,
they believed, and non-slaveholding whites were leading the revolt. John
Brown's raid had a dramatic effect on South Carolina politics and the push
toward secession. The master class sincerely believed that abolitionism was
pervading the country, infecting the minds of even southern whites. In the
wake of Harpers Ferry, therefore, vigilance committees became even more
singularly focused on controlling the speeches and actions of white men and
women, whether northern abolitionists, southern sympathizers, or suspicious immigrants. Slaveholders became so apprehensive that some of them
even proposed lifting the ban on slave testimony in courtrooms in hopes of
convicting troublemaking white incendiaries. Ultimately, John Brown's raid
had a significant impact on apolitical Southerners who identified as cooperationists and Unionists. The ranks of these groups dwindled as fewer
southern whites felt safe living in slave societies.[17]

[16] Harris, *Plain Folk and Gentry*, 91; Johnson, *Towards a Patriarchal Republic*, 30; quoted
in Shugg, *Origins of Class Struggle*, 145–6; quoted in Williams, *Bitterly Divided*, 31.
[17] Channing, *Crisis of Fear*, 18; 57; 50; 56; 83.

By December of 1859, articles published in Charleston's newspapers attempted to organize vigilance committees in every ward of the city. Their stated aim included questioning or examining every single man in the city, to "learn whether he is for us or against us in the conflict now waged by the North against our property and our rights. ... The times demand that all men South should be above suspicion." *The Daily Courier* promised to mete out "proper treatment" to both abolitionists and sympathizers. Brought to a peak in the winter of 1859, this long "reign of terror" created new frenzy surrounding free thought and free speech. All of the policing, all of the censorship, and all of the ensuing violence, were direct results of racial slavery. By the new year of 1860, there were daily reports of slave rebellions from every part of the Deep South. The possibility of a bloody slave revolt preoccupied every slave-holder's mind, and by the end of the year pro-secession men charged that most non-slaveholders were latent abolitionists, and thus needed to be both feared and controlled.[18]

As a result of this sentiment, Minute Men volunteer groups also began to organize across the entire South, largely in response to Lincoln's election. Much like vigilance committees, Sally Hadden found, these groups served "the multiple purposes of augmenting local surveillance of suspicious whites and assisting the slave patrols with their increasingly important duties." And, like vigilance committees, the ranks of the Minute Men were filled with upper-middling class and affluent men who were generally slaveholders. In Selma, Alabama, for example, the typical Minute Man was in his 20s or 30s, owned slaves, and worked in the professional or business community. Needless to say, Minute Men commonly used violent tactics. After reports of white abolitionists "exciting" the slaves in Georgia, one local chapter tarred and feathered several suspects.[19]

These groups were necessary, claimed the *Vicksburg Weekly Citizen,* just in case the government needed to "resort to drastic measures to insure secession." Another South Carolinian editorialist expressed his hope that these committees would "at least ... rid us of many vagabonds, too lazy to work, and depraved enough to do mischief." Even the president of the Mississippi Secession Convention, W.S. Barry, suggested that "a stiff limb

---

[18] Channing, *Crisis of Fear*, quoted on 34; 36; 35; 272; 23; 256.
[19] Barney, *The Secessionist Impulse*, 207; Hadden, *Slave Patrols*, 172; Barney, *The Secessionist Impulse*, 208.

and a strong rope vigorously applied" should quiet anyone who was opposed to "our work." These committees did their best to protect slave-holders from poor whites, who might try to incite the slaves to rebel. By August of 1860, the northern press was reporting that in "the Southern States a poor white man dare not speak, write, or print his sentiments. . . . If he does, he is mobbed, or driven from their borders. The entire South is now under a worse than martial law."[20]

Several other secretive, paramilitary style groups formed in the decade before the War, including what appears to be a precursor to the Ku Klux Klan – the Knights of the Golden Circle. The Knights were described in a northern political pamphlet entitled "The Slaveholders' Conspiracy." This sixteen-page document, subtitled "Treason against Democratic Principles," claimed that the purpose of secession was two-fold. First, slave-holders would establish rule by aristocracy, casting off the vestiges of democracy. The plantation gentry wanted a government "based on the privilege of class . . . [and] have set down the expressed apprehension as to the security of slavery as a hypocritical pretext for revolution . . . [the] more absorbing motive was to establish an order of nobility, either with or without monarchy." Then, with complete control over the region, the slaveocracy would lord over both slave and white serf, growing richer and richer at the grave expense of the masses.[21]

This task proved harder than slave owners expected, critics noted, because the loyalty of poor whites and other non-slaveholders was mani-festly suspect, causing the slaveholders to employ even more violent means of coercion:

It has been repeatedly asserted that the South was a political unit on the question of attempted revolution. . . . It is not now necessary to delineate the quasi-military organization of the Knights of the Golden Circle, or their operations in cajoling and terrorizing the Southern population into acquiescence . . . the very means employed to enforce acquiescence afforded also the evidence that there was a strong under-current of aversion. . . . Flight or conformity became the condition precedent of safety, even for life. The bulk of the Southern population was as much conspired against as the Government at Washington; and force against the same population was rigorously called into requisition to consummate what fraud and political crime had concocted. This was the boasted unity of the South.

---

[20] Quoted in Johnson, *Towards a Patriarchal Republic*, 19; quoted in Planitzer, "A Dangerous Class," 358; quoted in Bolton, *Poor Whites*, 175; reprinted as "Lincoln Freesoilism," *Georgia Weekly Telegraph*, August 10, 1860, 1.

[21] The Democratic League, "The Slaveholders' Conspiracy against Democratic Principles," (N.P., 1864?), 2–3; 10; 4, in the Alfred Stone Collection, MDAH.

The Knights of the Golden Circle, therefore, and other paramilitary organizations like it, were essential in ensuring secession. Originally established as a secret organization in 1854, the Knights' main goal was to create a slaveholding empire that encompassed the American South, Mexico, and parts of Central America and the Caribbean – the so-called golden circle. According to John Hope Franklin, the Knights planned to center their empire in Havana, creating a "gigantic slave empire." The President of the organization claimed it had 115,000 members, and even vowed to invade Mexico by January 1, 1861. To achieve these ends, the Knights had to toss off the shackles of the U.S. Constitution, subdue the white masses, and start conquering new slaveholding territory. First, however, they had to secede from the Union – and they needed to suppress the voices and votes of non-slaveholders to do so.[22]

Slaveholder anxieties peaked during the holiday season. Clara Young, the wife of a prosperous planter, worried that "Christmas will soon be here & I suppose vigilant committees will be active and no doubt but in many instances will be too active, for both white & black." It seemed as if nothing could calm the fears of the master class. By January of 1861, a vigilance committee from Panola, Mississippi vowed to "take notice of, and punish all and every persons who may be guilty of any misdemeanor, or prove themselves untrue to the South, or Southern Rights, in any way whatever." Wealthy masters had completely taken over southern society. Circumventing both the government and the criminal justice system, they effectively abolished due process and the right to trial. Instead, affluent slave owners anxiously lorded over the region, meting out punishments whenever they felt compelled, and inching the nation closer and closer to Civil War. Thus, concluded Manisha Sinha, "An atmosphere of terror and vigilantism limited the scope of political dissent and helped propel the secession movement."[23]

To make matters even worse, the summer of 1860 was one of the driest, hottest seasons that Southerners had experienced. Although slaveholders were able to produce a bumper crop of cotton, the severe drought added great unease over food shortages, as the possibility of famine became evident by spring. With poor whites and other non-slaveholders

---

[22] *Ibid.*; Randolph B. Campbell, "Knights of the Golden Circle," *Handbook of Texas Online*, accessed July 11, 2013. Published by the Texas State Historical Association; Franklin, *The Militant South*, 125–6.

[23] Barney, *The Secessionist Impulse*, quoted on 212; quoted on 212, footnote 42; Sinha, *The Counterrevolution of Slavery*, 214.

experiencing difficulty feeding themselves and their families, incidents of backlash against the well-fed upper classes were hardly surprising. Threats of armed rebellion, for example, came from Barbour County, Alabama. "The suffering is confined chiefly to the poorer classes who have not the means of providing themselves with the wants of life," one official reported, "and we understand that if provision is not made immediately to secure those wants unto them, they will take them by force of arms from those who happen to have them."[24]

The South's grave economic inequalities, which had always functioned as a source of class tension, were now resurrected with a vengeance on the eve of Lincoln's election. According to William Barney, "Only the incessant reports of ubiquitous abolitionists plotting slave revolts, setting fires, and poisoning wells upset the South's equilibrium more severely than the drought." Of course, these things were all interconnected; class continued to divide white Southerners as slaveholders intensified their efforts to "out" unlikable or suspicious non-slaveholders as abolitionists. Over the course of two nights in Alabama, a journeyman harness maker allegedly held "improper conversations with slaves." He was immediately stripped down and severely whipped, while newspapers throughout the region clamored for his death. Around the same time, Hilery J. Lanier was found guilty of "slave tampering" in Georgetown, Mississippi. During a public meeting, the slave-owning mob concluded there was not enough evidence to convict Lanier in a court of law. Ordering Lanier to leave town within thirty days, the mob specified that every single day past thirty that Lanier remained in town, he would receive 100 lashes on his bare back.[25]

Even before the 1860 Presidential election, some of the Deep South's poor white men were already disenfranchised, and slaveholders had myriad ways to control the votes of others. As pro-slavery advocate Louisa McCord wrote to James Henry Hammond, "the assumed position of equality [for white men] even in the limited sense which we adopt is plainly a false one." Of course, as the issue over secession exploded in 1860 and 1861, wealthy slaveholders began once again lauding the benefits of limited rights and suffrage – specifically for lower-class white men. George McDuffie, a staunch defender of racial and class-based inequality, claimed that by allowing white laborers to vote, "whatever may be their color, you do not elevate them to the character of freemen,

---

[24] Barney, *The Secessionist Impulse*, 184; 153; 157; quoted on 158.
[25] *Ibid.*, 163; 169–70; 175–6.

but degrade liberty to their level." Slaveholder Laurence M. Keitt further praised the inequities inherent in the region, writing that the South, "with the principle of subordination, gradation, and harmonious inequality pervading her social system," was the best system of governance in the world. He worried that Republicans would spread "impalpable" notions of equality throughout the region, not only to free blacks and slaves, but to poor whites as well. And John Townsend, the owner of over 200 slaves on Edisto Island, argued for secession, railing against southern unionism and claiming that every unionist was an abolitionist. Republicans, Townsend worried, were "a radical democratic party" who favored redistributive policies like the Homestead Act. Slaveholders were hardly overreacting by attempting to prevent non-slaveholders from voting. As the U.S. Marshall from Charleston asked South Carolina's Congressman William Miles in February of 1860, "think you that 360,000 Slaveholders will dictate terms for 3,000,000 of non-slaveholders at the South[?] I fear not, I mistrust our own people more than I fear all of the efforts of the Abolitionists."[26]

Scholars generally consider the election of 1860 the most important presidential election in our nation's history. In the four-way race, Republican Abraham Lincoln, who was not listed on the majority of southern ballots, garnered all of the northern and western electoral votes, and just less than 40 percent of the nation's popular vote. The slaveholding South, on the other hand, split its vote between the remaining three candidates. The "northern" Democrat, Stephen Douglas, won only Missouri but still earned a sizable percentage of Dixie's popular vote. John C. Breckenridge, the pro-slavery, pro-expansionist southern Democrat, carried about 18 percent of the nation's votes, sweeping the Deep South and western cotton states. Finally, John Bell, a Tennessean from the new Constitutional Union party, mostly claimed the votes of conservative former Whigs in the Border States. Bell did not take a firm stance on the issue of slavery's expansion, which widened his appeal in the Upper South.[27]

Immediately following the announcement of Abraham Lincoln's victory, southern pro-slavery men began clamoring for secession, partly due to worries over the loyalty of poor whites and other non-slaveholders. The master class was soon proven correct in its doubts. In the few short weeks

---

[26] Sinha, *The Counterrevolution of Slavery*, quoted on 90; quoted on 35; quoted on 226; quoted on 233; Barney, *The Secessionist Impulse*, 48–9.
[27] Thomas A. Bailey et al., *The American Pageant*, 11th Ed. (New York: Houghton Mifflin, 1998), chapter 20 and appendix 29.

following the presidential election, a group of "working men" from Richmond, Virginia organized a meeting to oppose secession. Another mechanics' association soon followed suit, railing against the "folly and sinister selfishness of the demagogues of the South." Some poor whites throughout the region made their political thoughts well known through other types of organizations. A band of non-slaveholders in southwest Alabama and southeast Mississippi deemed themselves "the Friends Z. Society." Described by one historian as a "mysterious poor man's abolitionist society," the Friends Z. Society reportedly had one hundred members. They adamantly opposed secession and even threatened "class warfare" if it "ever occurred." As the reality of disunion neared and the situation intensified, the master class began preparing for the worst. And mobilization to suppress the poor white vote began in earnest.[28]

Before resorting to drastic measures, though, wealthy slaveholders could use their dominant position in society to subtly shame or publicly humiliate poorer whites into talking, thinking, or voting a certain way. A man who supported anything less than immediate secession would summarily be branded as a traitor or a coward. Not only were these brands shameful, they also carried risks of mob and vigilante violence. Masters attempted to circumvent political power from the large majority of non-slaveholding voters using bribery, lies, and intimidation to make sure secession passed. Some poor whites took the slaveholders' cheapest bait, drinking themselves into intoxicating stupors before stumbling to the polls with a big crowd, too drunk to recognize the significance of their actions. Near Jackson, Mississippi, one candidate reported that "the 'rag-tag and bobtail' of creation were pulled in to vote the secession ticket. Whiskey was freely given; promises of corn and meat were made. Threats were made." Even Northerners realized that secession could possibly succeed – given the persuasive nature of spirituous liquors. As one Pennsylvania paper reported, a "jug of whiskey and the scare-crow of abolition was sufficient to identify them with secession and its bloody work." Poor whites should be pitied "deeply," the paper opined, "for they are of the most part the ignorant dupes of designing and desperate leaders."[29]

[28] Planitzer, "A Dangerous Class," 507; Williams, *Bitterly Divided*, 9; Barney, *The Secessionist Impulse*, 123; quoted in Bolton, *Poor Whites*, 233, note 41. Also see Stephanie McCurry, *Confederate Reckoning: Power and Politics in the Civil War South* (Cambridge: Harvard University Press, 2010).

[29] Johnson, *Towards a Patriarchal Republic*, 98; Bolton, *Poor Whites*, 166; "Preaching to the Secessionists," *The Christian Recorder*, March 22, 1862; Bolton, *Poor Whites*, 164; Shugg, *Origins of Class Struggle*, 164.

The road to disunion, therefore, was quite rocky. Far from a democratic mandate, secession was orchestrated by the master class over the protests – or at least the against the wishes – of hundreds of thousands of slaveless whites. In areas of the South where voters held few slaves, as in the piney woods and wiregrass regions, and in the northern foothills and mountains of Appalachia, secession was opposed decisively. These voting returns correspond with information on the poorest sections, where between two-thirds and three-fourths of voters wanted to remain in the Union. As Michael Johnson noted about Georgia, support for secession waned as voter turnout increased. The vast majority of southern whites did not own slaves, and were not eager to secede and possibly go to war to protect the property rights of a much more affluent minority.[30]

Even though official returns from the Deep South showed about 40 percent of the popular vote in convention elections was *against* secession, fraud was so rampant that the number is basically meaningless. Non-slaveholding white Southerners had precious few reasons to support disunion. In pushing for secession, masters channeled as much racial fear into their politics as possible, scaring and threatening their fellow citizens into acquiescence. Young, affluent lawyers led the separatist charge in Alabama and Mississippi, while in South Carolina, wealthy planters led the way toward disunion. Regardless of their professions, one thing was clear. Secession, the Confederacy, and Civil War were all overwhelmingly the creations of one small class of Americans: wealthy southern slaveholders.[31]

South Carolina, of course, blazed the trail toward secession, withdrawing from the Union just a month after Lincoln's election. It was the first slave state to secede for several reasons. The "vanguard determination of the state's political elite, the lack of organized opposition, an apparent disunionist majority among the citizenry, tactics of intimidation and terror, and hopeless apathy of outnumbered unionists," Manisha Sinha wrote, "made the state's secession a relentless juggernaut." The small farmers and poor whites in the mountainous part of the state had historically opposed nullification and now ardently resisted secession. To be sure, the unionism of Appalachians "worried secessionists." As one South

[30] Johnson, *Towards a Patriarchal Republic*, 66; 76; 74.
[31] Williams, *Bitterly Divided*, 36; Barney, *The Secessionist Impulse*, 230; 297; Sinha, *The Counterrevolution of Slavery*, 222. Seymore M. Lipset, "The Emergence of the One-Party South—The Election of 1860," *Political Man* (New York: Anchor, 1960), 377; 376; 377; 378; 383.

Carolinian warned, "when the battle comes in earnest ... and we find ourselves fairly embarked in a contest which will shake the world, you will find an element of great weakness in our non-slaveholding population."[32]

The second state to secede was Mississippi. As in many parts of the Deep South, lawyers ultimately led Mississippi out of the Union. During their efforts, there was certainly no lack of race-baiting. For instance, the two secessionist candidates from Attala County scandalously warned that Republicans were "in favor of abolishing all distinctions in social position and in civil and political rights between negroes and white men and women." Aside from fear tactics, Mississippi's secessionists also used outright fraud. When a Methodist minister from the state asked for a Union ticket, he "was informed that none had been printed, and that it would be advisable to vote a secession ticket." Furthermore, low voter turnout likely helped increase the number of secessionist representatives in the Magnolia state. While about 80 percent of Mississippi's registered electors voted in the presidential election, the turnout for the secession convention vote was much lower. Only slightly more than one-half (55 percent) of Mississippians who voted in the presidential election of 1860 actually voted for or against secession. Likewise, in Louisiana more than one-quarter of the citizens who voted in November missed the vote on disunion. The fewer people voting, the better secession did. Many poor and lower-middling class whites had long harbored an intense distrust of government, and bothered infrequently with civic activities like voting. They spent lifetimes noticing how little political power they actually possessed, and probably believed that no matter how they voted, power-ful slaveholders would rule in accordance with their own economic interests. Any apathy that poorer whites may have had towards the secession elections was understandable.[33]

Alabama's voter turnout for the convention was similar to its western neighbor's turnout. Out of the 79 percent of eligible Alabamans who voted in the presidential election, only about three-quarters of them returned to the polls to vote on secession. The cooperationists would have won, claimed a local paper, "except for bad management in two

---

[32] Sinha, *The Counterrevolution of Slavery*, 221–2; 135; 212; quoted on 212.

[33] Barney, *The Secessionist Impulse*, 312; quoted on 260; Williams, *Bitterly Divided*, quoted on 35; Barney, *The Secessionist Impulse*, 191; Bolton, *Poor Whites*, 164; Shugg, *Origins of Class Struggle*, 164; Barney, *The Secessionist Impulse*, 268: "Measured against the presidential vote, 20% of the Alabama voters and 40% of those in Mississippi did not bother to vote in December."

counties." As Alabama's convention neared, one politician rated the parties as having similar number of votes. However, by January 10, Mississippi had seceded, and the next day Florida followed, leaving Alabama with little choice. The state was nearly surrounded by secessionist states. Cooperationists were bitter but unwilling to put up more of a fight. Even though the state ultimately seceded, the opposition to joining the Confederacy was clear. Much like South Carolina and Georgia, Alabama's less affluent mountain and foothill whites, who were overwhelmingly non-slaveholders, adamantly opposed secession. As Barney put it, "The mountain whites, deeply resentful of the planters' wealth and privileges, did not hate slavery so much as they did the second-class citizenship to which it relegated them."[34]

Georgia seceded eight days after Alabama. While records show that secession may actually have been defeated by about 1,000 votes, Governor Joseph Brown lied about the results of the election, proudly proclaiming that the state had voted itself out of the Union. Still, as Michael Johnson declared almost forty years ago, by even "consenting to the secession election, secessionists revealed that they could not escape the internal crisis of the South. Instead ... they hoped to overcome it." Indeed, in Georgia the internal crisis was particularly evident. A majority of non-slaveholding voters had supported Breckenridge but then opposed secession. The master class instead achieved disunion by fraudulent means.[35]

Furthermore, as Drew Faust pointed out, most historians tend to overlook the fact that the secession conventions ushered in more than just a break with the Union. Delegates were actually in charge of writing the new state constitutions. Their proposals demonstrate that slaveholders were prepared to get rid of the guise of white democracy if it meant protecting their own economic interests. By creating a vision of new southern nation-states based on the maintenance and expansion of the institution of slavery, the region's masters revealed that they desired a form of government based on property holding and wealth – a rule *by* slaveholders and *for* slaveholders, all at the expense of the poor. Georgia's convention attempted to reduce the number of legislators and appoint (not elect) justices. North Carolina's judiciary committee called for property qualifications for certain governmental jobs and exempted other

---

[34] Barney, *The Secessionist Impulse*, 191; Escott, *After Secession*, 26; quoted on 26; Barney, *The Secessionist Impulse*, 302; 271.
[35] Williams, *Bitterly Divided*, 39; Johnson, *Towards a Patriarchal Republic*, 87; Escott, *After Secession*, 30.

offices from popular elections. Virginia proposed similar measures, and also sought to restrict voting to tax payers. Alabama and Arkansas endeavored to have all judges appointed, as elections "by the people" would produce "mere instruments of popular prejudice," as the justices' robes "were placed on their shoulders by the votes of a fanatical people." At every turn, southern slaveholders were revealing their anti-democratic desires. They ultimately created a centralized, slaveholder-dominated republic with a president who served six-year terms. The oligarchic tenets embedded in the Confederate Constitution led Faust to conclude that in the Deep South, "it was not the electorate but something very close to Genovese's ruling class that led the state[s] out of the Union . . . secession was necessary precisely because the hegemony of slaveholders was not secure." Still, slaveholders were ultimately able to turn secession into what Johnson termed a "double revolution: a revolution for home rule – to eliminate the external threat; and a conservative revolution for those who ruled at home – to prevent the political realization of the internal threat."[36]

The ultimate choice of disunion, therefore, was a choice made by the master class. By the early 1860s, the Deep South's slaveholding interests were using every possible method to force people with no ties to slavery to support the institution. Politics became dominated, as Shugg wrote, by "farce and fraud; the knife, the sling-shot, the brass knuckles determining . . . who shall occupy and administer the [public] offices." Poor whites, along with many other non-slave owners, made it completely clear that they opposed disunion. The state conventions, of course, were all dominated by the master class, who deliberately chose to ignore public will. While proving the efficacy of manipulative violence, slave owners simultaneously invoked more concern from Northerners. To Americans residing in free states, it seemed as if a small but powerful band of slaveholders were the only Southerners desiring disunion. Poor whites certainly did not want war. They had no desire to fight and die to protect an institution that had long injured their own prosperity and well-being. Despite all of the weight scholars have afforded white supremacy, it was simply not enough to unite the white South over slavery and disunion.[37]

[36] Drew Gilpin Faust, *The Creation of Confederate Nationalism: Ideology and Identity in the Civil War South* (Baton Rouge: Louisiana University Press, 1988), 34–8; 37; Johnson, *Towards a Patriarchal Republic*, xx.
[37] Shugg, *Origins of Class Struggle*, 147; Williams, *Bitterly Divided*, 2–3; Stephen V. Ash, "Poor Whites in the Occupied South," *Journal of Southern History* 57, (1991): 40; Johnson, *Towards a Patriarchal Republic*, 69.

While the scholarship on poor whites during the Civil War is still in relative infancy, pioneers in the field like Charles Bolton and Timothy Lockley have offered several reasons why poor whites would decide to fight and die for the South's slaveocracy – a class whose economic interests fundamentally clashed with their own. The current historical consensus hinges on three main points. First, poor whites had kinship ties with middling farmers and even planters, as well as other social ties to the upper classes. Second, many less affluent whites persisted in believing that through hard work and perseverance, they could move up the economic ladder and perhaps someday become slaveholders themselves. And third, racism often tainted poor whites' decision-making skills, helping to prevent the formation of true color-blind class consciousness.[38]

Although the first point has some considerable validity, the second and third arguments will likely lose favor in the near future. Instead, widely employed legal and extralegal means aimed to force dissenters to join the armed forces. Cases of imprisonment, lynching, and even murder for desertion and avoiding conscription were prevalent throughout the South. For the most part, the underwhelming support for secession had its roots in the severe class inequalities of the late antebellum period. The poor whites who did not support secession were generally better described as anti-Confederate than pro-Union. Feelings and beliefs about the Confederacy likely ran the gamut from apathy to hatred, but one thing was clear: a majority of poor white men had no burning desire to fight for the South from the start, and others were unwilling to fight for more than a year or two. Recently, historians such as Victoria Bynum and David Williams have shown that the South really did experience an "Inner Civil War" over the course of the actual one, and subsequent generations of scholars will surely uncover even more evidence of this internal disharmony.[39]

There were many colorful names for the anti-Confederates, from deserters and mossbacks to jayhawkers and abolitionists. Certainly, the most principled of the objectors, the abolitionists, came from all classes of white Southerners, but the impoverished caused the slaveholders the most

---

[38] Bolton, *Poor Whites*, and Lockley, *Lines in the Sand*.

[39] Victoria E. Bynum, *The Long Shadow of the Civil War: Southern Dissent and its Legacies* (Chapel Hill: University of North Carolina Press, 2010), and Williams, *Bitterly Divided*. For a discussion over pro-Union versus anti-Confederate or anti-authoritarian, see Barney, *The Secessionist Impulse*, 312. Some areas – especially where Union occupation occurred early – experienced changes in loyalties of the people. See Judkin Browning, *Shifting Loyalties: The Union Occupation of Eastern North Carolina* (Chapel Hill: University of North Carolina Press, 2011).

worry. Even the great Georgia statesman T.R.R. Cobb warned his fellow legislators to "Notice the anxious look when the traveling pedlar lingers too long in a conversation at the door with the servant who turns the bolt – the watchful gaze when the slave tarries long with the wandering artist who professes merely to furnish him with a picture." Masters were becoming increasingly fearful of whites who had no real stake in slavery, as evidenced by an Atlanta-area grand jury who decreed that all beggars were to "be promptly sent [to the Poor House] for support, and all transient beggars be arrested as vagrants, and sent back from whence they came, or otherwise *summarily disposed of*, as in that garb they may be the means of much mischief in these troublous times, by transmitting information to our enemies, and otherwise." Indeed, even the slave patrols amped up their policing duties, carefully monitoring the actions and conversations of both blacks and poor whites.[40]

By 1860 Alabama's slave patrols had the "authority to apprehend any white person who may be found ... consorting with slaves, or loitering about negro cabins." Furthermore, in the absence of the patrol, "any three freeholders or slaveholders" could arrest the white person who ignored segregation, giving propertied white men unprecedented authority to imprison lawfully other whites. Anxieties grew so intense that just a few weeks after Lincoln's election, South Carolina's Governor William Gist called upon the state's officials to punish "summarily and severely, if not with death, any person that circulates incendiary documents, avows himself an abolitionist, or ... attempts to create insubordination or insurrection among the slaves." While these laws seemed harsh in letter, they were nonetheless deemed necessary to prevent a massive rebellion involving slaves and poor whites. By the summer of 1861, slave conspiracies, "all of them involving whites," were uncovered in three Mississippi counties. In southwest Georgia a vigilance committee "uncovered plans for a slave uprising." The revolt was supposed "to be led by several local whites." And non-slaveholder Osborne Burson was arrested near Atlanta in March of the same year, for declaring that "negroes were as free as he was and that he would have voted for Lincoln had he a chance to do so, and if he had a chance he would assist in freeing them." Slave owners were in a racial frenzy. Just a few days after the secessionist ordinance passed, one Georgia politician "proposed that the governor accept the service of between fifteen and fifty men in each county and commission

---

[40] Johnson, *Towards a Patriarchal Republic*, 37; "Presentments of the Grand Jury," *Southern Confederacy* (GA), April 24, 1861, 1, italics added.

them as a 'Mounted Military Police'" to patrol the activities of suspected southern abolitionists.[41]

While historians will never know how many abolitionists inhabited the Deep South at any point, the number of southern Unionists is slightly easier to quantify. Although the majority of Unionists were from Upper South states, Unionist organizations existed all throughout the southernmost region as well. Including African Americans who served as Union soldiers, nearly half a million Southerners fought against the slaveholders. And there was certainly a class element among white Unionists, as they tended to be even poorer than common Confederate soldiers.[42]

Many of the vigilance committees that sprang up during the secession debates helped quiet "unionist dissent." When a Unionist candidate attempted to run for office in North Carolina, he was threatened with lynching. Even his supporters were mobbed at the polls, and summarily intimidated with promises of death. Masters used these tactics commonly enough to create an atmosphere of fear throughout the region. One transient poor white was arrested shortly after secession for "refusing to do military duty and vagrancy." The local sheriff offered to release the man from jail on one condition: that he enlist with the local regiment. And in northeastern Mississippi, an area with a high percentage of poor whites, coercion seemed common. One anti-Confederate from Chickasaw County "opposed the war all I could but when it forced itself on us I with several others volunteered in the Southern army as we thought we would be forced to join if we did not go."[43]

Rather than simply choosing to support the Confederacy, most poor whites doubtless felt they had little or no choice *but* to support the war effort because they were largely at the mercy of the slave owners. Because the master class completely controlled the southern legal system, they rendered poor whites essentially powerless. Slaveholders could coerce the poor to join the Confederate Army with the threat of jail time for vagrancy or some other trumped up charge. Other poor whites fell victim to vigilante "justice" or were simply banished from the region. Yet these punitive and criminal statutes were not the only laws invoking the ire of the lower classes. Almost immediately after secession, the divisions that had always existed between white Southerners once again became tense.

---

[41] Planitzer, "A Dangerous Class," 35; 408; Williams, *Bitterly Divided*, 50; Johnson, *Towards a Patriarchal Republic*, 133; 134.

[42] Williams, *Bitterly Divided*, 48; 242; 151.

[43] Bolton, *Poor Whites*, 151; quoted on 158; quoted on 176.

There was certainly no strong sense of Confederate nationalism in the early part of 1861. Even after the Montgomery Convention, when the Deep South delegates attempted to moderate their extreme views concerning slavery to appeal to the states in the Upper South, poor whites were not enthusiastic about fighting to protect the interests of slaveholders. Despite not agreeing (or even identifying with) the Confederacy, however, large numbers of Southerners obviously did not defect into the Union Army. Instead, a type of silent rebellion erupted, as many non-slaveholders showed no support for the slaveholders' cause. Still, nearly three-quarters of all enumerated southern white men served in the Confederate forces. Because most poor whites opposed secession, few were volunteers. They had to be forced to fight to preserve the riches of the master class – riches that seemed to always come at their expense.[44]

Joseph Glatthaar's research confirmed the strong ties between Confederate volunteers and their involvement in slavery. In 1861, almost half of all the South's enlistees "either lived with slaveholders or were slave owners themselves." The non-slaveholding volunteers sold crops to, worked for, or rented land from slave owners. Therefore, Glatthaar concluded, "the vast majority of the volunteers of 1861 had a direct connection to slavery. For slaveholder and non-slaveholder alike, slavery lay at the heart of the Confederate nation." These findings align nicely with the research of Hugh Bailey, who examined the antithesis of this slavery-induced patriotism. Studying Confederate disloyalty in Alabama, he contended that even in the Deep South, non-slaveholders held strong Unionist and anti-Confederate sympathies well before Fort Sumter:

It has long been recognized that disloyalty to the Confederacy became widespread in a number of the 'hill counties' of Alabama by the spring of 1862 and that this region remained a cancer in the side of the Confederacy for the remainder of the war. It is not generally recognized, however, that from secession active disaffection was widely prevalent in this area of poor land and small farmers.

In fact, Unionist voters were so decisively opposed to secession, Bailey asserted, that they "organized themselves to prevent enlistment and frequently asserted that if they fought it would be for Lincoln." James B. Bell, a non-slaveholding Unionist from Winston County, Alabama, wrote to his son Henry, a Confederate sympathizer, in April of 1861. After confirming the rest of the family's devotion to Lincoln, and thus, to the Union, the elder Bell warned that "All [the slaveholders] want is to get

---

[44] Escott, *After Secession*, 32; 33; 99; Forret, *Race Relations*, 223.

you pumped up and go to fight for their infernal negroes." James Bell clearly understood the genesis of secession and the cause of disunion, and he was certainly not planning to give his life to protect the vast wealth of the master class, who never showed any interest in well-being of poorer whites in the first place. In reality, Bell concluded, "after you do their fighting you may kiss their hind parts for all they care."[45]

Just a few months after the battles commenced, the *New York Times* remarked that the Confederate Army "is composed of the very *elite* of the South. ... Only a small portion of it has been drafted from the class of *poor whites*, who are too listless and degraded to be of any reliance if brought into the field." Two years later, however, the same paper reported that poor whites comprised "the rank and file of the rebellion." This drastic change in the South's soldiery, of course, resulted from the passage of the Conscription Acts, Substitution Act, and the Twenty Negro Act. Yet out of the poor whites forced to fight for the Confederacy, the *Times* contended, "nine-tenths of them do not know what they are fighting for, do not know what they are fighting against. A majority of them do not know anything." Even more shockingly, "hundreds of them never saw the American flag in their lives until they saw it march into Vicksburgh in triumph. ... But poor and ignorant as they are, let them express their own free minds, and they will, almost to a man, demand a speedy termination of this war." Poor whites had little interest in the Confederacy. Indeed, "It is only by bayonets that this army is kept together."[46]

Noting that Confederate poor whites were "blindly fighting against their own interests," Moncure Conway wrote that as "the soldiers of the North go farther South, they will find the population more and more definitely divided into three classes: viz. the slaveholders, the slaves, and the poor whites." As these class lines hardened, so too did the resolve of poorer dissenters, who did not want to fight a war in which they had no

---

[45] Joseph T. Glatthaar, *General Lee's Army: From Victory to Defeat* (New York: The Free Press, 2008), 20; Hugh C. Bailey, "Disloyalty in Early Confederate Alabama," *Journal of Southern History* 23, No. 4 (Nov. 1957): 522; 523; quoted on 524–5. Also see Georgia Lee Tatum, *Disloyalty in the Confederacy* (Chapel Hill: University of North Carolina press, 1934); Scott A. MacKenzie, "The Slaveholders' War: The Secession Crisis in Kanawha County, Western Virginia, 1860–1861," *West Virginia History*, New Series, Vol. 4, No. 1 (Spring 2010): 33–57, and Mark A. Weitz, *A Higher Duty: Desertion among Georgia Troops during the Civil War* (Lincoln: University of Nebraska Press, 2000).

[46] "Continuation of the War," Reprinted from *New York Times* in *Savannah Republican*, Aug. 9, 1861, 1; "Another Speech, Strong and Emphatic, by Gen. Logan," *New York Times*, Aug. 1, 1863.

interest. A little more than half a year after battles had started, slaves in Port Royal, South Carolina reported "that many poor white men were dragged off in chains to join the army." After coming into contact with Confederate troops after the Battle of Fort Donelson, Yankees described the impoverished men as "pinched and hungry, as if they had been upon short commons for months. . . . They had all the outlines of poor, ignorant and deluded men, who have been seduced into the rebellion by their demagogue leaders." Many of them "do not hesitate to declare that they were forced or deluded into taking up arms. The most false and abominable representations were made to them, and being mainly unable to read, they were not able to detect the baseness of the men who led off in the rebellion."

Given the illiteracy and semi-literacy of the majority of the poorer Southerners, certainly some of them were too uninformed – or deliberately misinformed – to make an intelligent decision about whether or not to support the Confederacy. Fed lies about racial uprisings, impending black domination, and the North's supposed plan to affect these ends, impoverished whites had few (if any) resources at their disposal to understand the possible implications of secession and war. Likely because they lived in a more socially egalitarian society because of lower levels of slaves and slaveholders, poorer whites in the Upper South tended to articulate class issues more clearly. This led, of course, to more men becoming Unionists. As one journalist stationed in North Carolina reported in early 1862, "The free-labor feeling I can affirm deliberately . . . is a prevalent one in all that portion of the State which is not within the Union lines. As to the Union men, we are chiefly non-slaveholders, they are pretty nearly unanimous in their hatred of an institution, to extend and perpetuate which, to the utter ruin of all other interests, they believe to be the prime cause of the rebellion." In strong, clear language, the correspondent daringly penned the words that every slaveholder dreaded. "There can be no mistake that a genuine Anti-Slavery, free-labor spirit has become quite general among the poor white men," he marveled, and "They have come to see how it is that Slavery entails ignorance and poverty upon them and their children, and how they have been made the actual white helots of the institution." Quite encouraged by the entire situation, the writer boasted that emancipation "will not only free the slaves, but [would also] free the 'poor white trash' . . . and make them the permanent friends of the Union."[47]

---

[47] "The Proclamation of the Non-slaveholders," *New York Times*, Nov. 14, 1862.

With the implementation of the southern draft, of course, the compos-
ition of the Confederate Army changed. Poor whites immediately became
the primary targets of the draft. The Conscription Act, passed April 16,
1862, declared that all white men from 18 to 35 years old were subject to
serving three years in the Confederate Army. Although certain categories
of laborers were exempt from the draft, they would be sent into combat
the moment they attempted to strike. Industrialists particularly delighted
in this loophole, finding it an efficient way to both control and underpay
their labor force. Few poor men wanted to fight in this incredibly bloody,
deadly war, and the spate of desertions after the Conscription Act
revealed the will of the people. As E.B. Seabrook wrote in 1867, even
before secession many poor whites completely opposed the idea of war.
After years of fighting the bloody conflict, "when the length of the
struggle and their increasing sufferings had abated their fires of their
patriotism, large numbers deserted, a fact, it is well known, which had
much to do with the ultimate failure of the cause."[48]

Less than six months after the draft, the Confederate Congress quietly
passed the Twenty Negro Act, exempting from service any planter with
more than nineteen slaves. Unsurprisingly, this one law brought mounting
class tensions closer to a head by emphatically affirming the non-slaveholders' refrain of "a rich man's war and a poor man's fight." The law's
blatant protection and privileging of the region's richest slave owners
surely spurred more rounds of mass desertion. Elsie Posey, who spent
her childhood enslaved in Mississippi, reported that the Twenty Negro
Act "accounts for Jones County's record as the 'Free State of Jones' and
for Covington County's famous 'Deserter's End Lake.'" Shortly after the
passage of the law, James Seddon, the Confederate Secretary of War,
attempted to spare the southern government the ire it would surely earn
from lower-class whites. Realizing the severity of the shortage of man-
power on non-slaveholders' farms, he recommended to Jefferson Davis
that the Confederacy "should exempt soldiers on whom several helpless
dependents relied for food." The slaveholding Confederate government,
however, never reacted to Seddon's request. This refusal, combined with
the failure to deal with monetary hoarding and speculation by the southern elite, comprised two of the most significant mistakes of the

---

[48] Mark V. Wetherington, *Plain Folk's Fight: The Civil War and Reconstruction in Piney
Woods Georgia* (Chapel Hill: University of North Carolina Press, 2005), 126; Williams,
Bitterly Divided, 84; E. B. Seabrook, "Poor Whites of the South," *The Galaxy Volume*,
Issue 6 (Oct. 1867): 689.

Confederate government. By targeting poorer whites such Confederate laws exacerbated already tense class relations – and ultimately helped draw the war to a close.[49]

All in all, more than 100,000 Confederates deserted over the course of the war. These men came from all socio-economic backgrounds, but most were from the lower-middling and poorer classes. Ella Lonn claimed that some of the southern privates "were ignorant of the real issues at stake and were but little identified with the struggle." Undeniably, she wrote, "The illiterate backwoodsman ... almost cut off from the mass of his fellow-men, was little interested in the economic aspect of the war, as he could see nothing in it for himself. When dragged from his farm plot into the Southern army, he often proved a passive Union sympathizer, as he was ready to fall back into his neutrality as deserter at the first opportunity." The poverty and lack of education of many deserters was evident in the remarks of several northern officers. One stated that "Quite a number of deserters come in daily ... and generally [are] so ignorant that little reliable information can be obtained from them." In 1864, Union General Carl Schurtz was stationed near Missionary Ridge, Tennessee. When he awoke one morning, his camp was so overrun with deserters that he "could hardly walk," he wrote. "Most of them were from Alabama and were from the poor, ignorant class."[50]

For deserters, of course, the specter of punishment always loomed. Men of wealth and means often escaped any penalties for desertion, while the poor suffered harsh punishments. According to Lonn, during the first few years of the war enlisted men were "too precious to be shot or hanged" for desertion, so officers resorted to "truly cruel and unusual forms of punishment" like "shaving the head, riding wooden horses, being drummed out of the service, flogging, wearing barrel-shirts, gagging, bucking, and branding." In one instance, twenty soldiers from North Carolina were charged with desertion near Richmond. Although

---

[49] David C. Downing, *A South Divided: Portraits of Dissent in the Confederacy* (Nashvivlle: Cumberland House, 2007), 115; 113; Elsie Posey, *American Slave*, Supplement, Series 1, Part 4 (MS), 1738; Escott, *After Secession*, 151; quoted on 152; Bell Irvin Wiley, *The Plain People of the Confederacy* (1943; reprint, Columbia: University of South Carolina Press, 2000), 69.

[50] Ella Lonn, *Desertion during the Civil War* (1928; reprint, Lincoln: University of Nebraska Press, 1998), vi: One out of every seven Union soldiers and one of every nine in the Confederate Army deserted. *Ibid.*, 123; 3; quoted on 3; quoted in Georgia Lee Tatum, *Disloyalty in the Confederacy* (1934; reprint, Lincoln: University of Nebraska Press, 2000), 69.

the penalties for all the offenders are unknown, one man "was sentenced to receive thirty-nine lashes on his bare back, to be branded in the left hand with the letter D, and to be put at hard labor on the public works for three months, with ball and chain weighing twelve pounds attached to the left leg." However, by 1863 southern officers increasingly resorted to the death penalty for deserters. They simply needed to incentivize and intimidate other men enough to remain within the ranks.[51]

Still another class-based Confederate law allowed rich Southerners to hire substitutes to take their places in the armed forces. Hiring a substitute was extremely expensive. Soon after the draft began substitutes could command $500, and by the middle of the war, a prospective soldier could charge thousands. In some parts of the region, substitutes reportedly received as much as $10,000. Since the average hireling charged far less than that, the practice remained widespread. One officer claimed that "four fifths of his deserters were substitutes, who deserted within twenty-four hours of being received at his headquarters." Desertion eventually became so common that the War Department commanded that substitutes be examined for their physical and moral capabilities. The entire process then had to be approved by the commanding general. This order, however, did little to curb such a popular transaction. In just two months of 1863, the small county of Chickasaw, Mississippi, recorded thirteen substitutions. Many of the substitutes were young sons of poor white women, some of whom were war widows and some of whom were abandoned. Repeatedly, these illiterate women left their marks, attesting to the fact that their sons were somewhere close to 16 years old. These impoverished children were then marched off to war to die in the stead of wealthy slaveholders, perpetuating the grave inequalities that had long marked the Deep South's society.[52]

Overall, the ability to hire a substitute allowed at least 50,000 of the South's wealthiest men to avoid military service. Some credible estimates claim that over 150,000 affluent Southerners hired someone to serve in their stead. But even this total falls far short of the actual number who used their personal fortunes to sidestep serving in the war. Sons of slaveholders could easily bribe conscript officers, and Army surgeons sold medical exemptions. These means of circumventing the draft were

[51] Lonn, *Desertion*, 51; 57; "Flogging in the Army," *Semi-Weekly Standard*, Jan. 27, 1863, 3; Lonn, *Desertion*, 58.
[52] Williams, *Bitterly Divided*, 57; quoted in Lonn, *Desertion*, 7; *Ibid.*; Chickasaw County, Mississippi, Substitutes, 1863, MDAH.

generally much cheaper than hiring a substitute, and afforded countless rich men other ways to shift the burden of war even more disproportionally onto the shoulders of the poor and lower-middling classes.[53]

While many poor white men simply joined or were drafted into the military and then deserted and returned back home, there were likely tens of thousands of men who evaded the draft purposely, or who lived away from mainstream society and were thus never drafted in the first place. By refusing to fight and die for slavery, these "layouts" had to spend the Civil War in hiding, whether in heavily wooded areas, swamplands, or small river islands. They were sometimes dubbed "mossbacks," because as they hid from Confederate troops, plant material would inevitably begin growing on their clothes. Overwhelmingly non-slaveholders, these men hunted and fished and survived on roots and berries. Using rockets and horns to alert each other to danger, the mossbacks would simply retreat farther back into the woods and swamps as Confederate forces approached. They became a great nuisance to southern leaders, who consistently attempted to arrest, impress, or kill them. Almost every southern newspaper reported the names of local deserters and layouts in the paper, urging citizens to turn in their friends, family, and neighbors for treason. One paper out of Albany, Georgia, publicized the names of over a dozen recent deserters, ordering the "good men of the country . . . to keep an eye on such men."[54]

For many of the deserters and layouts, banding together with other men in the same predicament brought additional protection and a sense of comradery. In some areas, wrote Lonn, deserters "were plied with a boldness and immunity which seems almost incredible." Throughout the Appalachian part of South Carolina and all over Mississippi, groups of forty to fifty men "would stack their arms, set out a picket guard," and continue their daily work as normal. As the Civil War raged on, bands of anti-Confederates and Unionists sometimes plotted to amass likeminded men in organized troops. One such group skirmished with Confederate forces in northern Georgia in early 1863. According to the *New York Times*, southern troops were "sent to put down the disaffection in that region. ... There are strong elements of disaffection, rebellion and revolution against the Confederacy all over the South among the poor whites, but they cannot be availed of as Union elements until the rebel Government is overthrown." Still another secret society began in East

Tennessee and spread throughout Alabama. Its members vowed to lay down arms on Christmas Day, 1864, to "achieve peace" by finally putting "an end to the war."[55]

Writing in 1891, a journalist named David Dodge wrote an expose on "The Cave-Dwellers of the Confederacy," proposing that most of these men had a deep disaffection for the secessionist slaveholders, and this "manifested itself in a dogged determination not to serve in the Confederate ranks." Although some of the cave dwellers were small slaveholders, they were "entirely out of sympathy with the slaveholding class in general." Two years into the carnage and destruction, these anti-Confederates began hiding out in ways they "had learned from runaway slaves." For the men without access to swamps or mountains, there was one main way to survive:

He either enlarged and concealed some natural cavity, or dug a cave in which he hid by day, to sally out under cover of darkness in quest of poultry, pigs, sheep, fruit, roasting-ears, watermelons, and other good things in season. If he feared pursuit by dogs, he rubbed the soles of his feet with onions or odorous herbs in order to confuse the scent. If moderately wary or skillful, he found little difficulty in remaining "out" till the crops were "laid by" and all the heavy work was over, or till cold weather drove him back to a snugger berth in the quarters.[56]

The wives of deserters had a harder time than the men, Dodge held, as they lived in constant worry for their husbands' safety, "for the sight of armed men seeking his capture or death was almost an every-day occurrence." Left to head the household without the help of slaves, these women had to raise and tend to the crops used to feed their families. "Then, after a hard day's work," Dodge noted, "food had to be prepared in the dead hours of night and smuggled out to the men in hiding. In short, her lot was but another proof of the truism that, after all, it is woman who has to bear the brunt of the ills that befall mankind." Of course, he penned, poorer white women were not the sole saviors of these cave dwellers, as "More than one deserter owed not only his comfort, but his liberty, if not his life, to the fidelity and cunning of some trusty slave."[57]

---

[55] Lonn, *Desertion*, 75; "Troubles in Georgia," *New York Times*, Feb. 11, 1863; Lonn, *Desertion*, 27: The "full flood" of desertion began in the fall of 1864 and continued until the close of the war.

[56] David Dodge, "The Cave-Dwellers of the Confederacy," *The Atlantic Monthly* (Oct. 1891): 514–22, Web.

[57] *Ibid.*

Several freed slaves also recalled stories of poor whites who refused to join the war effort or had deserted. Sallie Paul said that in North Carolina "There been plenty white folks that wouldn't never fight against the Yankees without they couldn't get out of it. They slip off and hide in pits they dig in the woods and the bays. Some of them say they didn't have no slaves and they weren't going to fight." One freedman from Alabama explained just how extreme conscription became: in the early part of the war the Confederacy asked for volunteers, but "then a little later when the south needed more men to fight, Jeff Davis's officers would go through the streets, and grab up the white men and put ropes around their wrists like they was taking them off to jail. And all the while they was just taking them off to the war. They made all the white men go." Jim Allen remembered that slave owners "would track the runaways with dogs and sometimes a white scalawag or slacker would be caught [by] 'dogging duty.' I saw as many deserters as I see corn stalks over in that field. They would hide out in day time and steal at night." Still other former slaves recalled helping feed the war's deserters. Mississippian Jeff Rayford told his interviewer that "men would hide out to keep from going to war. I cooked and carried many a pan of food to these men in the Pearl River swamp. This I did for one man regularly. All I had to do was to carry the food down after dark, and … pretty soon he would step out from behind a tree and say, 'Here Jeff' and then I would hand it to him and run back to the house."[58]

In Georgia, deserters scattered through the heavily forested area west of the Ocmulgee River as early as 1862. A few years later, the entire area was in open revolt. Gum Swamp, another densely wooded area in Pulaski and Telfair counties, provided another refuge. Because Confederate troops could not easily traverse the swamps or make it out to the small islands the deserters inhabited, they instead stole the men's guns and horses and occasionally harassed their families. In Mississippi and Louisiana, Shugg wrote, these "'draft-dodgers' were especially numerous" around the Pearl River, where "scarcely five hundred men were drafted from these piney woods."[59]

On the Mississippi River, deserters took over several small islands, leading one former slave to recall that a white "bandit named Coe settled

---

[58] Sallie Paul, *American Slave*, Vol. 3, Pt. 3 (SC), 233; Downing, *A South Divided*, 116; Tom McAlpin, *American Slave*, Vol. 6, Pt. 1 (AL), 270; Jim Allen, *Ibid.*, Vol. 6 (MS), Supplement Series 1, Pt. 1, 58; Jeff Rayford, *Ibid.*, Supplement, Series 1, Pt. 4 (MS), 1801–2.

[59] Wetherington, *Plain Folk's Fight*, 223; 222; Shugg, *Origins of Class Struggle*, 178–9.

on" Island No. 76. Coe apparently "gathered around him a large number of negroes. He became a terror to all the neighboring country. He and the negroes descended on the plantations and carried off everything." But Coe's anti-Confederate actions were not unique, as the former bondsman remembered "there were also other renegade white men with him whose names I will not mention." Indeed, many non-slaveholders joined anti-war organizations, while others formed semi-violent "tory" or "layout gangs." These bands of men could be highly destructive to the South's infrastructure, burning bridges, jails, and government buildings, attacking supply trains, and generally stealing from plantations whenever they got the chance. Emboldened anti-Confederates even began harassing conscript officers and other government officials. According to David Williams, by 1864 these men had "all but eliminated Confederate control" in the Deep South's hills and piney woods.[60]

Anti-Confederates and Union sympathizers were numerous enough to have taken over several areas of the Deep South by the end of the war. Weatherington found that in South Georgia, the backwoods areas "became contested ground" early on, with the homes of renegades "subjected to search-and-seizure sweeps ... Loyalists feared an anti-Confederate uprising." In South Carolina, the hill country around Greenville, Pickens, and Spartanburg was overrun with deserters, while in the piney woods of Louisiana, jayhawkers claimed to have established an anti-Confederate "government." Some southern counties even took the Confederacy's stance on secession literally, arguing that if the states could secede from the Union, then counties and districts could secede from states. In northern Alabama, the "Free State of Winston" seceded from the slave South, and in southern Mississippi, the "Free State of Jones" was established. Considered the heart of the Confederacy, Alabama and Mississippi ironically sustained some of the most passionate and well-organized opposition to the slaveholding oligarchy.[61]

One particularly large group of 700 to 800 men followed the infamous McLeod brothers throughout the two states. The McLeods, non-slaveholding yeomen, were avowed Unionists who "compared the slaves to the children of Israel and said they were meant to be free." The leaders

---

[60] Holt Collier, *American Slave*, Vol. 7, (MS), Part 2, 470; Williams, *Bitterly Divided*, 5.

[61] Wetherington, *Plain Folk's Fight*, 221; Williams, *Bitterly Divided*, 161; Shugg, *Origins of Class Struggle*, 180; Williams, *Bitterly Divided*, 49; Victoria Bynum, *The Free State of Jones: Mississippi's Longest Civil War* (Chapel Hill: University of North Carolina Press, 2003).

purported that their followers were ready and willing to start fighting against the slave owners. By 1864, the lower part of Mississippi had become so overrun with anti-Confederates and deserters that the tax quartermaster apologized to his superiors for not being able to perform his job properly, as the men had "overrun and taken possession of the country." Northern troops undoubtedly took note of the unionism – both latent and overt – among white non-slaveholding Southerners. In 1865, Yankee sergeant Richard W. Surby and his men stopped to eat at a modest log cabin in Mississippi's piney woods. The local women promptly welcomed them, unfurled a U.S. flag, and "wished aloud that their menfolk, hiding in the woods, might join them in their feast."[62]

Multiple sources report that poor whites, like blacks, were extremely helpful in providing Yankee troops with information about the Confederacy. Because planters had used the war as an opportunity to expand their fortunes by continuing to raise cotton and tobacco instead of growing food, poor white soldiers and their families were left to suffer from hunger and near-starvation. According to some estimates, the hardships on the home front became so dire that by late 1863, almost half of the Confederate army had deserted. On November 26, 1863, Secretary of War Seddon reported to President Davis that the Army is "generally a little more than a half, never two-thirds, of the numbers in the ranks." Just over a year later, Confederate J.B. Jones wrote that resentment over furloughs, combined with the exemption of wealthy planters, had created a "rapidly growing Emancipation Party."[63]

Certainly by 1864, the Confederate leadership fully recognized the need to ease class tensions as much as possible. Congress began reigning in some of the more profligate exemptions, like the Twenty Negro Act. The practice of hiring a substitute was finally officially discontinued. Furthermore, in an unprecedented effort to appease the poor and middling classes, southern politicians even established price controls. By this time, however, these tempered measures were vastly insufficient, and came much too late. Desertion levels had continued to climb following Gettysburg and Vicksburg. By the end of war, only 160,000 men were present out of a total of 359,000 whose names were on the muster rolls. Recent historians have even uncovered evidence that by the final years of the war, slaves and white anti-Confederates were cooperating in an

---

[62] Bolton, *Poor Whites*, 178; quoted in Williams, *Bitterly Divided*, 157; quoted in Bynum, *Long Shadow*, 3–4.
[63] Quoted in Williams, *Bitterly Divided*, 146; 3.

organized opposition to the southern government. The South truly was responsible for its own demise. Slaveholders had created a war to protect their own wealth and privilege. Then they expected non-slaveholders to carry the burden of the war; to give life, limb, and sanity to preserve an institution that only negatively impacted them. Hundreds of thousands of southern men evaded the draft or defected. As Bell Irvin Wiley wrote, this fact "was probably due ... to the conviction that they were being discriminated against by the privileged class."[64]

Unsurprisingly, near the end of the war, bread riots erupted in many southern cities and towns. The mobs of rioting women were ridiculed universally in the press for their poverty. One Alabama editor described the starving women as "prostitutes, plug uglies ... and those who have always been a nuisance to the community," while a Georgia paper complained about "loafers, vagrants, and loose women." Many poor whites initially hailed the invading troops as saviors, especially because Union commanders provided direct, material relief, supplying them with food and other provisions. By connecting with poor and non-slaveholding whites, Ash concluded, Yankee servicemen "endeavored to bring out [their] latent unionism ... by smiting the aristocracy." To many Northerners, plans to uplift and educate southern poor whites were seen as the key to reuniting the country, since poor white illiteracy and ignorance had "enabled secessionist demagogues to dupe" them in the first place.[65]

Still, while a sizable percentage of non-slaveholders had been drafted into the Confederate Army, and another portion were forced to join against their wills, there remained many lower-class white men who chose – by their own volition – to fight for slaveholders. In reality, there were numerous reasons why they cast their lot with the Confederacy. The master class's fear mongering surely helped convince a number of them that maintaining slavery would keep their families safe and their wages stable. By playing to their basest, most irrational anxieties, masters successfully used racism to push reluctant poor whites into an unsustainable war. Moreover, many of these men, who oftentimes lived hand to mouth during slavery, actually looked forward to the prospect of making a steady wage in the Confederate military. Even a private's low pay of $11 a month was more than most impoverished whites could make at

---

[64] Bynum, *Long Shadow*, 5; Downing, *A South Divided*, 115; Hahn, *A Nation under Our Feet*, 88; Wiley, *The Plain People*, viii.

[65] Quoted in Escott, *After Secession*, 127; 251; Williams, *Bitterly Divided*, 106; 100; Ash, "Poor Whites," 45–7.

home. And a consistent pay period of several months or years was likely attractive, too.[66]

Other poor whites were seemingly coerced into enlisting due to the fact that they depended upon certain slaveholders for employment, land rental, or loans. Some simply concluded that allying with the powerful master class was in their best interest. Yet another often-overlooked incentive for antebellum era men to join the armed forces was the historic precedent of the government granting land to veterans. In the decade between 1845 and 1855, multiple congressional acts deeded over sixty million acres of public land to more than 400,000 veterans, widows, and their heirs. Although only about 5 percent of the land claimants actually settled on the deeded lands, others made quick cash by selling their titles to brokers and speculators. This land giveaway was surely viewed as a likely bonus by men of fighting age, who usually realized that Congress had granted Mexican War volunteers (ranking below officers) 160 acre plots.[67]

Finally, cravings for honor and respect undoubtedly led some poor white men to try to prove their own self-worth and masculinity through combat. And once the war actually began, slaveholders could shift their campaign of racial hysteria into a campaign about honor and patriotism. Once the fighting commenced, the region's politicians could stop talking about miscegenation and race wars and begin talking about heroism and virility. And poor white men, who had spent most of their lives without a sense of honor, finally found a way to feel valued by their society. By protecting their homes, families, and communities, poor whites were able to elevate their social status. Furthermore, as David Potter found, most Southerners had more loyalty to the war and the troops than to the Confederacy itself, largely due to their emotional attachments to "home." These men identified themselves primarily by locality, not nationality. This type of localized identification was probably even more intense for the poorest Southerners, who lacked the means to learn about larger concepts like nationalism. Their worlds were limited, as was the intensity of their patriotism. As James Cobb wrote, the term "'my country' could refer not to the Confederacy or even to the South but to his own particular geographic and emotional realm of existence and experience, whether he defined that as his state or his local community, or

---

[66] Gorn, "'Gouge and Bite," 18–43. Williams, *Bitterly Divided*, 44.
[67] James W. Oberly, *Sixty Million Acres: American Veterans and the Public Lands before the Civil War* (Kent, OH: Kent State University Press, 1990).

simply 'the loved ones who call upon me to defend their homes from pillage.'"[68]

George Reed, once enslaved in Biloxi, Mississippi, told a story that revealed the importance of honor among poor white men in the Old South. Jim Hudson, a Hattiesburg native, "wouldn't go to war, nor [would] any of his brothers. So they joined up with the other white men in the woods that didn't want to go to war. They had their tick-tacking signals and the Confederate troops sent to make them join the army, never could catch them for a long time." After some time, Reed continued, Lem Williams, Jim's neighbor and best friend, "got tired of hiding out in the woods. 'Let's join up with the Confederate troops,' Lem says, 'then after the war is over we *can be somebody*. This way we never can.'" But Jim refused to fight. After Lem joined up with the local regiment, he led the troops to the hiding places of the other defectors, including his former best friend. When the Confederates got to Jim's house Lem chased the unarmed man into the woods and shot him down in cold blood. "Them buckshots made a patch of little holes in Jim's back about [as] big as your hand," Reed remembered, "They toted Jim into the house and he lived two, three hours, talking most [of] the time that *he had never hurt no humans*; that they must see after his wife and children."[69]

But men like Jim Hudson were still in the minority. Even though poor whites knew that slavery kept them in a state of dependency, even though they saw how slavery drove down their wages and disrupted their family lives, even though they were thoroughly marginalized within the southern economic system, some of them ultimately supported the slaveholders' war. The North, and indeed, the United States of America, might once have had a potentially game-changing ally in the South's poor whites. Yet when war comes, and violence begins, everything changes. Priorities undergo cataclysmic reorganization, once unimaginable alliances form, and society is ruled – if for a brief moment – by fear, not logic. One Atlanta journalist attempted to explain in 1870 why so many poor whites chose to fight for the South: "Thousands of our best men ... had opposed the war of secession inaugurated by Democratic politicians for the perpetuation of a party dynasty; they had denounced the Charleston Convention as a treasonable body, and held up its leaders to the execration of the public." However, as soon as "the fighting commenced, they very naturally submitted their better judgment to an impulse, and took up

---

[68] Potter is discussed in Cobb, *Away Down South*, 57.
[69] George Reed, *American Slave*, Supplement, Series 1, Part 4 (MS), 1810–1, italics added.

arms in defense of their native section." In short, these men had families to protect, and honor to gain.[70]

Mere days after the fighting ceased, a wealthy pro-slavery Southerner murdered Abraham Lincoln. Northern papers struggled to make sense of the nation's carnage and destruction, its immense suffering and loss. Deeming the American Civil War "A Class Revolution," the *New York Times* contended that "from the beginning of the war [we] urged that this struggle was essentially a struggle between a class – the slave aristocracy and the people." Even the newly appointed southern-born President, Andrew Johnson, prophesized before secession that "a base aristocracy, founded on slavery, who had long weighed on the poor and middle classes of the South, were now striving to overthrow all the franchises of the people on this continent, and were striking a blow at universal democracy."[71]

The slave regime of the Old South needs to be remembered for what it was. For a large percentage of white Southerners, slavery was deeply harmful. It spurred forces that drove down their wages, took their jobs, pushed them off of the land, denied them civil rights, and kept them languishing in cycles of poverty. In 1867, Union General John Pope wrote a letter to Ulysses Grant, expressing his concerns about how the Civil War – and the causes of the Confederacy – would be remembered in history.

The rebellion was the result of a tremendous conspiracy, to destroy the nation's life. It sought to obliterate civil liberty throughout the South – to reduce the Southern white laborer to the condition of the free negro, and the free negro to slavery; to re-open the African slave trade, and to establish over the South the despotism of an oligarchy founded alone on slavery, and the interests and ambition of those interested in slave property. How cruel and remorseless its career was—how little it respected individual rights and the common laws of humanity when they stood in the way of its remorseless schemes.[72]

When the war ended, however, it quickly became evident that former slaves were not the only Southerners who benefitted from new-found forms of freedom. Just as Hinton Helper argued that poor whites suffered a "second degree of slavery" in the antebellum period, the post-war era freed poor whites in several very significant ways. Most importantly, poor white workers were finally able to compete in a free-labor economy, albeit

[70] "Speech of Hon. Foster Bledgett," *Daily Atlanta Intelligencer*, Nov. 12, 1870, 2.
[71] "A Class Revolution," *Ibid.*, April 29, 1865.
[72] "General Pope's Letter," *Georgia Weekly Opinion*, Sept. 3, 1867, 4.

a surplus labor one, which at least provided them with a potential opportunity to improve their economic situation. "But another great element of productive power in the South is now to be brought into action," one Georgia paper opined, "the labor of poor white men who have heretofore been completely idle for want of employment. They will find agricultural labor to be creditable, in the absence of negro slavery, as well as highly remunerative."[73]

The pre-war plight of the Deep South's poor whites thus demonstrated that the tentacles of slavery extended into every aspect of southern life, and shaped even the worlds of people who had no involvement in the peculiar institution. As Mildred Mell wrote, "with the disintegration of the plantation-slave economy, the poor whites were no longer theoretically 'outside.' A free-labor economy, in theory, meant the disappearance of barriers which had kept them from sharing in the division of labor." Even former slaves recognized the ways in which black emancipation benefitted poor whites. Daniel Goddard reckoned that "Lincoln was raised up for a specific purpose, to end slavery, which was a menace to both whites and blacks." And Tom Woods, once enslaved in Florence, Alabama, explained in detail how the lives of poor whites changed after the Civil War: "if the nigger hadn't been set free this country wouldn't ever been what it is now! Poor white folks wouldn't never had a chance. The slaveholders had most of the money and the land and they wouldn't let the poor white folks have a chance to own any land or anything else to speak of. These white folks wasn't much better off than we was." Poor whites, Woods continued, "had to work hard and they had to worry about food, clothes, and shelter. ... Lots of slaveowners wouldn't allow them on their farms among their slaves without orders from the overseer. I don't know why, unless he was afraid they would stir up discontent among the niggers." Woods then correctly concluded that "White folks as well as niggers profited by emancipation." Indeed, the emancipation of African Americans heralded many new socioeconomic freedoms for poor white Southerners. Just as black slavery kept poor whites down, black freedom lifted them up.[74]

---

[73] "The South," *Daily Intelligencer*, Nov. 28, 1865, 1.
[74] Mell, "A Definitive Study," 2–3; Daniel Goddard, *American Slave*, Vol. 2, Pt. 2, 151; Tom W. Woods, *Ibid.*, Vol. 7, Pt. 1, 354.

Conclusion: A Dual Emancipation

Rejoice in a nobler emancipation, which has stricken the fetters from millions of our own race, and given an earnest of a better destiny to a class which has suffered fatally and long.

– E.B. Seabrook[1]

The blunting effects of slavery upon the slaveholder's moral perceptions are known and conceded the world over; and a privileged class, an aristocracy, is but a band of slaveholders under another name.

– Mark Twain[2]

Immediately following the news of emancipation, joyous freedmen and women gathered in every Deep South city and town in a near-ecstatic state of celebration. For generations they had prayed, hoped, and even fought to escape bondage. Reports of freedom unleashed renewed optimism among African Americans, many of whom envisioned a black community that was independent, self-governing, and largely autonomous. Freedom – emancipation – had been the primary dream of every black man, woman, and child who suffered through the horrors of slavery. Yet after a few short, jubilant years filled with the reuniting of families, the construction of new churches and schools, and the endowment of basic citizenship and suffrage rights, blacks found themselves at the bottom of free society, just one step removed from bondage. Facing a demographic catastrophe

---

[1] E.B. Seabrook, "The Poor Whites of the South," *The Galaxy* Volume 04 Issue 6 (Oct. 1867): 690, Web.

[2] Mark Twain, *A Connecticut Yankee in King Arthur's Court* I (Charles L. Webster & Co., 1889), Chapter XXV, Web.

wrought by disease and homelessness, freedmen experienced a devolution of once hopeful expectations. Indeed, in no more than a decade after emancipation, many African Americans were questioning the severe limitations that the region's whites were continually placing upon their "freedom." Famously describing the Reconstruction experience of the South's blacks, W.E.B. DuBois wrote, "The slave went free; stood a brief moment in the sun; then moved back again toward slavery."[3]

When judged comparatively with other nations' emancipatory histories, America's experience is unique. While African Americans were the only freed slaves to be granted political rights so soon after emancipation, those rights were limited for a people without land, wealth, or job prospects. Most of the enslaved were freed with little more than the clothes on their backs. Eventually black men were ostensibly awarded the rights of citizenship, but even that was inconsequential when they were jobless and their families were suffering from hunger and want. Newly granted civil rights sometimes rang hollow to people who were left – unprotected – to suffer the violence of vigilante groups like the Ku Klux Klan. The soon-neutralized Fourteenth and Fifteenth Amendments could not help almost 4 million Americans whose first concern was finding a way to earn a living wage and gain self-sufficiency.

According to Jim Downs, "the exigencies of war and the massive dislocation triggered by emancipation" caused tens of thousands of African Americans to perish from illness during the early years of Reconstruction. Given the utter chaos resulting from a homefront war, health conditions for freedmen were terrible. "Measles, fever, and diphtheria developed because of the overcrowded and unsanitary conditions" at refugee camps, Downs wrote, and in the few years following freedom smallpox and Asiatic cholera ravaged the entire population of former slaves. The United States government, however, did not attempt to deal with these epidemics in any meaningful way. These crises in public health prematurely ended the lives of untold thousands of blacks, causing their first years of emancipation to be fraught with pain, grief, and misery. African Americans' suffering was so prolonged and widespread that Downs proposed dropping the term "emancipation" altogether. Instead, he claimed, the "'process of emancipation' would be a more apt way to their experiences."[4]

---

[3] DuBois, *Black Reconstruction in America.*
[4] Jim Downs, *Sick from Freedom: African-Americans Illness and Suffering during the Civil War and Reconstruction* (New York: Oxford University Press, 2012), 7; 162–3; 96; 113; 14.

By the time of the Great Depression, several former slaves mourned retroactively for the freedom they had been promised, but felt they had never received. Keeping in mind that the formerly enslaved were being interviewed almost three generations after the fact, and that they obviously knew their white interviewers wanted them to downplay the horrors of slavery (and thus, the benefits of emancipation), their responses still warrant consideration. Many freedmen and women felt as if they had received absolutely no recompense for decades – indeed, generations – of slavery. Now upward of at least 70 years old, they concluded that the conditions they experienced throughout the postbellum period had been generally bleak and sometimes miserable, and that economically and materially, their lives had not significantly improved from the days of slavery. While they obviously appreciated certain aspects of emancipation, and fully recognized all of the benefits they had received from freedom, they also knew that nominal legal freedom never ended their struggles as impoverished blacks in a white-dominated world. Walter Calloway told his interviewer that African Americans had "never been what I call free . . . if they're all like me they still have to work just as hard, and sometimes have less." A Mississippi woman agreed. "We all had a hard time then and we still have a hard time," she lamented. "There is nothing in this old world but hard time for black folks." Minerva Wells remembered that shortly after learning of their emancipation, former slaves "were told we would be free to go and to work for wages and [be] given homes and stuff and the men could vote. But the whole country was so torn up and ruined until everybody had a hard time for several years after it was all over with."[5]

The horrors of a protracted, bloody war, combined with the destruction of the South's entire social, political, and economic system, led to one of the most intense, violent eras in the nation's history. "It seems like the white people can't get over us being free, and they do everything to hold us down all the time," one man observed. Instead of enjoying emancipation and building new lives, "we have to just keep on bowing and scraping when we are around white folks like we did when we were slaves. They had us down and kept us down." Jefferson Franklin Henry, who spent his childhood enslaved in Georgia, purported that after emancipation, "Negroes was free but they weren't allowed to act like free

---

[5] Walter Calloway, *American Slave*, Vol. 6 (AL), Pt. 1, 53; Harriet Miller, *Ibid.*, Vol. 9 (MS), Supplement, Series 1, Pt. 4, 1505; Minerva Wells, *Ibid.*, Vol. 10 (MS), Supplement, Series 1, Pt. 5, 2261.

people." James Southall echoed these sentiments, remembering "We lived in a sort of bondage for a long time." And Annie Groves Scott of Lyonsville, South Carolina recalled working just as hard after the Civil War as she did before it. "Wore myself out after freedom," she reported, "and got kind of tired of hearing folks yelling about Grant and Lincoln setting us free."[6]

Yet during early Reconstruction, while many former slaves questioned the actual socioeconomic benefits of their emancipation, poor whites experienced a time of mostly positive change. Before the Civil War, poor whites had functioned as social pariahs in the Deep South because they had no real place or stake in the slave system, and thus actually stood to threaten it. With emancipation, however, poor whites were finally granted at least enough of the privileges of whiteness to get them off the bottom rung of society, which would now be occupied by blacks. Just as Hinton Helper claimed that poor whites suffered a "second degree of slavery" during the antebellum period, the postbellum era freed poor southern whites in several important ways. With the region in economic ruin, poor whites were no longer effectively barred from land ownership. A small percentage were even able to take advantage of the former slaveholders' financial troubles, remaining in the Deep South and buying small plots of plantation land to farm. Moreover, the Homestead Act of 1862, along with the Southern Homestead Act of 1866, allowed tens of thousands of poor whites finally to join the ranks of landholders. Many poor whites migrated westward, to seek new opportunities and economic independence.[7]

For those poor whites who remained landless, there were still tangible improvements in their daily lives following the destruction of slavery. Most importantly, poor white workers were finally able to compete in a free labor economy, which at least provided them with a potential opportunity to improve their economic situation. Poor whites certainly gained more consistent employment, and thus the freedom to live in two-parent, family-centered households for the majority of the year. At the same time, black emancipation signaled the end of the virtual imprisonment of thousands of poor southern whites, whose existence outside the slave system had threatened the antebellum social hierarchy. The swift change in the race of the typical southern convict – overwhelmingly white during

---

[6] Allen V. Manning, *Ibid.*, Vol. 7 (OK), 222; Jefferson Franklin Henry, *Ibid.*, Vol. 12 (GA), Pt. 2, 191; James Southall, *Ibid.*, Vol. 7 (OK), 308; Annie Groves Scott, *Ibid.*, Supplement, Series I, Vol. 12 (OK), 273.

[7] Helper, *The Impending Crisis of the South*, 32–3.

slavery, overwhelmingly black after emancipation – meant that impoverished whites were no longer the primary targets of the criminal justice system. Although some of their newfound freedoms would be tempered or even suspended in later years, early Reconstruction served as a time of hope for many of the Deep South's poor whites, just as it did for African Americans.

Indeed, the idea of "freedom for poor whites" had become so commonplace in the New South that, up until the revisionist work of Frank Owsley, historians unhesitatingly used the term "emancipation" to describe poor whites' postbellum situation. The "dual nature of emancipation" has been discussed by more recent scholars like Stephen Ash, Robert Gilmour, and Jeff Forret, who accurately concluded that "poor white gains often came at the freedpeople's expense." Because the lower classes were finally able to begin enjoying some of the privileges of whiteness, Forret contended, once surprisingly fluid "racial lines hardened." Ash similarly found that "The conquest of the South by northern armies during the Civil War began the liberation of the region's poor whites as well as its enslaved blacks. In pursuing the extraordinary opportunities thus presented, slaves and poor whites followed remarkably parallel – but not congruent – paths, celebrated kindred victories, and stumbled over like obstacles." Therefore, he wrote, "both encountered revolutionary possibilities beyond mere liberation, only to see those possibilities eventually thwarted by powerful countervailing forces." Unfortunately, after a few brief years of expanded opportunities and inclusion in the privileges of whiteness, most poor whites became re-ensnared in poverty. Their economic ascension may have ultimately failed, but they still gained certain permanent benefits from black emancipation.[8]

Despite the continued concentration of southern wealth, there were fewer barriers to land ownership for poor whites following the Thirteenth Amendment. Although the majority of masters' wealth was lost with the freedom of their slaves, the federal government allowed all but a very few former slaveholding Confederates to keep their land. By maintaining ownership of most of the Deep South's remaining capital, former slaveholders were able to adapt to the new economic structure of the region by

---

[8] Ash, "Poor Whites"; Robert Arthur Gilmour, "The Other Emancipation: Studies in the Society and Economy of Alabama Whites during Reconstruction," (Ph.D. Diss., Johns Hopkins, 1972); Forret, *Race Relations*, 228–9; Ash, "Poor Whites," 39–40. See William M. Brewer, "Poor Whites and Negroes in the South since the Civil War," *Journal of Negro History* 15, No. 1 (Jan. 1930): 32.

earning their primary income as landholders. In their transition from laborlords to landlords, Gavin Wright penned, "farmers now reoriented their investments and their politics toward raising land yields and land values ... [they] began to push for markets, towns, railroads, and eventually factories." As landlords, these men finally felt a reason to invest in their local communities. But while newly freed African Americans waited for their storied recompense of 40 acres and a mule, poor whites were slowly but surely entering the ranks of small landholders. For those poor whites who remained in the Deep South, opportunities for land ownership that had not existed before the Civil War suddenly sprung up. Ash found that some plantation owners, "hurt financially by the loss of their slaves ... were anxious to sell off excess acreage; and therein lay opportunity" for less affluent whites. While some thrifty, hard-working poor whites were able to purchase their land the old-fashioned way, many more were the beneficiaries of the largest entitlement program in the entire history of the United States of America: the Homestead Acts.[9]

Southern slaveholders had successfully prevented the passage of the Homestead Act during the late antebellum period. Fearing a nation of small, independent farmers who would ostensibly become anti-slavery proponents, the master class had used their weighty political power to table any discussion of agrarian plans and land grants. As soon as the pro-slavery men seceded, abandoning their seats in the legislature, the push for the Homestead Act was renewed. The original Act granted about 246 million acres of western land – an area close to the land mass of both California and Texas – to individual Americans, virtually for free. As Trina Williams explained,

The new law established a three-fold homestead acquisition process: filing an application, improving the land, and filing for deed of title. Any U.S. citizen, or intended citizen, who had never borne arms against the U.S. Government could file an application and lay claim to 160 acres of surveyed Government land. For the next 5 years, the homesteader had to live on the land and improve it by building a 12-by-14 dwelling and growing crops. After 5 years, the homesteader could file for his patent (or deed of title) by submitting proof of residency and the required improvements to a local land office.

Because the Homestead Act was signed into law by Lincoln in May 1862, however, few people from the Deep South initially received any benefit from it. Yet given that it remained in place until 1934, tens if not hundreds

---

[9] Wright, *Old South, New South*, 47; Soltow, *Men and Wealth*, 141; Wright, *Old South*, 34.

of thousands of southern poor whites became landowners following the close of the Civil War. By the end of the Act, over 1.6 million homestead applications had been processed. Williams estimated that about 10 percent of all the land in the entire United States was given to homesteaders for little more than a filing fee. Thus, for many poor whites who had longed to leave the South but never had the means to emigrate, the Homestead Act offered them a chance to start fresh, often in places unstained by the legacy of slavery.[10]

A year after Appomattox, the Southern Homestead Act sought to accomplish the same objectives as the original act on a much smaller scale. Opening 46 million acres of public domain land in Alabama, Arkansas, Florida, Louisiana, and Mississippi, the guidelines to claiming land were similar to the original Homestead Act. At first, the Southern Homestead Act was proposed to make self-sufficient farmers out of freedmen, but the aims of the law were never fully realized, and the federal government's failure to make a significant proportion of African Americans landowners would have dire consequences for decades to come. As Claude Oubre wrote, "The tragedy of Reconstruction is the failure of the black masses to acquire land, since without the economic security provided by land ownership the freemen were soon deprived of the political and civil rights which they had won." Owning land would have been the only realistic way for African Americans to achieve a level of self-sufficiency after generations of slavery. Yet to the great detriment of U.S. race relations, Oubre rightly concluded that land reform – at least in regards to black Americans – must be judged as a complete failure.[11]

While the Freedman's Bureau had initially been in charge of land policy relating to former slaves, it never had authority over more than about twenty percent of the region's land. Moreover, President Andrew Johnson issued an amnesty proclamation giving almost all southern land back to the former slaveholders. When it became obvious that the Bureau had been rendered powerless to effect real change, Radical Republicans in Congress began pushing for a Homestead Act specifically aimed to give

---

[10] Williams, "The Homestead Act," 1; 6; "Homestead Act," National Archives, http:// www.archives.gov/education/lessons/homestead-act/; Williams, "The Homestead Act," 1.

[11] *Ibid.*; Williams, "The Homestead Act," 6; 1; Claude F. Oubre, *Forty Acres and A Mule: The Freedmen's Bureau and Black Land Ownership* (Baton Rouge: Louisiana University Press, 1978), 197.

federal land to ex-slaves. Spurred on by the efforts of Union General Oliver Otis Howard, the Southern Homestead Act passed in the summer of 1866. During the first year of the Act, land was exclusively offered to African Americans and loyal whites, but after 1867, landless former Confederates could apply. Although the law ostensibly offered a solution to the region's land problem without removing any owners from their property, in reality, only unoccupied, often un-farmable land remained. Much of the Southern Homestead land was either covered with swamps, heavily wooded, or lay very far from transportation routes.[12]

Even with these qualifications, the passage of the Southern Homestead Act gave the region's poor population reason for hope, as land ownership could turn the dream of self-sufficiency into a reality. Ultimately, of course, the Southern Homestead Act fell far short of its objectives as far as African Americans were concerned. According to Oubre, there were several reasons for this failure. Perhaps most importantly, African Americans had already entered into contractual year-long contracts with employers. Although many of these jobs had been arranged under the Freedman's Bureau, blacks were locked into these contracts until the very date (January 1, 1867) that they stopped receiving special benefits from the Act. Finally, it was incredibly hard to administratively arrange homesteading, especially for people with no cash and no experience in dealing with bureaucracy. Most southern states had only one land office, meaning that for most poor families, the cost of accomplishing the administrative duties was more than the filing fees for the actual land.[13]

Homesteading activity varied greatly by state, and was also sporadic from year to year. Perhaps due to the Southern Homestead Act's disorganized, haphazard administration, Congress repealed it in 1876, exactly a decade after its start date (much unlike the long-lived Homestead Act of 1862). As Trina Williams found, under the Southern Act approximately 67,600 applications were made, but at most only about 27,800 applicants received final patent, totaling about 6 percent of the land originally offered. Using the few reports left by these bureaucratic offices, it is nearly impossible to calculate how many white individuals, as opposed to businesses, received land under the southern version of the Act. However, it is much easier to calculate the number of black beneficiaries. Williams estimated that fewer than 5,500 of the 27,800 final patents were ever awarded to African Americans. Other records indicate that less than

---

[12] Oubre, *Forty Acres*, 31; Foner, *Reconstruction*, 246.
[13] Katherine C. Mooney, Foreword, in Oubre, *Forty Acres*, n.p., Oubre, *Forty Acres*, 90.

4,000 freed people received land. "Either way," Williams concluded, "the reality is that few homesteads were granted to Black claimants."[14]

By the end of Reconstruction, therefore, thousands of poor whites had succeeded in becoming landowners, and many others would follow in their footsteps over the next few decades. Indeed, by essentially giving away land to individuals, the Homestead Acts were the most extensive, radical, redistributive governmental policy in American history. The number of original (1862) Homestead-recipient descendants living in 2000 was estimated to be around 46 million people, about one-quarter of the U.S. adult population. These beneficiaries, of course, were overwhelmingly white. Largely denied these wealth entitlements, blacks were essentially left landless after years (and generations) of unpaid, coerced, and brutalized labor. As sociologist Thomas Shapiro pointed out, if that many Americans can potentially trace their "legacy of property ownership" to these entitlement programs, modern-day issues like "upward mobility, economic stability, class status, and wealth" need to be understood as directly related "to one national policy – a policy that in practice essentially excluded African Americans."[15]

Without the widespread redistribution of southern land among the freedmen, African Americans were all but doomed to recurrent indebtedness and poverty. For poor whites who remained landless, the Civil War did not revolutionize their economic circumstances, but it did offer them new job opportunities. With slavery abolished, poor whites were finally able to sell their labor in a free market. Long shut out of many of the region's labor opportunities, they at last had the chance to work without having to compete with slaves, for jobs *or* for wages. Gavin Wright thus accurately deemed emancipation "an economic revolution," noting that "A popular metaphor among regional spokesmen during the 1870s and 1880s was the notion that slavery had enslaved whites as well as blacks by stifling economic energies in various ways." For so many years, manual labor had been degraded within the slaveholding South, especially in areas with high percentages of slaves.[16]

[14] Williams, "The Homestead Act," 10. Eric Foner used the lower estimate: "By 1869 only 4,000 black families had even attempted to take advantage of the act, three quarters of them in sparsely populated Florida, and many of these subsequently lost their land." Foner, *Reconstruction*, 246.

[15] Gilmour, *Other Emancipation*, 121, footnote 2; Williams, "The Homestead Act," 8; Thomas M. Shapiro. *The Hidden Cost of Being African American: How Wealth Perpetuates Inequality* (New York: Oxford University Press, 2004), 190.

[16] Bolton, *Poor Whites*, 182; Wright, *Old South*, 18.

By way of contrast, Wilbur Fisk Tillett wrote in 1887, "If the Old South had a contempt for the worker, the New South has a greater contempt for the do-nothing and the idler." With the massive upheaval of the southern work force, however, poor whites finally, albeit briefly, perhaps, had a modicum of power with which to negotiate labor terms. This shift, in turn, forced more affluent whites to at least pay homage to the "honor" inherent in hard work. As E.B. Seabook confirmed just two years into Reconstruction, "Already [poor whites'] services are, for the first time, in general demand, and simultaneously all over the country many of them have been taken into employment." Now that all labor was supposed to be dignified, and all laborers could possess a sense of honor, poor whites "are recovering the place from which too long they have been driven, and ... they will stretch upward from it to higher aims and better attainments." Although poor whites' options in the labor market were still limited, at least the prospect of agricultural labor was once again open to them.[17]

African Americans did not fare as well. The plantation economy did indeed survive black emancipation. This fact became undeniable in the organization and implementation of the post-bellum criminal justice system. Just as African Americans had taken over poor whites' old place at the bottom of free society in terms of land policy and labor, a similar scenario played out in state and local legal matters. Deep South legislatures passed new constitutions between 1865 and 1866. With slavery over, the updated documents were based on Black Codes restricting African Americans from almost every privilege of freedom. These repressive statutes prompted the federal Civil Rights Act of 1866, which anticipated the Fourteenth Amendment and forced the Old Confederacy to give at least an appearance of having accepted emancipation, primarily by changing the wording of laws that blatantly targeted blacks. Although the new state Constitutions did not single out ex-slaves in letter, the intent of the region's new laws was quite clear. If former masters could no longer lord over enslaved African Americans, they would at least create a path whereby the most "dangerous" and disruptive freed people could be returned to legally sanctioned bondage. By drastically increasing the severity of criminal punishments, broadening the statutes of behavioral crimes, and effectively preventing jury service

---

[17] Wilbur Fisk Tillett, "The White Man of the New South," *Century Magazine* (March 1887): 769; Seabrook, "The Poor Whites," 690; Gilmour, *Other Emancipation*, ii.

by blacks, southern whites were able to quickly reclaim a good deal of social control over freedmen and women.[18]

Following emancipation, then, the number of people arrested in the Deep South rose significantly as the substance and enforcement of certain laws changed substantially. In stark contrast to the antebellum period, the vast majority of those now arrested were black. To keep up with the rapid pace of arrests, cities and towns that did not have police forces before the war quickly established professional, uniformed forces during Reconstruction. Atlanta, Augusta, Nashville, Memphis, and Richmond created formal police departments. The undeniable proportion of race-based arrests caused concern, even during the initial years of freedom. In one petition to the Georgia's Freedmen's Bureau, the blatant racism of a particular judge was called into question after he punished several African Americans for speaking "disrespectfully" to whites. Indeed, the petitioners lamented, "the condition of the freed people is worse than slavery."[19]

By the mid-1870s, Georgia's Greene and Chatham Counties recorded alarming levels of racial discrepancy in convictions. While 60 percent of arrested whites would eventually be convicted, the proportion rose to 80 percent for arrested blacks. Local southern officials became so heavily invested in policing the freedmen that by January 1875, the *Greensboro Herald* warned of a "heavy increase" in state convicts that fall, because local jails across the region were already filled to capacity. Emancipation did, of course, provide the theoretical framework of black freedom, and laid the groundwork for a path towards citizenship. The Thirteenth Amendment also provided the former slaveholders with a "slavery" loophole: involuntary servitude was completely legal in conjunction with criminal convictions. African Americans' path toward citizenship would be long and hard, with many obstacles along the way. Despite idealistic promises from the federal government, overturning an entrenched system of racial slavery was a momentous task. Unless local governments were purged of Confederate sympathizers, true emancipation for southern blacks was nearly impossible. Hahn rightly concluded that "Vagrancy ordinances, apprenticeship laws, antienticement statutes, stiff licensing fees, heavy taxes, the eradication of common-use rights on unenclosed

---

[18] Jay R. Mandle, *The Roots of Black Poverty: The Southern Plantation Economy after the Civil War* (Durham: Duke University Press, 1978), 15. Furthermore, just as antebellum child apprenticeship laws allowed poor white children to be taken from their homes and forced to labor for individual citizens, the postbellum version of these laws, of course, targeted African American children. Foner, *Reconstruction*, 200; 201.

[19] Ayers, *Vengeance and Justice*, 168; quoted on 154.

land, and the multiplication of designated 'crimes' against property constructed a distinct status of black subservience and a legal apparatus that
denied freedpeople access to economic independence."[20]

In 1868, Allen Thomas was the first person sent to Georgia's penitentiary for vagrancy following the Civil War. A 45 year old from Dooly
County, Thomas differed from the state's antebellum vagrants in two
extremely important ways. First, Thomas was African American. Second,
instead of the usual one- to four-year sentence handed down to poor
white vagrants during the antebellum period, Thomas was sentenced to
"natural life." Unfortunately, little else is known about Thomas. He died
in prison, less than a year after his conviction. Yet his arrest symbolizes
the refocusing of the Deep South's criminal justice system following
emancipation. In Georgia, for example, postbellum vagrancy laws crim-
inalized people "who have not some visible and known means of a fair,
honest and reputable livelihood," meaning freedmen who left the employ
of their plantations. It also included people "without a fixed abode,"
qualifying all newly freed, and usually homeless, blacks. The vagrant
category extended to anyone involved in trading or buying stolen property, presumably property carried off plantations by these uncompensated
laborers. Finally, the statute deemed it lawful for "any person to arrest
said vagrants," effectively giving even the poorest whites legal authority
over blacks. After arrest, vagrants could be fined, imprisoned, or sentenced to work on "public works or roads." Alternatively, they could "be
bound out to some person" for a year, for a bond not exceeding $300.
This short-term master would agree to provide food, clothing, and medical attention, making the black vagrant's virtual slavery complete.[21]

No longer masters, former slaveholders used institutionalized ways to
reassert their power. They began aggressively enforcing laws enacted
strictly to control the purchasing and distribution of liquor, to regulate
individuals' private sexual lives, and to dictate how and where people
could spend their leisure time. After the initial few years following the

---

[20] *Ibid.*, quoted on 174; 179; Hahn, *A Nation under our Feet*, 235.
[21] State of Georgia Board of Corrections, Inmate Administration Division: Central Registration of Convicts, 1817–68, GDAH; *Acts of the General Assembly of the State of
Georgia*, Passed in Milledgeville, at an annual session in December 1865, and January,
February, and March 1866: 234. Several scholars have written about vagrancy in the
post-war context. See Schmidt, *Free to Work*, and Mary Farmer-Kaiser, "'Are They Not
in Some Sorts Vagrants?': Gender and the Efforts of the Freedman's Bureau to Combat
Vagrancy in the Reconstruction South." *Georgia Historical Quarterly* 68, No. 1 (Spring
2004): 25–49.

war, the Deep South once again had a labor surplus. Local officials were not incarcerating people because they needed laborers. Instead, there was a distinct continuity before and after the war: southern criminal statutes' intended purpose was the maintenance of elite social control over the masses. Just as poor whites had been singled out for prosecution for nonviolent, behavioral crimes in the antebellum period, so too were blacks in the postbellum period. As one Union soldier stationed in Meridian, Mississippi wrote of the former slaveholders, "It is their hope, and intention, under the guise of vagrant laws, &c, to restore all of slavery but its name."[22]

Because the vast majority of people arrested in the post-war Deep South were black, scholars like Alex Lichtenstein and Lawrence Friedman have demonstrated that post-emancipation statutes were specifically intended to keep freedmen trapped in a type of bondage. Friedman wrote that post-war arrests "played a sinister role in the system of race oppression." The southern legislatures may not have been able to single out African Americans in letter, but law enforcement officials across the former Confederacy clearly understood the statutes' intended targets. Complicating this plan of criminal prosecution, however, was the fact that most southern prisons had fallen apart during the war. Georgia and Mississippi had turned their prisons into munitions factories during the fighting, while others had simply fallen too far into states of disrepair. Many local jails had suffered similar fates, or had been burned down or otherwise destroyed by invading soldiers or disgruntled Southerners, both black and white.

To deal with this lack of infrastructure, the old master class returned to convict leasing. In short, localities leased convicts to the highest bidder, who had then had the right to their labor. Although poor white debtors and convicts had been hired out for their labor to the highest bidder under slavery, the system become much more brutal when the convicts were African American. Generally not abolished until the Progressive Era, convict leasing was, in Lichtenstein's words, "a fiscally conservative means of coping with a new burden: the ex-slaves who were emancipated from the dominion of the slaveholder only to be subject to the authority of the state." The racial disparity apparent in the disproportionate numbers of black convicts during early Reconstruction

---

[22] Quoted in Amy Dru Stanley, *From Bondage to Contract: Wage Labor, Marriage, and the Market in the Age of Slave Emancipation* (New York: Cambridge University Press, 1998), 126.

remained consistent throughout the remainder of the century. As late as 1908, Georgia's African American prisoners outnumbered white convicts almost ten to one.[23]

In many instances, convict leasing was akin to a death sentence. Several journalists confirmed the brutal history of convict labor in the Deep South. One activist attempted to reveal the inhumanity and racism inherent in the system. During the late 1860s and early 1870s in Alabama, even official reports showed that one-third of all convicts died each year. Some of this rapid increase was because of the dangerous nature of railroad construction, but the rest could be contributed to the brutal, violent nature of punishing the workers – a form of labor control directly carried over from slavery. One prison bureaucrat bluntly remarked that "if tombstones were erected over the graves of all the convicts who fell either by the bullet of the overseer or his guards during the construction of one of the railroads, it would be one continuous graveyard from one end to the other." Mississippi fared no better. The average yearly death rate for black convicts in that state was around 11 percent in the years from 1880 to 1885. White convict death rates hovered at half that level. By 1887, the annual rates of death for African American prisoners had risen to an astonishing 16 percent. Blacks had unquestionably taken over poor whites' place as the intended targets of a particularly brutal legal system, a tradition that the rest of America eventually would adopt and perpetuate.[24]

Forced into another type of bondage, African Americans surely harbored some resentment toward all whites. Likewise, as poor whites were slowly but steadily included in the privileges of whiteness, their anger toward blacks seemed to become more apparent and more vicious. Some of the most important developments of the post-bellum era, therefore, concern the significant change in social relations between poor whites and blacks. Recognizing the slaveholders as their respective oppressors, the Deep South's poor whites, free blacks, and slaves had once shared similar class concerns. As Eugene Genovese wrote in his essay on poor whites in 1977, although slaveholders ultimately "succeeded in driving a deep wedge" between impoverished whites and blacks, "the hints of mutual sympathy and compassion in a world in which so much

[23] Friedman, *Crime and Punishment*, 95; Lichtenstein, *Twice the Work of Free Labor*, 3; 15.
[24] Clarissa Olds Keeler, *The Crime of Crimes: Or The Convict System Unmasked* (Washington, D.C.: Pentecostal Era Co., 1907), quoted on 7; Woodward, *Origins*, 214.

conspired to sow distrust and hatred suggest that the Reconstruction era was not fated to end as it did." Certainly, he believed, "A wiser and firmer social polity directed toward building interracial unity would have encountered enormous obstacles, but it would have had more on which to build than historians have yet investigated." Poor whites began as pariahs in the antebellum era because they had no real place in the slave system and therefore actually threatened it. With the emancipation of African Americans, poor whites were finally brought into the system of white privilege, albeit at the bottom. This inclusion nonetheless placed them higher on the southern social hierarchy than freedmen, and they gained certain legal, political, and social advantages solely based upon race. Both blacks and poor whites were better off after emancipation, but both were still constrained by historical and contemporary economic and social forces that, especially when manipulated by those atop the economic and political pyramid, made their respective interests seem contradictory.

After emancipation, of course, African Americans became the only race in America ever to start out – as an entire people – with close to zero wealth. With no saved, inheritable wealth and assets, loans were nearly impossible to secure. Foreclosure, homelessness, and hunger were only one illness or one accident away. Without ever owning land, and thus, having nothing else upon which to build or generate wealth, the majority of freedmen had little real chance of breaking the cycles of poverty created by slavery. Without the prospect of earning a living wage, or the opportunity to secure a job in the first place, millions of African Americans struggled through generations of hunger and want. Jane Johnson had spent her childhood as a slave in South Carolina, and understood the realities of severe poverty. She even linked the experiences of impoverished whites before the Civil War to those of impoverished blacks after emancipation:

There was a heap of poor white folks in slavery time, and some of them lived mighty hard, worse than the slaves sometimes. . . . They say slavery was wrong but what about hard times? That is the worst kind of slavery, I think. All this hollering round about freedom they have, shucks, all that kind of talk ain't nothing. When you have work and some money in your pocket so you can go to the store and buy some meat and bread, then you have the best freedom there is, don't tell me.

Many freedmen believed that this poverty – a direct consequence of slavery – was responsible for a degree of deterioration within the black community. The inability to provide for a family had to have been extremely demoralizing for African Americans, much like it was for impoverished whites in the antebellum period. Years after gaining free-dom, some former slaves still grieved the fact that younger generations of African Americans seemed unable to extricate themselves from debt, poverty, and the criminal justice system. Dempsey Pitts of Mississippi lamented that black parents were only able to "bring up their children for three things – The County Farm, the Penitentiary, and the Gallows." Charlie Davenport also found little substantial difference between slavery and extreme poverty. African Americans, he maintained, were "all in debt and chained down to something same as we slaves were." Therefore, in an observation that might have resonated with many poor whites as well, Davenport concluded, "there ain't no such thing as freedom. We're all tied down to something."[25]

The South, of course, remains the poorest region in America today, and the Deep South is the poorest region *within* that region. The eco-nomic consequences of slavery among African Americans accounts for a good bit of this disparity, but certainly not all. Slavery's cruel grip extended widely, damaging the lives of poorer whites who would never benefit from the institution. Pushed off the land, and having to compete with unpaid, brutalized slave labor, a significant portion of whites wallowed in extreme poverty, too, and the vestiges of this impoverish-ment are still evident today. The stain of slavery, it seems, is much more widespread and lasting than many scholars have admitted.

In certain tragic respects, then, the nineteenth-century South offered ominous foreshadowings of twenty-first-century America. From an eco-nomic perspective, the extreme inequality of wealth and privilege remains striking, a direct reminder of the toll of unrestrained capitalism. During the antebellum period, very few poor whites could ever hope to rise above the economic class into which they were born. Today, people born into poverty rarely will be able to lift themselves out of the lower classes. For African Americans, the savage consequences of history, policy, and racism have rendered prospects of economic ascension grimmer still. Finally, the current crisis of the criminal justice system is a matter worthy of moral outrage, akin to the righteous indignation of the abolitionists. The tacit acceptance of most Americans concerning the blatant, systemic racism inherent in our legal system – from search, to arrest, to charge, to council, to jury selection, to conviction, to sentence – proves that the

[25] Jane Johnson, *Ibid.*, Vol. 3 (SC), Pt. 3, 51; Dempsey Pitts, *Ibid.*, Vol. 9 (MS), Supplement, Series 1, Pt. 4, 1723; Charlie Davenport, *Ibid.*, Vol. 6 (MS), Supplement, Series 1, Pt. 2, 572.

violent legacies of the past are still painfully evident. The fact that one out of every three young black men is bound to the incarceral state convincingly demonstrates that the shackles of slavery are not far removed. Indeed, for some Americans, the chains were never truly broken.[26]

As the social theorist C.L.R. James eloquently penned, "The cruelties of property and privilege are always more ferocious than the revenges of poverty and oppression. For the one aims at perpetuating resented injustice, the other is merely a momentary passion soon appeased." His sentiments seem to hold true years later, as increasing economic disparity continues to lead to other types of inequity, both social and political. The conversation over the United States's extreme (and growing) inequality is long overdue, and, more clearly now than ever, a subject of not simply regional but truly national urgency. "Anyone who has ever struggled with poverty," James Baldwin lamented, "knows how extremely expensive it is to be poor."[27]

---

[26] Michelle Alexander, *The New Jim Crow: Mass Incarceration in the Age of Colorblindness* (New York: New Press, 2010), 9. Also see Angela Y. Davis, *Are Prisons Obsolete?* (New York: Seven Stories, 2003) and Holloway, *Living in Infamy*.

[27] Quoted in Hahn, *A Nation under our Feet*, 265; James A. Baldwin quote, online at http://www.chronicpoverty.org/uploads.

Appendix: Numbers, Percentages, and the Census

Only within the past twenty-five years have revisionist scholars focused specifically on poor whites, but questions over who qualified as poor, as well as problems with inaccurate census returns, prevented a precise estimate. The most commonly accepted definition of poor whites remains Charles Bolton's, who claimed that they comprised between 30 and 50 percent of the South's white population. Because there were slightly more than 8 million whites in what would eventually become the Confederacy, Bolton's estimates meant there were somewhere between 2.5 and 4 million poor whites in 1860. Yet even with more nuanced definitions of poor whites, past estimates are very likely on the low side. Bolton recently revealed that even he surely underestimated their numbers. Census records, he said, had "always under-counted the poor and the mobile, and that was undoubtedly true in the antebellum period." As Ulrich B. Phillips confirmed, "These listless, uncouth, shambling refugees from the world of competition were never enumerated." Thus, while census records may provide relatively accurate numbers of masters, landholding yeomen, and slaves, poor whites were generally much harder to count, throwing percentage totals off for the entire southern population. As any historian who has spent time working with antebellum census records can confirm, poor whites frequently show up in one census, then disappear in the next, perhaps resurfacing years later in subsequent enumerations. Census taking in antebellum America was haphazard, with very little oversight by the federal government. Poor whites often lived in the backwoods and on the fringes of society. Their homes may not have been close to main roads and therefore were not visited by census takers. Some poor whites were so distrustful of government that they simply avoided anyone who approached their homes, especially when they suspected that the officials had come to tax them.[1]

Johnson J. Hooper, a popular humorist of the late antebellum era, wrote a short story describing his time as a census taker in Alabama. Most Southerners held the "popular impression" that a "tremendous tax would soon follow" the census taker's visit, Hooper remarked, and "the consequence was, that the information sought by him was either withheld entirely, or given with great reluctance." Reviled as "chicken men," census marshals were wrongly believed to tax every last cow, loom, and chicken owned, and many people thus declined to give accurate information, if they gave any information at all. "The returns, therefore ... exhibit a very imperfect view of the wealth and industrial progress of the country," Johnson continued. Public revulsion toward the enumerators became so bad, in fact, that "in some portions of the country the excitement against the unfortunate officers ... made it almost dangerous for them to proceed with the business of taking the census; and bitter were the taunts, threats, and abuse which they received on all hands." He contended that the worst offenders were often older women residing in rural areas.

Recalling one antagonistic encounter near Tallapoosa, Alabama, the census-taking Johnson asked a widow for "the age, sex, and complexion of each member of her family." After vigorously refusing to answer his questions, the old woman finally, albeit incompletely, complied, defiantly stating, "I've got five in family, and they are all between five and a hundred years old; they are all a plaguy sight whiter than you, and whether they are he or she, is none of your consarns." Although Johnson's sketch may have been slightly exaggerated, its underlying premises – that census taking was fraught with inaccuracies, and that ordinary people were generally hesitant to give personal information to the government – were invariably true.[2]

In an 1881 article entitled "The Alleged Census Frauds in the South," Henry Gannett, a census geographer, revealed that several federal enumerations prior to 1880 had been rife with errors, with the 1860 and

---

[1] Bolton, *Poor Whites* 5; Conversation between Charles Bolton and Keri Leigh Merritt at the 2011 Southern Historical Association in Baltimore, Maryland. Repeated with email permission from Dr. Bolton, dated 2/18/14; quoted in Brown, "A Vagabond's Tale," 801.

[2] Johnson J. Hooper, *Some Adventures of Captain Simon Suggs, Late of the Tallapoosa Volunteers; Together with 'Taking the Census,'" and Other Alabama Sketches* (Philadelphia: Carey & Hart, 1845), 149–53.

1870 censuses being the most imprecise. Mistakes were easy to make, Gannett found, because the system was structured in a rather unorganized, patronage-centered way. Beginning with the 1850 census, all subsequent enumerations were run similarly: official U.S. marshals had the "duty of supervision" over the locally appointed marshals who actually went around recording people's information. Most of the supervising marshals, therefore, "were non-residents, had little local knowledge, and no local pride or interest. The enumerators, known as assistant marshals, were appointed by the marshals without authority from the central office." The majority of these appointments, of course, were political patronage positions given to the area's local elite, who in turn had their own reasons for deciding what questions would be asked, and to whom. It was hardly surprising that Francis Walker, Superintendent of the 1870 Census, referred to the "'general' practice in parts of the South of marshals 'taking the census' at election and court days instead of visiting each dwelling." By controlling this information, the Deep South's upper classes gained still another form of political power. Census returns, just like all other primary sources, need to be viewed in historical context, with the recognition that they were riddled with errors at best, and were deliberately censored and manipulated by the people in power at worst.[3]

Instead, most scholars of antebellum America continue to rely on census returns as if they are factually sound, even though a bevy of research has disproved their accuracy. According to Donald DeBats, the administrator for the 1870 census admitted that "the censuses of 1850, 1860, and of 1870 are loaded with bad statistics." The average enumeration during these decades could last from weeks to months, and DeBats estimated that between 6 and 15 percent of adult white male residents were never counted by enumerators. Finding "important differences in the social and political characteristics of the enumerated and the nonenumerated," DeBats contended that the people missing from census records were less likely to own land, and generally had less wealth. Often more transient and not well established, the uncounted were also "somewhat more inclined to vote against the dominant political party." DeBats concluded that the rather large discrepancies found in census returns should challenge two assumptions about the post-Jacksonian United States. First, scholars need to reassess the socioeconomic makeup

---

[3] Henry Gannett, "The Alleged Census Frauds in the South," *International Review* 10 (1881): 465; J. David Hacker, "New Estimates of Census Coverage in the United States, 1850–1930," *Social Science History* 37, No. 1 (Spring 2013): 76.

of the country and, thus, the importance and rigidity of class lines. Second, voter participation in nineteenth-century America requires a reexamination, as underenumeration invariably requires statisticians to "lower our estimates of past electoral turnout."[4]

In a study published the same year as DeBats', Peter Knights similarly claimed that census undercounts between 1850 and 1880 varied from 11 to 14.6 percent. Moreover, Knights also recognized that those enumerated "represented a rather well educated portion of society, most likely familiar with the purpose of a census and experienced in replying to it." Thus, he asked, "should not underenumeration among illiterates or newcomers unsure of the purpose of the census have been much higher?" In still a more recent assessment, J. David Hacker reached analogous conclusions, describing most of nineteenth-century census taking as "an ad hoc measure ... until the 1880 census the Census Office had no control over the field enumeration, which was administered by federal marshals." During previous counts, he claimed, censuses missed a large percentage of immigrants, but also at least 10 percent of native-born whites, most often the "residents of large cities or rapidly growing frontier areas; the very young; the poor; and the 'floating' population of boarders, lodgers, and servants." Given all of these studies, it is safe to assume that among the landless, slaveless poor whites of the Deep South, *at least* 10 to 15 percent were never enumerated in a given year. In all likelihood, the number is probably even higher due to poor whites' transience, poverty, and disdain for government, as well as the influx of white immigrants to the South in the two decades prior to Civil War. As Knights put it, "It is sloppy technique for historians to be less critical of the census than of other sources they employ. ... Modern census administrators in civilized countries struggle to push underenumeration rates below 5 percent," he bemoaned, "yet many historians who deal with nineteenth-century censuses (designed by politicians, enumerated by their hack appointees, and hand-tallied by bored clerks) seemingly never entertain the thought that many lives slipped through the fingers of those amateur statisticians somewhere along the way."[5]

---

[4] Donald A. DeBats, "Hide and Seek: The Historian and Nineteenth-Century Social Accounting," *Social Science History* 15, No.4 (Winter 1991): 545; 546; 560; 557; 561; 548; 547; In a 1988 study, Richard Steckel estimated that 10 to 15 percent of America's population was unenumerated for those census years. Still, most of these studies come from the North – the rural South and West may have had even less accurate counts.

[5] Peter R. Knights, "Potholes in the Road of Improvement? Estimating Census Underenumeration by Longitudinal Tracing: U.S. Censuses, 1850–1880," *Social Science History* 15,

With so many poor whites unenumerated, historians will never truly know what percentage of the white population poor whites comprised. Yet scholars know with relative accuracy that slaveholders accounted for about a quarter of the South's enumerated white population on the eve of secession. This number was down from 36 percent just a decade earlier. Not only were fewer Southerners *becoming* slaveholders, but out of people who had once owned slaves, a growing percentage was unable to *remain* part of the master class. Wealth – in the form of land, cash, or slaves – was becoming more and more concentrated. In the cotton Deep South, William Barney found, "approximately 40 percent of the slaves, farm value, cotton output, and total agricultural wealth were controlled by the top 5 percent of the farming population." Figures like these ultimately led Barney to deem secession a "result of the oligarchic concentration of wealth."[6]

These statistics, of course, varied somewhat from state to state, and even within different sections of single states. In the mountains, piney woods, and wiregrass regions, where percentages of slaves were low, landholding rates differed from high slave, plantation-belt areas. In North Carolina's central Piedmont, Bolton used census records to determine that "Landless farmers and laborers headed from 26 to 30 percent of the area's agricultural households. In addition, over 60 percent of the small group of nonagricultural households in the region – primarily headed by women and artisans – did not own land. All told, landless whites headed from 30 to 40 percent of the free households." Y.I. Shinoda arrived at an even higher number. Studying nine North Carolina counties scattered across different geographical areas, Shinoda determined that 47 percent of enumerated white families were landless in 1860.[7]

South Carolina's demographics were the most extreme of all the slave states, as it held the distinction of having the highest percentage of slaves (57 percent), as well as the highest percentage of slaveholders. By the

No. 4 (Winter 1991): 521; Hacker, "New Estimates," 95; 80; 76; Knights, "Potholes in the Road of Improvement?," 517–8; see also Margo J. Anderson, *The American Census: A Social History* (New Haven: Yale University Press, 1988). There is much work left to be completed on the accuracy of the South's census records.

[6] Boles, *The South through Time*, 221; Barney, *The Secessionist Impulse*, 4.

[7] Bolton, *Poor Whites*, 12; Y.I. Shinoda, "Lands and Slaves in North Carolina in 1860," (Ph.D. diss, University of North Carolina, 1971), quoted in *Ibid.*, 192, footnote 9: Moreover, "Blanche Henry Clark, in *The Tennessee Yeoman, 1840–1860* (Nashville: Vanderbilt, 1942), 9, finds that 47 percent of Tennessee non-slaveholders in 1850 were either farm laborers, squatters, or tenants."

1850s, slightly more than one-half of the state's enumerated white citizens owned slaves, making it the first state with that distinction. Only the Appalachian districts of Pendleton, Greenville, and Spartanburg contained populations with less than 20 percent slaves. As Manisha Sinha's research indicated, the state's slaveholding rates were so high in part because many poor, landless whites had migrated west. From 1830 to 1850, South Carolina's white population actually decreased as many small farmers lost their land and then moved to places like Alabama, Mississippi, and Texas. Even after this wave of migration, however, a large proportion of South Carolina's whites remained landless and poor. Industrialist William Gregg estimated their numbers at one-third of the total white population in the 1850s, enough to alarm slaveholders over increasing class tensions. Stephanie McCurry's totals for Beaufort, a coastal city between Charleston and Savannah, support Gregg's assertion. She found that 35 percent of enumerated whites were landless and slaveless.[8]

In neighboring Georgia, about one-third of the enumerated white population owned slaves. In his study of Augusta's hinterlands, William Harris estimated that poor whites made up 30 to 40 percent of the region's white population. "Laborers, tenant farmers, and women in factory or other semi-skilled work accounted for most of the household heads among the poor," he wrote. As more sparsely settled western states, Mississippi and Alabama nonetheless had socioeconomic profiles similar to the older state of Georgia. Bolton found that somewhere between 40 and 50 percent of families in northeastern Mississippi qualified as poor whites. Christopher Olsen determined that about 20 percent of Mississippi's enumerated white *male* household heads owned neither land nor slaves, and William Barney also used the census to estimate that 20 to 25 percent of the enumerated white population was landless. Alabama's numbers were comparable.[9]

The proportion of poor whites in these states, however, was greatly underestimated due to several factors. First, Olsen only counted male household heads, while many poor white families were headed by females

---

[8] Total percentages of slaves in each state were compiled from information from the 1860 census, found online at http://www.civil-war.net/pages/1860_census.html. Sinha, *The Counterrevolution of Slavery*, 12; 12; 11; quoted in Russel, "The Effects of Slavery," 122; McCurry, *Masters of Small Worlds*.

[9] James C. Cobb, *Georgia Odyssey* (Athens: University of Georgia Press, 1997), 19; Harris, *Plain Folk*, 77 (Harris defined "poor" as owning less than $250 in property); Wallenstein, *From Slave South to New South*, 14; 19.

for at least parts of the year. Furthermore, the prevalence of squatters in newly acquired western states certainly threw off landholding counts. Census takers were hardly cross-checking county records and deed books to confirm landownership. Finally, the inaccuracies of enumeration were compounded in recently settled rural areas. In all likelihood, population totals in Alabama and Mississippi were probably closer to Louisiana's distribution, where three out of five white families lacked the means to own land. Roger Shugg claimed that a "surprising minority could hardly have been anything but squatters."[10]

Finally, large influxes of European immigrants arrived in the Deep South throughout the 1840s and 1850s, adding to the impoverished white population. Undercounted in the census records perhaps at an even higher rate than native poor whites, immigrants helped add to the growing ranks of poor whites in the few years prior to secession. Indeed, by 1860, census records listed foreigners as comprising nearly 45 percent of New Orleans' white population, more than one-third of the white populations of Savannah, Memphis, Louisville, and Mobile, 27 percent of Charleston's whites, and 22 percent of Richmond's. Even in Montgomery, Alabama – far removed from port cities and towns along the Mississippi River – immigrants made up at least 13 percent of the enumerated white population. More importantly, their numbers were increasing every year.[11]

Given all of this information, I have chosen to use the most restrained estimate possible by arguing that truly impoverished whites comprised approximately one-third of the white population in the Deep South. Although I personally believe that their numbers were even higher, there is simply no way to prove any approximation. Historians' lowest possible estimates of poor whites generally range from 25 to 30 percent, and the lowest possible percentage of those not enumerated in the census records was between 10 and 15 percent of whites. Out of these propertyless whites, however, some of them were sons of slave- and property-holders who had not received their inheritances yet. Others were young professionals – doctors, lawyers, and merchants – about to enter the ranks of the middling classes. Still, as Lee Soltow determined, these upwardly mobile landless whites could only account for 5 to 10 percent of the population "at best." Considering these disparate factors, scholars may safely (and conservatively) assume that by 1860, about one-third of antebellum Deep

---

[10] Shugg, *Origins of Class Struggle*, 86.
[11] Eaton, *The Freedom of Thought Struggle*, 238. By comparison, most major northern cities were about half foreign-born.

South whites were truly, cyclically poor. They had very few opportunities to overcome their economic station. Renting homes and land, Bolton wrote, "was a permanent way of life" for these people. With so few poor whites ever approaching the "verge of prosperity or even land owner- ship," it was nearly impossible for them to rise out of the class into which they had been born. For the vast majority of these people, upward mobility was an unattainable dream. Poverty was almost always a life sentence.[12]

[12] Soltow, *Men and Wealth*, 24; Bolton, *Poor Whites*, 13; 12.

Index

Abbott, John, 55, 115, 144–145, 274–275, 280
Abney, Matthew M., 129
abolitionism
  and alcohol, 206–208
  allegations of, 278
  and appeals to poor whites, 25–26
  and censorship (*see* censorship)
  and class consciousness, 53
  and Homestead Act, 58–61, 298
  and plight of poor whites, 53
  and Republican Party, 298
  suppressed through lack of education, 149–150
  and vigiliante violence, 281–283, 297
  and westward migration, 267–268
  and white slavery, 263–264. *See also* Helper, Hinton
Adams, James, 104, 287
agrarian consolidation, 42, 45, 49–52
agrarian reform
  land grants to veterans, 319. *See also* Homestead Act
Albert (enslaved man), 263
alcohol
  and abolitionism, allegations of, 206–208
  abuse of, 204–205
  access to, 206
  Blue Laws, origins of, 203
  and criminal charges, 220
  and domestic abuse, 133–134
  and dram shops, 202
  employer concerns about, 76

  as escapism, 202–203, 205, 208
  and fear of insurrection, 207
  and interracial interactions, 202, 206–208, 251–252, 280
  and jaundice, 254
  and labor disruptions, 203
  and politics, 176–177
  prevalence of, 201–203
  and prostitution, 207
  and respectability, 202, 206
  and secession, 299
  and taverns, 202
  and vagrancy, 188–189, 191, 194, 197–198, 203
  and violence, 141–142, 203–206
  and women, 202
Allen, Jim, 315
Allen, John, 198
Allen, Thomas, 334
Allen, Washington, 200
Allston, R.F.W., 228
American Union Commission, 160–161
Amey (enslaved woman), 211
Andrews, Samuel, 125
apprenticeship, 41
  as punishment, 127–128. *See also* children
associations
  for mechanics, 100
  response to, 287–288
  and secession, opposition to, 298–299
  on slave labor, 288
Attaway, Addison, 205

CPSIA information can be obtained
at www.ICGtesting.com
Printed in the USA
LVOW10s0927150418
573543LV00023B/351/P